The Recognition of Henry David Thoreau

Henry David Thoreau
From a daguerreotype taken in 1856 by B. E. Maxham

The
Recognition
of
HENRY DAVID THOREAU

Selected Criticism Since 1848

Edited by
WENDELL GLICK

Ann Arbor
THE UNIVERSITY OF MICHIGAN PRESS

Permissions

Grateful acknowledgment is made to the following individuals and publishers for kind permission to reprint materials:

To Raymond Adams and *Studies in Philology* for "Thoreau's Mock-Heroics and the American Natural History Writers," from *Studies in Philology*, Vol. 52 (1955).

To John C. Broderick and Duke University Press for "The Movement of Thoreau's Prose," from *American Literature*, Vol. 33 (1961).

To the Houghton Mifflin Company for Reginald Cook's "The Sinews of *Walden*," from *Passage to Walden*.

To The University of Massachusetts Press for Richard Drinnon's "Thoreau's Politics of the Upright Man," from *Thoreau in Our Season*, edited by John Hicks.

To Norman Foerster for "The Humanism of Thoreau."

To Walter Harding for "Thoreau's Fame Abroad."

To the Hall of Fame for Great Americans at New York University for the photograph of Malvina Hoffman's bronze of Thoreau.

To Stanley Edgar Hyman and The World Publishing Company for "Henry Thoreau in Our Time," from *The Promised End*. Copyright © by Stanley Edgar Hyman.

To Joseph Wood Krutch and *The New York Times* for "The Steady Fascination of Thoreau." © 1951 by The New York Times Company. Reprinted by permission.

To The Macmillan Company for Archibald MacMechan's "Thoreau." Reprinted with permission of The Macmillan Company from *Cambridge History of American Literature*, Vol. II. Copyright 1917 by Cambridge University Press. Copyright 1945 by The Macmillan Company.

To Oxford University Press for F. O. Matthiessen's "Thinking in Images," from *American Renaissance*. Copyright 1941 by Oxford University Press, Inc. Reprinted by permission.

To Joseph Moldenhauer and *The Graduate Journal* for "Paradox in *Walden*."

To Lewis Mumford for "The Dawn," from *The Golden Day*.

To Harcourt, Brace & World, Inc. for "Henry Thoreau/Transcendental Economist," from *Main Currents in American Thought*, Vol. II, by Vernon L. Parrington, copyright 1927, 1930, by Harcourt, Brace & World, Inc.; renewed, 1955, 1958, by Vernon L. Parrington, Jr., Louise P. Tucker, and Elizabeth P. Thomas. Reprinted by permission of the publisher.

To Gilbert Seldes for his "Thoreau."

To Willard Odell Shepard for Odell Shepard's "The Paradox of Thoreau."

To Mark Van Doren for "Position," from *Henry David Thoreau/A Critical Study*. Copyright © 1916 by Mark Van Doren. Reprinted by permission of Mark Van Doren.

To Mrs. N. C. Wyeth for N. C. Wyeth's "Thoreau, His Critics, and the Public."

Preface

Though Emerson lamented in his eulogy at Thoreau's funeral that "the country knows not yet, or in the least part, how great a son it has lost," not even Emerson himself could have been more than dimly aware of the magnitude of Thoreau's accomplishment. Thoreau had published but two books in his lifetime. *A Week on the Concord and Merrimack Rivers* (1849) had received mixed notices: one anonymous reviewer in *Godey's Lady's Book* had attributed it to Whittier; another in the London *Athenaeum* had dismissed it as one of "the worst offshoots of Carlyle and Emerson"; George Ripley, though offended by the book's "pantheism," had praised its "freshness" and "originality." *Walden* (1854) had fared better; some reviewers had discerned genius in it, though as a rule they had deplored the hubris and eccentricity of the book's author, one suggesting crustily that such authors as Mr. Thoreau would have no audience to write for if all men, as he had done, eschewed matrimony and withdrew to the shores of ponds. The anonymous writer of Thoreau's obituary notice for the New York *Tribune* probably reflected the consensus of the limited public who had read Thoreau when he spoke of him as "the genial writer on the natural scenery of New England," though attributing geniality to Thoreau must have raised not a few Concord eyebrows. Most readers of Emerson's eulogy, it is fair to say, probably discounted Emerson's 1862 prediction of Thoreau's future stature as funereal superlative.

Nor did Emerson live to see his prediction fulfilled. In 1882, when Emerson died, it was by no means certain that Thoreau would survive the attacks, largely *ad hominem*, of such contemporaries as Lowell, or the hypersensitive reactions of such loyal but unperceptive friends as Ellery Channing and Frank Sanborn. What was needed—and what most of Thoreau's nineteenth-century defenders were too much imprisoned by their own age to supply—were perceptive appraisals of the dimensions of Thoreau's humanism; of the real, not apocryphal, reasons why he had withdrawn to Walden Pond; of his deep and genuine concern for the wastage of human life he perceived going on about him; of his apprehension of the tragedy of man's serving ignoble ends under the mistaken assumption that all his options are foreclosed; and, finally, of Thoreau's unique genius in marrying the English tongue to his thoughts.

Not all of Thoreau's early interpreters, it is true, were victims of the obtuseness which afflicted the majority. To the common estimate that Thoreau was an "oddity," a "Yankee Diogenes," a "rural humbug" and foil to the "town humbug," P. T. Barnum, a significant few refused to acquiesce. Lydia Child, for example, argued for the "simple grandeur of Mr. Thoreau's position," chiding the "scholars [who] are often as blind as others to any new elevation of the soul." She might with considerable justice have chid them for being *more* blind; it was not from the scholars, but from writers like herself, George Eliot, and others, that the most sensitive contemporary criticism of Thoreau derived. Thoreau had to wait until the next century for such academic interpreters as John Macy, Norman Foerster, Raymond Adams, Francis O. Matthiessen, and Reginald Cook, to vindicate Emerson in his prediction. Not until the twentieth century was two decades gone did Thoreau shed for good such labels as "naturalist," "minor essayist," "skulker," "disciple of Emerson," and take his place with Melville and Whitman, whose fate it was to suffer from the imperceptivity of the same generation of critics. Not until the twentieth century did Thoreau emerge, ironically, from the investiture of coldness and stoicism with which Emerson as funeral eulogist and as editor had garbed him.

There is a wry sort of justice in the fact that Thoreau was perhaps the best defender of his own posthumous reputation until the centenary of his birth in 1917. For the bulk of the work by which he is now remembered was still in manuscript at the time of his death; and relatives and friends like his sister Sophia, Ellery Channing, and Emerson, wasted little time in beginning the task of putting it into print. Five books quarried from Thoreau's manuscripts or collected from periodicals were issued by Ticknor and Fields in the four years following Thoreau's death: *Excursions* (1863); *The Maine Woods* (1864); *Cape Cod* (1865); *Letters to Various Persons* (1865), edited by Emerson with the intent of reflecting Thoreau's stoicism; and *A Yankee In Canada With Anti-Slavery and Reform Papers* (1866). This succession of books elicited at least thirty-six reviews, as John Broderick has shown; and though many of them represent Thoreau as a transcendental naturalist maimed by personal eccentricities, they at least served, along with the reprinting of *Walden* in 1863, 1864, and 1866, to keep interest in Thoreau alive. Publication by Houghton Mifflin of the Riverside Edition of his works in 1893-94, edited by H. G. O. Blake, H. E. Scudder, and F. B. Sanborn, served also as a stimulant to Thoreau's reputation, as did publication of the more ambitious Walden Edition, which included the *Journals*, edited by Bradford Torrey and Sanborn in 1906.

The period between the first posthumous flush of Thoreau publication with its attendant critical reaction, and the Houghton Mifflin issuance of the Riverside Edition of Thoreau in 1893-94, was the critical period in the recognition of Thoreau; or, as Professor Raymond Adams phrased it at the centennial of Thoreau's death in 1962 when Thoreau was inducted into the New York University Hall of Fame for Great Americans, it was "the day Thoreau didn't die." Lowell's *ad hominem* charge that Thoreau's "whole life was a search for the doctor" had been widely promulgated and believed: Lowell's long evaluation of Thoreau which began as a review of the *Letters to Various Persons* echoed down through dozens of reviews and appraisals of Thoreau in the 1870's and 1880's. Who, after all, possessed the prestige to refute the most influential critic of the time? And had not Emerson himself upbraided Thoreau for his churlish negativism? The puny voices of such partisans as Ellery Channing (*Thoreau, the Poet-Naturalist*, 1873), Bronson Alcott, Emerson's "tedious archangel" (*Concord Days*, 1872), and that well-meaning dilettante, Franklin Sanborn, were simply not equal to the major task of lifting the Lowell stigma. And when the prestigious Robert Louis Stevenson chimed in from England in 1880 with his charge that Thoreau had been a "skulker" as Emerson in his eulogy had implied, critical esteem for Thoreau based on anything more than his acute observation of nature seemed to have reached its nadir.

For forty years after Lowell delivered his judgment of Thoreau, the academic critics, who might have reopened the question of Thoreau's importance, showed little inclination to do so. Charles Richardson (1887) classified Thoreau as a lunar reflection of Emerson, who "fell far short of the master's work, not, of course, in quantity alone, but also in quality." E. P. Whipple in the same year praised Webster as a master of English prose style, but neglected even to mention Thoreau in his survey of American literature. Walter Bronson, though admitting in his *Short History of American Literature* (1900) that "the flavor of his best work is exceedingly fine," classified Thoreau nonetheless with the "minor American authors." George E. Woodberry, in his *America in Literature* (1903), treated Emerson and Longfellow as the most fitting representatives of the "literary age of Boston." Richard T. Burton (1904) considered Bryant and Lowell appropriate for inclusion in a study of *Literary Leaders of America*, but not Thoreau. The pattern of academic neglect persisted. W. C. Brownell in his *American Prose Masters* (1909) included Cooper, Hawthorne, Emerson, Poe, Lowell, and Henry James; but omitted Thoreau. As late as 1912, William B. Cairns in his *History of American Literature* was still condescending: though Thoreau was "one of the few American writers whose fame has steadily increased," Cairns observed, "his eccentricities prevent him from ranking with the greatest American essayists." Most American literary historians were either cowed by Lowell or anesthetized by tradition or both. Had the succoring of Thoreau's reputation depended upon *academic* recognition between 1880 and 1916, renascence would have been long delayed. Fortunately, it did not.

From two unexpected quarters about 1890 a long recoil against Lowell began—from England and Mid-West America —and when it had run its course, Thoreau had won admittance to the highest pantheon of American writers, while Lowell's reputation had receded into the dusty recesses now occupied by his Brahmin contemporaries. The price Lowell paid for challenging Thoreau's claim to eminence may well have been, to a degree at least, the sacrifice of his own. Something more than coincidence is required to explain the reverse correlation in the movement of the reputations of Lowell and Thoreau in this century: Thoreau, ironically, is now one of the touchstones by which Lowell as critic is judged; and one of the most conspicuous nails in the coffin of Lowell's current reputation is his maligning of Thoreau's genius.

Spearheading critical interest in Thoreau in England was A. H. Japp, who published in 1877 under the pseudonym H. A. Page the second biography of Thoreau (*Thoreau: His Life and Aims*), an attempt to redress the misunderstanding "boldly repeated, recently, by high authorities, who should have known better" that "Thoreau was a morbid egotist, a sentimentalist, a solitary." Nothing, protested Dr. Japp, "could have been farther from the truth"; and when Stevenson, following Emerson, depicted Thoreau three years later as a man of "negative superiorities," Japp promptly remonstrated with him and prevailed upon him to retract his charge. But it was H. S. Salt, of all the English critics, who did the most to deflect Thoreau criticism from its inordinate preoccupation with the man and to point it in the direction of the palpable ingredients of Thoreau's modern fame. Three-quarters of a century after he wrote *The Life of Henry David Thoreau* (1890), his incisive comments have the ring of modernity about them. On this side of the Atlantic, simultaneously, Dr. Samuel A. Jones, an Ann Arbor physician, ridiculed the allegation that Thoreau was a carbon copy of Emerson, and urged his fellow-countrymen to "read the writings of a rare man, a flesh-and-blood reality, whose whole life was one strenuous endeavor to apprehend— *lay hold of*—eternity." In 1901, Jones edited and published in Detroit, with the assistance of Edwin B. Hill, the first collection of Thoreau criticism, *Pertaining to Thoreau*. Salt and Jones, and such other *fin de siècle* critics as Bradford Torrey, Gilbert Coleman, and John Macy, cleared the way for the twentieth-century reappraisal of Thoreau by releasing Thoreau criticism from three crippling *ad hominem* misconceptions: that Thoreau was a diminutive Emerson, as Lowell had alleged; that Thoreau's chief significance was to be found in his studies of flora and fauna, as Channing had alleged; that Thoreau had been an introverted, cold-blooded, "skulker," as both Emerson and Stevenson had to some extent alleged. "The true Thoreau," Stevenson had observed in his reevaluation of 1885, "still remains to be depicted," and John Macy also warned (in 1908) that "the man is not yet fully understood." But the spade-work had been begun; and though there would be frequent demurs, particularly from academic historians, as Thoreau's fame climbed steadily through the twentieth century and the many dimensions of his genius were uncovered, it would shortly be impossible to dismiss him with flippant epithets. Gilbert Coleman was no more than a decade in the vanguard of the criticism of his day when he wrote in 1906 that "probably no writer in America can lay claim to a sounder foundation for fame than Thoreau," and then went on to advise would-be critics:

> Thoreau is too valuable a possession, not only to American literature but to all literature, to be dealt with in an inappreciative or superficial manner by any critic, however witty or brilliant. His is a complex nature, not readily understood, and it is sometimes difficult to see with his vision. It is for this reason that those who would approach him in a critical spirit should approach him with caution and with sympathy. His is one of the rare cases known in literature where a noble spirit, a witty and inspiring mind, and a moral force of great value and attractiveness, have been brought together in one man.

Modern criticism of Thoreau can be said to have begun with Mark Van Doren's astringent volume in 1916. To Van Doren, Thoreau inhabited a vacuum and spent his life adroitly defending his choice of habitation, with the result that his "main product was nothing, and his main effort vain." Yet despite his unconcealed dislike for Thoreau, Van Doren ended his *Henry David Thoreau / A Critical Study* with the grudging admission that "Thoreau has demonstrated some of the meannesses of the demands of Time and Matter, and furnished the spirit and will for social criticism; he has made men acute critics, if not sensible shepherds, of their own sentiments." Subsequent writers on Thoreau in the period of academic reevaluation from 1917 to 1941 as a rule found Thoreau easier to praise. Though Archibald MacMechan in *The Cambridge History of American Literature* (1917) was perceptibly reserved and even obtuse, the power of *Walden* and the purity of Thoreau's style did not escape him. But to Norman Foerster must go the credit for having written the criticism at the centenary of Thoreau's birth that has been proved by time to have been most prophetic and just: with keen critical prescience, Foerster cut through fifty years of timorous acquiescence to Emerson and Lowell, of *ad hominem* attacks and defenses, to focus cleanly upon the qualities of Thoreau's mind and art which to later critics have proved to be the crucial ones. Foerster discerned the complexities in a writer whom most previous critics had attempted to explain in terms of single epithets and simple phrases; after the publication of his four seminal critical essays (1917-23), the old simplistic shibboleths became rapidly obsolete.

Prophetic also were the insights of N. C. Wyeth, who sensed in 1919 what so many readers have later discerned in Thoreau: the absorbing relevance of his writings to life in the twentieth century. Though he had grown up in the shadow of Concord, Wyeth remarked, and had been made to "feel a strong distaste for Thoreau," he discovered upon reading Thoreau "blisters and plasters in great variety and of warranted strength to make a man repent the lowness of his aims and the vulgarity of his satisfactions." A tradition of readers who turn to Thoreau for his therapeutic ventilation of American values has followed Wyeth, not the least being E. B. White and Howard Mumford Jones. Odell Shepard, like Wyeth, interpreted Thoreau as a "practical philosopher, constantly asking and trying to answer the most important question of all: how to live"; and lamented, in 1920, the loss America had incurred from having been "bemused these sixty years by a mere legend about him."

The 1920's and 1930's brought a conspicuously broadened apprehension of the many facets of Thoreau's genius, a widening of his audience and a sharpening of his fame: Leon Bazalgette's "novelized biography," *Henry Thoreau, Sauvage*, was translated into English by Van Wyk Brooks in 1924; Lewis Mumford, viewing Thoreau as one of the most influential contributors to American national self-knowledge, credited him with accepting, as the early pioneer had not, the challenge to "meet the expectation of the land," and of thus helping to precipitate "the dawn" of "the golden day" in American experience and culture. Brooks Atkinson wrote in 1927 his *Henry Thoreau, the Cosmic Yankee*, a thoroughly readable biography which helped satisfy the increasing curiosity about Thoreau among lay readers. Vernon Louis Parrington in 1930 was the forerunner of many analyses during the 1930's of Thoreau's political and economic thought; H. M. Tomlinson took up the question of Thoreau's style; A. E. Christy examined his Orientalism; F. Lorch explored the "organic" element in his poetry; Bartholow Crawford issued his *Henry David Thoreau* (1934) in the American Writers Series. Throughout the 1930's Canby wrote prolifically, beginning with his long study of Thoreau in *Classic Americans: A Study of Eminent American Writers from Irving to Whitman* (1931), which depicts Thoreau as "a great writer as well as a great man" and "one of the masters of English prose, purer, stronger, racier, closer to a genuine life rhythm, than any of his contemporaries in England or America"; and ending the decade with his biography of Thoreau (1939) which achieved the popularity of the best-seller lists. No collection of criticism can do more than suggest the mushrooming interest in Thoreau during this period (to what degree stimulated by the Great Depression no one can say): reprinted here is Gilbert Seldes' essay on Thoreau written for John Macy's *American Writers on American Literature* which suggests the solidity of Thoreau's reputation; omitted are such narrower studies as those of Christy, and of the Marxist critics, who gave inadvertent testimony to Thoreau's achieved stature by using him, as it were, to buttress their own critical and political predilections. By the outbreak of World War II, it is fair to say, the question as to whether Thoreau should rank with the half dozen or so major American writers of assured fame was no longer open; and critics, beginning with Matthiessen in *American Renaissance* (1941), set themselves to identifying and examining the facets of Thoreau's genius that would explain his rise to eminence.

Hiram M. Stanley, writing in *The Dial* in 1896 of "Thoreau as a Prose Writer," distinguished five styles in Thoreau's writing, ranging from "the adolescent, diffuse, romantic style of 'The Week'" to the "perfectly sound, sensible, sober style of the essay on 'Wild Apples.'" He lamented "the unfulfilled promise of an artist uniquely great in animal and landscape word painting," yet predicted that "despite the incompleteness and immaturity of his actual performance . . . appreciation of him is bound to grow." His prediction has been proved right, but how rudimentary his perception was of the complexities of Thoreau's art has become apparent only since Matthiessen developed his thesis in 1941 that *Walden,* far from being a glue and paste mosaic of sketches, is an "organic" unity, informed by subtle symbolism, and grounded upon a well integrated theory of art. "When, as a writer," Matthiessen observed, Thoreau "could fuse his thought and his observation by means of a symbol, which was not just suggested but designed in sharp detail, he was able, in Coleridge's phrase, to 'elicit truth as at a flash.'" "Thinking in images," Matthiessen contended, made it possible for Thoreau to exploit the possibilities for metaphorical expression and to demonstrate the unity he as a transcendentalist felt between the world of the senses and that of the spirit. Thoreau himself had provided a warrant for the critical vivisections of his prose that flooded the journals during the 1940's and 1950's in the wake of Matthiessen's pioneering studies, with such statements as the following contained in a letter to Emerson in July 1843:

> In writing conversation should be folded many times thick. It is the height of art that on the first perusal plain common sense should appear—on the second severe truth —and on the third beauty—and having these warrants for its depth and reality, we may then enjoy the beauty forever more.

The relationship between such statements as this and that of Robert Frost that a poem should begin in delight and end in wisdom has not gone unnoticed. Frost himself acknowledged his indebtedness to Thoreau. Studies of the influence of Thoreau upon other writers and upon world leaders have multiplied in the past two decades, and they are an important aspect of Thoreau's recognition. Exigencies of space, regrettably, preclude reprinting a sample of them in this collection.

To the influence of Matthiessen may be attributed in part the failure of any single school of criticism of the middle of the century to dominate the approaches to Thoreau. Though Matthiessen stimulated the several schools to apply their methodology to Thoreau, his insistence that "judgment of art is unavoidably both an aesthetic and a social act, and the critic's sense of social responsibility gives him a deeper thirst for meaning" provided a broad middle stance among the critical redoubts of liberals, humanists, new critics, myth critics, and Freudians. The selection of contemporary essays which concludes this volume has been made from this broad, middle ground.

To typify the solidity of Thoreau's current fame, this anthology includes the work of such established academic scholars as Raymond Adams, Joseph Wood Krutch, and Reginald Cook, whose names have long been associated with that of Thoreau. It includes Stanley Edgar Hyman's "Henry Thoreau in Our Time," one of the best known interpretative essays on Thoreau of the past quarter century. It reprints the study of Thoreau's European fame by Walter Harding, along with essays from John Broderick and Joseph Moldenhauer, younger but well established analysts of Thoreau's style. It concludes with Richard Drinnon's recent study of the relevance of Thoreau's political thought to this age and time. Terminating the collection with a study of Thoreau's activism seems appropriate for a writer who remarked on the title page of his greatest book that his purpose was to "crow like chanticleer . . . if only to wake my neighbors up."

––––––––

Because Thoreau's present fame rests primarily on his prose, no studies of his poetry are included. Arrangement of the selections is chronological. In all substantive matters, the original texts have been followed. In a few cases, long quotations from Thoreau, or biographical information about Thoreau which lacks relevance to the purpose of this volume, has been elided. In each case the elision has been indicated. Obvious accidental errors have been silently corrected.

Gratefully acknowledged is the assistance of Misses Leila Neilson, Jo Lynn Matko, Diane Poupard, Pam De Rocker, and Pam Zimmermann of the several libraries of the University of Minnesota, and that of Mrs. Robert Owens of the Duluth Public Library. Acknowledged also with appreciation is the grant of a summer research award by the Graduate School of the University of Minnesota which made possible the preparation of this volume.

Contents

First Revaluations: 1890-1916

The Rise to Fame: 1917-41

Mid-Century Insights and Appraisals: 1941 to the Present

I do not suppose that I have attained to obscurity, but I should be proud if no more fatal fault were found with my pages on this score than was found with the Walden ice. Southern customers objected to its blue color, which is the evidence of its purity, as if it were muddy, and preferred the Cambridge ice, which is white, but tastes of weeds. The purity men love is like the mists which envelop the earth, and not like the azure ether beyond.

"Conclusion," *Walden*

Ad Hominem:
Emersonian Eccentric
and Naturalist
1848-90

It is a ridiculous demand which England and America make, that
you shall speak so that they can understand you. Neither men nor
toadstools grow so.

"Conclusion," Walden

JAMES RUSSELL LOWELL (1819-91), abolitionist, poet, editor, and critic, was the first of Thoreau's contemporaries to accord Thoreau critical recognition, *A Fable for Critics* being published in 1848. Which of the blanks in the passage quoted refers to Thoreau and which to Thoreau's close friend, Ellery Channing, is debatable; but both men are charged with imitating the "mystagogue," Emerson. Of far greater impact upon Thoreau's nineteenth-century reputation was Lowell's long, posthumous, *ad hominem* appraisal of Thoreau published in 1865.

From
A Fable for Critics

JAMES RUSSELL LOWELL

The Poetical Works of James Russell Lowell, Riverside Edition, Vol. 3 (Boston and New York: Houghton Mifflin Company, 1890), 41-42.

He [Emerson] has imitators in scores, who omit
No part of the man but his wisdom and wit,—
Who go carefully o'er the sky-blue of his brain,
And when he has skimmed it once, skim it again;
If at all they resemble him, you may be sure it is
Because their shoals mirror his mists and obscurities,
As a mud-puddle seems deep as heaven for a minute,
While a cloud that floats o'er is reflected within it.

There comes ————, for instance; to see him's rare sport,
Tread in Emerson's tracks with legs painfully short;
How he jumps, how he strains, and gets red in the face,
To keep step with the mystagogue's natural pace!
He follows as close as a stick to a rocket,
His fingers exploring the prophet's each pocket.
Fie, for shame, brother bard; with good fruit of your own,
Can't you let Neighbor Emerson's orchards alone?
Besides, 't is no use, you'll not find e'en a core,—
———— has picked up all the windfalls before.

A Notice of
A Week on the Concord
and Merrimack Rivers

ANONYMOUS

Godey's Lady's Book, Vol. 39 (September, 1849), 223.

Those who have read "Margaret Smith's Journal," will be at no loss in settling the authorship of this clever and interesting work. Mr. Whittier touches all his themes with the true poet's wand; all show forms of beauty and gleams of light that, like the sunbeams on the far-off mountain, make the cold and rugged landscape appear soft and charming. It is just the book to read in the idleness of summer, when wishing to enjoy the pleasures of journeying, without the inconvenience which the actual packing up and going off in hot steamboats and dusty cars occasion. Read it, and see.

Review of
A Week on the Concord
and Merrimack Rivers

ANONYMOUS

London Athenaeum, No. 1149 (October 27, 1849), 1086.

A Week on the Concord and Merrimack Rivers. By Henry D. Thoreau. —One of Mr. Chapman's importations from the United States. The Concord and Merrimack are not rivers which would be likely to yield much matter of interest to the traveller—even if he sought for it, —which Mr. Thoreau does not. His pages are the record of a week of pic-nicing, and boating—and the vagrant thoughts and fancies to which a man of education and reading habits may give himself up in "hours of idleness." The book would therefore be better described as a series of essays on love, poetry, religion—and so on. The matter is for the most part poor enough; but there are a few things in the volume, scattered here and there, which suggest that the writer is a man with a habit of original thinking, which with more careful culture may produce a richer harvest in some future season. The manner is that of the worst offshoots of Carlyle and Emerson: all Mr. Thoreau's best things are spoilt in the utterance. If he would trust in his own genius, he has that to say which might command a larger audience. But imitations of an imitation! The world is too old and the prophets are too many for such things to have a chance of a public hearing in these days.

Review of
Walden

ANONYMOUS

Graham's Magazine, Vol. 45 (September, 1854), 298-300.

Whatever may be thought or said of this curious volume, nobody can deny its claims to individuality of opinion, sentiment, and expression. Sometimes strikingly original, sometimes merely eccentric and odd, it is always racy and stimulating. The author, an educated gentleman, disgusted with the compliances and compromises which society enjoins on those to whom it gives "a living," goes off alone into Concord woods, builds his own house, cooks his own victuals, makes and mends his own clothes, works, reads, thinks as he pleases, and writes this book to chronicle his success in the experiment. Mr. Thoreau, it is well known, belongs to the class of transcendentalists who lay the greatest stress on the "I," and knows no limitation on the exercise of the rights of that important pronoun. The customs, manners, occupations, religion, of society, he "goes out" from, and brings them before his own inward tribunal for judgment. He differs from all mankind with wonderful composure; and without any of the fuss of the come-outers, goes beyond them in asserting the autocracy of the individual. Making himself the measure of truth, he is apt to think that "difference from me is the measure of absurdity;" and occasionally he obtains a startling paradox, by the simple inversion of a stagnant truism.

WALDEN;

OR,

LIFE IN THE WOODS.

By HENRY D. THOREAU,

AUTHOR OF "A WEEK ON THE CONCORD AND MERRIMACK RIVERS."

I do not propose to write an ode to dejection, but to brag as lustily as chanticleer in the
morning, standing on his roost, if only to wake my neighbors up. — Page 92.

BOSTON:
TICKNOR AND FIELDS.
M DCCC LIV.

The title page of *Walden*, 1854

He likes to say that four and four makes nine, in order to assert his independence of the contemptible trammels of the world's arithmetic. He has a philosophical flare and gibe for most axioms, and snaps his fingers in the face of the most accredited proprieties and "do-me-*goodisms*" of conventional life. But if he has the wildness of the woods about him, he has their sweetness also. Through all the audacities of his eccentric protests, a careful eye can easily discern the movement of a powerful and accomplished mind. He has evidently read the best books, and talked with the best people. His love for nature, and his eye for nature, are altogether beyond the ordinary love and insight of nature's priests; and his descriptions have a kind of De Foe-like accuracy and reality in their eloquence, peculiar to himself among all American writers. We feel, in reading him, that such a man has earned the right to speak of nature, for he has taken her in all moods, and given the same "frolic welcome" to her "thunder and her sunshine."

But we doubt if anybody can speak so well of Mr. Thoreau as Mr. Thoreau himself. He has devoted so much of his life to the perusal of his own consciousness, that we feel it would be a kind of impertinence to substitute our impressions for his knowledge. . . . [There follows a lengthy series of extracts from *Walden.*]

We fear that our extracts have not done justice to the attractiveness of this curious and original volume. We might easily fill a page with short, sharp, quotable sentences, embodying some flash of wit or humor, some scrap of quaint or elevated wisdom, or some odd or beautiful image. Every chapter in the book is stamped with sincerity. It is genuine and genial throughout. Even its freaks of thought are full of suggestions. When the author turns his eye seriously on an object, no matter how remote from the sphere of ordinary observation, he commonly sees into it and through it. He has a good deal of Mr. Emerson's piercing quality of mind, which he exercises on the more elusive and flitting phenomena of consciousness, with a metaphysician's subtilty, and a poet's expressiveness. And as regards the somewhat presumptuous manner in which he dogmatizes, the reader will soon learn to pardon it for the real wealth of individual thinking by which it is accompanied, always remembering that Mr. Thoreau, in the words of his own

noble enough to inspire those whom we would so benefit with nobleness. External bondage is trifling compared with the bondage of an ignoble soul. Such things are often said, doubtless, in pulpits and elsewhere, but the men who say them are too apt to live just with the crowd, and so their words come more and more to ring with a hollow sound.

It is refreshing to find in these books the sentiments of one man whose aim manifestly is to *live*, and not to waste his time upon the externals of living. Educated at Cambridge, in the way called liberal, he seems determined to make a liberal life of it, and not to become the slave of any calling, for the sake of earning a reputable livelihood or of being regarded as a useful member of society. He evidently considers it his first business to become more and more a living, advancing soul, knowing that thus alone (though he desires to think as little as possible about that) can he be, in any proper sense, useful to others. Mr. Thoreau's view of life has been called selfish. His own words, under the head of "Philanthropy" in Walden, are the amplest defense against this charge, to those who can appreciate them. In a deeper sense than we commonly think, charity begins at home. The man who, with any fidelity, obeys his own genius, serves men infinitely more by so doing, becoming an encouragement, a strengthener, a fountain of inspiration to them, than if he were to turn aside from his path and exhaust his energies in striving to meet their superficial needs. As a thing by the way, aside from our proper work, we may seek to remove external obstacles from the path of our neighbours, but no man can help them much who makes that his main business, instead of seeking evermore, with all his energies, to reach the loftiest point which his imagination sets before him, thus adding to the stock of true nobleness in the world.

But suppose all men should pursue Mr. Thoreau's course, it is asked triumphantly, as though, then, we should be sure to go back to barbarism. Let it be considered, in the first place, that no man could pursue his course who was a mere superficial imitator, any more than it would be a real imitation of Christ if all men were to make it their main business to go about preaching the Gospel to each other. Is it progress toward barbarism to simplify one's outward life for the sake of coming closer to Nature and to the realm of ideas? Is it civilization and refinement to be occupied evermore with adding to our material conveniences, comforts and luxuries, to make ourselves not so much living members as dead tools of society, in some bank, shop, office, pulpit or kitchen? If men were to follow in Mr. Thoreau's steps, by being more obedient to their loftiest instincts, there would, indeed, be a falling off in the splendor of our houses, in the richness of our furniture and dress, in the luxury of our tables, but how poor are these things in comparison with the new grandeur and beauty which would appear in the souls of men. What fresh and inspiring conversation should we have, instead of the wearisome gossip, which now meets us at every turn. Men toil on, wearing out body or soul, or both, that they may accumulate a needless amount of the externals of living; that they may win the regard of those no wiser than themselves; their natures become warped and hardened to their pursuits; they get fainter and fainter glimpses of the glory of the world, and, by and by, comes into their richly-adorned parlours some wise and beautiful soul, like the writer of these books, who, speaking from the fullness of his inward life, makes their luxuries appear vulgar, showing that, in a direct way, he has obtained the essence of that which his entertainers have been vainly seeking for at such a terrible expense.

It seems remarkable that these books have received no more adequate notice in our Literary Journals. But the class of scholars are often as blind as others to any new elevation of soul. In Putnam's Magazine, Mr. Thoreau is spoken of as an oddity, as the Yankee Diogenes, as though the really ridiculous oddity were not in us of the "starched shirt-collar" rather than in this devotee of Nature and Thought. Some have praised the originality and profound sympathy with which he views natural objects. We might as well stop with praising Jesus for the happy use he has made of the lilies of the field. The fact of surpassing interest for us is the simple grandeur of Mr. Thoreau's position —a position open to us all, and of which this sympathy with Nature is but a single result. This is seen in the less descriptive, more purely thoughtful passages, such as that upon Friendship in the "Wednesday" of the "Week," and in those upon "Solitude," "What I Lived for," and "Higher Laws," in "Walden," as well as in many others in both books. We do not believe that, in the whole course of literature, ancient and modern, so noble a discourse upon Friendship can be produced as that which Mr. Thoreau has given us. It points to a relation, to be sure, which, from the ordinary level of our lives, may seem remote and dreamy. But it is our thirst for, and glimpses of, such things which indicate the greatness of our nature, which give the purest charm and colouring to our lives. The striking peculiarity of Mr. Thoreau's attitude is, that while he is no religionist, and while he is eminently practical in regard to the material economics of life, he yet manifestly feels, through and through, that the loftiest dreams of the imagination are the solidest realities, and so the only foundation for us to build upon, while the affairs in which men are everywhere busying themselves so intensely are comparatively the merest froth and foam.

GEORGE ELIOT (1819-80), English novelist, was born Mary Ann Evans. From 1851 to 1853 she was assistant editor of the *Westminster Review*, in which she published her review of *Walden*. Not until 1857 was she to publish the first of the novels upon which her fame now rests.

Review of
Walden

GEORGE ELIOT

Westminster Review, Vol. 65 (January, 1856), 302-3. Excerpts from *Walden* have been deleted.

In a volume called *Walden*; or, *Life in the Woods*, published last year, but quite interesting enough to make it worth while for us to break our rule by a retrospective notice—we have a bit of pure American life (not the 'go a-head' species, but its opposite pole), animated by that energetic, yet calm spirit of innovation, that practical as well as theoretic independence of formulae, which is peculiar to some of the finer American minds. The writer tells us how he chose, for some years, to be a stoic of the woods; how he built his house; how he earned the necessaries of his simple life by cultivating a bit of ground. He tells his system of diet, his studies, his reflections, and his observations of natural phenomena. These last are not only made by a keen eye, but have their interest enhanced by passing through the medium of a deep poetic sensibility; and, indeed, we feel throughout the book the presence of a refined as well as a hardy mind. People—very wise in their own eyes—who would have every man's life ordered according to a particular pattern, and who are intolerant of every existence the utility of which is not palpable to them, may pooh-pooh Mr. Thoreau and this episode in his history, as unpractical and dreamy. Instead of contesting their opinion ourselves, we will let Mr. Thoreau speak for himself. There is plenty of sturdy sense mingled with his unworldliness. . . .

Thoreau's Obituary

ANONYMOUS

New York *Tribune*, 10 May 1862.

Henry D. Thoreau, the genial writer on the natural scenery of New England, died at Concord, Massachusetts on Tuesday, May 6th, after a protracted illness of more than eighteen months. He was a native of Boston, but moved with his family at the age of five years to Concord, where he has since resided. He graduated at Harvard College in 1837, and was nearly forty-five years old at the time of his death. His writings include *A Week on the Concord and Merrimack Rivers*; *Walden, or Life in the Woods*; and various contributions to the periodical literature of the day. They are remarkable for their freedom and originality of thought, their quaint humor, and their warm sympathy with all the manifold aspects of nature. His disease was consumption, and, as we are informed, 'his humor and cheerful courage did not forsake him during his sickness, and he met death as gayly as Theramenes in Xenophon's story.' Mr. Thoreau, in spite of the racy individuality of his character, was much beloved and respected by his townsmen, and his writings have numerous admirers. He was honored with a public funeral from the Town Hall of Concord, on Friday, the 9th, inst.

GEORGE WILLIAM CURTIS (1824-92) was a participant in the Brook Farm experiment and a correspondent for Horace Greeley's New York *Tribune*. He became a propagandist for woman's rights and for the antislavery movement after 1856, edited *Harper's Weekly* after 1863, and contributed for many years to the "Editor's Easy Chair" column of *Harper's Magazine*.

Editor's Easy Chair

GEORGE WILLIAM CURTIS

Harper's Monthly, Vol. 25 (July, 1862), 270-71. A quotation from *Walden* has been deleted.

The name of Henry Thoreau is known to very few persons beyond those who personally knew him; but it will be known long and well in our literature, and can not fade from the memories of all who ever saw him. He was a plain New England man, who sighed neither for old England nor for Greece and Rome. In the woods and pastures of a region in no way remarkable for its natural beauty or for cultivation he found all the company he cared for, and believed that the birds and beasts and flowers he knew were certainly as good, and the men and women perhaps even better, than he could have found in any other place at any other time.

The story of his life is perfectly simple. He had an aptitude for study, graduated at Cambridge, returned to his home in Concord, Massachusetts, and worked as a land-surveyor, while he studied as his inclinations led; built a shanty or cottage by the side of a pretty pond, where he lived quite alone at an expense of about seventy dollars a year; was as faithful a student of nature as he was of Greek literature and Hindoo philosophy; was a most accurate observer, and became known to naturalists and valued by them; had a shrewd mother-wit; but upon the whole he seemed to think that civilization had gone astray; that much fine wisdom had perished with the Indians, and had not been replaced; that the Stoics were the true heroes, and the Hindoo Vedas and Norse Eddas the most interesting religious legends.

He was a man of singular rectitude, independence, and sagacity. Mr. Emerson says of him that no one was so entirely uninfluenced by the ordinary motives of human action. He wished neither riches, nor fame, nor influence. He cared to be himself only, and he held the world and modern times successfully at bay. But he was entirely unobtrusive. Once or twice only, by the urgent request of others, he spoke in public, but without especial success, for he was in no degree magnetic or impassioned, and his intellectual habit was solitary and severe. He was truly at home in the woods or on the water, and yet he was so much more than a naturalist merely, like Cotton or any of the amiable observers of birds and animals, that he is to be thought of as a naturalist only in the largest sense. He was quite as much thinker as he was observer, and he was familiar with the best literature. His chapter on Reading, in his "Walden, or Life in the Woods," is as good as any thing ever written upon the subject. . . .

This book, the record of his residence, his thoughts, and observations during the time he lived in the woods upon the shore of Walden Pond, in Concord, Massachusetts, is of the very best of its kind in any literature. He lived in his cottage about two years. For the rest of his life his home was in the village. "I found," he says, "that by working about six weeks in a year I could meet all the expenses of living. The whole of my winters, as well as most of my summers, I had free and clear for study." The cheerful humor with which he details his woodland experience is racy and delightful. "Many a traveler came out of his way to see me and the inside of my house, and, as an excuse for calling, asked for a glass of water. I told them that I drank at the pond, and pointed thither, offering to lend them a dipper." "Restless committed men, whose time was all taken up in getting a living or keeping it; ministers who spoke of God as if they enjoyed a monopoly of the subject, who could not bear all kinds of opinions; doctors, lawyers, uneasy housekeepers, who pried into my cupboard and bed when I was out —how came Mrs.—— to know that my sheets were not as clean as hers?—young men who had ceased to be young, and had concluded that it was safest to follow the beaten track of the professions—all these generally said that it was not possible to do so much good in my position. Ay! there was the rub. The old and infirm and the timid, of whatever age or sex, thought most of sickness, and sudden accident, and death; to them life

seemed full of danger—what danger is there if you don't think
of any?—and they thought that a prudent man would carefully
select the safest position, where Dr. B—— might be on hand
at a moment's warning. To them the village was literally a
com-munity, a league for mutual defense; and you would
suppose that they would not go a huckleberrying without a
medicine-chest. The amount of it is, if a man is alive there is
always *danger* that he may die, though the danger must be
allowed to be less in proportion as he is dead-and-alive to
begin with. A man sits as many risks as he runs."

Thoreau was a Stoic, but he was in no sense a cynic. His
neighbors in the village thought him odd and whimsical, but
his practical skill as a surveyor and in wood-craft was known
to them. No man was his enemy, and some of the best men were
his fastest friends. But his life was essentially solitary and reserved. Careless of appearances in later days, when his hair and
beard were long, if you had seen him in the woods you might
have fancied Orson passing by; but had you stopped to talk
with him, you would have felt that you had seen the shepherd
of Admetus's flock, or chatted with a wiser Jacques. For some
time past he had been sinking under a consumption. He made
a journey to the West a year ago, but in vain; and returned to
die quietly at home.

It was my good fortune to see him again, last November,
when he came into the library of a friend to borrow a volume
of Pliny's letters. He was much wasted, and his doom was
clear. But he talked in the old strain of wise gravity without
either sentiment or sadness. His conversation fell upon the
Indians of this country, of our obligations to them, and our in-
gratitude. It was by far the best talk about Indians I have ever
heard or read; and somewhere among his papers, it is to be
hoped, some monument of his knowledge of them and regard
for them survives.

Mr. Thoreau was the neighbor and intimate friend of Mr.
Emerson, who read a discourse at his funeral. "Referring to
the Alpine flower *Adelweiss*, or noble-purity, which the young
Switzers sometimes lose their lives in plucking from its perilous
heights, he said: 'Could we pierce to where he is, we should
see him wearing profuse chaplets of it, for it belonged to him.'
Where there is knowledge, where there is virtue, where there

is beauty, where there is progress, there is now his home." In a poem called "Woodnotes," published nearly twenty years ago, Mr. Emerson had already said what he doubtless felt of this valued and faithful friend. The lines will be new to many of our readers to whom the author is not known as a poet, although few men have written such true poetry:

> "The water-courses were my guide;
> I traveled grateful by their side,
> Or through their channel dry;
> They led me through the thicket damp,
> Through brake and fern, the beavers' camp,
> Through beds of granite cut my road,
> And their resistless friendship showed;
> The falling waters led me,
> The foodful waters fed me,
> And brought me to the lowest land,
> Unerring to the ocean sand.
> The moss upon the forest bark
> Was pole-star when the night was dark;
> The purple berries in the wood
> Supplied me necessary food;
> For Nature ever faithful is
> To such as trust her faithfulness.
> When the forest shall mislead me,
> When the night and morning lie,
> When sea and land refuse to feed me,
> 'Twill be time enough to die;
> Then will yet my mother yield
> A pillow in her greenest field,
> Nor the June flowers scorn to cover
> The clay of their departed lover."

RALPH WALDO EMERSON (1803-82), fourteen years Thoreau's senior, was the most highly esteemed of the transcendentalists and an intimate of Thoreau throughout the younger man's adult life. Emerson delivered the address at the funeral services for Thoreau on May 6, 1862; and later printed the address with some changes in the *Atlantic Monthly*. Emerson's emphasis upon Thoreau's asceticism and stoicism evoked many rejoiners.

Thoreau

RALPH WALDO EMERSON

Atlantic Monthly, Vol. 10 (August, 1862), 239-49. A section of quotations from Thoreau has been deleted.

Henry David Thoreau was the last male descendant of a French ancestor who came to this country from the Isle of Guernsey. His character exhibited occasional traits drawn from this blood, in singular combination with a very strong Saxon genius.

He was born in Concord, Massachusetts, on the 12th of July, 1817. He was graduated at Harvard College in 1837, but without any literary distinction. An iconoclast in literature, he seldom thanked colleges for their service to him, holding them in small esteem, whilst yet his debt to them was important. After leaving the University, he joined his brother in teaching a private school, which he soon renounced. His father was a manufacturer of lead-pencils, and Henry applied himself for a time to this craft, believing he could make a better pencil than was then in use. After completing his experiments, he exhibited his work to chemists and artists in Boston, and having obtained their certificates to its excellence and to its equality with the best London manufacture, he returned home contented. His friends congratulated him that he had now opened his way to fortune. But he replied that he should never make another pencil. "Why should I? I would not do again what I have done once." He resumed his endless walks and miscellaneous studies, making every day some new acquaintance with Nature, though as yet never speaking of zoölogy or botany, since, though very studious of natural facts, he was incurious of technical and textual science.

At this time, a strong, healthy youth, fresh from college, whilst all his companions were choosing their profession, or eager to begin some lucrative employment, it was inevitable that his thoughts should be exercised on the same question, and it required rare decision to refuse all the accustomed paths and keep his solitary freedom at the cost of disappointing the natural expectations of his family and friends: all the more difficult that he had a perfect probity, was exact in securing his own independence, and in holding every man to the like duty. But Thoreau never faltered. He was a born protestant. He declined to give up his large ambition of knowledge and action for any narrow craft or profession, aiming at a much more comprehensive calling, the art of living well. If he slighted and defied the opinions of others, it was only that he was more intent to reconcile his practice with his own belief. Never idle or self-indulgent, he preferred, when he wanted money, earning it by some piece of manual labor agreeable to him, as building a boat or a fence, planting, grafting, surveying or other short work, to any long engagements. With his hardy habits and few wants, his skill in wood-craft, and his powerful arithmetic, he was very competent to live in any part of the world. It would cost him less time to supply his wants than another. He was therefore secure of his leisure.

A natural skill for mensuration, growing out of his mathematical knowledge and his habit of ascertaining the measures and distances of objects which interested him, the size of trees, the depth and extent of ponds and rivers, the height of mountains and the air-line distance of his favorite summits,—this, and his intimate knowledge of the territory about Concord, made him drift into the profession of land-surveyor. It had the advantage for him that it led him continually into new and secluded grounds, and helped his studies of Nature. His accuracy and skill in this work were readily appreciated, and he found all the employment he wanted.

He could easily solve the problems of the surveyor, but he was daily beset with graver questions, which he manfully confronted. He interrogated every custom, and wished to settle all his practice on an ideal foundation. He was a protestant *à outrance*, and few lives contain so many renunciations. He was bred to no profession; he never married; he lived alone; he never went to church; he never voted; he refused to pay a tax to the State; he ate no flesh, he drank no wine, he never knew the use of tobacco; and, though a naturalist, he used neither trap nor gun. He chose, wisely no doubt for himself, to be the bachelor of thought and Nature. He had no talent for wealth, and knew how to be poor without the least hint of squalor or inelegance. Perhaps he fell into his way of living without forecasting it much, but approved it with later wisdom. "I am often reminded," he wrote in his journal, "that if I had bestowed on me the wealth of Crœsus, my aims must be still the same, and my means essentially the same." He had no temptations to fight against,—no appetites, no passions, no taste for elegant trifles. A fine house, dress, the manners and talk of highly cultivated people were all thrown away on him. He much preferred a good Indian, and considered these refinements as impediments to conversation, wishing to meet his companion on the simplest terms. He declined invitations to dinner-parties, because there each was in every one's way, and he could not meet the individuals to any purpose. "They make their pride," he said, "in making their dinner cost much; I make my pride in making my dinner cost little." When asked at table what dish he preferred, he answered, "The nearest." He did not like the taste of wine, and never had a vice in his life. He said,—"I have a faint recollection of pleasure derived from smoking dried lily-stems, before I was a man. I had commonly a supply of these. I have never smoked anything more noxious."

He chose to be rich by making his wants few, and supplying them himself. In his travels, he used the railroad only to get over so much country as was unimportant to the present purpose, walking hundreds of miles, avoiding taverns, buying a lodging in farmers' and fishermen's houses, as cheaper, and more agreeable to him, and because there he could better find the men and the information he wanted.

There was somewhat military in his nature, not to be subdued, always manly and able, but rarely tender, as if he did not feel himself except in opposition. He wanted a fallacy to expose, a blunder to pillory, I may say required a little sense of victory, a roll of the drum, to call his powers into full exercise. It cost him nothing to say No; indeed he found it much easier than to say Yes. It seemed as if his first instinct on hearing a proposition was to controvert it, so impatient was he of the limitations of our daily thought. This habit, of course, is a little chilling to the social affections; and though the companion would in the end acquit him of any malice or untruth, yet it mars conversation. Hence, no equal companion stood in affectionate relations with one so pure and guileless. "I love Henry," said one of his friends, "but I cannot like him; and as for taking his arm, I should as soon think of taking the arm of an elm-tree."

Yet, hermit and stoic as he was, he was really fond of sympathy, and threw himself heartily and childlike into the company of young people whom he loved, and whom he delighted to entertain, as he only could, with the varied and endless anecdotes of his experiences by field and river: and he was always ready to lead a huckleberry-party or a search for chestnuts or grapes. Talking, one day, of a public discourse, Henry remarked that whatever succeeded with the audience was bad. I said, "Who would not like to write something which all can read, like Robinson Crusoe? and who does not see with regret that his page is not solid with a right materialistic treatment, which delights everybody?" Henry objected, of course, and vaunted the better lectures which reached only a few persons. But, at supper, a young girl, understanding that he was to lecture at the Lyceum, sharply asked him, "Whether his lecture would be a nice, interesting story, such as she wished to hear, or whether it was one of those old philosophical things that she did not care about." Henry turned to her, and bethought himself, and, I saw, was trying to believe that he had matter that might fit her and her brother, who were to sit up and go to the lecture, if it was a good one for them.

He was a speaker and actor of the truth, born such, and was ever running into dramatic situations from this cause. In any circumstance it interested all bystanders to know what part Henry would take, and what he would say; and he did not disappoint expectation, but used an original judgment on each emergency. In 1845 he built himself a small framed house on the shores of Walden Pond, and lived there two years alone, a life of labor and study. This action was quite native and fit for him. No one who knew him would tax him with affectation. He was more unlike his neighbors in his thought than in his action. As soon as he had exhausted the advantages of that solitude, he abandoned it. In 1847, not approving some uses to which the public expenditure was applied, he refused to pay his town tax, and was put in jail. A friend paid the tax for him, and he was released. The like annoyance was threatened the next year. But as his friends paid the tax, notwithstanding his protest, I believe he ceased to resist. No opposition or ridicule had any weight with him. He coldly and fully stated his opinion without affecting to believe that it was the opinion of the company. It was of no consequence if every one present held the opposite opinion. On one occasion he went to the University Library to procure some books. The librarian refused to lend them. Mr. Thoreau repaired to the President, who stated to him the rules and usages, which permitted the loan of books to resident graduates, to clergymen who were alumni, and to some others resident within a circle of ten miles' radius from the College. Mr. Thoreau explained to the President that the railroad had destroyed the old scale of distances,—that the library was useless, yes, and President and College useless, on the terms of his rules,—that the one benefit he owed to the College was its library,—that, at this moment, not only his want of books was imperative, but he wanted a large number of books, and assured him that he, Thoreau, and not the librarian, was the proper custodian of these. In short, the President found the petitioner so formidable, and the rules getting to look so ridiculous, that he ended by giving him a privilege which in his hands proved unlimited thereafter.

No truer American existed than Thoreau. His preference of his country and condition was genuine, and his aversation from English and European manners and tastes almost reached contempt. He listened impatiently to news or *bonmots* gleaned from London circles; and though he tried to be civil, these anecdotes fatigued him. The men were all imitating each other, and on a small mould. Why can they not live as far apart as possible, and each be a man by himself? What he sought was the most energetic nature; and he wished to go to Oregon, not to London. "In every part of Great Britain," he wrote in his diary, "are discovered traces of the Romans, their funereal urns, their camps, their roads, their dwellings. But New England, at least, is not based on any Roman ruins. We have not to lay the foundations of our houses on the ashes of a former civilization."

But idealist as he was, standing for abolition of slavery, abolition of tariffs, almost for abolition of government, it is needless to say he found himself not only unrepresented in actual politics, but almost equally opposed to every class of reformers. Yet he paid the tribute of his uniform respect to the Anti-Slavery party. One man, whose personal acquaintance he had formed, he honored with exceptional regard. Before the first friendly word had been spoken for Captain John Brown, he sent notices to most houses in Concord that he would speak in a public hall on the condition and character of John Brown, on Sunday evening, and invited all people to come. The Republican Committee, the Abolitionist Committee, sent him word that it was premature and not advisable. He replied,— "I did not send to you for advice, but to announce that I am to speak." The hall was filled at an early hour by people of all parties, and his earnest eulogy of the hero was heard by all respectfully, by many with a sympathy that surprised themselves.

It was said of Plotinus that he was ashamed of his body, and 't is very likely he had good reason for it,—that his body was a bad servant, and he had not skill in dealing with the material world, as happens often to men of abstract intellect. But Mr. Thoreau was equipped with a most adapted and serviceable body. He was of short stature, firmly built, of light complexion, with strong, serious blue eyes, and a grave aspect,—his face covered in the late years with a becoming beard. His senses were acute, his frame well-knit and hardy, his hands strong and skilful in the use of tools. And there was a wonderful fitness of body and mind. He could pace sixteen rods more accurately than another man could measure them with rod and chain. He could find his path in the woods at night, he said, better by his feet than his eyes. He could estimate the measure of a tree very well by his eye; he could estimate the weight of a calf or a pig, like a dealer. From a box containing a bushel or more of loose pencils, he could take up with his hands fast enough just a dozen pencils at every grasp. He was a good swimmer, runner, skater, boatman, and would probably outwalk most countrymen in a day's journey. And the relation of body to mind was still finer than we have indicated. He said he wanted every stride his legs made. The length of his walk uniformly made the length of his writing. If shut up in the house he did not write at all.

He had a strong common sense, like that which Rose Flammock, the weaver's daughter in Scott's romance, commends in her father, as resembling a yardstick, which, whilst it measures dowlas and diaper, can equally well measure tapestry and cloth of gold. He had always a new resource. When I was planting forest trees, and had procured half a peck of acorns, he said that only a small portion of them would be sound, and proceeded to examine them and select the sound ones. But finding this took time, he said, "I think if you put them all into water the good ones will sink;" which experiment we tried with success. He could plan a garden or a house or a barn; would have been competent to lead a "Pacific Exploring Expedition;" could give judicious counsel in the gravest private or public affairs.

He lived for the day, not cumbered and mortified by his memory. If he brought you yesterday a new proposition, he would bring you to-day another not less revolutionary. A very industrious man, and setting, like all highly organized men, a high value on his time, he seemed the only man of leisure in town, always ready for any excursion that promised well, or for conversation prolonged into late hours. His trenchant sense was never stopped by his rules of daily prudence, but was always up to the new occasion. He liked and used the simplest food, yet, when some one urged a vegetable diet, Thoreau thought all diets a very small matter, saying that "the man who shoots the buffalo lives better than the man who boards at the Graham House." He said,—"You can sleep near the railroad, and never be disturbed: Nature knows very well what sounds are worth attending to, and has made up her mind not to hear the railroad-whistle. But things respect the devout mind, and a mental ecstasy was never interrupted." He noted what repeatedly befell him, that, after receiving from a distance a rare plant, he would presently find the same in his own haunts. And those pieces of luck which happen only to good players happened to him. One day, walking with a stranger, who inquired where Indian arrow-heads could be found, he replied, "Everywhere," and, stooping forward, picked one on the instant from the ground. At Mount Washington, in Tuckerman's Ravine,

Thoreau had a bad fall, and sprained his foot. As he was in the act of getting up from his fall, he saw for the first time the leaves of the *Arnica mollis.*

His robust common sense, armed with stout hands, keen perceptions and strong will, cannot yet account for the superiority which shone in his simple and hidden life. I must add the cardinal fact, that there was an excellent wisdom in him, proper to a rare class of men, which showed him the material world as a means and symbol. This discovery, which sometimes yields to poets a certain casual and interrupted light, serving for the ornament of their writing, was in him an unsleeping insight; and whatever faults or obstructions of temperament might cloud it, he was not disobedient to the heavenly vision. In his youth, he said, one day, "The other world is all my art; my pencils will draw no other; my jack-knife will cut nothing else; I do not use it as a means." This was the muse and genius that ruled his opinions, conversation, studies, work and course of life. This made him a searching judge of men. At first glance he measured his companion, and, though insensible to some fine traits of culture, could very well report his weight and calibre. And this made the impression of genius which his conversation sometimes gave.

He understood the matter in hand at a glance, and saw the limitations and poverty of those he talked with, so that nothing seemed concealed from such terrible eyes. I have repeatedly known young men of sensibility converted in a moment to the belief that this was the man they were in search of, the man of men, who could tell them all they should do. His own dealing with them was never affectionate, but superior, didactic, scorning their petty ways,—very slowly conceding, or not conceding at all, the promise of his society at their houses, or even at his own. "Would he not walk with them?" "He did not know. There was nothing so important to him as his walk; he had no walks to throw away on company." Visits were offered him from respectful parties, but he declined them. Admiring friends offered to carry him at their own cost to the Yellowstone River,—to the West Indies,—to South America. But though nothing could be more grave or considered than his refusals, they remind one, in quite new relations, of that fop Brummel's reply to the gentleman who offered him his carriage in a shower, "But where will *you* ride, then?"—and what accusing silences, and what searching and irresistible speeches, battering down all defences, his companions can remember!

Mr. Thoreau dedicated his genius with such entire love to the fields, hills and waters of his native town, that he made them known and interesting to all reading Americans, and to people over the sea. The river on whose banks he was born and died he knew from its springs to its confluence with the Merrimack. He had made summer and winter observations on it for many years, and at every hour of the day and night. The result of the recent survey of the Water Commissioners appointed by the State of Massachusetts he had reached by his private experiments, several years earlier. Every fact which occurs in the bed, on the banks or in the air over it; the fishes, and their spawning and nests, their manners, their food; the shad-flies which fill the air on a certain evening once a year, and which are snapped at by the fishes so ravenously that many of these die of repletion; the conical heaps of small stones on the river-shallows, the huge nests of small fishes, one of which will sometimes overfill a cart; the birds which frequent the stream, heron, duck, sheldrake, loon, osprey; the snake, musk-rat, otter, woodchuck and fox, on the banks; the turtle, frog, hyla and cricket, which make the banks vocal,—were all known to him, and, as it were, townsmen and fellow creatures; so that he felt an absurdity or violence in any narrative of one of these by itself apart, and still more of its dimensions on an inch-rule, or in the exhibition of its skeleton, or the specimen of a squirrel or a bird in brandy. He liked to speak of the manners of the river, as itself a lawful creature, yet with exactness, and always to an observed fact. As he knew the river, so the ponds in this region.

One of the weapons he used, more important to him than microscope or alcohol-receiver to other investigators, was a whim which grew on him by indulgence, yet appeared in gravest statement, namely, of extolling his own town and neighborhood as the most favored centre for natural observation. He remarked that the Flora of Massachusetts embraced almost all the important plants of America,—most of the oaks, most of the willows, the best pines, the ash, the maple, the beech, the nuts. He returned Kane's Arctic Voyage to a friend of whom he had borrowed it, with the remark, that "Most of the phenomena noted might be observed in Concord." He seemed a little envious of the Pole, for the coincident sunrise and sunset, or five minutes' day after six months: a splendid fact, which Annursnuc had never afforded him. He found red snow in one of his walks, and told me that he expected to find yet the *Victoria regia* in Concord. He was the attorney of the indigenous plants, and owned to a preference of the weeds to the imported plants, as of the Indian to the civilized man, and noticed, with pleasure, that the willow bean-poles of his neighbor had grown more than his beans. "See these weeds," he said, "which have been hoed at by a million farmers all spring and summer, and yet have prevailed, and just now come out triumphant over all lanes, pastures, fields and gardens, such is their vigor. We have insulted them with low names, too,—as Pigweed, Wormwood, Chickweed, Shad-blossom." He says, "They have brave names, too,—Ambrosia, Stellaria, Amelanchier, Amaranth, etc."

I think his fancy for referring everything to the meridian of Concord did not grow out of any ignorance or depreciation of other longitudes or latitudes, but was rather a playful expression of his conviction of the indifferency of all places, and that the best place for each is where he stands. He expressed it once in this wise: "I think nothing is to be hoped from you, if this bit of mould under your feet is not sweeter to you to eat than any other in this world, or in any world."

The other weapon with which he conquered all obstacles in science was patience. He knew how to sit immovable, a part of the rock he rested on, until the bird, the reptile, the fish, which had retired from him, should come back and resume its habits, nay, moved by curiosity, should come to him and watch him.

It was a pleasure and a privilege to walk with him. He knew the country like a fox or a bird, and passed through it as freely by paths of his own. He knew every track in the snow or on the ground, and what creature had taken this path before him. One must submit abjectly to such a guide, and the reward was great. Under his arm he carried an old music-book to press plants; in his pocket, his diary and pencil, a spyglass for birds, microscope, jack-knife and twine. He wore a straw hat, stout shoes, strong gray trousers, to brave scrub-oaks and smilax, and to climb a tree for a hawk's or a squirrel's nest. He waded into the pool for the water-plants, and his strong legs were no insignificant part of his armor. On the day I speak of he looked for the Menyanthes, detected it across the wide pool, and, on examination of the florets, decided that it had been in flower five days. He drew out of his breast-pocket his diary, and read the names of all the plants that should bloom on this day, whereof he kept account as a banker when his notes fall due. The Cypripedium not due till to-morrow. He thought that, if waked up from a trance, in this swamp, he could tell by the plants what time of the year it was within two days. . . .

No college ever offered him a diploma, or a professor's chair; no academy made him its corresponding secretary, its discoverer or even its member. Perhaps these learned bodies feared the satire of his presence. Yet so much knowledge of Nature's secret and genius few others possessed; none in a more large and religious synthesis. For not a particle of respect had he to the opinions of any man or body of men, but homage solely to the truth itself; and as he discovered everywhere among doctors some leaning of courtesy, it discredited them. He grew to be revered and admired by his townsmen, who had at first known him only as an oddity. The farmers who employed him as a surveyor soon discovered his rare accuracy and skill, his knowledge of their lands, of trees, of birds, of Indian remains and the like, which enabled him to tell every farmer more than he knew before of his own farm; so that he began to feel a little as if Mr. Thoreau had better rights in his land than he. They felt, too, the superiority of character which addressed all men with a native authority.

Indian relics abound in Concord,—arrowheads, stone chisels, pestles and fragments of pottery; and on the river-bank, large heaps of clam-shells and ashes mark spots which the savages frequented. These, and every circumstance touching the Indian, were important in his eyes. His visits to Maine were chiefly for love of the Indian. He had the satisfaction of seeing the manufacture of the bark canoe, as well as of trying his hand in its management on the rapids. He was inquisitive about the

making of the stone arrow-head, and in his last days charged
a youth setting out for the Rocky Mountains to find an Indian
who could tell him that: "It was well worth a visit to California
to learn it." Occasionally, a small party of Penobscot Indians
would visit Concord, and pitch their tents for a few weeks in
summer on the river-bank. He failed not to make acquaintance
with the best of them; though he well knew that asking questions of Indians is like catechizing beavers and rabbits. In his
last visit to Maine he had great satisfaction from Joseph Polis,
an intelligent Indian of Oldtown, who was his guide for some
weeks.

He was equally interested in every natural fact. The depth
of his perception found likeness of law throughout Nature, and
I know not any genius who so swiftly inferred universal law
from the single fact. He was no pedant of a department. His
eye was open to beauty, and his ear to music. He found these,
not in rare conditions, but wheresoever he went. He thought
the best of music was in single strains; and he found poetic
suggestion in the humming of the telegraph-wire.

His poetry might be bad or good; he no doubt wanted a
lyric facility and technical skill, but he had the source of
poetry in his spiritual perception. He was a good reader and
critic, and his judgment on poetry was to the ground of it. He
could not be deceived as to the presence or absence of the
poetic element in any composition, and his thirst for this made
him negligent and perhaps scornful of superficial graces. He
would pass by many delicate rhythms, but he would have
detected every live stanza or line in a volume and knew very
well where to find an equal poetic charm in prose. He was so
enamoured of the spiritual beauty that he held all actual
written poems in very light esteem in the comparison. He admired Æschylus and Pindar; but when some one was com-
mending them, he said that Æschylus and the Greeks, in describing Apollo and Orpheus, had given no song, or no good
one. "They ought not to have moved trees, but to have chanted
to the gods such a hymn as would have sung all their old ideas
out of their heads, and new ones in." His own verses are often
rude and defective. The gold does not yet run pure, is drossy
and crude. The thyme and marjoram are not yet honey. But
if he want lyric fineness and technical merits, if he have not

the poetic temperament, he never lacks the causal thought, showing that his genius was better than his talent. He knew the worth of the Imagination for the uplifting and consolation of human life, and liked to throw every thought into a symbol. The fact you tell is of no value, but only the impression. For this reason his presence was poetic, always piqued the curiosity to know more deeply the secrets of his mind. He had many reserves, an unwillingness to exhibit to profane eyes what was still sacred in his own, and knew well how to throw a poetic veil over his experience. All readers of Walden will remember his mythical record of his disappointments:—

"I long ago lost a hound, a bay horse and a turtle-dove, and am still on their trail. Many are the travellers I have spoken concerning them, describing their tracks, and what calls they answered to. I have met one or two who have heard the hound, and the tramp of the horse, and even seen the dove disappear behind a cloud; and they seemed as anxious to recover them as if they had lost them themselves."

His riddles were worth the reading, and I confide that if at any time I do not understand the expression, it is yet just. Such was the wealth of his truth that it was not worth his while to use words in vain. His poem entitled "Sympathy" reveals the tenderness under that triple steel of stoicism, and the intellectual subtilty it could animate. His classic poem on "Smoke" suggests Simonides, but is better than any poem of Simonides. His biography is in his verses. His habitual thought makes all his poetry a hymn to the Cause of causes, the Spirit which vivifies and controls his own:—

> "I hearing get, who had but ears,
>   And sight, who had but eyes before;
> I moments live, who lived but years,
>   And truth discern, who knew but learning's lore."

And still more in these religious lines:—

> "Now chiefly is my natal hour,
>   And only now my prime of life;
> I will not doubt the love untold,
>   Which not my worth nor want have bought,

Which wooed me young, and wooes me old,
And to this evening hath me brought."

Whilst he used in his writings a certain petulance of remark in reference to churches or churchmen, he was a person
of a rare, tender and absolute religion, a person incapable of
any profanation, by act or by thought. Of course, the same
isolation which belonged to his original thinking and living
detached him from the social religious forms. This is neither
to be censured nor regretted. Aristotle long ago explained it,
when he said, "One who surpasses his fellow citizens in virtue
is no longer a part of the city. Their law is not for him, since he
is a law to himself."

Thoreau was sincerity itself, and might fortify the convictions of prophets in the ethical laws by his holy living. It
was an affirmative experience which refused to be set aside. A
truth-speaker he, capable of the most deep and strict conversation; a physician to the wounds of any soul; a friend, knowing
not only the secret of friendship, but almost worshipped by
those few persons who resorted to him as their confessor and
prophet, and knew the deep value of his mind and great
heart. He thought that without religion or devotion of some
kind nothing great was ever accomplished: and he thought
that the bigoted sectarian had better bear this in mind.

His virtues, of course, sometimes ran into extremes. It
was easy to trace to the inexorable demand on all for exact
truth that austerity which made this willing hermit more solitary even than he wished. Himself of a perfect probity, he
required not less of others. He had a disgust at crime, and no
worldly success would cover it. He detected paltering as
readily in dignified and prosperous persons as in beggars, and
with equal scorn. Such dangerous frankness was in his dealing
that his admirers called him "that terrible Thoreau," as if he
spoke when silent, and was still present when he had departed.
I think the severity of his ideal interfered to deprive him of a
healthy sufficiency of human society.

The habit of a realist to find things the reverse of their
appearance inclined him to put every statement in a paradox.
A certain habit of antagonism defaced his earlier writings,—a
trick of rhetoric not quite outgrown in his later, of substituting

for the obvious word and thought its diametrical opposite. He praised wild mountains and winter forests for their domestic air, in snow and ice he would find sultriness, and commended the wilderness for resembling Rome and Paris. "It was so dry, that you might call it wet."

The tendency to magnify the moment, to read all the laws of Nature in the one object or one combination under your eye, is of course comic to those who do not share the philosopher's perception of identity. To him there was no such thing as size. The pond was a small ocean; the Atlantic, a large Walden Pond. He referred every minute fact to cosmical laws. Though he meant to be just, he seemed haunted by a certain chronic assumption that the science of the day pretended completeness, and he had just found out that the *savans* had neglected to discriminate a particular botanical variety, had failed to describe the seeds or count the sepals. "That is to say," we replied, "the blockheads were not born in Concord; but who said they were? It was their unspeakable misfortune to be born in London, or Paris, or Rome; but, poor fellows, they did what they could, considering that they never saw Bateman's Pond, or Nine-Acre Corner, or Becky Stow's Swamp; besides, what were you sent into the world for, but to add this observation?"

Had his genius been only contemplative, he had been fitted to his life, but with his energy and practical ability he seemed born for great enterprise and for command; and I so much regret the loss of his rare powers of action, that I cannot help counting it a fault in him that he had no ambition. Wanting this, instead of engineering for all America, he was the captain of a huckleberry-party. Pounding beans is good to the end of pounding empires one of these days; but if, at the end of years, it is still only beans!

But these foibles, real or apparent, were fast vanishing in the incessant growth of a spirit so robust and wise, and which effaced its defeats with new triumphs. His study of Nature was a perpetual ornament to him, and inspired his friends with curiosity to see the world through his eyes, and to hear his adventures. They possessed every kind of interest.

He had many elegancies of his own, whilst he scoffed at conventional elegance. Thus, he could not bear to hear the sound of his own steps, the grit of gravel; and therefore never willingly walked in the road, but in the grass, on mountains and in woods. His senses were acute, and he remarked that by night every dwelling-house gives out bad air, like a slaughter-house. He liked the pure fragrance of melilot. He honored certain plants with special regard, and, over all, the pond-lily,— then, the gentian, and the *Mikania scandens,* and "life-everlasting," and a bass-tree which he visited every year when it bloomed, in the middle of July. He thought the scent a more oracular inquisition than the sight,—more oracular and trustworthy. The scent, of course, reveals what is concealed from the other senses. By it he detected earthiness. He delighted in echoes, and said they were almost the only kind of kindred voices that he heard. He loved Nature so well, was so happy in her solitude, that he became very jealous of cities and the sad work which their refinements and artifices made with man and his dwelling. The axe was always destroying his forest. "Thank God," he said, "they cannot cut down the clouds!" "All kinds of figures are drawn on the blue ground with this fibrous white paint." . . .

There is a flower known to botanists, one of the same genus with our summer plant called "Life-Everlasting," a *Gnaphalium* like that, which grows on the most inaccessible cliffs of the Tyrolese mountains, where the chamois dare hardly venture, and which the hunter, tempted by its beauty, and by his love (for it is immensely valued by the Swiss maidens), climbs the cliffs to gather, and is sometimes found dead at the foot, with the flower in his hand. It is called by botanists the *Gnaphalium leontopodium,* but by the Swiss *Edelweisse,* which signifies *Noble Purity.* Thoreau seemed to me living in the hope to gather this plant, which belonged to him of right. The scale on which his studies proceeded was so large as to require longevity, and we were the less prepared for his sudden disappearance. The country knows not yet, or in the least part, how great a son it has lost. It seems an injury that he should leave in the midst his broken task which none else can finish, a kind of indignity to so noble a soul that he should depart out of Nature before yet he has been really shown to his peers for what he is. But he, at least, is content. His soul was made for the noblest society; he had in a short life exhausted the capabilities of this world; wherever there is knowledge, wherever there is virtue, wherever there is beauty, he will find a home.

THOMAS WENTWORTH HIGGINSON (1823-1911), best known as the "preceptor" of Emily Dickinson, was also the biographer of Whittier, Longfellow, and Margaret Fuller. Many of his critical judgments, once held in high repute, have now been superseded: Higginson based his faith in Thoreau's eventual recognition, for instance, upon Thoreau's studies of nature.

Review of
The Maine Woods

THOMAS WENTWORTH HIGGINSON

Atlantic Monthly, Vol. 14 (September, 1864), 386-87.

The steadily growing fame of Thoreau has this characteristic, that it is, like his culture, a purely American product, and is no pale reflection of the cheap glories of an English reprint. Whether he would have gained or lost by a more cosmopolitan training or criticism is not the question now; but certain it is that neither of these things went to the making of his fame. Classical and Oriental reading he had; but beyond these he cared for nothing which the men and meadows of Concord could not give, and for this voluntary abnegation, half whimsical, half sublime, the world repaid him with life-long obscurity, and will yet repay him with permanent renown.

His choice of subjects, too, involves the same double recompense; for no books are less dazzling or more immortal than those whose theme is external Nature. Nothing else wears so well. History becomes so rapidly overlaid with details, and its aspects change so fast, that the most elaborate work soon grows obsolete; while a thoroughly sincere and careful book on Nature cannot be superseded, and lives forever. Its basis is real and permanent. There will always be birds and flowers, nights and mornings. The infinite fascinations of mountains and of forests will outlast this war, and the next, and the race that makes the war. The same solidity of material which has guaranteed permanence to the fame of Izaak Walton and White of

Selborne will as surely secure that of Thoreau, who excels each of these writers upon his own ground, while superadding a wider culture, a loftier thought, and a fine, though fantastic, literary skill. All men may not love Nature, but all men ultimately love her lovers. And of those lovers, past or present, Thoreau is the most profound in his devotion, and the most richly repaid.

Against these great merits are to be set, no doubt, some formidable literary defects: an occasional mistiness of expression, like the summit of Katahdin, as he himself describes it,— one vast fog, with here and there a rock protruding; also, an occasional sandy barrenness, like his beloved Cape Cod. In truth, he never quite completed the transition from the observer to the artist. With the power of constructing sentences as perfectly graceful as a hemlock-bough, he yet displays the most wayward aptitude for literary caterpillars' nests and all manner of disfigurements. The same want of artistic habit appears also in his wilful disregard of all rules of proportion. He depicts an Indian, for instance, with such minute observation and admirable verbal skill that one feels as if neither Catlin, nor Schoolcraft ever saw the actual creature; but though the table-talk of the aboriginal may seem for a time more suggestive than that of Coleridge or Macaulay, yet there is a point beyond which his, like theirs, becomes a bore.

In addition to these drawbacks, one finds in Thoreau an unnecessary defiance of tone, and a very resolute non-appreciation of many things which a larger mental digestion can assimilate without discomfort. In his dealings with Nature he is sweet, genial, patient, wise. In his dealings with men he exasperates himself over the least divergence from the desired type. Before any over-tendency to the amenities and luxuries of civilization, in particular, he becomes unreasonable and relentless. Hence there appears something hard and ungenial in his views of life, utterly out of keeping with the delicate tenderness which he shows in the woods. The housekeeping of bees and birds he finds noble and beautiful, but for the home and cradle of the humblest human pair he can scarcely be said to have even toleration; a farmer's barn he considers a cumbrous and pitiable appendage, and he lectures the Irishwomen in their shanties for their undue share of the elegancies of life. With infinite faith in the tendencies of mineral and vegetable nature, in human nature he shows no practical trust, and must even be severe upon the babies in the Maine log-huts for playing with wooden dolls instead of pine-cones. It is, indeed, noticeable that he seems to love every other living animal more unreservedly than the horse,—as if this poor sophisticated creature, though still a quadruped and a brother, had been so vitiated by undue intimacy with man as to have become little better than if he wore broadcloth and voted.

Yet there was not in Thoreau one trait of the misanthrope; his solitary life at Walden was not chosen because he loved man less, but because he loved Nature more; and any young poet or naturalist might envy the opportunities it gave him. But his intellectual habits showed always a tendency to exaggeration, and he spent much mental force in fighting shadows. Church and State, war and politics,—a man of solid vigor must find room in his philosophy to tolerate these matters for a time, even if he cannot cordially embrace them. But Thoreau, a celibate, and at times a hermit, brought the Protestant extreme to match the Roman Catholic, and though he did not personally ignore one duty of domestic life, he yet held a system which would have excluded wife and child, house and property. His example is noble and useful to all high-minded young people, but only when interpreted by a philosophy less exclusive than his own. In urging his one social panacea, "Simplify, I say, simplify," he failed to see that all steps in moral or material organization are really efforts after the same process he recommends. The sewing-machine is a more complex affair than the needle, but it simplifies every woman's life, and helps her to that same comparative freedom from care which Thoreau would seek only by reverting to the Indian blanket.

But many-sided men do not move in battalions, and even a one-sided philosopher may be a boon to think of, if he be as noble as Thoreau. His very defects are higher than many men's virtues, and his most fantastic moralizings will bear reading without doing harm, especially during a Presidential campaign. Of his books, "Walden" will probably be permanently reckoned as the best, as being the most full and deliberate exhibition of the author's mind, and as extracting the most from the least material. It is also the most uniform in texture, and the most complete in plan, while the "Week" has no unity but that of the chronological epoch it covers,—a week which is probably the most comprehensive on record, ranging from the Bhagvat-Geetha to the "good time coming,"—and the "Excursions" no unity but that of the covers which comprise them, being, indeed, a compilation of his earliest and latest essays. Which of his four volumes contains his finest writing it would really be hard to say; but in structure the present book comes nearest to "Walden"; it is within its limits a perfect monograph of the Maine woods. All that has been previously written fails to portray so vividly the mysterious life of the lonely forest,—the grandeur of Katahdin or Ktaadn, that hermit-mountain,—and the wild and adventurous navigation of those Northern water-courses whose perils make the boating of the Adirondack region seem safe and tame. The book is also more unexceptionably healthy in its tone than any of its predecessors, and it is pleasant to find the author, on emerging from his explorations, admitting that the confines of civilization afford, after all, the best residence, and that the wilderness is of most value as "a resource and a background."

There yet remain for publication Thoreau's adventures on Cape Cod; his few public addresses on passing events, especially those on the Burns Rescue and the John-Brown affair, which were certainly among the very ablest productions called forth by those exciting occasions; his poems; and his private letters to his friend Blake, of Worcester, and to others,—letters which certainly contain some of his toughest, and perhaps also some of his finest writing. All these deserve, and must one day receive, preservation. He who reads most books reads that which has a merely temporary interest, and will be presently superseded by something better; but Nature has waited many centuries for Thoreau, and we can hardly expect to see, during this generation, another mortal so favored with her confidence.

Thoreau

JAMES RUSSELL LOWELL

North American Review, Vol. 101 (October, 1865), 597-608. A lengthy introductory comment on transcendentalism has been deleted.

Among the pistillate plants kindled to fruitage by the Emersonian pollen, Thoreau is thus far the most remarkable; and it is something eminently fitting that his posthumous works should be offered us by Emerson, for they are strawberries from his own garden. A singular mixture of varieties, indeed, there is;—alpine, some of them, with the flavor of rare mountain air; others wood, tasting of sunny roadside banks or shy openings in the forest; and not a few seedlings swollen hugely by culture, but lacking the fine natural aroma of the more modest kinds. Strange books these are of his, and interesting in many ways,—instructive chiefly as showing how considerable a crop may be raised on a comparatively narrow close of mind, and how much a man may make of his life if he will assiduously follow it, though perhaps never truly finding it at last.

I have just been renewing my recollection of Mr. Thoreau's writings, and have read through his six volumes in the order of their production. I shall try to give an adequate report of their impression upon me both as critic and as mere reader. He seems to me to have been a man with so high a conceit of himself that he accepted without questioning, and insisted on our accepting, his defects and weaknesses of character as virtues and powers peculiar to himself. Was he indolent, he finds none of the activities which attract or employ the rest of mankind worthy of him. Was he wanting in the qualities that make success, it is success that is contemptible, and not himself that lacks persistency and purpose. Was he poor, money was an unmixed evil. Did his life seem a selfish one, he condemns doing good as one of the weakest of superstitions. To be of use was with him the most killing bait of the wily tempter Uselessness. He had no faculty of generalization from outside of himself, or at least no experience which would supply the material of such, and he makes his own whim the law, his own range the horizon of the universe. He condemns a world, the hollowness of whose satisfactions he had never had the means of testing, and we recognize Apemantus behind the mask of Timon. He had little active imagination; of the receptive he had much. His appreciation is of the highest quality; his critical power, from want of continuity of mind, very limited and inadequate. He somewhere cites a simile from Ossian, as an example of the superiority of the old poetry to the new, though, even were the historic evidence less convincing, the sentimental melancholy of those poems should be conclusive of their modernness. He had none of the artistic mastery which controls a great work to the serene balance of completeness, but exquisite mechanical skill in the shaping of sentences and paragraphs, or (more rarely) short bits of verse for the expression of a detached thought, sentiment, or image. His works give one the feeling of a sky full of stars,—something impressive and exhilarating certainly, something high overhead and freckled thickly with spots of isolated brightness; but whether these have any mutual relation with each other, or have any concern with our mundane matters, is for the most part matter of conjecture,—astrology as yet, and not astronomy.

It is curious, considering what Thoreau afterwards became, that he was not by nature an observer. He only saw the things he looked for, and was less poet than naturalist. Till he built his Walden shanty, he did not know that the hickory grew in Concord. Till he went to Maine, he had never seen the phosphorescent wood, a phenomenon early familiar to most country boys. At forty he speaks of the seeding of the pine as a new discovery, though one should have thought that its gold-dust of blowing pollen might have earlier drawn his eye. Neither his attention nor his genius was of the spontaneous kind. He discovered nothing. He thought everything a discovery of his own, from moonlight to the planting of acorns and nuts by squirrels. This is a defect in his character, but one of his chief charms as a writer. Everything grows fresh under his hand. He delved in his mind and nature; he planted them with all manner of native and foreign seeds, and reaped assiduously. He was not merely solitary, he would be isolated, and succeeded at last in almost persuading himself that he was autochthonous. He valued everything in proportion as he fancied it to be exclusively his own. He complains in "Walden" that there is no one in Concord with whom he could talk of Oriental literature, though the man was living within two miles of his hut who had introduced him to it. This intellectual selfishness becomes sometimes almost painful in reading him. He lacked that generosity of "communication" which Johnson admired in Burke. De Quincey tells us that Wordsworth was impatient when any one else spoke of mountains, as if he had a peculiar property in them. And we can readily understand why it should be so: no one is satisfied with another's appreciation of his mistress. But Thoreau seems to have prized a lofty way of thinking (often we should be inclined to call it a remote one) not so much because it was good in itself as because he wished few to share it with him. It seems now and then as if he did not seek to lure others up "above our lower region of turmoil," but to leave his own name cut on the mountain peak as the first climber. This itch of originality infects his thought and style. To be misty is not to be mystic. He turns commonplaces end for end, and fancies it makes something new of them. As we walk down Park Street, our eye is caught by Dr. Winship's dumb-bells, one of which bears an inscription testifying that it is the heaviest ever put up at arm's length by any athlete; and in reading Mr. Thoreau's books we cannot help feeling as if he sometimes invited our attention to a particular sophism or paradox as the biggest yet maintained by any single writer. He seeks, at all risks, for perversity of thought, and revives the age of *concetti* while he fancies himself going back to a pre-classical nature. "A day," he says, "passed in the society of those Greek sages, such as described in the Banquet of Xenophon, would not be comparable with the dry wit of decayed cranberry-vines and the fresh Attic salt of the moss-beds." It is not so much the True that he loves as the Out-of-the-Way. As the Brazen Age shows itself in other men by exaggeration of phrase, so in him by extravagance of statement. He wishes always to trump your suit and to *ruff* when you least expect it. Do you love Nature because she is beautiful? He will find a better argument in her ugliness. Are you tired of the artificial man? He instantly dresses you up an ideal in a Penobscot Indian, and attributes to this creature of his other-wise-mindedness as peculiarities things that are common to all woodsmen, white or red, and this simply because he has not studied the pale-faced variety.

This notion of an absolute originality, as if one could have a patent-right in it, is an absurdity. A man cannot escape in thought, any more than he can in language, from the past and the present. As no one ever invents a word, and yet language somehow grows by general contribution and necessity, so it is with thought. Mr. Thoreau seems to me to insist in public on going back to flint and steel, when there is a match-box in his pocket which he knows very well how to use at a pinch. Originality consists in power of digesting and assimilating thought, so that they become part of our life and substance. Montaigne, for example, is one of the most original authors, though he helped himself to ideas in every direction. But they turn to blood and coloring in his style, and give a freshness of complexion that is forever charming. In Thoreau much seems yet to be foreign and unassimilated, showing itself in symptoms of indigestion. A preacher-up of Nature, we now and then detect under the surly and stoic garb something of the sophist and the sentimentalizer. I am far from implying that this was conscious on his part. But it is much easier for a man to impose on himself when he measures only with himself. A greater familiarity with ordinary men would have done Thoreau good, by showing him how many fine qualities are common to the race. The radical vice of his theory of life was that he confounded physical with spiritual remoteness from men. A man is far enough withdrawn from his fellows if he keep himself clear of their weaknesses. He is not so truly withdrawn as exiled, if he refuse to share in their strength. "Solitude," says Cowley, "can be well fitted and set right but upon a very few persons. They must have enough knowledge of the world to see the vanity of it, and enough virtue to despise all vanity." It is a morbid self-consciousness that pronounces the world of men empty and worthless before trying it, the instinctive evasion of one who is sensible of some innate weakness, and retorts the accusation of it before any has made it but himself. To a healthy mind, the world is a constant challenge of opportunity. Mr. Thoreau had not a healthy mind, or he would not have been so fond of prescribing. His whole life was a search for the doctor. The old mystics had a wiser sense of favors that have been done him by roadside and riverbrink and woodland walk, as if to kiss and tell were no longer treachery, it will be a positive refreshment to meet a man who is as superbly indifferent to Nature as she is to him. By and by we shall have John Smith, of No. −12 −12th Street, advertising that he is not the J. S. who saw a cowlily on Thursday last, as he never saw one in his life, would not see one if he could, and is prepared to prove an alibi on the day in question.

Solitary communion with Nature does not seem to have been sanitary or sweetening in its influence on Thoreau's character. On the contrary, his letters show him more cynical as he grew older. While he studied with respectful attention the minks and woodchucks, his neighbors, he looked with utter contempt on the august drama of destiny of which his country was the scene, and on which the curtain had already risen. He was converting us back to a state of nature "so eloquently," as Voltaire said of Rousseau, "that he almost persuaded us to go on all fours," while the wiser fates were making it possible for us to walk erect for the first time. Had he conversed more with his fellows, his sympathies would have widened with the assurance that his peculiar genius had more appreciation, and his writings a larger circle of readers, or at least a warmer one, than he dreamed of. We have the highest testimony[1] to the natural sweetness, sincerity, and nobleness of his temper, and in his books an equally irrefragable one to the rare quality of his mind. He was not a strong thinker, but a sensitive feeler. Yet his mind strikes us as cold and wintry in its purity. A light snow has fallen everywhere in which he seems to come on the track of the shier sensations that would elsewhere leave no trace. We think greater compression would have done more for his fame. A feeling of sameness comes over us as we read so much. Trifles are recorded with an over-minute punctuality and conscientiousness of detail. He registers the state of his personal thermometer thirteen times a day. We cannot help thinking sometimes of the man who

> "Watches, starves, freezes, and sweats
> To learn but catechisms and alphabets
> Of unconcerning things, matters of fact,"

[1] Mr. Emerson, in the Biographical Sketch prefixed to the *Excursions*.

and sometimes of the saying of the Persian poet, that "when the owl would boast, he boasts of catching mice at the edge of a hole." We could readily part with some of his affectations. It was well enough for Pythagoras to say, once for all, "When I was Euphorbus at the siege of Troy"; not so well for Thoreau to travesty it into "When I was a shepherd on the plains of Assyria." A naïve thing said over again is anything but naïve. But with every exception, there is no writing comparable with Thoreau's in kind, that is comparable with it in degree where it is best; where it disengages itself, that is, from the tangled roots and dead leaves of a second-hand Orientalism, and runs limpid and smooth and broadening as it runs, a mirror for whatever is grand and lovely in both worlds.

George Sand says neatly, that "Art is not a study of positive reality," (*actuality* were the fitter word,) "but a seeking after ideal truth." It would be doing very inadequate justice to Thoreau if we left it to be inferred that this ideal element did not exist in him, and that too in larger proportion, if less obtrusive, than his nature-worship. He took nature as the mountain-path to an ideal world. If the path wind a good deal, if he record too faithfully every trip over a root, if he botanize somewhat wearisomely, he gives us now and then superb outlooks from some jutting crag, and brings us out at last into an illimitable ether, where the breathing is not difficult for those who have any true touch of the climbing spirit. His shanty-life was a mere impossibility, so far as his own conception of it goes, as an entire independency of mankind. The tub of Diogenes had a sounder bottom. Thoreau's experiment actually presupposed all that complicated civilization which it theoretically abjured. He squatted on another man's land; he borrows an axe; his boards, his nails, his bricks, his mortar, his books, his lamp, his fish-hooks, his plough, his hoe, all turn state's evidence against him as an accomplice in the sin of that artificial civilization which rendered it possible that such a person as Henry D. Thoreau should exist at all. *Magnis tamen excidit ausis.* His aim was a noble and a useful one, in the direction of "plain living and high thinking." It was a practical sermon on Emerson's text that "things are in the saddle and ride mankind," an attempt to solve Carlyle's problem (condensed from Johnson) labor when it lay in the way of his object; and complaint he was never known to utter on his own account.

No hard logical line ought to be laid to his utterances in the sphere of personal opinion or liking. He confessedly wrote without regard to abstract consistency. His whole life was determined by sympathy, though he sometimes seemed cynical. We are fain to think, indeed, that under his brusqueness there lay a suppressed humorous questioning of his reader's capacity and consequent right to understand him and to offer sympathy. If, on this account, he may be said to have sacrificed popularity, he paid the penalty, which people often pay in actual life for too consciously hiding their true feelings under a veil of indifference; and it is much if we find that the cynical manner seldom intruded on the real nature.

The story of Thoreau's life has a value, too, inasmuch as we see in him how the tendency of culture, and of theoretic speculation towards rationalistic indifference, and a general unconcern in the fate of others, may be checked by a genuine love of Nature, and by the self-denials she can prompt in the regard that she conveys and enforces for the individual life and for freedom. The practical lesson of a true Transcendentalism, faithfully applied, must issue thus,—and it is the same whether we see it in St. Francis, in the saintly Eckhart, in William Law or in the naturalist Thoreau. All life is sanctified by the relation in which it is seen to the source of life,—an idea which lies close to the Christian spirit, however much a fixed and rationalized dogmatic relation to it may tend to dessicate and render bare and arid those spaces of the individual nature which can bloom and blossom only through sympathy and emotions that ally themselves with what is strictly mystical.

It was through Nature, to which he retreated, that Thoreau recovered his philanthropic interests,—his love of mankind, which he might have come near to losing through the spirit of culture which can only encourage cynicism and weariness in view of artificial conventions and pretexts. Thoreau would have shrunk with loathing horror from the touch of that savant who, as Agassiz seriously assures us, said to him that the age of real civilization would have begun when you health. I cannot lay my hands on the passage in which he explains his abstinence from tea and coffee, but I am sure I have the meaning correctly. It is this: He thought it bad economy and worthy of no true virtuoso to spoil the natural rapture of the morning with such muddy stimulants; let him but see the sun rise, and he was already sufficiently inspirited for the labors of the day. That may be reason good enough to abstain from tea; but when we go on to find the same man, on the same or similar grounds, abstain from nearly everything that his neighbors innocently and pleasurably use, and from the rubs and trials of human society itself into the bargain, we recognize that valetudinarian healthfulness which is more delicate than sickness itself. We need have no respect for a state of artificial training. True health is to be able to do without it. Shakespeare, we can imagine, might begin the day upon a quart of ale, and yet enjoy the sunrise to the full as much as Thoreau, and commemorate his enjoyment in vastly better verses. A man who must separate himself from his neighbors' habits in order to be happy, is in much the same case with one who requires to take opium for the same purpose. What we want to see is one who can breast into the world, do a man's work, and still preserve his first and pure enjoyment of existence.

Thoreau's faculties were of a piece with his moral shyness; for they were all delicacies. He could guide himself about the woods on the darkest night by the touch of his feet. He could pick up at once an exact dozen of pencils by the feeling, pace distances with accuracy, and gauge cubic contents by the eye. His smell was so dainty that he could perceive the fœtor of dwelling-houses as he passed them by at night; his palate so unsophisticated that, like a child, he disliked the taste of wine—or perhaps, living in America, had never tasted any that was good; and his knowledge of nature was so complete and curious that he could have told the time of year, within a day or so, by the aspect of the plants. In his dealings with animals, he was the original of Hawthorne's Donatello. He pulled the woodchuck out of its hole by the tail; the hunted fox came to him for protection; wild squirrels have been seen to nestle in his waistcoat; he would thrust his arm into a pool and bring forth a bright, panting fish, lying undismayed in the palm of his hand. There were few things that he could not do. He could make a house, a boat, a pencil, or a book. He was a surveyor, a scholar, a natural historian. He could run, walk, climb, skate, swim, and manage a boat. The smallest occasion served to display his physical accomplishment; and a manufacturer, from merely observing his dexterity with the window of a railway carriage, offered him a situation on the spot. "The only fruit of much living," he observes, "is the ability to do some slight thing better." But such was the exactitude of his senses, so alive was he in every fibre, that it seems as if the maxim should be changed in his case, for he could do most things with unusual perfection. And perhaps he had an approving eye to himself when he wrote: "Though the youth at last grows indifferent, the laws of the universe are not indifferent, *but are forever on the side of the most sensitive.*"

II

Thoreau had decided, it would seem, from the very first to lead a life of self-improvement: the needle did not tremble as with richer natures, but pointed steadily north; and as he saw duty and inclination in one, he turned all his strength in that direction. He was met upon the threshold by a common difficulty. In this world, in spite of its many agreeable features, even the most sensitive must undergo some drudgery to live. It is not possible to devote your time to study and meditation without what are quaintly but happily denominated private means; these absent, a man must contrive to earn his bread by some service to the public such as the public cares to pay him for; or, as Thoreau loved to put it, Apollo must serve Admetus. This was to Thoreau even a sourer necessity than it is to most; there was a love of freedom, a strain of the wild man, in his nature, that rebelled with violence against the yoke of custom; and he was so eager to cultivate himself and to be happy in his own society, that he could consent with difficulty even to the interruptions of friendship. "*Such are my engagements to myself* that I dare not promise," he once wrote in answer to an invitation; and the italics are his own. Marcus Aurelius found time to study virtue, and between whiles to conduct the imperial affairs of Rome; but Thoreau is so busy improving himself, that he must think twice about a morning call. And now imagine him condemned for eight hours a day to some uncongenial and unmeaning business! He shrank from the very look of the mechanical in life; all should, if possible, be sweetly spontaneous and swimmingly progressive. Thus he learned to make lead-pencils, and, when he had gained the best certificate and his friends began to congratulate him on his establishment in life calmly announced that he should never make another. "Why should I?" said he; "I would not do again what I have done once." For when a thing has once been done as well as it wants to be, it is of no further interest to the self-improver. Yet in after years, and when it became needful to support his family, he returned patiently to this mechanical art—a step more than worthy of himself.

The pencils seem to have been Apollo's first experiment in the service of Admetus; but others followed. "I have thoroughly tried school-keeping," he writes, "and found that my expenses were in proportion, or rather out of proportion, to my income; for I was obliged to dress and train, not to say think and believe, accordingly, and I lost my time into the bargain. As I did not teach for the benefit of my fellowmen, but simply for a livelihood, this was a failure. I have tried trade, but I found that it would take ten years to get under way in that, and that then I should probably be on my way to the devil." Nothing, indeed, can surpass his scorn for all so-called business. Upon that subject gall squirts from him at a touch. "The whole enterprise of this nation is not illustrated by a thought," he writes; "it is not warmed by a sentiment; there is nothing in it for which a man should lay down his life, nor even his gloves." And again: "If our merchants did not most of them fail, and the banks too, my faith in the old laws of this world would be staggered. The statement that ninety-six in a hundred doing such business surely break down is perhaps the sweetest fact that statistics have revealed." The wish was probably father to the figures; but there is something enlivening in a hatred of so genuine a brand, hot as Corsican revenge, and sneering like Voltaire.

Pencils, school-keeping, and trade being thus discarded one after another, Thoreau, with a stroke of strategy, turned the position. He saw his way to get his board and lodging for practically nothing; and Admetus never got less work out of any servant since the world began. It was his ambition to be an oriental philosopher; but he was always a very Yankee sort of oriental. Even in the peculiar attitude in which he stood to money, his system of personal economics, as we may call it, he displayed a vast amount of truly down-East calculation, and he adopted poverty like a piece of business. Yet his system is based on one or two ideas which, I believe, come naturally to all thoughtful youths, and are only pounded out of them by city uncles. Indeed, something essentially youthful distinguishes all Thoreau's knock-down blows at current opinion. Like the posers of a child, they leave the orthodox in a kind of speechless agony. These know the thing is nonsense. They are sure there must be an answer, yet somehow cannot find it. So it is with his system of economy. He cuts through the subject on so new a plane that the accepted arguments apply no longer; he attacks it in a new dialect where there are no catchwords ready made for the defender; after you have been boxing for years on a polite, gladiatorial convention, here is an assailant who does not scruple to hit below the belt.

"The cost of a thing," says he, "is *the amount of what I will call life* which is required to be exchanged for it, immediately or in the long run." I have been accustomed to put it to myself, perhaps more clearly, that the price we have to pay for money is paid in liberty. Between these two ways of it, at least, the reader will probably not fail to find a third definition of his own; and it follows, on one or other, that a man may pay too dearly for his livelihood, by giving, in Thoreau's terms, his whole life for it, or, in mine, bartering for it the whole of his available liberty, and becoming a slave till death. There are two questions to be considered—the quality of what we buy, and the price we have to pay for it. Do you want a thousand a year, a two thousand a year, or a ten thousand a year livelihood? and can you afford the one you want? It is a matter of taste; it is not in the least degree a question of duty, though commonly supposed so. But there is no authority for that view anywhere. It is nowhere in the Bible. It is true that we might do a vast amount of good if we were wealthy, but it is also highly improbable; not many do; and the art of growing rich is not only quite distinct from that of doing good, but the practice of the one does not at all train a man for practising the other. "Money might be of great service to me," writes Thoreau; "but the difficulty now is that I do not improve my opportunities, and therefore I am not prepared to have my opportunities increased." It is a mere illusion that, above a certain income, the personal desires will be satisfied and leave a wider margin for the generous impulse. It is as difficult to be generous, or anything else, except perhaps a member of Parliament, on thirty thousand as on two hundred a year.

Now Thoreau's tastes were well defined. He loved to be free, to be master of his times and seasons, to indulge the mind rather than the body; he preferred long rambles to rich dinners, his own reflections to the consideration of society, and an easy, calm, unfettered, active life among green trees to dull toiling at the counter of a bank. And such being his inclination he determined to gratify it. A poor man must save off something; he determined to save off his livelihood. "When a man has attained those things which are necessary to life," he writes, "there is another alternative than to obtain the superfluities; *he may adventure on life now*, his vacation from humbler toil having commenced." Thoreau would get shelter, some kind of covering for his body, and necessary daily bread; even these he should get as cheaply as possible; and then, his vacation from humbler toil having commenced, devote himself to oriental philosophers, the study of nature, and the work of self-improvement.

Prudence, which bids us all go to the ant for wisdom and hoard against the day of sickness, was not a favorite with Thoreau. He preferred that other, whose name is so much misappropriated: Faith. When he had secured the necessaries of the moment, he would not reckon up possible accidents or torment himself with trouble for the future. He had no toleration for the man "who ventures to live only by the aid of the mutual insurance company, which has promised to bury him decently." He would trust himself a little to the world. "We may safely trust a good deal more than we do," says he. "How much is not done by us! or what if we had been taken sick?" And then, with a stab of satire, he describes contemporary mankind in a phrase: "All the day long on the alert, at night we unwillingly say our prayers and commit ourselves to uncertainties." It is not likely that the public will be much affected by Thoreau, when they blink the direct injunctions of the religion they profess; and yet, whether we will or no, we make the same hazardous ventures; we back our own health and the honesty of our neighbors for all that we are worth; and it is chilling to think how many must lose their wager.

In 1845, twenty-eight years old, an age by which the liveliest have usually declined into some conformity with the world, Thoreau, with a capital of something less than five pounds and a borrowed axe, walked forth into the woods by Walden Pond, and began his new experiment in life. He built himself a dwelling, and returned the axe, he says with characteristic and workman-like pride, sharper than when he borrowed it; he reclaimed a patch, where he cultivated beans, peas, potatoes, and sweet corn; he had his bread to bake, his farm to dig, and for the matter of six weeks in the summer he worked at surveying, carpentry, or some other of his numerous dexterities, for hire. For more than five years, this was all that he required to do for his support, and he had the winter and most of the summer at his entire disposal. For six weeks of occupation, a little cooking and a little gentle hygienic gardening, the man, you may say, had as good as stolen his livelihood. Or we must rather allow that he had done far better; for the thief himself is continually and busily occupied; and even one born to inherit a million will have more calls upon his time than Thoreau. Well might he say, "What old people tell you you cannot do, you try and find you can." And how surprising is his conclusion: "I am convinced that *to maintain oneself on this earth is not a hardship, but a pastime,* if we will live simply and wisely; *as the pursuits of simpler nations are still the sports of the more artificial.*"

When he had enough of that kind of life, he showed the same simplicity in giving it up as in beginning it. There are some who could have done the one, but, vanity forbidding, not the other; and that is perhaps the story of the hermits; but Thoreau made no fetich of his own example, and did what he wanted squarely. And five years is long enough for an experiment and to prove the success of transcendental Yankeeism. It is not his frugality which is worthy of note; for, to begin with, that was inborn, and therefore inimitable by others who are differently constituted; and again, it was no new thing, but has often been equalled by poor Scotch students at the universities. The point is the sanity of his view of life, and the insight with which he recognized the position of money, and thought out for himself the problem of riches and a livelihood. Apart from his eccentricities, he had perceived, and was acting on, a truth of universal application. For money enters in two different characters into the scheme of life. A certain amount, varying with the number and empire of our desires, is a true necessary to each one of us in the present order of society; but beyond that amount, money is a commodity to be bought or not to be bought, a luxury in which we may either indulge or stint ourselves, like any other. And there are many luxuries that we may legitimately prefer to it, such as a grateful conscience, a country life, or the woman of our inclination. Trite, flat, and obvious as this conclusion may appear, we have only to look round us in society to see how scantily it has been recognized; and perhaps even ourselves, after a little reflection, may decide to spend a trifle less for money, and indulge ourselves a trifle more in the article of freedom.

III

"To have done anything by which you earned money merely," says Thoreau, "is to be" (have been, he means) "idle and worse." There are two passages in his letters, both, oddly enough, relating to firewood, which must be brought together to be rightly understood. So taken, they contain between them the marrow of all good sense on the subject of work in its relation to something broader than mere livelihood. Here is the first: "I suppose I have burned up a good-sized tree to-night— and for what? I settled with Mr. Tarbell for it the other day; but that wasn't the final settlement. I got off cheaply from him. At last one will say: 'Let us see, how much wood did you burn, sir?' And I shall shudder to think that the next question will be, 'What did you do while you were warm?' " Even after we have settled with Admetus in the person of Mr. Tarbell, there comes, you see, a further question. It is not enough to have earned our livelihood. Either the earning itself should have been service-able to mankind, or something else must follow. To live is some-times very difficult, but it is never meritorious in itself; and we must have a reason to allege to our own conscience why we should continue to exist upon this crowded earth. If Thoreau had simply dwelt in his house at Walden, a lover of trees, birds, and fishes, and the open air and virtue, a reader of wise books, an idle, selfish self-improver, he would have managed to cheat Admetus, but, to cling to metaphor, the devil would have had him in the end. Those who can avoid toil altogether and dwell in the Arcadia of private means, and even those who can, by abstinence, reduce the necessary amount of it to some six weeks a year, having the more liberty, have only the higher moral obligation to be up and doing in the interest of man.

The second passage is this: "There is a far more important and warming heat, commonly lost, which precedes the burning of the wood. It is the smoke of industry, which is incense. I had been so thoroughly warmed in body and spirit, that when at length my fuel was housed, I came near selling it to the ash-man, as if I had extracted all its heat." Industry is, in itself and when properly chosen, delightful and profitable to the worker; and when your toil has been a pleasure, you have not, as Tho-reau says, "earned money merely," but money, health, delight, and moral profit, all in one. "We must heap up a great pile of doing for a small diameter of being," he says in another place; and then exclaims, "How admirably the artist is made to ac-complish his self-culture by devotion to his art!" We may escape uncongenial toil, only to devote ourselves to that which is con-genial. It is only to transact some higher business that even Apollo dare play the truant from Admetus. We must all work for the sake of work; we must all work, as Thoreau says again, in any "absorbing pursuit—it does not much matter what, so it be honest;" but the most profitable work is that which combines into one continued effort the largest proportion of the powers and desires of a man's nature; that into which he will plunge with ardor, and from which he will desist with reluctance; in which he will know the weariness of fatigue, but not that of satiety; and which will be ever fresh, pleasing, and stimulating to his taste. Such work holds a man together, braced at all points; it does not suffer him to doze or wander; it keeps him actively conscious of himself, yet raised among superior interests; it gives him the profit of industry with the pleasures of a pastime. This is what his art should be to the true artist, and that to a degree unknown in other and less intimate pursuits. For other professions stand apart from the human business of life; but an art has its seat at the centre of the artist's doings and sufferings, deals directly with his experiences, teaches him the lessons of his own fortunes and mishaps, and becomes a part of his biography. So says Goethe:

> "Spät erklingt was früh erklang;
> Glück und Unglück wird Gesang."

Now Thoreau's art was literature; and it was one of which he had conceived most ambitiously. He loved and believed in good books. He said well, "Life is not habitually seen from any common platform so truly and unexaggerated as in the light of literature." But the literature he loved was of the heroic order. "Books, not which afford us a cowering enjoyment, but in which each thought is of unusual daring; such as an idle man cannot read, and a timid one would not be entertained by, which even make us dangerous to existing institutions—such I call good books." He did not think them easy to be read. "The heroic books," he says, "even if printed in the character of our mother-tongue, will always be in a language dead to degenerate times; and we must laboriously seek the meaning of each word and line, conjecturing a larger sense than common use permits out of what wisdom and valor and generosity we have." Nor does he suppose that such books are easily written. "Great prose, of equal elevation, commands our respect more than great verse," says he, "since it implies a more permanent and level height, a life more pervaded with the grandeur of the thought. The poet often only makes an irruption, like the Parthian, and is off again, shooting while he retreats; but the prose writer has conquered like a Roman and settled colonies." We may ask ourselves, almost with dismay, whether such works exist at all but in the imagination of the student. For the bulk of the best of books is apt to be made up with ballast; and those in which energy of thought is combined with any stateliness of utterance may be almost counted on the fingers. Looking round in English for a book that should answer Thoreau's two demands of a style like poetry and sense that shall be both original and inspiriting, I come to Milton's *Areopagitica*, and can name no other instance for the moment. Two things at least are plain: that if a man will condescend to nothing more commonplace in the way of reading, he must not look to have a large library; and that if he proposes himself to write in a similar vein, he will find his work cut out for him.

Thoreau composed seemingly while he walked, or at least exercise and composition were with him intimately connected; for we are told that "the length of his walk uniformly made the length of his writing." He speaks in one place of "plainness and vigor, the ornaments of style," which is rather too paradoxical to be comprehensively true. In another he remarks: "As for style of writing, if one has anything to say it drops from him simply as a stone falls to the ground." We must conjecture a very large sense indeed for the phrase "if one has anything to say." When truth flows from a man, fittingly clothed in style and without conscious effort, it is because the effort has been made and the work practically completed before he sat down to write. It is only out of fulness of thinking that expression drops perfect like a ripe fruit; and when Thoreau wrote so nonchalantly at his desk, it was because he had been vigorously active during his walk. For neither clearness, compression, nor beauty of language come to any living creature till after a busy and a prolonged acquaintance with the subject on hand. Easy writers are those who, like Walter Scott, choose to remain contented with a less degree of perfection than is legitimately within the compass of their powers. We hear of Shakespeare and his clean manuscript; but in face of the evidence of the style itself and of the various editions of *Hamlet*, this merely proves that Messrs. Hemming and Condell were unacquainted with the common enough phenomenon called a fair copy. He who would recast a tragedy already given to the world must frequently and earnestly have revised details in the study. Thoreau himself, and in spite of his protestations, is an instance of even extreme research in one direction; and his effort after heroic utterance is proved not only by the occasional finish, but by the determined exaggeration of his style. "I trust you realize what an exaggerator I am—that I lay myself out to exaggerate," he writes. And again, hinting at the explanation: "Who that has heard a strain of music feared lest he should speak extravagantly any more forever?" And yet once more, in his essay on Carlyle, and this time with his meaning well in hand: "No truth, we think, was ever expressed but with this sort of emphasis, that for the time there seemed to be no other." Thus Thoreau was an exaggerative and a parabolical writer, not because he loved the literature of the East, but from a desire that people should understand and realize what he was writing. He was near the truth upon the general question; but in his own particular method, it appears to me, he wandered. Literature is not less a conventional art than painting or sculpture; and it is the least striking, as it is the most comprehensive of the three. To hear a strain of music, to see a beautiful woman, a river, a great city, or a starry night, is to make a man despair of his Lilliputian arts in language. Now, to gain that emphasis which seems denied to us by the very nature of the medium, the proper method of literature is by selection, which is a kind of negative exaggeration. It is the right of the literary artist, as Thoreau was on the point of seeing, to leave out whatever does not suit his purpose. Thus we extract the pure gold; and thus the well-written story of a noble life becomes, by its very omissions, more thrilling to the reader. But to go beyond this, like Thoreau, and to exaggerate directly, is to leave the saner classical tradition, and to put the reader on his guard. And when you write the whole for the half, you do not express your thought more forcibly, but only express a different thought which is not yours.

Thoreau's true subject was the pursuit of self-improvement combined with an unfriendly criticism of life as it goes on in our societies; it is there that he best displays the freshness and surprising trenchancy of his intellect; it is there that his style becomes plain and vigorous, and therefore, according to his own formula, ornamental. Yet he did not care to follow this vein singly, but must drop into it by the way in books of a different purport. *Walden, or Life in the Woods, A Week on the Concord and Merrimack Rivers, The Maine Woods,*—such are the titles he affects. He was probably reminded by his delicate critical perception that the true business of literature is with narrative; in reasoned narrative, and there alone, that art enjoys all its advantages, and suffers least from its defects. Dry precept and disembodied disquisition, as they can only be read with an effort of abstraction, can never convey a perfectly complete or a perfectly natural impression. Truth, even in literature, must be clothed with flesh and blood, or it cannot tell its whole story to the reader. Hence the effect of anecdote on simple minds; and hence good biographies and works of high, imaginative art, are not only far more entertaining, but far more edifying, than books of theory or precept. Now Thoreau could not clothe his opinions in the garment of art, for that was not his talent; but he sought to gain the same elbow-room for himself, and to afford a similar relief to his readers, by mingling his thoughts with a record of experience.

Again, he was a lover of nature. The quality which we should call mystery in a painting, and which belongs so particularly to the aspect of the external world and to its influence upon our feelings, was one which he was never weary of attempting to reproduce in his books. The seeming significance of nature's appearances, their unchanging strangeness to the senses, and the thrilling response which they waken in the mind of man, continued to surprise and stimulate his spirits. It appeared to him, I think, that if we could only write near enough to the facts, and yet with no pedestrian calm, but ardently, we might transfer the glamour of reality direct upon our pages; and that, if it were once thus captured and expressed, a new and instructive relation might appear between men's thoughts and the phenomena of nature. This was the eagle that he pursued all his life long, like a schoolboy with a butterfly net. Hear him to a friend: "Let me suggest a theme for you—to state to yourself precisely and completely what that walk over the mountains amounted to for you, returning to this essay again and again until you are satisfied that all that was important in your experience is in it. Don't suppose that you can tell it precisely the first dozen times you try, but at 'em again; especially when, after a sufficient pause, you suspect that you are touching the heart or summit of the matter, reiterate your blows there, and account for the mountain to yourself. Not that the story need be long, but it will take a long while to make it short." Such was the method, not consistent for a man whose meanings were to "drop from him as a stone falls to the ground." Perhaps the most successful work that Thoreau ever accomplished in this direction is to be found in the passages relating to fish in the *Week*. These are remarkable for a vivid truth of impression and a happy suitability of language, not frequently surpassed.

Whatever Thoreau tried to do was tried in fair, square prose, with sentences solidly built, and no help from bastard rhythms. Moreover, there is a progression—I cannot call it a progress—in his work toward a more and more strictly prosaic level, until at last he sinks into the bathos of the prosy. Emerson mentions having once remarked to Thoreau: "Who would not like to write something which all can read, like *Robinson Crusoe?* and who does not see with regret that his page is not solid with a right materialistic treatment which delights everybody?" I must say in passing that it is not the right materialistic treatment which delights the world in *Robinson*, but the romantic and philosophic interest of the fable. The same treatment does quite the reverse of delighting us when it is applied, in *Colonel Jack*, to the management of a plantation. But I cannot help suspecting Thoreau to have been influenced either by this identical remark or by some other closely similar in meaning. He began to fall more and more into a detailed materialistic treatment; he went into the business doggedly, as one who should make a guide-book; he not only chronicled what had been important in his own experience, but whatever might have been important in the experience of anybody else; not only what had affected him, but all that he saw or heard. His ardor had grown less, or perhaps it was inconsistent with a right materialistic treatment to display such emotions as he felt; and, to complete the eventful change, he chose, from a sense of moral dignity, to gut these later works of the saving quality of humor. He was not one of those authors who have learned, in his own words, "to leave out their dulness." He inflicts his full quantity upon the reader in such books as *Cape Cod*, or *The Yankee in Canada*. Of the latter he confessed that he had not managed to get much of himself into it. Heaven knows he had not, nor yet much of Canada, we may hope. "Nothing," he says somewhere, "can shock a brave man but dulness." Well, there are few spots more shocking to the brave than the pages of *The Yankee in Canada*.

There are but three books of his that will be read with much pleasure: the *Week, Walden,* and the collected letters. As to his poetry, Emerson's word shall suffice for us, it is so accurate and so prettily said: "The thyme and marjoram are not yet honey." In this, as in his prose, he relied greatly on the goodwill of the reader, and wrote throughout in faith. It was an exercise of faith to suppose that many would understand the sense of his best work, or that any could be exhilarated by the dreary chronicling of his worst. "But," as he says, "the gods do not hear any rude or discordant sound, as we learn from the echo; and I know that the nature toward which I launch these sounds is so rich that it will modulate anew and wonderfully improve my rudest strain."

IV

"What means the fact," he cries, "that a soul which has lost all hope for itself can inspire in another listening soul such an infinite confidence in it, even while it is expressing its despair?" The question is an echo and an illustration of the words last quoted; and it forms the key-note of his thoughts on friendship. No one else, to my knowledge, has spoken in so high and just a spirit of the kindly relations; and I doubt whether it be a draw-back that these lessons should come from one in many ways so unfitted to be a teacher in this branch. The very coldness and egoism of his own intercourse gave him a clearer insight into the intellectual basis of our warm, mutual tolerations; and testimony to their worth comes with added force from one who was solitary and disobliging, and of whom a friend remarked, with equal wit and wisdom, "I love Henry, but I cannot like him."

He can hardly be persuaded to make any distinction between love and friendship; in such rarefied and freezing air, upon the mountain-tops of meditation, had he taught himself to breathe. He was, indeed, too accurate an observer not to have remarked that "there exists already a natural disinterestedness and liberality" between men and women; yet, he thought, "friendship is no respecter of sex." Perhaps there is a sense in which the words are true; but they were spoken in ignorance; and perhaps we shall have put the matter most correctly, if we call love a foundation for a nearer and freer degree of friendship than can be possible without it. For there are delicacies, eternal between persons of the same sex, which are melted and disappear in the warmth of love.

To both, if they are to be right, he attributes the same nature and condition. "We are not what we are," says he, "nor do we treat or esteem each other for such, but for what we are capable of being." "A friend is one who incessantly pays us the compliment of expecting all the virtues from us, and who can appreciate them in us." "The friend asks no return but that his friend will religiously accept and wear and not disgrace his apotheosis of him." "It is the merit and preservation of friendship that it takes place on a level higher than the actual characters of the parties would seem to warrant." This is to put friendship on a pedestal indeed; and yet the root of the matter is there; and the last sentence, in particular, is like a light in a dark place, and makes many mysteries plain. We are different with different friends; yet if we look closely we shall find that every such relation reposes on some particular apotheosis of oneself; with each friend, although we could not distinguish it in words from any other, we have at least one special reputation to preserve: and it is thus that we run, when mortified, to our friend or the woman that we love, not to hear ourselves called better, but to be better men in point of fact. We seek this society to flatter ourselves with our own good conduct. And hence any falsehood in the relation, any incomplete or perverted understanding, will spoil even the pleasure of these visits. Thus says Thoreau again: "Only lovers know the value of truth." And yet again: "They ask for words and deeds, when a true relation is word and deed."

But it follows that since they are neither of them so good as the other hopes, and each is, in a very honest manner, playing a part above his powers, such an intercourse must often be disappointing to both. "We may bid farewell sooner than complain," says Thoreau, "for our complaint is too well grounded to be uttered." "We have not so good a right to hate any as our friend."

> "It were treason to our love
> And a sin to God above,
> One iota to abate
> Of a pure, impartial hate."

Love is not blind, nor yet forgiving. "O yes, believe me," as the song says, "Love has eyes!" The nearer the intimacy, the more cuttingly do we feel the unworthiness of those we love; and because you love one, and would die for that love to-morrow, you have not forgiven, and you never will forgive, that friend's misconduct. If you want a person's faults, go to those who love him. They will not tell you, but they know. And herein lies the magnanimous courage of love, that it endures this knowledge without change.

It required a cold, distant personality like that of Thoreau, perhaps, to recognize and certainly to utter this truth; for a more human love makes it a point of honor not to acknowledge those faults of which it is most conscious. But his point of view is both high and dry. He has no illusions; he does not give way to love any more than to hatred, but preserves them both with care like valuable curiosities. A more bald-headed picture of life, if I may so express myself, has seldom been presented. He is an egoist; he does not remember, or does not think it worth while to remark, that, in these near intimacies, we are ninety-nine times disappointed in our beggarly selves for once that we are disappointed in our friend; that it is we who seem most frequently undeserving of the love that unites us; and that it is by our friend's conduct that we are continually rebuked and yet strengthened for a fresh endeavor. Thoreau is dry, priggish, and selfish. It is profit he is after in these intimacies; moral profit, certainly, but still profit to himself. If you will be the sort of friend I want, he remarks naïvely, "my education cannot dispense with your society." His education! as though a friend were a dictionary. And with all this, not one word about pleasure, or laughter, or kisses, or any quality of flesh and blood. It was not inappropriate, surely, that he had such close relations with the fish. We can understand the friend already quoted, when he cried: "As for taking his arm, I would as soon think of taking the arm of an elm-tree!"

As a matter of fact he experienced but a broken enjoyment in his intimacies. He says he has been perpetually on the brink of the sort of intercourse he wanted, and yet never completely attained it. And what else had he to expect when he would not, in a happy phrase of Carlyle's, "nestle down into it"? Truly, so it will be always if you only stroll in upon your friends as you might stroll in to see a cricket match; and even then not simply for the pleasure of the thing, but with some after-thought of self-improvement, as though you had come to the cricket match to bet. It was his theory that people saw each other too frequently, so that their curiosity was not properly whetted, nor had they anything fresh to communicate; but friendship must be something else than a society for mutual improvement—indeed, it must only be that by the way, and to some extent unconsciously; and if Thoreau had been a man instead of a manner of elm-tree, he would have felt that he saw his friends too seldom, and have reaped benefits unknown to his philosophy from a more sustained and easy intercourse. We might remind him of his own words about love: "We should have no reserve; we should give the whole of ourselves to that business. But commonly men have not imagination enough to be thus employed about a human being, but must be coopering a barrel, forsooth." Ay, or reading oriental philosophers. It is not the nature of the rival occupation, it is the fact that you suffer it to be a rival, that renders loving intimacy impossible. Nothing is given for nothing in this world; there can be no true love, even on your own side, without devotion; devotion is the exercise of love, by which it grows; but if you will give enough of that, if you will pay the price in a sufficient "amount of what you call life," why then, indeed, whether with wife or comrade, you may have months and even years of such easy, natural, pleasurable, and yet improving intercourse as shall make time a moment and kindness a delight.

The secret of his retirement lies not in misanthropy, of which he had no tincture, but part in his engrossing design of self-improvement and part in the real deficiencies of social intercourse. He was not so much difficult about his fellow human beings as he could not tolerate the terms of their association. He could take to a man for any genuine qualities, as we see by his admirable sketch of the Canadian woodcutter in *Walden;* but he would not consent, in his own words, to "feebly fabulate and paddle in the social slush." It seemed to him, I think, that society is precisely the reverse of friendship, in that it takes place on a lower level than the characters of any of the parties would warrant us to expect. The society talk of even the most brilliant man is of greatly less account than what you will get from him in (as the French say) a little committee. And Thoreau wanted geniality; he had not enough of the superficial, even at command; he could not swoop into a parlor and, in the naval phrase, "cut out" a human being from that dreary port; nor had he inclination for the task. I suspect he loved books and nature as well and near as warmly as he loved his fellow-creatures,—a melancholy, lean degeneration of the human character.

"As for the dispute about solitude and society," he thus sums up: "Any comparison is impertinent. It is an idling down on the plain at the base of the mountain instead of climbing steadily to its top. Of course you will be glad of all the society you can get to go up with? Will you go to glory with me? is the burden of the song. It is not that we love to be alone, but that we love to soar, and when we do soar the company grows thinner and thinner till there is none at all. It is either the tribune on the plain, a sermon on the mount, or a very private ecstasy still higher up. Use all the society that will abet you." But surely it is no very extravagant opinion that it is better to give than to receive, to serve than to use our companions; and above all, where there is no question of service upon either side, that it is good to enjoy their company like a natural man. It is curious and in some ways dispiriting that a writer may be always best corrected out of his own mouth; and so, to conclude, here is another passage from Thoreau which seems aimed directly at himself: "Do not be too moral; you may cheat yourself out of much life so. . . . *All fables, indeed, have their morals; but the innocent enjoy the story.*"

v

"The only obligation," says he, "which I have a right to assume is to do at any time what I think right." "Why should we ever go abroad, even across the way, to ask a neighbor's advice?" "There is a nearer neighbor within, who is incessantly telling us how we should behave. *But we wait for the neighbor without to tell us of some false, easier way.*" "The greater part of what my neighbors call good I believe in my soul to be bad." To be what we are, and to become what we are capable of becoming, is the only end of life. It is "when we fall behind ourselves" that "we are cursed with duties and the neglect of duties." "I love the wild," he says, "not less than the good." And again: "The life of a good man will hardly improve us more than the life of a freebooter, for the inevitable laws appear as plainly in the infringement as in the observance, and" (mark this) "*our lives are sustained by a nearly equal expense of virtue of some kind.*" Even although he were a prig, it will be owned he could announce a startling doctrine. "As for doing good," he writes elsewhere, "that is one of the professions that are full. Moreover, I have tried it fairly, and, strange as it may seem, am satisfied that it does not agree with my constitution. Probably I should not conscientiously and deliberately forsake my particular calling to do the good which society demands of me, to save the universe from annihilation; and I believe that a like but infinitely greater steadfastness elsewhere is all that now preserves it. If you should ever be betrayed into any of these philanthropies, do not let your left hand know what your right hand does, for it is not worth knowing." Elsewhere he returns upon the subject, and explains his meaning thus: "If I ever *did* a man any good in their sense, of course it was something exceptional and insignificant compared with the good or evil I am constantly doing by being what I am."

There is a rude nobility, like that of a barbarian king, in this unshaken confidence in himself and indifference to the wants, thoughts, or sufferings of others. In his whole works I find no trace of pity. This was partly the result of theory, for he held the world too mysterious to be criticised, and asks conclusively: "What right have I to grieve who have not ceased to wonder?" But it sprang still more from constitutional indifference and superiority; and he grew up healthy, composed, and unconscious from among life's horrors, like a green bay-tree from a field of battle. It was from this lack in himself that he failed to do justice to the spirit of Christ; for while he could glean more meaning from individual precepts than any score of Christians, yet he conceived life in such a different hope, and viewed it with such contrary emotions, that the sense and purport of the doctrine as a whole seems to have passed him by or left him unimpressed. He could understand the idealism of the Christian view, but he was himself so unaffectedly un-human that he did not recognize the human intention and essence of that teaching. Hence he complained that Christ did not leave us a rule that was proper and sufficient for this world, not having conceived the nature of the rule that was laid down; for things of that character that are sufficiently unacceptable become positively non-existent to the mind. But perhaps we shall best appreciate the defect in Thoreau by seeing it supplied in the case of Whitman. For the one, I feel confident, is the disciple of the other; it is what Thoreau clearly whispered that Whitman so uproariously bawls; it is the same doctrine, but with how immense a difference! the same argument, but used to what a new conclusion! Thoreau had plenty of humor until he tutored himself out of it, and so forfeited that best birthright of a sensible man; Whitman, in that respect, seems to have been sent into the world naked and unashamed; and yet by a strange consummation, it is the theory of the former that is arid, abstract, and claustral. Of these two philosophies so nearly identical at bottom, the one pursues Self-improvement—a churlish, mangy dog; the other is up with the morning, in the best of health, and following the nymph Happiness, buxom, blithe, and debonair. Happiness, at least, is not solitary; it joys to communicate; it loves others, for it depends on them for its existence; it sanctions and encourages to all delights that are not unkind in themselves; if it lived to a thousand, it would not make excision of a single humorous passage; and while the self-improver dwindles toward the prig, and, if he be not of an excellent constitution, may even grow deformed into an Obermann, the very name and appearance of a happy man breathe of good-nature, and help the rest of us to live.

In the case of Thoreau, so great a show of doctrine demands some outcome in the field of action. If nothing were to be done but build a shanty beside Walden Pond, we have heard altogether too much of these declarations of independence. That the man wrote some books is nothing to the purpose, for the same has been done in a suburban villa. That he kept himself happy is perhaps a sufficient excuse, but it is disappointing to the reader. We may be unjust, but when a man despises commerce and philanthropy alike, and has views of good so soaring that he must take himself apart from mankind for their cultivation, we will not be content without some striking act. It was not Thoreau's fault if he were not martyred; had the occasion come, he would have made a noble ending. As it is, he did once seek to interfere in the world's course; he made one practical appearance on the stage of affairs; and a strange one it was, and strangely characteristic of the nobility and the eccentricity of the man. It was forced on him by his calm but radical opposition to negro slavery. "Voting for the right is doing nothing for it," he saw; "it is only expressing to men feebly your desire that it should prevail." For his part, he would not "for an instant recognize the political organization for *his* government which is the *slave's* government also." "I do not hesitate to say," he adds, "that those who call themselves Abolitionists should at once effectually withdraw their support, both in person and property, from the government of Massachusetts." That is what he did: in 1843 he ceased to pay the poll-tax. The highway-tax he paid, for he said he was as desirous to be a good neighbor as to be a bad subject; but no more poll-tax to the State of Massachusetts. Thoreau had now seceded, and was a polity unto himself; or, as he explains it with admirable sense, "In fact, I quietly declare war with the State after my fashion, though I will still make what use and get what advantage of her I can, as is usual in such cases." He was put in prison; but that was a part of his design. "Under a government which imprisons any unjustly, the true place for a just man is also a prison. I know this well, that if one thousand, if one hundred, if ten men whom I could name—ay, if *one* HONEST man, in this State of Massachusetts, *ceasing to hold slaves*, were actually to withdraw from this copartnership, and be locked up in the county jail therefor, it would be the abolition of slavery in America. For it matters not how small the beginning may seem to be; what is once well done is done forever." Such was his theory of civil disobedience.

And the upshot? A friend paid the tax for him; continued year by year to pay it in the sequel; and Thoreau was free to walk the woods unmolested. It was a *fiasco*, but to me it does not seem laughable; even those who joined in the laughter at the moment would be insensibly affected by this quaint instance of a good man's horror for injustice. We may compute the worth of that one night's imprisonment as outweighing half a hundred voters at some subsequent election: and if Thoreau had possessed as great a power of persuasion as (let us say) Falstaff, if he had counted a party however small, if his example had been followed by a hundred or by thirty of his fellows, I cannot but believe it would have greatly precipitated the era of freedom and justice. We feel the misdeeds of our country with so little fervor, for we are not witnesses to the suffering they cause; but when we see them wake an active horror in our fellowman, when we see a neighbor prefer to lie in prison rather than be so much as passively implicated in their perpetration, even the dullest of us will begin to realize them with a quicker pulse.

Not far from twenty years later, when Captain John Brown was taken at Harper's Ferry, Thoreau was the first to come forward in his defence. The committees wrote to him unanimously that his action was premature. "I did not send to you for advice," said he, "but to announce that I was to speak." I have used the word "defence;" in truth he did not seek to defend him, even declared it would be better for the good cause that he should die; but he praised his action as I think Brown would have liked to hear it praised.

Thus this singularly eccentric and independent mind, wedded to a character of so much strength, singleness, and purity, pursued its own path of self-improvement for more than half a century, part gymnosophist, part backwoodsman; and thus did it come twice, though in a subaltern attitude, into the field of political history.

NOTE.—For many facts in the above essay, among which I may mention the incident of the squirrel, I am indebted to *Thoreau: His Life and Aims*, by J. A. Page, or, as is well known, Dr. Japp.

Thoreau
From
Preface, By Way of Criticism

ROBERT LOUIS STEVENSON

Familiar Studies of Men and Books (New York: Charles Scribner's Sons, 1911), pp. 9-12.

Here is an admirable instance of the "point of view" forced throughout, and of too earnest reflection on imperfect facts. Upon me this pure, narrow, sunnily-ascetic Thoreau had exercised a great charm. I have scarce written ten sentences since I was introduced to him, but his influence might be somewhere detected by a close observer. Still it was as a writer that I had made his acquaintance; I took him on his own explicit terms; and when I learned details of his life, they were, by the nature of the case and my own *parti-pris*, read even with a certain violence in terms of his writings. There could scarce be a perversion more justifiable than that; yet it was still a perversion.

The study, indeed, raised so much ire in the breast of Dr. Japp (H. A. Page), Thoreau's sincere and learned disciple, that had either of us been men, I please myself with thinking, of less temper and justice, the difference might have made us enemies instead of making us friends. To him who knew the man from the inside, many of my statements sounded like inversions made on purpose; and yet when we came to talk of them together, and he had understood how I was looking at the man through the books, while he had long since learned to read the books through the man, I believe he understood the spirit in which I had been led astray.

On two most important points, Dr. Japp added to my knowledge, and with the same blow fairly demolished that part of my criticism. First, if Thoreau were content to dwell by Walden Pond, it was not merely with designs of self-improvement, but to serve mankind in the highest sense. Hither came the fleeing slave; thence was he despatched along the road to freedom. That shanty in the woods was a station in the great Underground Railroad; that adroit and philosophic solitary was an ardent worker, soul and body, in that so much more than honorable movement, which, if atonement were possible for nations, should have gone far to wipe away the guilt of slavery. But in history sin always meets with condign punishment; the generation passes, the offence remains, and the innocent must suffer. No underground railroad could atone for slavery, even as no bills in Parliament can redeem the ancient wrongs of Ireland. But here at least is a new light shed on the Walden episode.

Second, it appears, and the point is capital, that Thoreau was once fairly and manfully in love, and, with perhaps too much aping of the angel, relinquished the woman to his brother. Even though the brother were like to die of it, we have not yet heard the last opinion of the woman. But be that as it may, we have here the explanation of the "rarified and freezing air" in which I complained that he had taught himself to breathe. Reading the man through the books, I took his professions in good faith. He made a dupe of me, even as he was seeking to make a dupe of himself, wrestling philosophy to the needs of his own sorrow. But in the light of this new fact, those pages, seemingly so cold, are seen to be alive with feeling. What appeared to be a lack of interest in the philosopher turns out to have been a touching insincerity of the man to his own heart; and that fine-spun airy theory of friendship, so devoid, as I complained, of any quality of flesh and blood, a mere anodyne to lull his pains. The most temperate of living critics once remarked a passage of my own with a cross and the words, "This seems nonsense." It not only seemed; it was so. It was a private bravado of my own, which I had so often repeated to keep up my spirits, that I had grown at last wholly to believe it, and had ended by setting it down as a contribution to the theory of life. So with the more icy parts of this philosophy of Thoreau's. He was affecting the Spartanism he had not; and the old sentimental wound still bled afresh, while he deceived himself with reasons.

Thoreau's theory, in short, was one thing and himself another: of the first, the reader will find what I believe to be a pretty faithful statement and a fairly just criticism in the study; of the second he will find but a contorted shadow. So much of the man as fitted nicely with his doctrines, in the photographer's phrase came out. But that large part which lay outside and beyond, for which he had found or sought no formula, on which perhaps his philosophy even looked askance, is wanting in my study, as it was wanting in the guide I followed. In some ways a less serious writer, in all ways a nobler man, the true Thoreau still remains to be depicted.

WILLIAM SLOANE KENNEDY (1850-1929) is perhaps best known for his early, spirited defense of Walt Whitman, though he was the biographer of Longfellow, Whittier, Holmes, and John Burroughs, and a student of natural history. The influence of Thoreau's "rugged energy, his fine idealism, the purity and honesty, and manliness of his life," Kennedy predicted, "shall for generations breathe through the literature and the life of America like a strengthening ocean breeze."

A New Estimate
of Thoreau

WILLIAM SLOANE KENNEDY

The Penn Monthly, Vol. 11 (October, 1880), 794-808.

Of the true significance of Thoreau's life in its wide and universal relations, of its relation to democracy, (as a protest against the social and political tyranny of the majority—that most colossal and menacing of all the dangers that threaten the existence of popular government) of its relation to religion, war, labor and capital, patriotism, and to that tendency of modern times to simplify life, which was first voiced in Europe by Rousseau—of the true value and significance of his life and work in all these respects, no one, it seems to me, has yet adequately treated. Mr. H. A. Page's *Study of Thoreau* is good in its way, but is certainly weak in philosophical grasp and breadth of treatment. Mr. James Russell Lowell's essay is caustic and shrewd, and not without kindliness, but is, on the whole, unsympathetic; he never reached the Thoreau point of view. His warm and hearty social instincts led him to look with abhorrence upon Thoreau, the stoic and cynic. The considerable number of biting and bitter sarcasms and harsh paradoxes, scattered throughout Thoreau's book, are pretty hard to digest, it must be confessed. Mr. Lowell evidently had an *animus* against Thoreau on account of these things.* The same may be said of Mr. Alger, who has a brief criticism of Thoreau in his *Genius of Solitude*. Mr. A. B. Alcott and Robert Collyer have each written short appreciative sketches of their friend. Mr. T. W. Higginson's essay is a very kindly estimate of Thoreau; but it does not profess to be an exhaustive psychological analy-

---

* Now and then, and only now and then, do we recognize in Thoreau moods that remind us of Diogenes, Timon or Apemantus. Mr. Lowell seems to have thought that in these occasional moods he had found the key to Thoreau's whole character. He thought that in them the mask slipped aside. The natural face itself, he mistook for a mask. His critical opera-glass was not properly focussed. It seems fitting to say a word, here at the very start, upon the special theme of the isolation and egoism of Thoreau which were perplexing to many. We may admit that he was often too stiff and crusty and cynical in his attitude toward men—and blame him for that defect of nature, if we choose; but his isolation from society, or the mass of men, I think we cannot blame, but must, on the contrary regard as both necessary and laudable.

To substitute this position, let me quote two or three paragraphs from Mr. John Morley's *Rousseau;* they throw light upon Thoreau's life as well as upon that of Rousseau:—"Geographical loneliness," says Morley, "is to some men a condition of their fullest strength." And again: "There are some natures in which all emotion is so entirely associated with the ideal, that real and particular manifestations of it are repugnant to them as something alien." And once again he says: "There is no more rash idea of the right composition of a society than one which leads us to denounce a type of character for no better reason than that, if it were universal, society would go to pieces."

sis. Mr. R. W. Emerson's biographical sketch is, of course, inimitable; but it, too, is rather a characterization of its subject as an individual, than as the product of a special phasis of civilization.[*]

It will be the special object of this paper to treat of Thoreau in his attitude towards society,—and secondarily, to give an estimate of his personal character and of his writings, and this without any very formal separation of the subjects in the treatment.

To approach our task: Here is a certain phenomenon called Thoreau; the first thing to do is to account for him, to uncover the long filamental roots that run out from his life, far back into the past, and out on every side into the fabric of contemporary society. That society is a little too modest in its rejection of Thoreau. He is one of its fruits; let it then accept him, and fairly and candidly try to explain him. Without doubt, the result of the examination will be far more honorable to him than was supposed, and at the same time productive of wholesome effects upon society, in leading it to see itself in new and startling aspects.

Thoreau, the solitaire, is no new phenomenon, although he happened to be so in America. A practical, money-getting nation, naturally looked with some perplexity upon the advent in its midst of a pure and solitary mystic who looked with

---

[*] Mr. Henry James, in his study of Hawthorne, characterizes Thoreau as "imperfect, unfinished, inartistic," and "parochial." Surely, this can hardly be called criticism: it is little more than opinion *ab extra*, the wondering stare of an alien mind. It is Teniers estimating Turner. It is Goethe judging Richter. Thoreau's work is "unfinished, inartistic" is it? Well, so is Turner's work, and Shakespeare's work, in one sense. The *Slave Ship* is not a Dutch canal scene, and *Hamlet* is not the *Essay on Man*, and a water-fall is not a mill-sluice, and the crumbling maroon and red gold cloud-bars of sunset do not remind you of a theatre-curtain;—what a pity!—Thoreau was "parochial." Yes, he was as parochial as Socrates was, as Kant, Wordsworth, Sir Walter Scott, Burns, and Cowper were, but in no other sense. He was an austere thinker and not a gay butterfly-worldling, a Stoic and not an Epicurean, a satirist and not a popular favorite. It is not absolutely necessary that the thinker should travel much, and especially not the mystic. All we require of such, is catholicity and breadth in their reading and thinking. Thoreau, as is well known, was thoroughly read in the Ethnic Scriptures, in Greek literature, and in old English poetry. But he was pre-eminently antiquarian, autochthonous, patriotic—loving his country with manly devotion and enthusiasm. Mr. James aspires, I believe, to be cosmopolitan. But it is surely better to be patriotic first, and cosmopolitan second, than to be cosmopolitan first, and patriotic last, or not at all.

indifference, if not with contempt, upon the precious wealth which most of them spend their lives in accumulating. They thought him a fool, of diseased mind. But the story of such lives as his may be read in the literatures of all the olden countries of the globe. He takes his place with the great throng of sensitive geniuses, whom the hard blows of the world have always driven to nature and to books. The possession of rarer mental powers than the mass of men have, has always driven the possessor into some degree of solitude, and always will. For solitude frees from envy and affords quiet. The more fragile the flower, the more easily are its ethereal petals withered and torn. But it is in the great *Sturm und Drang* phasis of social upheavals through which we have been passing for the last hundred years, that the greatest number of tragical breaks with society has occurred. The transition from Feudalism to Democracy is yet far from being completed. In the shuffling and rearranging of the pieces in the great human kaleidoscope there are many fatal misunderstandings and collisions. This is the outward aspect of things. But in the mind too is revolution, a complete *bouleversement* of the whole mental furniture.

It is a period when the bloom of self-consciousness is opening out in the minds of men over vast areas of society —as beds of river lilies, smitten by the rays of the morning sun, flash open their white petals far and wide in response to the warm stimulus of the light. With the dawning of a consciousness of self upon the mind—a consciousness of its worth and power—comes the demand for self-government, come a thousand gnarring wants and unsatisfiable desires; hence arise, often, wild and sombre yearnings and broodings; then appear in literature, the Werthers, the Schoppes, the Manfreds, the Fausts; and in actual life, the Shelleys, St. Pierres, Rousseaus, and Thoreaus. It seems almost impossible for a poor and sensitive genius to live a *perfectly noble* life in the midst of society in a modern democracy, partaking as he must of its deep unrest, its melancholy introspection, and its fierce ambition. Generally the result of his mental struggle is that he is depressed in spirit and driven back upon himself, unable to endure the harsh treatment of society. If he is brooding and melancholy, we have a Maurice de Guerin, a Chopin; if he have elasticity of mental fibre and doubtless energy of will, we have an Angelo, a Thoreau. From the former class we have the tender and pensive elegiac strains, as well as bitter complaints; from the latter we have no unmanly moanings, but accents of cheerful stoicism, as well as words of warning, reproof, and scourging satire. Both of these classes of idealists, however, scandalize society by their withdrawal from it. The mass of men have thick skins and stout lungs; they rather enjoy the blows of society than otherwise, and easily breathe its dense air. They cannot see why to the sensitive genius that should be misery and death, which to them is only a pleasant stimulus. They see that nearly all appear to be tolerably well content in society; the conclusion is that the delicately-organized genius has an unhealthy mind, forsooth! This is but an old song. Idealists have always seemed mad or diseased to those unable to understand them. The Teuton shudders at the idea of cold-water baths and fresh air, and the "well-mixed" man of society shudders at the bracing austerity of manners of the idealist. In the case of the Teutons, the really normal man, the man of glowing and robust health, is the exceptional man of baths and fresh air, such as Goethe was; and in society the really robust and healthy man is the idealist. The spell of illusion seems to be so woven over the minds of many, that they are unable to distinguish between the unhealthy and morbid dreamer, and the real prophet of a higher life among them, such as Thoreau was among his countrymen. It is such men as he who compel us to recognize the fact that society, as it is now constituted, is not altogether lovely in itself, but is all blotched and tainted with imperfections.*

---

* This is the message Thoreau spoke to his fellow men. He was, in one phase of his character, the Socrates of the American Attica. One spoke in the streets of Athens what the other speaks in his books. If one is dauntless and unsparing in his denunciation of falsehood and pretence, so is the other. If Socrates did not despair of men notwithstanding their faults, neither did Thoreau. Like Socrates, he set about with restless energy and matchless determination to prove that life is noble. *The one great lesson which he wished to teach is, that life is worth living. He demonstrated, triumphantly and forever, that this life of ours may be of infinite value and joy, even when lived under circumstances ordinarily regarded as most discouraging.* This lesson has been taught many a time in other lands; the world had its Jean Paul, its Cervantes, its Samuel Johnson. But Thoreau is the first great American teacher of this lesson in life, unless we except Benjamin Franklin. Henceforth, no American who knows his books can reasonably despair. He is one of the saviours of the coming generations.

If Thoreau had done nothing more than point out the unloveliness of society in many of its aspects, without any attempt to better it himself, his life would have been of as little value as it is by many supposed to have been. But nothing could be farther from the truth than such a view of his life and work. No truer patriot, no truer man has ever breathed the air of this new world. By his fine Spartan life he taught us how to live. The influence of his rugged energy, his fine idealism, the purity and honesty, and manliness of his life, shall for generations breathe through the literature and the life of America like a strengthening ocean breeze, adding tone, toughness, elasticity, and richest Attic sparkle to the thought of men. His influence is almost wholly hygienic and sanative to those who know how to read him,—avoiding his hobbies, and passing by his too morbid dislike of men. Why is it that the lives of such men as Alcott and Thoreau excite such warm opposition in some quarters? Is it not partly because there are many who keenly feel the rebuke which such lives imply? It does not do to be too good in this world; it excites envy. Then there is often a curious and not very laudable feeling of irritation at seeing something successfully accomplished, which people had voted well nigh impossible. The problem of the reconcilement of labor and culture, is one of these, and it has been worked out in Concord, Massachusetts.

When will men learn to be entirely generous and just in their judgments of their fellows? A man of wide and Catholic sympathies will not be offended by the few eccentricities and prejudices that another may have, but will smilingly pass them over, if at the same time he finds the true and manly ring, and sterling worth of character. What is wonderful in Thoreau's case is, that he accomplished so much. What we want in order to save society from moral rottenness is, fifty thousand Henry Thoreaus in the class of farmers and mechanics. If in every generation there were even five hundred men in a nation, who, starting with next to no capital, could roll up such a fortune as he did in culture, manliness, and purity and sweetness of character, and dying, leave behind them such fragrant memories and such pregnant and stimulating writings, then would it be madness to ever despair of the future of Democracy.

To the fellow-citizens of Thoreau I would say: Let us

cherish the memory of this saintliest of men. He is one of our saviours, if we would but see it. Fitting it were to strew our costliest flowers as a votive offering upon the grave of one of the truest, manliest hearts that ever beat, to plant around the now neglected spot that holds his dust the wild, rich weeds and plants he loved so passing well, and to inscribe, perhaps, upon his monument such words as these: "Here lies one whose only crime it was to be too pure and stainless in his life, and to love too well the meadows, woods and streams."

If in the years to come the lovers of Henry Thoreau in this country, are not counted by tens of thousands, (as they are now by hundreds) then might we well be tempted to think meanly of our America. Alas! shall men forever continue to run after every charlatan who can dazzle their eyes with cunning mask and bedizened coat, and pass unheeded by the great and genuine souls in their midst? If to be great means to always speak the truth, to be faithful in friendship, industrious, frugal, patriotic, dauntless in moral courage, cultured, a teacher of men, and an enthusiastic scientific student, if it means this, then was he of whom we are speaking a great man. He was not only great, this plain-dressed, plain-speaking, plain-souled Thoreau, but he was the richest man in all the wide Americas. For when he came to maturity of years, he was presented by a certain enchanter, with a pass-key to a far-stretching, sunlit garden called Nature, which contains the larger part of the real wealth of the world. A ticket to this garden is for life, and is really a deed in fee-simple of the whole estate. Thoreau was the happy possessor of one of these deeds.

His patriotism was deep and strong—knit into the very fibre of his being. He was patriotic in his own way, however. He loved not so much the people in the abstract and philanthropic sense, as he did individual friends. He was in love with the brown soil, the azure sky, the clouds, the honest rocks, the artless flowers and shrubs in their charming and unconscious beauty; trees, rivers, lakes and hills—all these he loved with a passionateness such as no other American, with whom we are acquainted, ever felt. He loved nature, and he loved good men; he prized above all, liberty and justice. If the testimony of his friends to the warmth and tenderness of his affection were not more than sufficient to prove his love of men, his Anti-Slavery papers would put it beyond doubt. It is touching and pathetic to read of the kind of terror, the paralysis of mind and the gloom which came over him at the time of the enforcement of the Fugitive Slave Law by the delivering up of Anthony Burns on the part of the Massachusetts civil officers. He said he could not enjoy nature as before. Life seemed worth much less to him in Massachusetts than formerly. No more terrible indignation was ever put into words than we find in his patriotic papers. His sentences cut like a knife; they draw blood. His feelings are at a white heat, but his words are as quiet and measured as if he were speaking upon an indifferent theme. His hearers and readers at that time must have writhed under the steady fusillade of his scorching sarcasms and bitter reproaches.

There are sentences in these Anti-Slavery papers which deserve to be engraved in gold and set in diamonds, to be hung up in every court of justice in America. He says of John Brown: "He did not go to the college called Harvard. * * * He would have left a Greek accent slanting the wrong way, and righted up a falling man." Here are a few sentences from his article on Civil Disobedience: "It is not desirable to cultivate a respect for the law so much as for the right." "It is not so important that many should be as good as you, as that there be some absolute goodness somewhere, for that will leaven the whole lump." "There are nine hundred and ninety-nine patrons of virtue to one virtuous man."

On the theme of Friendship, Thoreau (in his *Week*), has said some of the most subtle things that have ever been uttered. These, taken in connection with his *Letters*, show how rich and pure his affections were—only they tell us that his friendships were for idealized persons, rather than for the actual persons themselves in all the grossness and imperfection of the flesh.

Thoreau's finely-strung and vibrant nature led him to shun as much as possible the gross real. He yearned to live wholly in the ideal. He fled from the jangle and jar of clashing interests. Far up along the azure cliffs of life he moved, breathing an atmosphere not respirable by the mass of men. His life was pure and simple as that of the Alpine herdsman, and he drank from the streams of truth and joy, whose sources lie above the clouds.

It often happens that in reading the biography of a person, we peruse hundreds of pages without getting an insight into the character; but we read on in search of that one touch which shall reveal to us, as in a flash of light, the whole picture, the whole character. In my own experience it has usually been a few strokes of portrait painting, or some single characteristic act that has done this. The light was flashed upon Thoreau's life for me by a few sentences in a late newspaper article on Thoreau, by Robert Collyer. He says of him:

He was "rather slender, but of a fine mould, and with a presence which touched you with a feeling of perfect purity, as newly opened roses do. And it was a clear rose-tinted face he turned to you, delicate to look at as the face of a girl, and great gray eyes, the seer's eyes, full of quiet sunshine." There are volumes in these words. Among other things they tell the story of his friendships, of the ideality which necessarily characterized them. I remember that one of Thoreau's most intimate friends, Mr. H. G. O. Blake, told me that their friendship was wholly of this ideal nature. Some of the sentences on Friendship in the *Week*, cannot be quoted too often. He says of friendship, that it is something that all men are continually thinking about, planning for, and dreaming about, and yet nobody talks about it. Of two friends he says: "The one's love is exactly balanced and represented by the other. Persons are only the vessels which contain the nectar, and the hydrostatic paradox is the symbol of love's law." He subtly says that there is something wild, primeval, pagan, and godlike about noble friendship; if it is merely Christian, it becomes charity and not friendship. Again: "We must accept or refuse one another as we are. I could tame a hyena more easily than my friend. He is a material which no tool of mine will work." Again he says: "The constitutional differences which always exist, and are obstacles to a perfect friendship, are forever a forbidden theme to the lips of my friend." Again: "My friend is my real brother." And in another connection: "The lover learns at last that there is no person quite transparent and trustworthy, but every one has a devil in him that is capable of any crime in the long run. Yet, as an Oriental philosopher has said: 'Although the friendship between good men is interrupted, their principles remain unaltered. The stalk of the lotus may be broken and the fibers remain connected.' " Finally, on the influence of time upon a true friendship, he exquisitely says: "Time shall foster, and adorn, and consecrate our Friendship, no less than the ruins of temples."

Those who refuse to believe that Thoreau cherished warm and humanitarian sympathies beneath his stoical exterior, will, of course, see in his passion for the wild in nature, nothing but confirmation of their conviction that he had only a cold and repellant disposition. A deep and permanent love of the wild is something so rare, that most people are inclined to regard it as an uncanny thing, and as triumphant proof of a soured and disappointed nature. But it is nothing of the kind. In and of itself, if it is not carried to excess, it is one of the chief sources of freshness and originality. In all rural poetry it is the indispensable condition of success. As Thoreau himself says: "He would be a poet who would impress the winds and the streams into his service, to speak for him; who nailed words to their primitive senses; * * who derived his words as often as he used them,—transplanted them to his page with earth adhering to their roots." And, again, he says: "In literature it is only the wild that attracts us. Dullness is but another name for tameness. * * All good things are wild and free." Thoreau's praise of the wild, as contrasted with the tame and factitious, was undoubtedly extreme. It was his nature to always attempt to see what could be said upon the unpopular or opposite side of any question. This arose, I think, not so much from a love of singularity, or from obstinacy, as from a love of strict justice, and a desire to help the weaker side. He was always for the under dog in the fight. It must be continually borne in mind that his exaggeration of solitude and the wild, as sources of happiness, was made with deliberate purpose. He says in his paper on walking, that he wishes to make an extreme statement, if so he may make an emphatic one, for "there are enough champions of civilization." I regard this passage as the key to Thoreau's whole life conduct. His circumstances, and his taste as a naturalist having led him to the forests and the fields, and to Spar-

tan simplicity of life, he saw that the sources of enjoyment to
be found there were, to a great extent, unknown to his countrymen; that the pernicious habit of all classes of crowding into
great cities in search of happiness, is the cause of untold
amounts of vice and misery. And so he gradually came to feel
that his mission to men was to recall them to the simple pleasures of rural life. He did this work, and did it well. His books
have restored to sane and healthy views of life many a de-
spondent soul. They are not to be devoured all at once, in a
month, or in three months. They must be read in parts, in the
warm days of Summer and Autumn, in the open fields, in the
mountain camp, or by the sea. You are to resort to them for
their bracing and restorative effects upon the *ennuyé* and
blasé mind, just as you resort to mountain, field, or sea for invigorating air and sunshine. His best book, of course, is *Walden*; America has produced no more fascinating work. Next to
this I would rank in order of merit, his *Anti-Slavery and Reform
Papers*, his *Letters*, and his *Week on the Concord and Merrimack Rivers*. The *Maine Woods, Cape Cod*, and *A Yankee in
Canada* would be enjoyed best, I think, as itineraries, or pocket
guide-books.

The *Yankee in Canada*, and portions of the *Maine Woods*,
and the *Cape Cod*, are about as dry reading for most people,
it must be confessed, as it is possible to find: these portions of
his works are not at all equal to the rest.*

In the *Hippolytos* of Euripides, Hippolytos (who ardently
loves the chase, and the sweet, wild solitudes of nature) is made
to utter this invocation: "Hail, O most beauteous of virgins in
Olympus, Dian! For thee, my mistress, bear I this wreathed
garland from the pure mead, where neither does the shepherd
think fit to feed his flocks, nor yet came iron there, but the bee

---

* A characteristic of all of his books is their grave monotony. They lack humor,
as has often been said. Hence, it is wearisome to read in them long at a time.
This partly arises, also, from the richness and originality of the thought, making
it necessary to ponder long over a few sentences. If you read very long at
once, you will also tire of the uniformly negative attitude toward society which
he assumes. Then he chronicles too many trifles. These are the faults of his
style. But it by no means follows that his books are uninteresting on account
of these few faults, and are not the most valuable reading to be found in
literature.

ranges over the pure and vernal mead, and Reverence waters
it with river-dews." Because he neglected to do homage to
Venus, and preferred to live the hardy life of the huntsman in
forest and field, Hippolytos came to a violent and cruel death
through the machinations of the enraged goddess. So, until
lately, it seemed as if the American votary of Dian, the author
of *Walden,* would meet his death at the hands of the modern
worshippers of Venus—only death in a milder form, namely,
that of cold neglect. But a rare and holy life can no more be
prevented from diffusing its influence through society, than
the sun at dawn can be prevented from throwing "his faire
fresh-quilted colors through the sky," and filling the whole
land with light. As early as 1866, in an article on Walt Whitman, in the October number of the *Fortnightly Review,* Mr. M.
D. Conway predicted that Henry David Thoreau, though then
neglected, would one day be widely read and loved. His pre-
sentiment is already receiving its confirmation. He is coming
to be admiringly read for that very ferity, that fresh sylvan
flavor as of crushed wild grapes, and scent of earth and moss,
with which the pages of his books are redolent, and which,
strange to say, at first experience of it, causes a shudder to
pass through the frame of the morbid and enervated reader
who lives under glass in the hot air of city houses. There is a
passage in Thoreau's *Excursions,* which I never read without
feeling a strange, slow thrill of pleasure creeping throughout
my entire body. There is such a glow of courage and joy; such
an elixir of life; such a subtle therapeutic virtue in the words,
that I am unable to imagine an atrabilious humor so dense as
that it would not be immediately dissipated by a sympathetic
and intelligent perusal of them. "Surely," says he, "good courage will not flag here on the Atlantic border as long as we are
flanked by the Fur Countries. There is enough in that sound
to cheer one under any circumstances. The spruce, the hem-
lock, and the pine will not countenance despair. Methinks some
creeds in vestries and churches do forget the hunter wrapped
in furs by the Great Slave Lake, and that the Esquimaux sledges
are drawn by dogs, and in the twilight of the northern night,
the hunter does not give over to follow the seal and walrus on
the ice." There is also balm for the hurt minds of this forlorn

and bewildered age in the following hearty words, or rather in their implication: "We fancy that this din of religion, literature, and of philosophy, which is heard in the pulpits, the lyceums, and parlors, vibrates through the universe, and is as catholic a sound as the creaking of the earth's axle; but if a man sleep soundly, he will forget it all between sunset and dawn." We gradually become aware in reading Thoreau's pages of the deep but quiet joy in which his life was steeped. It is a peculiar kind of joy, however,—not Italian gaiety, but sedate New England cheerfulness. "Surely, joy is the condition of life," says he. "Men tire me when I am not constantly greeted and refreshed as by the flux of sparkling streams." This joy wells forth not only in his prose writings, but more especially in his poems; as in those poems on *Mist, Smoke,* and *Haze,* by which English literature is so much enriched, and also in the stirring lines on the "tumultuous silence" of that far-off azure fleet—Monadnock and the Peterboro hills. A man who is not happy does not write poetry like this.

His religion was a cheerful and reverent mysticism. His attitude in respect of the details of the infinite life was one of suspended judgment, as that of every man ought to be. With the imbecilities and pretences of conventional religion he clashed, as, again, every true man must. In his sparring with the Church, he struck out from the shoulder, hit hard, and hit in the face like a man. There is no shilly-shallying; no shuffling. No quarter is given, and none is asked. The truth must out. Hypocrisy, Christian casuistry and sophistry, cant and the thousand vices which they breed, are sources of pain to every knightly and heroic soul; he at least will fight his fight with them, come what may, and in battle against them flash in their eyes the lightnings of his ethereal-tempered sword of truth. Accordingly, in his very first book (the *Week*), we have such sentences as these: "There is more religion in men's science than there is science in their religion." "Christianity has dreamed a sad dream and does not yet welcome the morning with joy. The mother tells her falsehoods to her child, but, thank Heaven, the child does not grow up in its parents' shadow." "A healthy man with steady employment, as wood-chopping at fifty cents a cord, and a camp in the woods, will not be a good subject for Christianity." "The church is a sort of hospital for men's souls, and as full of quackery as the hospital for their bodies." Of course, such sentences as these will be misunderstood by very many estimable Christians. It is to be feared that they will be misled by them, and will refuse to believe what is true about Thoreau, namely, that he was really one of the purest of Christians, one whom Christ would have loved with all the warmth of his lofty and kindred soul. Thoreau speaks here, as usual, with exaggerated emphasis. We know from other parts of his writings (see especially his little essay on Prayers,) that he had a most devout nature. In the passage I have quoted he is speaking only of conventional and Pharisaic religion. The Christianity of the mass of the male population of Europe and America is but a wretched parody of the religion of Jesus. It wholly misses its essential spirit, which is a reverent and tender mysticism, and a love that abhors war and strife. Thoreau, in this respect, was the truest of Christians. So are Quakers; and (as respects war), no other sect is really Christian. The other so-called Christian sects, and the "Christian" nations, are notorious as the most turbulent brawlers upon the face of the globe. In this connection read the following lines of Thoreau on spades *vs.* swords, as honorable trophies of conquest. They would serve admirably, I think, as a shibboleth by which to test the true Christian: "The weapons," says he, "with which we have gained our most important victories, [and] which should be handed down as heirlooms from father to son, are not the sword and the lance, but the bushwhack, the turf-cutter, the spade, and the bog-hoe, rusted with the blood of many a meadow, and begrimed with the dust of many a hard-fought field."

Thoreau has been loosely and vaguely compared with Rousseau. But it is a trite saying, that analogies in such cases are generally misleading. While there is a great deal in common between Thoreau and Rousseau, there is much more, it seems to me, wherein they differ. Rousseau was a man of large, intuitive, and humanitarian sympathies, a man of a tropical nature, with quivering sensibilities, with quiet and simple tastes; and yet withal a brooding and unhealthy sensualist, indolent in the highest degree, and of so irresolute a will, that he never, to the end of his life, became master of himself.

Thoreau stands in the sharpest antithesis to most of this. His humanitarian sympathies were not so strong. Such books as the *New Heloisa*, the *Social Contract*, and *Emilius*, could not have been written by one of Thoreau's make and habits. He had not Rousseau's fervid imagination; he was no dreamer like him, but active, resolute, alert, alive in every fibre of him; a man objective and inductive in his methods of work, whereas Rousseau was lazily subjective, and by his brilliant but pernicious dreams, the cause of more misery to France than any of her own sons before or since.

Rousseau, moreover, had an unclean and prurient imagination. Thoreau, on the contrary, reveals in a letter of his upon the subject of chastity, that he had a nature as pure and translucent as that of a vestal virgin—a purity, as rare and costly in quality as that of the snow-white lily of Japan, perfumed, golden-grained, and drenched with morning dew. Rousseau and Thoreau were alike in their idealism, their sensitiveness, their desire to simplify life by a return to nature, their love of quiet pleasures, and their detestation of pedantry and tyranny. They were alike, I say, in their undisguised preference for the homely virtues of the primitive life, the wild life. Each was driven into this attitude toward society by the difficulty, if not impossibility, of living a perfectly noble life within its limits. Now most persons have no hesitation in saying, that it would be better for such idealists if they would make some concessions to society, some compromise with it. But here is just where such persons are mistaken. These rare souls feel instinctively that they are only strong, are only fulfilling their destiny when they are keeping their lives as stainless as a cloudless morning sky. No sadder thing, surely, could happen to society than to have its prophets and idealists subjected to the conventional moral standards, however high those standards may be for society itself. The desire of some of Mr. Thoreau's friends to relieve him from the unpopularity which his stern reproofs of society have given him, to tame his magnificent wildness, and represent him as a good and regular citizen (only a little eccentric) —this desire of his friends, I say, springs from the most laudable motives, but still is based, it seems to me, upon an error as to the real facts in the case, an error as to the real value and significance of his life and work. As to the facts—one could quote from his books hundreds of passages to prove how irksome the mass of men were to him, and what intense delight he took in finding places about Concord, in the Maine woods, and elsewhere, where the work of man had not caused that deformity in the landscape which so often attends his footsteps, especially in a new country. To quote but one instance; in his *Winter Walk*, he says: "The chicadee and nut-hatch are more inspiring society than statesmen and philosophers, and we shall return to these last as to more vulgar companions."

There is not the least doubt but that he would have seen a great deal to admire in the declaration Rousseau made, in one of his *Discourses*, to the effect that if he were chief of an African tribe, he would set up on his frontiers a gallows, on which he would hang the first civilized man who should venture to cross over into his territory, as well as the first native who should dare to pass out of it. Now, what *is* the significance of such extreme statements as these? What do they mean? What gives them their value?—for value they have, and that a high one. They mean that society is morally imperfect and unlovely to thousands of men; their value lies in the fact that they form a bright mirror, in which society may see its faults, and so be enabled to correct them. Let it, at its peril, refuse to take the reproof which a glance into the mirror gives. Let it, rather, strengthen itself by repeated glances. Let us not be disobedient to the heavenly vision. Do we not go up to the silence and soothing serenity of lofty mountain heights, that we may receive strength and inspiration for the struggle of life? Yet the grandeur of the heights humbles us, and the thin air is with difficulty respired.

But people say: "Is it not much better to stay in Society and improve it, rather than to stand outside of it and point out its faults?" I answer, "Yes, for you and me, perhaps, but not for all. For how can anything be seen in its *ensemble*—in its true proportions and relations—unless *some one* views it wholly from the outside? Thoreau, happening to be a naturalist in taste, found his work outside of society. This was well for him.

It would not be well for the majority of us, for the simple reason that the isolated and primitive life is not, and never can be,
best for the development of mankind as a whole. The solutions
of the problems of society are to be found in society itself. The
perfect adjustment of man to his surroundings must come from
combined toil. But this perfect adjustment is a thing of the
far-off future. In the meantime, let us not refuse to see that
now and then peculiarly constituted individuals may—nay,
must—live their highest life by communings with nature in
"her unspeakable rural solitudes," "along the cool, sequestered
vale of life," "far from the madding crowd's ignoble strife," and
even apart from that delightful social intercourse which imparts
strength and courage to most of us.

First Revaluations: 1890-1916

You will pardon some obscurities, for there are more secrets in my trade than in most men's, and yet not voluntarily kept, but inseparable from its very nature.

"Economy," *Walden*

HENRY STEPHENS SALT (1851-1939), a prolific writer and critic, wrote biographies of Shelley, Richard Jefferies, James Thomson, and De Quincey, as well as of Thoreau. Friend of Shaw, W. H. Hudson, Thomas Hardy, George Meredith, G. K. Chesterton, and the literati of his day, Salt was influential in introducing Thoreau to English readers. In 1935, looking back upon *The Life of Henry David Thoreau* which he had published in 1890, Salt wrote to Professor Raymond Adams, the distinguished American interpreter of Thoreau, that the chief fault of the book was its overemphasis upon the influence of Emerson on Thoreau. Salt had concluded, he told Professor Adams, that of the two men, Thoreau was the "greater" (*The Thoreau Society Bulletin*, No. 29, October, 1949).

Conclusion

HENRY S. SALT

The Life of Henry David Thoreau (London: Richard Bentley & Son, 1890; reprinted by Archon Books, Hamden, Conn., 1968), pp. 282-98.

Thus, as we have seen, the most vigorous protest ever raised against that artificiality in life and literature which constitutes one of the chief dangers of our complex civilisation proceeded not from some sleepy old-world province, which might have been expected to be unable to keep pace with a progressive age, but from the heart of the busiest and most advanced nation on the globe—it is to Yankeeland that we owe the example and the teaching of the Walden hermit and bachelor of nature. The personality of Thoreau is so singular and so unique that it seems useless to attempt, as some have done, to draw out any elaborate parallel between his character and that of other social, or un-social, reformers, who have protested against some prevalent tendency in the age in which they lived. Those who are interested in seeking for literary prototypes may perhaps, in this case, find one in Abraham Cowley, a member of that school of gnomic poets with which Thoreau was so familiar, and moreover a zealous lover of the peace and solitude of nature. He lived in close retirement during the later years of his life, and his death, which, like Thoreau's, was due to a cold caught while he was botanising, is attributed by his biographer to "his very delight in the country and the fields, which he had long fancied above all other pleasures." Some of Cowley's remarks in his essays on solitude are conceived in a spirit very similar to that of Thoreau. "The First Minister of State," he says, "has not so much business in public as a wise man in private; if the one has little leisure to be alone, the other has less leisure to be in company; the one has but part of the affairs of one nation, the other all the works of God and nature under his consideration"; and elsewhere he expresses the wish that men could "unravel all they have woven, that we might have our woods and our innocence again, instead of our castles and our policies." But these parallels, between two men of widely different periods and purposes, can contain nothing more than slight and superficial resemblances. Nor, except for his general connection with Emerson and the transcendentalists, is it more easy to match Thoreau with any ethical writer of his own generation.[1]

As a poet-naturalist, however, Thoreau is distinctly akin to Richard Jefferies and one or two other writers of the same school. Jefferies' character was richer and more sensuous than Thoreau's, but they had the same mystic religious temperament, the same impatience of tradition and conventionality, the same passionate love of woods and fields and streams, and the same gift of brilliant language in which to record their observations. It is curious to compare these modern devotees of country life with the old-fashioned naturalists of whom Izaak Walton and Gilbert White are the most illustrious examples. While the honest old angler prattles on contentedly, like the babbling streams by which he spent his days, with here and there a pious reflection on the beneficence of Providence and the adaptation of means to ends, and while the kindly naturalist of Selborne devotes himself absolutely and unreservedly to the work of chronicling the fauna and flora of the district about which he writes, these later authors have brought to the treatment of similar subjects a far deeper insight into the beauty and pathos of nature, and a power of poetical description which was not dreamed of by their simple yet not less devoted predecessors. It is mainly to Thoreau in America, and to Jefferies in

---

[1] It is interesting to observe that of late years a body of social reformers has arisen in England whose doctrines are largely in accord with those of Thoreau. *England's Ideal*, a volume of essays published in 1887 by Edward Carpenter, is worthy to rank with *Walden* in the literature of "plain living and high thinking."

England, that we owe the recognition and study of what may be called the poetry of natural history—a style of thought and writing which is peculiar to the last thirty or forty years. The study of nature has, of course, been from time immemorial one of the great subjects of poetry, but, so far, it was nature in its more general aspects; it was not till comparatively recent years that there was discovered to be poetry also in the accurate and patient observation of natural phenomena. We have now learnt that natural history, which was formerly regarded as a grave and meritorious study of a distinctly prosaic kind, may be made to yield material for the most imaginative and poetical reflections.

When Thoreau died in 1862, Richard Jefferies was a boy of fourteen, busily engaged among his native Wiltshire Downs in laying the foundation of his wonderful knowledge of outdoor life. As far as I am aware, there is no mention of Thoreau in his writings, nor any indication that he had read him; yet one is often struck by suggestive resemblances in their manner of thought. Take, for instance, that half-serious, half-whimsical contention of Thoreau's, which has probably been more misunderstood than any other of his sayings—that Concord, in its natural features, contains all the phenomena that travellers have noted elsewhere—and compare it with the following opinion expressed by Jefferies. "I found that the reeds, and ferns, and various growths through which I pushed my way, explained to me the jungles of India, the swamps of Central Africa, and the backwoods of America; all the vegetation of the world. Representatives exist in our own woods, hedges, and fields, or by the shore of inland waters. It was the same with flowers. I think I am scientifically accurate in saying that every known plant has a relative of the same species or genus growing wild in this country. . . . It has long been one of my fancies that this country is an epitome of the natural world, and that if any one has come really into contact with its productions, and is familiar with them, and what they mean and represent, then he has a knowledge of all that exists on the earth."[1] In reading these words, one has a difficulty in remembering that they were not written by Thoreau.

The association of Thoreau's name with the district in

---

[1] *The Life of the Fields*; essay on "Sport and Science."

which he lived and died is likely to become closer and closer as the years go on. Great nature-lovers, it has been truly remarked, have the faculty of stamping the impress of their own character on whole regions of country, so that there are certain places which belong by supreme and indisputable right to certain persons who have made them peculiarly and perpetually their own. As the Lake District is inseparably connected with the names of the poets who dwelt and wrote there; as the Scotch border-land owns close allegiance to Scott, and the Ayrshire fields to Burns; and as the little Hampshire village of Selborne is the inalienable property of Gilbert White—so the thoughts of those who visit Concord turn inevitably to Thoreau. "Thoreau's affections and genius," says one of his admirers, "were so indissolubly bound up with this country that now he is gone he presents himself to my mind as one of these local genii or deified men whom the Scandinavian mythology gave as guardians to the northern coasts and mountains. These beings kept off murrain from the cattle and sickness from men. They made the nights sweet and salubrious, and the days productive. If Thoreau had lived in the early ages of Greece, he would have taken his place in the popular imagination along with his favourite god Pan."

That a personality so stubbornly and aggressively independent as Thoreau's would be a stumbling-block to many critics, good and bad alike, might have been foreseen, and indeed *was* foreseen, from the first. "What an easy task it would be," said one who understood him unusually well,[1] "for a lively and not entirely scrupulous pen to ridicule his notions, and raise such a cloud of ink in the clear medium as entirely to obscure his true and noble traits." Just three months after these prophetic words were written appeared Mr. Lowell's criticism of Thoreau in the *North American Review*, in which, while paying reluctant tribute to his literary mastership, he made merry over his character and ethical opinions, holding up to ridicule his supposed conceit, indolence, selfishness, misanthropy, valetudinarianism, and lack of humour. "The radical vice of his theory of life," says Mr. Lowell, "was that he confounded physical with spiritual remoteness from men. One is

[1] John Weiss, *Christian Examiner*, July 1865.

far enough withdrawn from his fellows if he keep himself clear of their weaknesses." That a confusion of physical with spiritual remoteness should be attributed to Thoreau of all writers is an astounding piece of criticism which must have made many a reader of *Walden* rub his eyes; for one of the truths emphasised in that book with peculiar insistence is that it is possible to be farthest removed from a man at the very time when one is nearest to him in the body. Indeed, Mr. Lowell has himself manifested the weakness of his own assertion by stating, on the same page of the same article, that Thoreau's Walden shanty was a sham, because his actual remoteness from his townsmen was there so inconsiderable. He once saw, he says, "a genuine solitary, who spent his winters 150 miles beyond all human communication." In other words, he blames Thoreau first for living as much as two miles from his fellow-citizens, and then for not living as much as 150. Such captious criticism would be laughable enough in itself were it not for the fact that, coming with the authority of a great name, it has prejudiced many a reader against Thoreau's writings before he has made fair trial of them for himself.

"A skulker" is the phrase in which Mr. R. L. Stevenson summed up Thoreau's character in his essay in *Men and Books*; but as he himself admits in the later written preface that he had quite misread Thoreau through lack of sufficient knowledge of his life, there is no reason why admirers of *Walden* should feel much disturbed at the bestowal of that singularly inappropriate appellation. Other critics, again, while enjoying much of Thoreau's writing, have been haunted by a suspicion that he was the victim of a theatrical self-consciousness, and that he became a hermit rather to attract attention than to avoid it. "We have a mistrust of the sincerity of the St. Simeon Stylites," said a contemporary reviewer of *Walden*,[1] "and sus-

---

[1] *Putnam's Magazine*, Oct. 1854. See also Mr. Grant Allen's remarks in the *Fortnightly Review*, May 1888: "Like a true Pythagorean, he cultivated chiefly the domestic bean, finding it on the whole the cheapest food on which man can sustain life in the woods of Massachusetts. In all this I wish I could always feel quite sure that Thoreau was *au fond* thoroughly sincere." The statement of fact is here as unfortunate as the inference drawn from it. The Pythagoreans made a point of *not* eating beans, and Thoreau informs us that he was a Pythagorean in this respect, and exchanged his beans for other food.

pect that they come down from the pillars in the night-time when nobody is looking at them. Diogenes placed his tub where Alexander would be sure of seeing it, and Mr. Thoreau ingeniously confesses that he went out to dine." So inconceivable does it seem to those who have not considered, much less practised, a simple and frugal life, that a man should deliberately, and for his own pleasure, abandon what *they* believe to be luxuries and comforts, that critics are always discovering some far-fetched and non-existent object in the Walden experiment, while they miss its true and salutary lessons. "Thoreau," says Dr. E. W. Emerson, "is absurdly misconceived by most people. He did not wish that every one should live in isolated cabins in the woods, on Indian corn and beans and cranberries. His own Walden camping was but a short experimental episode, and even then this really very human and affectionate man constantly visited his friends in the village, and was a most dutiful son and affectionate brother. It is idle for cavilling Epicureans to announce as a great discovery that he sometimes took supper comfortably at a friend's house, or was too good a son to churlishly thumb back the cake that his good mother had specially made for him. He was not like the little men of that day who magnified trifles of diet until they could think of little else."

Thoreau's "lack of ambition" was another point that caused him to be much misunderstood—even Emerson gave his sanction to this rather futile complaint. "I cannot help counting it a fault in him," he said, "that he had no ambition. Wanting this, instead of engineering for all America, he was the captain of a huckleberry party. Pounding beans is good to the end of pounding empires one of these days; but if, at the end of years, it is still only beans!" But the obvious answer to this criticism is that, in Thoreau's case, it was *not* only beans. The chapter on "The Bean Field," in *Walden*, is one of the most imaginative and mystic in all his works—"it was no longer beans that I hoed," he says, "nor I that hoed beans"—for the object of his quest and labour was not the actual huckleberry nor the tangible bean, but the glorified and idealised fruit of a lifetime spent in communion with nature, which imparted to his writings a freshness and fragrance as of nature itself. In this matter

Thoreau was the wisest judge of his own powers, and conferred a far greater benefit on the human race by writing *Walden* than he could have done by engineering for all America. "No bribe," says Channing, "could have drawn him from his native fields, where his ambition was—a very honorable one—to fairly represent himself in his works, accomplishing as perfectly as lay in his power what he conceived his business. His eye and ear and hand fitted in with the special task he undertook—certainly as manifest a destiny as any man's ever was."

The conclusion of the whole matter is, that Thoreau is a hopeless subject for corrective criticism; it is easy to point out that he would have been wiser had he done this or had he omitted to do that; but the fact remains that he had a clear and definite object before him which he followed with inflexible earnestness, and that his very faults and limitations subserved the main purpose of his life. "There is a providence in his writings," says one of his best interpreters,[1] "which ought to protect him from the complaint that he was not somebody else. No man ever lived who paid more ardent and unselfish attention to his business. If pure minds are sent into the world upon errands, with strict injunction not to stray by other paths, Thoreau certainly was one of these elect. A great deal of criticism is inspired by the inability to perceive the function and predestined quality of the man who passes in review. It only succeeds in explaining the difference between him and the critic. Such a decided fact as a man of genius is ought to be gratefully accepted and interpreted."

That Thoreau's doctrines, no less than his character, have their shortcomings and imperfections, few will be disposed to deny. He could not realise, or perhaps did not care to realise, the immense scope and complexity of the whole social problem; he had scarcely the data or opportunities for doing so; and in any case his intensely individualistic nature would probably have incapacitated him. We therefore cannot look to him for any full and satisfactory solution of the difficulties by which our modern civilisation is surrounded, but it would be a great error to conclude that we are not to look to him at all. If it

---

[1] John Weiss, *Christian Examiner*, 1865.

is true that the deadlock resulting from the antagonism of labour and capital can never be relieved without external legislation, it is equally true that there can be no real regeneration of society without the self-improvement of the individual man; it is idle to assert that the one or the other must come first—*both* are necessary, and the two must be carried on side by side. In Thoreau the social instinct was deficient or undeveloped; but, on the other hand, he has set forth the gospel of the higher intellectual individualism with more force and ability than any modern writer; if it be but a half-truth that he preaches, it is none the less a half-truth of the utmost moment and significance.[1]

We have seen that he was not, like Emerson, a philosopher of wide far-reaching sympathies and cautious judicial temperament, but rather a prophet and monitor—outspoken, unsparing, trenchant, inexorable, irreconcilable. He addressed himself to the denunciation and correction of certain popular tendencies which he perceived to be mischievous and delusive, and preached what may be comprehensively termed a gospel of simplicity, in direct antagonism to the prevailing tone of a self-indulgent and artificial society. Who will venture to say that the protest was not needed then—that it is not still more needed now? "The years which have passed," says a well-known writer,[2] "since Thoreau came back out of Walden wood, to attend to his father's business of pencil-making, have added more than the previous century to the trappings and baggage of social life, which he held, and taught by precept and example, that men would be both better and happier for doing without. And while we succumb and fall year by year more under the dominion of these trappings, and life gets more and more overlaid with one kind and another of upholsteries, the idea of something simpler and nobler probably never haunted men's minds more than at this time." Herein lies the

---

[1] "As to Thoreau," says Edward Carpenter, "the real truth about him is that he was a thorough economist. He reduced life to its simplest terms, and having, so to speak, labor in his right hand and its reward in his left, he had no difficulty in seeing what was worth laboring for and what was not, and no hesitation in discarding things which he did not think *worth* the time or trouble of production."—*England's Ideal.*

[2] Mr. T. Hughes, *Academy,* 17th Nov. 1877.

strength of Thoreau's position, and the assurance of the ultimate recognition of the essential wisdom of his teaching—the
very excess of the evil, which turns our supposed comforts
into discomforts and our luxuries into burdens, must at last
induce us to listen to the voice of sobriety and reason.

As to the manner in which Thoreau expresses his convictions nothing more need here be said, except that his style is
justly adapted to his sentiments. His "knock-down blows at
current opinion" are likened by Mr. R. L. Stevenson to the
"posers" of a child, "which leave the orthodox in a kind of
speechless agony." "They know the thing is nonsense—they
are sure there must be an answer, yet somehow they cannot
find it." We may shrewdly doubt whether the conclusive
answer will ever be forthcoming; but it is something that
people should be at all aroused from the complacent lethargy
of custom and tradition. Thoreau is thus seen to have a quickening, stimulating, and, at times, exasperating effect as an
ethical teacher; it is no part of his object to prophesy smooth
things, to deal tenderly with the weaknesses of his readers, or
even to explain those features of his doctrine which, from
their novelty or unpopularity, are most likely to be misunderstood. This being so, his character and writings were certain
to prove as distasteful to some readers as they are attractive to
others; if he is a good deal misapplied at present, time will
set that right. "The generation he lectured so sharply," says
John Burroughs, "will not give the same heed to his words as
will the next and the next. The first effect of the reading of his
books upon many minds is irritation and disappointment; the
perception of their beauty and wisdom comes later on."

In conclusion, we see in Thoreau the extraordinary product of an extraordinary era—his strange, self-centred, solitary
figure, unique in the annals of literature, challenges attention
by its originality, audacity, and independence. He had, it has
been well remarked, "a constitutional *No* in him"; he renounced
much that other men held dear, and set his heart on objects
which to the world seemed valueless; it was part of his mission
to question, to deny, to contradict. But his genius was not only
of the negative and destructive order. In an age when not one
man in a thousand had a real sympathy with nature, he attained

to an almost miraculous acquaintance with her most cherished secrets; in an age of pessimism, when most men, as he himself expresses it, "lead lives of quiet desperation," he was filled with an absolute confidence in the justice and benevolence of his destiny; in an age of artificial complexity, when the ideal is unduly divorced from the practical, and society stands in false antagonism to nature, he, a devout pantheist, saw everywhere simplicity, oneness, relationship. In his view God was not to be considered apart from the material world, nor was man to be set above and aloof from the rest of creation and the lower forms of life; he tracked everywhere the same divine intelligence—"inanimate" nature there was none, since all was instinct with the same universal spirit. It was his purpose, in a word, "to civilise nature with the highest intuitions of the mind, which show her simplicity to restless and artificial men."

This ideal he pursued, as we have seen, with a rare courage, sincerity, and self-devotion. Whether he succeeded or failed in his endeavour is a question which time alone can fully answer. His example and doctrines were coldly and incredulously received during his lifetime by most of those with whom he came in contact, and his comparatively early death cut him off, in the prime of his vigour, from reaping the harvest he had sown with such patience and assiduity; so far his career, like that of most idealists, must be confessed a failure. But these are not the tests by which idealists, least of all Thoreau, can be judged. For he enjoyed, in the first place, that priceless and inalienable success which consists in perfect serenity of mind and contentment with one's own fortunes. "If the day and night," he says in *Walden*, "are such that you greet them with joy, and life emits a fragrance like flowers and sweet-scented herbs—is more elastic, starry, and immortal—that is your success." And, secondly, he had the assurance, which is seldom denied to a great man, that the true value of his work would ultimately be recognised and appreciated. During the quarter of a century that has passed since his death his fame has steadily increased both in America and England, and is destined to increase yet further.

The blemishes and mannerisms of Thoreau's character are written on its surface, easy to be read by the indifferent passerby who may miss the strong and sterling faculties that underlie them. His lack of geniality, his rusticity, his occasional littleness of tone and temper, his impatience of custom, degenerating sometimes into injustice, his too sensitive self-consciousness, his trick of over-statement in the expression of his views—these were incidental failings which did not mar the essential nobility of his nature. We shall do wisely in taking him just as he is, neither shutting our eyes to his defects nor greatly deploring their existence, but remembering that in so genuine and distinctive an individuality the faults have their due place and proportion no less than the virtues. Had he added the merits he lacked to those which he possessed, had he combined the social with the individual qualities, had he been more catholic in his philosophy and more guarded in his expression, then we might indeed have admired him more, but should scarcely have loved him so well, for his character, whatever it gained in fulness, would have missed the peculiar freshness and piquancy which are now its chief attraction—whatever else he might have been, he would not have been Thoreau.

SAMUEL ARTHUR JONES (1834-1912), a Michigan physician, compiled the first bibliography of Thoreau (1894), and edited the first volume of Thoreau criticism, *Pertaining to Thoreau* (1901), as well as a volume of the letters of Sophia and Henry Thoreau. "Time," Jones believed, "is doing its kindliest offices for Thoreau." Despite Lowell's "misrepresentations," "the seriousness of his life is being recognized."

Thoreau and His Biographers*

SAMUEL ARTHUR JONES

Lippincott's Monthly Magazine, Vol. 48 (August, 1891), 224-28.

What more delightful anticipation is there than when we cut the leaves of a new Life of an author whom we have long loved? And if the reading prove only a "bootless bene," how

---

*Thoreau, the Poet Naturalist. By Wm. Ellery Channing. Boston, 1873.
Thoreau: his Life and Aims. By H. A. Page. Boston, 1877.
Henry D. Thoreau. By F. B. Sanborn. Boston, 1883.
The Life of Henry David Thoreau. By H. S. Salt. London, 1890.

absurdly inefficacious do we find dear Mary Lamb's "shoeless pea"! Beyond question there is a special limbo for the inept biographer.

It is Thoreau's good fortune to have biographers who improve upon each other. The initiatory endeavor, by Channing, though published eleven years after Thoreau's death, was still too near that event to allow his chosen companion to write anything other than a rhapsody. For a more satisfactory glimpse of Thoreau the student was obliged to have recourse to Emerson's calmer obituary sketch. From it and the subsequent volume of "Letters," edited by Emerson, has been derived that conception of Thoreau which is at once the most general and the most unjust. It was Emerson's desire to display Thoreau as "a most perfect piece of stoicism." He elided from the letters the evidences of Thoreau's human tenderness so unsparingly that Sophia Thoreau remonstrated: "it did not seem quite honest to Henry." Mr. James T. Fields seconded her protest, and a few passages which evinced "some tokens of natural affection" were retained. Emerson, we are told, "fancied" that this pious interference of a bereaved sister "had marred his classic statue."

Channing's book is valuable as containing much of Thoreau's "Journal" that has not been published elsewhere; and many of his selections are of singular beauty. For instance, Thoreau is at Clematis Brook watching the dispersion of milkweed seeds as the summer breeze catches their silken wings, and he derives this corollary from so commonplace an incident: "Who could believe in the prophecies of a Daniel or of Miller, that the world would end this summer, while one milkweed with faith matured its seed?"

The succeeding Life by H. A. Page, now known as Dr. A. H. Japp, was written at too great a distance from its subject and too near Thoreau's books to be of any other use than to whet the reader's curiosity and make him eager for a more extended knowledge of its hero. Dr. Japp is the introducer and chief disseminator of the figment that the shanty at Walden was a station of the underground railroad. He infers this from a cursory statement of Channing's: "Not one slave alone was expedited to Canada by Thoreau's personal assistance." R. L.

Stevenson accepts this myth as the *raison d'être* for Thoreau's abode in Walden woods, and even Mr. Salt repeats the story in his excellent Life. The writer has made this a matter of special investigation, and the truth is that there were specially-prepared houses in "Old Concord" which afforded infinitely more secure resting- and hiding-places for the fugitive slave. Moreover, the survivors who managed Concord "station" declare that Thoreau's hut was not used for such a purpose.

With Mr. Sanborn's Life began the era of personal misrepresentation; and soon after its publication a highly-incensed lady called its unfortunate author to account in the Boston *Daily Advertiser.* We have not been able to learn the whereabouts of Mr. Sanborn's reply. Living in Concord, and having known Thoreau personally, Mr. Sanborn had at hand the materials for an interesting book; but it appears that he felt called upon to write at once Thoreau's biography, and a history of Concord, and at the same time to make "honorable mention" of all its worthies, living or dead, past, present, and to come. It is, however, an entertaining volume if you possess the patience to unravel it and the skill to follow an often-hidden trail. Lacking these qualities yourself, the book is still deserving of the encomium that Dr. John Brown says a Scotch shepherd awarded to a boiled sheep's-head: "There's a deal o' confused eatin' aboot it." But this Life has left a smart in the hearts of those who knew and loved the Thoreaus that needs only to be known to nullify the false witness.

Mr. Salt's Life is purely a labor of love. To him Thoreau's "gospel of simplicity" is both chart and compass: he is not so much an "admirer" as an earnest follower of the sincere man whose life he both writes and lives. When precept and practice go hand in hand and love walks with them, the printed page becomes refulgent. Mr. Salt has done more than any other writer, living or dead, to correct the errors that are current concerning Thoreau and to enable a just conception of his character to be made. Preceding this Life is an essay on Thoreau, *Temple Bar*, No. 78, p. 369, so felicitous that all students of Thoreau should read it; and since the appearance of the more formal Life Mr. Salt has published an "Introductory Note"*

---

* Anti-Slavery and Reform Papers. Swan, Sonnenschein & Co. London, 1890.

and a paper on "Thoreau's Gospel of Simplicity"† which form an all-sufficient reply to certain objections by Professor Nichol and James Russell Lowell. Writing in a foreign country, with only a scholar's access to his materials, and, of all who had known Thoreau personally, having met only Mr. Sanborn, Mr. Salt's Life is singularly correct. A few trivial mis-statements are found: its one great blemish is owing solely to his having accepted Mr. Sanborn's estimate of Thoreau's parents and their relatives as trustworthy. It is to be feared that Mr. Sanborn has judged Thoreau's father from the exterior alone,—a shallow judgment! John Thoreau had in his veins the blood of Huguenot, Covenanter, and Quaker,—an ancestral blending to be coveted; Mr. Sanborn could discern only a "little," "deaf," "plainly-clad," "unobtrusive," "unambitious," "plodding" man whose shrug and snuff-box were the only reminiscences of his French extraction. They who knew him believe that John Thoreau is to Mr. Sanborn like the cathedral window described by Hawthorne: "Standing without, you see no glory, nor can possibly imagine any; standing within, every ray of light reveals a harmony of unspeakable splendors." But it isn't the window's fault!

That Mrs. Thoreau, her sister, and her sisters-in-law were vilified, after every one of the name Thoreau was dead, the best blood in and of Concord will this day testify. *De mortuis nil nisi bonum* should also be read *nil nisi verum*. Alas that the printed page should still be able to reiterate the lie that has been branded in the market-place!

There is another feature of Mr. Sanborn's Life that perplexes the thoughtful reader,—namely, the exalted character which he ascribes to the Thoreau children. Not that their moral status is to be questioned: the puzzle is to explain the phenomenon. The fountain, according to Mr. Sanborn, rises *so* much higher than its source. A "plodding, unambitious" father, but children living up to the highest ideals. A mother given to "flashes of gossip and malice," yet growing up around her hearth-stone sons and daughters whom such an atmosphere would have stifled! The problem darkens when Mr. Sanborn says, "Perpetuity, indeed, and hereditary transmission of every-

† The Paternoster Review, March, 1891.

thing that by nature and good sense can be inherited, are among the characteristics of Concord." (Life, p. 38.)

The whole household—father, mother, Helen, John, Henry, Sophia: the last of their name in America—are gathered together on that little hill-top in Sleepy Hollow which the morning sun is the first to visit and the last to leave; and if the reader shall ever stand a pious pilgrim there in the solemn silence of a summer's night, shadows below and starlight above, he will be devoutly thankful that nothing of earth can break their peace.

No man's life can be fully written by a contemporary. *Pace tua*, James Boswell. If thine angry shade shall threaten vengeance, then shalt thou be referred to Dr. Birkbeck Hill, whose editorship has made old Ursus Major better known to us than ever he was to those who supped with him at the Mitre or helped him to beguile the nights he so dreaded. Death and time break the seals of reticences that are sacred to coevals, and posterity is permitted to make the most searching postmortem examinations. Meanwhile, the falsities that for a time batten on a dead man's memory one by one drop into oblivion, shrivelled by the light of Truth. Time is doing its kindliest offices for Thoreau. One after the other misrepresentations are being brought to judgment, and there is "reversal with costs." Lowell, the chief offender, is already condemned by all but the vulgar. Thoreau is no longer considered a "misanthrope," nor is he deemed a "hermit" who masqueraded at Walden Pond. The seriousness of his life is being recognized, his earnestness is seldom questioned, and the wisdom of his philosophy is more than suspected. Before the end of Plato's year he may find disciples in every deed.

That he was sincerity incarnate is the first necessary lesson to be learned concerning him. That he studied the problem of life as profoundly and as continually as did Marcus Aurelius, and that he lived it as regally, will soon be seen. Then it will be time to consider what was to him the outcome of his philosophy. It will be found that his religion grew out of his philosophy; not the philosophy from the religion. This reversal of the sacerdotal order produced precious fruit. He learned that life is not from the Divine *design* a soul-wearying struggle, but, truly lived, a pastime worthy of the soul. His spiritual ear discovered the source of the discords that mar the harmony of the psalm of life: "When we are weary with travel, we lay down our load and rest by the wayside. So, when we are weary with the burden of life, why do we not lay down this load of falsehoods which we have volunteered to sustain, and be refreshed as never mortal was? Let the beautiful laws prevail. Let us not weary ourselves by resisting them."

Volunteered to sustain. There is the hammer-stroke that buries the nail. The Eternal Unspeakable One is *not* the bungler: it is WE who will not "let the beautiful laws prevail." Thus devoutly doth he justify the ways of God to man.

He inculcated the supremest care of the body: "A man is never inspired unless his body is also." He insisted that man should accept his "genius"—the voice within—as the unerring guide: not Socrates was more obedient to his dæmon. He declares "that if one advances confidently in the direction of his dreams, and endeavors to live the life which he has imagined, he will meet with a success unexpected in common hours." Ay, more, "in proportion as he simplifies his life, the laws of the universe will appear less complex, and solitude will not be solitude, nor poverty poverty, nor weakness weakness. If you have built castles in the air, your work need not be lost; that is where they should be. Now put the foundations under them."

When our latter-day mad race for wealth, only wealth, shall have brought to us the inevitable result and a chastened people shall seek "the better way," it will be the "hermit" of Walden, not the Sage of Concord, that will lead them.

Though called away when his capabilities were at their highest and his cherished work undone, it is difficult to think of Thoreau's life as incomplete; still harder to believe with his distinguished friend that it was only "pounding beans." His end was presaged by that sublime outburst of supreme manhood, his defence of Captain John Brown "sick and in prison." When all other lips were sealed, Thoreau's flamed with living fire, for even God had touched them.

After that came the slow decay, and the sleep for one whom the grandest occasion in his life had found sufficient. But every vouchsafed moment was piously husbanded: manuscripts were arranged and essays revised before the hand had forever lost its cunning. One of these may be seen in Concord Library, and three handwritings are found in it,—his own with pen and ink, and, when he wearied, with the more convenient pencil, and, when too weak for even that, his sister Sophia wrote at his dictation.

He went forth at his prime, having "much to report on natural history," but obliged to take it all into the inexorable grave. Yet no repining; instead, the declaration from lips that were never sullied by a lie, "I am enjoying existence as much as ever, and regret nothing."

"A man's religion is the chief fact with regard to him." What was Thoreau's? He "rested quietly in God's palm." He was so filled with confidence in the Unspeakable One that he asked no curious questions; and, in our ignorance, perhaps that is the wisest attitude for any soul. Better than all, the moral grandeur of his exit shows that he had not only the courage but also the comfort of his convictions.

CHARLES C. ABBOTT (1843-1919), American archaeologist, naturalist, and novelist, was the author of more than thirty volumes, including a cyclopedia of natural history (1895). A naturalist himself, Abbott contended that Thoreau's permanent fame would not rest upon his studies of wild life.

Thoreau

CHARLES C. ABBOTT

Lippincott's Monthly Magazine, Vol. 55 (June, 1895), 852-55.

There are two of the many essays on Thoreau that are probably more read than all the others put together, and because of their authorship—Emerson and Lowell—have greater weight in the minds of readers than would any expression of opinion from any other source as to Thoreau as a man of letters or as a naturalist. But the world is not always wise in bowing down to greatness, for greatness is very sure, in the long run, to overestimate itself. Neither Emerson nor Lowell was fitted to the task they undertook, though they doubtless thought they were. It is true that

Emerson's article prefacing Thoreau's volume "Excursions" is a biographical sketch merely, but in it are phrases that are open to criticism. As an instance, take Emerson's estimate of Thoreau's ambition, or what he calls a lack of it. Now, so great is the influence carried with every word of Emerson that probably not one reader in a hundred but regrets that Thoreau preferred to be "captain of a huckleberry party" to leader of a political one, and that he held "pounding beans" to be better than "the pounding of empires." There is the error. What we sadly need is an infusion of intellect into the lower strata of man's activities. There will always be brains and to spare in the courts of professional life,—great leaders who will reach the artificial element that crowds the cities and happily leaves undisturbed the simple folk who live nearer to Nature. Thoreau would have been lost, or at best but one of many, had he overcome his repugnance to mere formality and met his neighbors in a dress-suit. We cannot imagine him acting any one of the innumerable white lies of modern society. In such slavish toggery he would have excited as much of ridicule as he now commands of admiration. In his lifelong battle for sincerity and simplicity, he knew the field upon which he was to fight; knew it better than any antagonist he met, and left it a conqueror.

As we glance over modern biography, we find there are countless examples of youth born in the ranks of the lowly who have aspired to better things and seized knowledge as a cable by which to draw themselves upward, and spent their remaining days at a higher level and in an atmosphere that was but a source of wonderment to their ancestors. This sounds very noble; it is noble; but in Thoreau's case there was an inversion of this order, and the intellectuality that Emerson deplored as dissipated was put to the very highest of uses, that of making the lower or simpler things of life shine out in their proper light. By thoughtfully pursuing the occupations he chose, he raised them to the rank of professions, and clothed with dignity labor that before was drudgery. The quickest way to send the world to perdition would be to make all men lead professional lives, and the positive curse under which we now rest is that the absurdity is taught by parents to infants, and by teachers to scholars, that the true or best life is that of the pre-eminently learned, and that no dignity or honor or worthy reward of any kind comes to him who lives closest to Nature, and so most remote from the centres of civilization. Pounding beans, which Emerson sneers at, would not be degrading or belittling or unworthy a man of brains, if here and there a man of mental force would show that his brain and brawn need not come into conflict. If, over the land, Thoreaus would demonstrate that a day of toil in the fields can be followed by an evening of rational, intellectual enjoyment, the world would quickly advance beyond the present stage of agitation and unrest, that needs a standing army to preserve even the semblance of order. If the philanthropists would attack the problem of intellectualizing work, the workman would be benefited indirectly more than any efforts directed at "the masses" will avail. No work that the world calls for should be looked upon by a favored few as beneath manhood. More mischief lurks in a sneer than about a cannon's mouth. Thoreau stands for two conditions which neither Emerson nor Lowell nor any great man of letters or of science or of political economy has ever dreamed of displaying upon his banner: Simplicity and Sincerity. This was an ambition far higher, far better fitted to secure the welfare of man and the permanency of his own fame (if he ever thought of the latter), than anything that Emerson ever thought of. Of course we must always bear in mind that Thoreau died before the youth of old age had commenced, and it is obviously unfair to pass too critically upon his writings. But two of the eleven volumes that complete his works were issued in his lifetime, and what he might have done with the mass that has since been printed, what omitted and what elaborated, cannot even be conjectured. That the best results should be realized, Thoreau should be read first, and what his critics have to say be considered subsequently; and it is to be regretted that, laudatory as is the biographical sketch by Emerson, it should have contained a single stricture. That stricture was not called for.

Lowell's essay on Thoreau, in the former's volume entitled "My Study Windows," though he claims his "most fruitful studies" to have been "in the open air," is eminently unjust. There was not the slightest trace of sympathy between the two men. Lowell is the reporter of the flower-garden; Thoreau, of the forest. Lowell can ride in a well-appointed boat down a safe stream, and report the graceful weeping willows that adorn its banks; Thoreau can sit cross-legged in a cranky canoe and tell in matchless language of the wild life that lives in dangerous rapids and lurks in the fastnesses of the untrodden wilderness. Lowell is tame, Thoreau is savage. The former tells us of a zoological garden; the latter of life in the haunts that Nature had provided. This being true, there lurked no cunning in Lowell's pen to tell the world who and what Thoreau really was. He simply gives us his own impressions, and they are erroneous. The well-known instance of Lowell, as editor, omitting from a manuscript of Thoreau's what he considered an objectionable passage, shows how widely apart these two men stood, and the act was an assumption on Lowell's part without excuse. What right, indeed, had he tacitly to assert that heaven lacked a feature Thoreau thought might be there? Neither of them knew, of course, one whit about the matter, but it is difficult to see why the bare-handed, sunburnt out-of-door Thoreau's opinion is not as worthy of consideration as that of his in-door, kid-gloved critic. It was a trivial matter, perhaps, but nevertheless a straw showing the direction of Lowell's thoughts,—that Thoreau, because of his being a champion of simplicity and a foe to half that which Lowell cherished as making life worth living, could be snubbed successfully. But the world is growing wiser. There is more freedom of thought than there was forty years ago, and perhaps no better evidence of true advance than the increase in numbers of those who now ponder as seriously over Thoreau's suggestive pages as they were once entertained by the polished periods of Lowell.

Extremes are necessary to effect great changes. No man ever yet drove a nail home, using only the exact force needed. There will always be an over-expenditure of enthusiasm. Thoreau always said more than he meant, knowing that, if he did not, his meaning would not reach home. He did not expect or wish a Walden hut to be built on the shore of every frog-pond. It was enough that his own experience should be an object-lesson for succeeding generations. We can carry a hermitage with us wherever we go, and meditate therein to our advantage. There are few men of culture but have or long to have their "den" where they are comparatively free from interruption. This is the meaning of Walden. He knew, well enough, that to be heard we must speak loudly to the deaf, and he shouted his best phrases where others have whispered and been unheeded. There is a roughness that is excusable on occasion. We do not ask the drowning man if his arm is sore when we firmly grasp it to save his life. If the reader is surprised at times at Thoreau's earnestness and plainness of speech, he must remember that he was a man with a purpose and held his moments at their full value. There was no time to study what others had decided as the best methods of recording thought; and yet who has given us better specimens of pure literature than he? There is no other writer of our country who leaves the mind in a more thoughtful state, when we close the volume, than he does. This is just the difference between Thoreau and his critic, Lowell. The latter keeps us in a pleasant frame of mind so long as we read, but Thoreau lingers long after we have laid aside his books.

A word more concerning Thoreau as a naturalist. He was busied with the wild life about Concord when "Science" was still occupied with the hunt for new species and content with a mere description of form and color. Evolution was but little discussed, and in New England much disregarded, because of the efforts of Agassiz to make it appear untrue. Thoreau made no practice of haunting museums, objects in alcohol, or stuffed with tow not appealing strongly to him; but he did care to know, and was successful in ascertaining, the habits of the animals he saw. It is true he was anxious to know the scientific name of a plant that he had found, and, learning it, felt his interest grow; but this does not seem to have been a need as to animal life. It was enough to know that a given fish was a chub or a perch. The bream built a nest, scooping a hollow in the sand. That this New England "bream" was a percoid, and not a cyprinoid as is the English bream, and that it had a dozen Latin names given by as many authors from Linné down, did not interest him. He knew the birds as creatures to be met in various places, each with habits of its own and its seasons of going and coming. This, rather than anatomy, was to him a matter of interest and importance. To-day such facts are found to have a bearing on philosophical zoology quite equal in importance to anatomical structure. Thoreau did not add greatly to our knowledge of wild life, but he did that which is of equal merit, showed how delightful was the pursuit of such knowledge, and, in a measure, how it might be obtained.

For many readers, perhaps for most, there is too little natural history in his books, too much of other matter. As we read, we feel at times a wish that he would sooner reach his conclusions on philosophical or political questions, because we are sure they will be followed by some bright reference to a bird or beast, simply phrased, yet so cunningly that the creature stands before us. Anybody can say or write, "I see a fox," but in Thoreau's books these same words are so framed in other matter that the animal leaps into view, and we see it dart over the snow, daintily carrying its splendid brush, perhaps looking partly over its shoulder at us, and leaving footprints that dot the author's pages, though he is eloquent over Greek poets, addresses a mountain, or weaves into splendid imagery the smoke that at sunrise he sees curling from his neighbor's chimney.

Thoreau had no predecessor and can have no successor. He was the product of conditions that can never again arise, for to expect another Concord with its galaxy of intellectual giants is utterly vain. He was one whose influence will last as long as our language shall remain.

HIRAM M. STANLEY (1854-1903) taught for many years at Lake Forest College. A scholar and researcher of broad interests, he contributed more than a score of articles in the fields of psychology, literature, religion, and education to such journals as *Science, The Psychological Review, The Philosophical Review,* and *The Educational Review.* A scientist himself, Stanley discerned that Thoreau's genius was not scientific: "Indeed," he asserted, "the spirit of science is in the directest opposition to Thoreau's; for while science does away with the personal equation, Thoreau magnifies it."

Thoreau as Prose Writer

HIRAM M. STANLEY

The Dial (Chicago), Vol. 21 (October 1896), 179-82.

Thoreau's prose writings, as published in complete form in eleven volumes, make it for the first time possible to come to any clear and full judgment concerning his character and place as a writer of artistic prose. What is Thoreau's best work? What is his rank among artists? If his life had been prolonged, would he have done better work than he actually accomplished? To these and the like interesting questions it is now possible to give some definite answer. Let us begin with the first, and consider what is Thoreau's best and most characteristic expression of himself.

"Walden" is usually pointed out as Thoreau's masterpiece. But while this is certainly a very brilliant piece of writing, and has a unity too often lacking in his other works, it yet affords but a slight clue to the real Thoreau; for here he addresses an inquiring public desirous of knowing in detail his hut-life by Walden pond, and in the whole course of the book he keeps this audience in mind, goes out to meet it, and by a most conspicuously popular style adapts himself to it. In lightsome mood, and with many a satirical stroke and humorous touch, he tells this Walden story. What can be finer, as a playful image, than his complaint that the "Iron Horse," "whose ear-rending neigh is heard throughout the town, has muddied the Boiling Spring with his foot, and he it is that has browsed off all the woods on Walden shore." But with all its excellence of style, "Walden" is comparatively superficial in both matter and manner. If we would find Thoreau's deeper self, we must search elsewhere.

Let us look then to the Journals, as printed in the four volumes entitled "Spring," "Summer," "Autumn," and "Winter." Here Thoreau writes merely for himself and to please himself, and so reveals his true self. The "journalizing," he says, is "an effort to expose my innermost and richest wares to light." The Journals are then, I take it, most important documents to help us in fully understanding and appreciating the real Thoreau and his art. Here we find, indeed, much treasure, both silver and gold; but also some base metal, both brass and pewter. As a specimen of his basest metal, we extract a few lines from his profuse and foolish musings on a big toadstool:

> Such growths ally our age to those earlier periods which geology reveals. I wondered if it had not some relation to the skunk, though not in odor, yet in its color and

the general impression it made. It suggests a vegetative force which may almost make men tremble for his dominion. It carries me back to the era of the formation of the coal measures, the age of the Saurus and the Pliosaurus, and when bull-frogs were as big as bulls. . . . Is it not a giant mildew or mold? In the warm, muggy night the surface of the earth is mildewed. The mold is the flower of humid darkness and ignorance. The pyramids and other monuments of Egypt are a vast mildew or toad-stool which have met with no light of day sufficient to waste them away.

This is mere sophomoric crudeness and callow maundering. And such slipshod thought is not infrequent in the Journals, though often in a measure redeemed by accuracy and purity of style. We have met with but one bad error in style, and this is so ludicrously bad that it is worth quoting. Describing the wintergreen blossom, Thoreau says, "It is a very pretty little chandelier of a flower, fit to adorn the forest floor." Possibly Thoreau's slight acquaintance with ball-rooms made him overlook the fact that chandeliers do not usually adorn floors.

But it is very pleasant to the patient searcher among the Journals to find amid the baser metals nuggets of purest gold; here and there he comes upon passages of descriptive literature of the highest order. Take, for instance, the description of the felling and dismembering of a giant pine by the lumberman. We can quote only the conclusion of this woodland tragedy. The tree felled, the chopper "Has measured it with his ax and marked off the small logs it will make. It is lumber. . . . When the fish-hawk in the spring revisits the banks of the Musketaquid, he will circle in vain to find his accustomed perch, and the hen-hawk will mourn for the pines lofty enough to protect her brood. . . . I hear no knell tolled, I see no procession of mourners in the streets or the woodland aisles. The squirrel has leaped to another tree, the hawk has circled farther off, and has now settled upon a new eyrie, but the woodman is preparing to lay his ax at the root of that also." This has genuine quality, as has also the following description of a bobolink's song:

I hear the note of a bobolink concealed in the top of an apple-tree behind me. Though this bird's full strain is ordinarily somewhat trivial, this one appears to be meditating a strain as yet unheard in meadow or orchard. *Paulo majora canamus.* He is just touching the strings of his theorbo, his glassichord, his water organ, and one or two notes globe themselves and fall in liquid bubbles from his harp within a vase of liquid melody, and when he lifted it out the notes fell like bubbles from the trembling strings. Methinks they are the most liquidy sweet and melodious sounds I ever heard. They are as refreshing to my ear as the first distant tinkling and gurgling of a rill to a thirsty man. Oh, never advance farther in your art; never let us hear your full strain, sir! But away he launches, and the meadow is all bespattered with melody. . . . It is the foretaste of such strains as never fell on mortal ears, to hear which we should rush to our doors and contribute all that we possess and are.

Where will you find anything finer in its way than this? It is truly, like the bobolink's, a large and noble strain. And many of Thoreau's descriptions of notes of birds and animals have a very rare quality, as when he writes of the cock's clarion, the blackbird's song, and the bullfrog's trump.

To show once more what Thoreau in his best mood can do, look at this little landscape sketch:

"The air is clear as if a cool, dewy brush had swept the meadows of all haze. A liquid coolness invests them, as if their midnight aspect were suddenly revealed to midday. The mountain outline is remarkably distinct, and the intermediate earth appears more than usually scooped out like a vast saucer sloping upwards to its sharp mountain rim. The mountains are washed in air."

This picture of pellucid air is remarkably artistic. Nought is florid or forced, but the expression is singularly close, clear, and grand. The phrase, "The mountains are washed in air," touches the sublime; it strikes the keynote of a Nature hymn. For the moment Thoreau soars the empyrean with eagle sweep.

We confess to enjoying such slight but exquisite sketches as these from the Journals far more than the elaborate and conscious efforts in "Walden." "Walden" is exoteric, the Journals are esoteric. "Walden" has not the deep seriousness, the solemn rapture, which pervades these records of daily life. Here we see more clearly than elsewhere how strongly Thoreau is thrilled and uplifted by nature's beauty. This "vision" affects him more "deeply and powerfully" than aught else. Hence he is a haunter of fields and rivers, of woods and hills; and, far withdrawing from the roar of modern mechanic life, he would "lurk," he says, "in crystalline thought, like the trout under the verdurous banks, where stray mankind should only see my bubble coming to the surface."

But though Thoreau often rises to rapture in his marvellously sensitive response to nature, he yet never attains real poetic expression. He has the raw material in plenty; but, as Emerson says, "thyme and marjoram are not yet honey." Thoreau regards the art of metre, rhyme, and rhythm as too much akin to artifice. He thinks that the "very scheme and form" of poetry is adopted at "a sacrifice of vital truth and poetry," and he refuses to make this sacrifice.

Thoreau has been called the "poet-naturalist." We have seen that he is not a poet, and it is equally plain that he is not a naturalist. Throughout his Journals, Thoreau iterates and re-iterates that he is not a scientist, and that science has no vital interest for him. Indeed, the spirit of science is in the directest opposition to Thoreau's; for while science does away with the personal equation, Thoreau magnifies it. He values nature not as a source of mere knowledge for its own sake, but as a fount of delight and inspiration which pours through his whole being. In all his close observation of nature, he seeks, not information, but beauty and sympathy. "In what book," he asks, "is this world and its beauty described? Who has plotted the steps toward the discovery of beauty? You must be in a different state from common. Your greatest success will be simply to conceive that such things are, and you will have no communication to make to the Royal Society." Thoreau thus shows an artist's dislike of cold, unimpressionable science. He desires above all things to feel deeply the supernal beauty of nature, and to give large expression of this emotion in living prose; in short, Thoreau is preëminently an artist, and in particular an impressionist of the open-air school. Out-of-doors is the subject of his art; there is his studio,—and, indeed, also his home, his theatre, his university, and his church.

But Thoreau is not equally open to all sides of nature. He lived for some time by the sea, and often visited its shore; yet, so far as we may judge from his writings, he was not much affected by the wondrous beauty and majesty of old ocean. He wandered over Cape Cod; he made excursions to the White Mountains, to the Maine woods, and to Canada; but his writings thereabout—and Thoreau is very faithful to himself in all his writing—are quite juiceless and uninspired. But let Thoreau once set foot on the well-beloved fields of Concord, walk in its forests, glide along its smooth-flowing river, and he at once utters a fresh, deep, and strong note. Even Monadnock and Wachusett thrill him chiefly as seen from Concord. All that is best in Thoreau's life and art centres in rural Concord; he is its literary *Genius loci;* he broods over its every phase, and voices his observation and meditation in sentences full of rarest insight and clearest beauty. Away from Concord he is ill at ease, and only partially receptive of the divine message of nature. "I am afraid," he says, "to travel much, or to famous places, lest it might completely dissipate the mind. Then I am sure that what we observe at home, if we observe anything, is of more importance than what we observe abroad. The far-fetched is of the least value."

Thoreau's writings show several styles. We distinguish five. First is the adolescent, diffuse, romantic style of "The Week." This work we find intensely wearisome in its smooth discursiveness and sophomoric sententiousness. Second, there is the dry, matter-of-fact style of the "Cape Cod," "Maine Woods," and "Yankee in Canada" narratives. Here he is objective and reportorial. Thoreau himself speaks of the "Canada story" as simply a "report" of what he saw, and as "not worth the time I took to tell it." This is, perhaps, too harsh a judgment; but still, all his stories of travel, though touched with a lucid simplicity, are yet on the whole quite meagre and commonplace. Again, we have the style of "Walden," brilliant, sketchy, charming, but never satisfying, because it both reveals and conceals. And again, we have the frank, plain, but often noble style of the best parts of the Journals and Letters. This writing is very concise and clear, often limpid, and generally slow of movement. However, the pine-tree episode, from which we have quoted, has much the swing of "Walden"; and in the Journals we find also the adolescent style, and even the dry narrative style, as in the account of the White Mountain trip. Lastly, we have the perfectly sound, sensible, sober style of the essay on "Wild Apples." This is a very delightful bit of prose, and, I think, quite the best complete work that Thoreau has left us. It shows that he could in his latter days give a unity of development and a mature expression, mellowed, withal, by a thoroughly genial humor—a humor wholly free from that satiric acidity which gives a bad taste to so much of Thoreau's production. The catalogue of the kinds of wild apples reminds one of Charles Lamb.

With whom shall we compare Thoreau as a painter of nature? Not with White of Selborne, for White is primarily a scientist, while Thoreau is above all and before all an artist. Not with Ruskin, for though both are artists, they are very diverse; Ruskin sees nature through the medium of the Bible and Turner, but Thoreau could allow neither priest nor painter to be his interpreter, and so he felt himself radically out of tune with the great art critic. And further, the rich and cloying style of Ruskin is altogether unlike the crystalline simplicity of Thoreau's best work. In his mind and art, Thoreau is much nearer to Wordsworth than to either White or Ruskin. Both Wordsworth and Thoreau are entirely individual and direct in their approach to nature, seeking at all times an unprepossessed impression, which they would express in the simplest and freest art,—Wordsworth, in prosaic poetry; Thoreau, in poetic prose. For both, nature is a source not merely of æsthetic but also of ethical inspiration, though Wordsworth has a mature strength and poise, an abiding rock-like solidity, quite foreign to Thoreau. Both are local in their sentiment, the Lake country being to Wordsworth what Concord was to Thoreau. For a particular comparison of work, read the description of the bobolink's song, before mentioned, and then read these lines of Wordsworth on a nightingale's song:

O Nightingale! thou surely art
A creature of a fiery heart;—
These notes of thine—they pierce and pierce;
Tumultuous harmony and fierce!
Thou sing'st as if the God of wine
Had helped thee to a Valentine;
A song in mockery and despite
Of shades, and dews, and silent Night;
And steady bliss, and all the loves
Now sleeping in these peaceful Groves.

The art of Wordsworth is here more perfect and eloquent than Thoreau's, but Thoreau excels in intimacy with nature and in fulness and closeness of expression. Thoreau is the more intense and thorough student of nature, and if he could have put his impression of the bobolink's song into adequate poetic form it would have been a nobler piece than Wordsworth's lines to a nightingale. Thoreau's matter is superior, but his manner is inferior.

What, then, is Thoreau's rank as literary artist? And has he, indeed, any permanent place in literature? We can with all safety predict that the greater part is perishable. It is plain enough that "The Week," the stories of the Cape Cod, Maine, and Canada excursions, and most of the "Miscellanies," are perishable third-rate work. "Walden" is certainly a brilliant piece of its kind, but that not the highest; and in the Journals we have a sketch-book containing some very beautiful studies, but no finished work. However, in my judgment the essay on "Wild Apples" shows Thoreau at his best, and in his true function; but even this needs pruning, and the theme is rather small and narrow. What an essay Thoreau could have given us on Bird-song! It would have been a classic. If Thoreau had lived his allotted span, he might have produced some wonderfully fine work on such lines; but as it is, we can only lament the unfulfilled promise of an artist uniquely great in animal and landscape word painting. Thoreau was undoubtedly one of those rarest visitors to our planet—a genius; and, what is more, a genius true to himself, who never swerved to the right or left in following out his bent. As such, appreciation of him is bound to grow, and that despite the incompleteness and immaturity of his actual performance. We may say with confidence that Thoreau's place, though small, is secure and permanent; he occupies a distinct but minor niche in the eternal Pantheon of Art.

BRADFORD TORREY (1843-1912), American ornithologist, wrote several popular books on birds. He is remembered today, however, for his editing of Thoreau's Journals, which first appeared as Volumes VII-XX of the Manuscript Edition (1906). Torrey was cheered in 1896 by Thoreau's increasing vogue, especially in England, and attributed it to "the loftiness and purity of his thought."

Thoreau

BRADFORD TORREY

Atlantic Monthly, Vol. 78 (December, 1896), 822-32. A long passage in which Thoreau's style is compared to that of Stevenson has been deleted.

It lay at the root of Thoreau's peculiarity that he insisted upon being himself. Having certain opinions, he held them; having certain tastes, he encouraged them; having a certain faculty, he made the most of it: all of which, natural and reasonable as it may sound, is as far as possible from what is expected of the average citizen, who may be almost what he will, to be sure, if he will first observe the golden rule of good society, to be "like other folks." Society is still a kind of self-constituted militia, a mutual protective association,—an army, in short; and in an army, as everybody knows, the first duty of man is to keep step.

What made matters worse in Thoreau's case was, that his tastes and opinions, on which he so stoutly insisted, were in themselves far out of the common. Not only would he be himself, but the "himself" was a very queer person. He liked solitude; in other words, he liked to think. He loved the society of trees and all manner of growing things. He found fellowship in them, they were of his kin; which is not at all the same as to say that he enjoyed looking at them as objects of beauty. He lived in a world of his own, a world of ideas, and was strangely indifferent to much that other men found absorbing. He could get along without a daily newspaper, but not without a daily walk. He spent hours and hours of honest daylight in what looked for all the world like idleness; and he did it on principle. He was more anxious to live well—according to an inward standard of his own—than to lodge well, or to dress well, or to stand well with his townsmen. A good name, even, was relatively unimportant. He found easy sundry New Testament scriptures which the church would still be stumbling over, only that it has long since worn a smooth path round them.

He set a low value on money. It *might* be of service to him, he once confessed, underscoring the doubt, but in general he accepted poverty as the better part. "We are often reminded," he said, "that if there were bestowed on us the wealth of Crœsus, our aims must still be the same, and our means essentially the same." Highly exalted aims they must have been, to bear such a test. Even the preacher is apt to find his health uncertain if by any chance a fortune drops into his lap. As for houses and lands, to Thoreau's mind they were often no better than incumbrances. Some of his wealthier neighbors were as good as in prison, he thought. In what sense were men to be called free, if their "property" had put them under bonds to stay in such a place and do only such and such things? Life was more than meat, as he reckoned, and having trained himself to "strict business habits" (his own words), he did not believe in swapping a better thing for a poorer one. To him it was amazing that hardheaded, sensible men should stand at a desk the greater part of their days, and "glimmer and rust, and finally go out there." "If they *know* anything," he exclaimed, "what under the sun do they do that for?" He speaks as if the question were unanswerable; but no doubt, some readers will think it easy enough, the only real difficulty being a deplorable scarcity of desks. For Thoreau's part, at any rate, other men might save dollars if they would; he meant to save his soul. It should not glimmer and rust and go out, if a manly endeavor was good for anything. And he saved it. To the end he kept it alive; and though he died young, he lived a long life and did a long life's work, and what is more to the present purpose, he left behind him a long memory.

His economies, which were so many and so rigorous, were

worthy of a man. In kind, they were such as any man must practice who, having a task assigned him, is set upon doing it. If the river is to run the mill, it must contract itself. Rightly considered, Thoreau's singularity consisted, not in his lodging in a cabin, nor in his wearing coarse clothes, nor in his non-observance of so-called social amenities, nor even in his passion for the wild, but in his view of the world and of his own place in it. He was a poet-naturalist, an idealist, an individualist, a transcendental philosopher, what you will; but first of all he was a prophet. "I am the voice of one crying in the wilderness," he might have said; and the locusts and wild honey followed as things of course. It followed, also, that the fathers neglected him,—stoning having gone out of fashion,—and the children garnish his sepulchre. A prophet is a very worthy person—after he is dead. Then come biographies, eulogies, and new editions of his works, including his journals and private letters. Fame is a plant that blossoms on graves; as a manual of such botany might say, "a late-flowering perennial, nowhere common, to be looked for in old cemeteries."

A prophet, a writer, a student of nature: this was Thoreau, and the three were one.

He preached faith, simplicity, devotion to the ideal; and with all a prophet's freedom he denounced everything antagonistic to these. He was not one of those nice people who are contented to speak handsomely of God and say nothing about the devil.

No man was more of a believer and less of a skeptic. Faith and hope, "infinite expectation," were his daily breath. Charity was his, also, but less conspicuously, and after a standard of his own, philanthropy being one of his prime aversions. He knew not the meaning of pessimism. The world was good. "I am grateful for what I am and have. My thanksgiving is perpetual." To the final hour existence was a boon to him. "For joy I could embrace the earth," he declared, though he seldom indulged himself in emotional expression; "I shall delight to be buried in it." "It was not possible to be sad in his presence," said his sister, speaking of his last illness. His may have been "a solitary and critical way of living," to quote Emerson's phrase, but in his work there is no trace of anything morbid or unwholesome. Some who would hesitate to rank themselves among his disciples keep by them a copy of Walden or the Week, to dip into for refreshment and invigoration when life runs low and desire begins to fail. Readers of this kind please him better, we may guess, if he knows of them, than those who skim his pages for the natural history and the scenery. Such is the fate of prophets. The fulminations and entreaties of Isaiah are now highly recommended as specimens of Oriental *belles-lettres*. And yet, worse things may happen to a man than to be partially appreciated. As Thoreau himself said: "It is the characteristic of great poems that they will yield of their sense in due proportion to the hasty and the deliberate reader. To the practical they will be common sense, and to the wise wisdom; as either the traveler may wet his lips, or an army may fill its watercasks at a full stream." His own was hardly a "full stream," perhaps; a mountain brook rather than one of the world's rivers; clear, cold, running from the spring, untainted by the swamp; less majestic than the Amazons, but not less unfailing, and for those who can climb, and who know the taste of purity, infinitely sweeter to drink from.

Simplicity of life and devotion to the ideal, the one a means to the other,—these he would preach, in season and, if possible, out of season. "Simplicity, simplicity, simplicity! I say, let your affairs be as two or three, and not a hundred or a thousand; instead of a million count half a dozen, and keep your accounts on your thumb-nail." This, which, after all, is nothing but the old doctrine of the one thing needful,—since it is one mark of a prophet that he deals not in novelties, but in truth,—all this spiritual economy is connected at the root with Thoreau's belief in free will, his vital assurance that the nobility or meanness of a man's life is left largely to his own choice. He may waste it on the trivial, or spend it on the essential. There is "no more encouraging fact than the unquestionable ability of man to elevate his life by a conscious endeavor." And what a man is inwardly, that to *him* will the world be outwardly; his mood affects the very "quality of the day." Could anything be truer or more finely suggested? For himself, Thoreau was resolved to get the best out of time as it passed. He refused to be hurried. The hour was too precious. "If the bell rings, why should we run?" Neither would he knowingly be put off with a sham,—as if there were nothing real! He would not "drive a nail into mere lath and plastering," he declared. Such a deed would keep him awake nights. A very reasonable and practical kind of doctrine, certainly, whether it be called transcendentalism or common sense. Perhaps we accuse it with a long word because of the obligation it lays us under.

And possibly it is for a similar reason that the world in general has agreed to regard Thoreau not as a preacher of righteousness, but as an interpreter of nature. For those who have settled down to take things as they are, having knocked under and gone with the stream, in Thoreau's language, it is pleasanter to read of beds of water-lilies flashing open at sunrise or of a squirrel's pranks upon a bough than of daily aspiration after an ideal excellence. Whatever the reason, Thoreau is to the many a man who lived out of doors, and wrote of outdoor things.

His attainments as a naturalist have been by turns exaggerated and belittled, one extreme following naturally upon the other. As for the exaggeration, nothing else was to be expected, things being as they were. It is what happens in every such case. If a man knows some of the birds, his neighbors, who know none of them, celebrate him at once as an ornithologist. If he is reputed to "analyze" flowers,—pull them to pieces under a pocket-lens, and by means of a key find out their polysyllabic names,—he straightway becomes famous as a botanist; all of which is a little as if the ticket-seller and the grocer's clerk should be hailed as financiers because of their facility in making change. Thoreau knew his local fauna and flora after a method of his own,—a method which, for lack of a better word, may be called sympathetic. Nobody was ever more successful in getting inside of a bird; and that, from his point of view and for his purpose,—and not less for ours who read him,—was the one important thing. After that it mattered little if some of his flying neighbors escaped his notice altogether, while others led him a vain chase year after year, and are still, in his published journals, a puzzle to all readers. Who knows what his night warbler was, or, with certainty, his seringo bird? The latter, indeed, a native of his own Concord hay-fields, he seems to have been pretty well acquainted with as a bird; its song was familiar to him, and less frequently he caught sight of the singer itself perched upon a fence-post or threading its way through the grass; but he had found no means of ascertaining its name, and so was driven to the primitive expedient of christening it with an invention of his own. His description of its appearance and notes leaves us in no great doubt about its identity; probably it was the savanna sparrow; but how completely in the dark he himself was upon this point may be gathered from an entry in his journal of 1854. He had gone to Nantucket, in late December, and there saw, running along the ruts, flocks of "a gray, bunting-like bird about the size of the snow-bunting. Can it be the seaside finch," he asks, "or the savanna sparrow, or the shore lark?" The man who has "named *all* the birds without a gun" is yet to be announced; the youngest reader of the present article will not live long enough to see him; and Thoreau's studies in this line, it is fair to add, were pursued under limitations and disadvantages to which the amateur of our later day is happily a stranger. Ornithologically, it is a long time since Thoreau's death, though it is less than thirty-five years.

If any be disposed to insist, as some have insisted, that he made no discoveries (he discovered a new way of writing about nature, for one thing), and was more curious than scientific in his spirit and method as an observer, it is perhaps sufficient to reply that he cultivated his own field. From first to last he refused the claims of science,—whether rightly or wrongly is not here in question,—and with the exception of one or two brief essays wrote nothing directly upon natural history. He worshiped Nature, even while he played the spy upon her, fearing her enchantments and "looking at her with the side of his eye." Run over the titles of his books: A Week on the Concord and Merrimack Rivers, Walden, The Maine Woods, Cape Cod, A Yankee in Canada, Excursions. The first two are studies in high and plain living,—practical philosophy, spiritual economy, the right use of society and solitude, books and nature. The rest are narratives of travel, with a record of what the traveler saw and thought and felt. In Excursions, to be sure, there is an early paper on The Natural History of Massachusetts, to which, by straining a point, we may add one on The Succession of Forest Trees, another on Autumnal Tints, and still another on Wild Apples. Elsewhere, though the landscape is always carefully studied, it is always a landscape with figures. In truth, while he wrote so much of outward nature, and so often seemed to find his fellow-mortals no better than intruders upon the scene, his real subject was man. "Man is all in all," he says; "Nature nothing but as she draws him out and reflects him." And again he said, "Any affecting human event may blind our eyes to natural objects." The latter sentence was written shortly after the death of John Brown, in whose fate Thoreau had been so completely absorbed that his old Concord world, when he came back to it, had almost a foreign look to him, and he saw with surprise that the little grebe was still diving in the river as of yore. With all his devotion to nature and philosophy, it was the "human event" that really concerned him. But then he had ideas of his own as to what constituted an event. As for men's so-called affairs, and all that passes current under the name of news, nothing could be less· eventful; for all such things he could never sufficiently express his contempt. "In proportion as our inward life fails," he says, "we go more constantly and desperately to the post-office." And he adds, in that peculiarly airy manner of his to which one is tempted sometimes to apply the old Yankee adjective "toplofty," "I would not run around the corner to see the world blow up." After which, the reader whose bump of incuriosity is less highly developed may console himself by remembering that when a powder-mill blew up in the next town, Thoreau, hearing the noise, ran downstairs, jumped into a wagon, and drove post-haste to the scene of the disaster. So true is it that it is

> "the most difficult of tasks to *keep*
> Heights which the soul is competent to gain."

Careful economist as Thoreau was, bravely as he trusted his own intuitions and kept to his own path, much as he preached simplicity and heroically as he practiced it, he shared the common lot and fell short of his own ideal. Life is never quite so simple as he tried to make it, and he, like other men, was conscious of a divided mind. He had by nature a bias toward the investigation of natural phenomena, a passion for particulars, which, if he had been less a poet and philosopher, might have made him a man of science. He knew it, and was inwardly chafed by it. Perhaps it was because of this chafing that he fell into the habit of speaking so almost spitefully of science and scientific men. Not to lay stress upon his frequent paradoxes about the superiority of superstition to knowledge, the advantages of astrology over astronomy, the slight importance of precision in matters of detail ("I can afford to be inaccurate"),—to say nothing of these things, which, taken as they were meant, are not without a measure of truth, and with which no lover of Thoreau will be much disposed to quarrel (those who cannot abide a paradox or a grain or two of exaggeration may as well let him alone), it is plain that in certain moods, especially in his later years, his own semi-scientific researches were felt to be a hindrance to the play of his higher faculties. "It is impossible for the same person to see things from the poet's point of view and that of the man of science," he writes in 1842. "Man cannot afford to be a naturalist," he says again, in 1853. "I feel that I am dissipated by so many observations. . . . Oh, for a little Lethe!" And a week afterward he takes up the same strain, in a tone of reminiscence that is of the very rarest with him. "Ah, those youthful days," he breaks out, "are they never to return? when the walker does not too enviously observe particulars, but sees, hears, scents, tastes, and feels only himself, the phenomena that showed themselves in him, his expanding body, his intellect and heart. No worm or insect, quadruped or bird, confined his view, but the unbounded universe was his. A bird has now become a mote in his eye." What devotee of natural science, if he be also a man of sensibility and imagination, does not feel the sincerity of this cry?

But having delivered himself thus passionately, what does the diarist set down next? Without a break he goes on: "Dug into what I take to be a woodchuck's burrow in the low knoll below the cliffs. It was in the side of the hill, and sloped gently downward at first diagonally into the hill about five feet, perhaps westerly, then turned and ran north about three feet, then northwest further into the hill four feet, then north again four feet, then northeast I know not how far, the last five feet, perhaps, ascending,"—with as much more of the same tenor and equally detailed. A laughable paragraph, surely, to follow a lament over a too envious observation of particulars; with its "perhaps" four times repeated, its five feet westerly, three feet northerly, and so on, like a conveyancer's description of a woodlot: and all about a hole in the ground which he "took to be" a woodchuck's burrow!

In vain shall a man bestir himself to run away from his own instincts. In vain, in such a warfare, shall he trust to the freedom of the will. Happily for himself, and happily for the world, Thoreau could never cease from his too envious observation. By inclination and habit he liked to see and do things for himself, as if they had never been seen or done before. That was one mark of his individualistic temper. He describes in his journal an experiment in making sugar from the sap of red maple trees. Here, too, he goes into the minutest details, not omitting the size of the holes he bored and the frequency with which the drops fell,—about as fast as his pulse beat. His father, he mentions (the son was then forty years old), chided him for wasting his time. There was no occasion for the experiment, the father thought; it was well known that the thing could be done; and as for the sugar, it could be bought cheaper at the village shop. "He said it took me from my studies," the journal records. "I said that I made it my study, and felt as if I had been to a university." (If fault-finding is in order, an individualist prefers to do it on his own account.) But whether the old gentleman or the son may be supposed to have been right in the present instance, there can be no doubt that by habits of this kind knowledge is made peculiarly one's own, and, old or new, keeps something of the freshness of discovery upon it. The critic may smile, but even he will not dispute the charm of writing done in such a spirit,—the very spirit in which the old books were written, in the childhood of the world. Even the edibility of white-oak acorns affected Thoreau, at the age of forty, as a new fact. So far as his feeling about it was concerned, the fruit might have been that morning created. "The whole world is sweeter" to him for having "discovered" it. "To have found two Indian gouges and tasted sweet acorns, is it not enough for one afternoon?" he asks himself. And the next day, shrewd economist and exaggerator that he is, he tastes his new dainty again, and behold, a second discovery. The acorns "appear to dry sweet"! One need not be a critic, but only a country-bred Yankee, to smile at this. But indeed, it is a relief to be able to smile now and then at one who held himself so high and aloof,—"a Switzer on the edge of the glacier," as he called himself; who found no wisdom too lofty for him, no companionship quite lofty enough; and who, in his longing for something better than the best, could exclaim. "Give me a sentence which no intelligence can understand." Not that we feel any diminution of our respect and affection; but it pleases us to have met our Switzer for once on something near our own level. In an author, as in a friend, an amiable weakness, if there be strength enough behind it, is only another point of attraction.

As a writer Thoreau is by himself. There are no other books like Walden and the Week. The reader may like them or leave them (unless he is pretty sure of himself, he may be advised to try Walden first), he will find nowhere else the same combination of pure nature and austere philosophy. It is hard even to see with what to compare them, or to conceive of any one else as having written them. If Marcus Aurelius, with half his sweetness of temper eliminated, and something of sharpness, together with liberal measures of cool intellectuality, injected, could have been united with Gilbert White rather less radically transformed, and if the resultant complex person had made it his business to write, we can perhaps imagine that his work would not have been in all respects unlike that of the sage of Walden; in saying which we have but taken a circuitous course back to our former position, that Thoreau was a man of his own kind.

He was an author from the beginning. Of that, as he said himself, he was never in doubt. His ceaseless observation of nature—which some have decried as lacking purpose and method—and his daily journal were deliberately chosen means to that end. "Here have I been these forty years learning the language of these fields that I may the better express myself."

That was what he aimed at, let his subject be what it might,—
to express *himself*. Few writers have ever treated their work
more seriously, or studied their art more industriously. He
talked sometimes, to be sure, as if there were no art about it.
To listen to him in such a mood, one might suppose that the
fact and the thought were the only things to be considered, and
that language followed of itself. Such was neither his belief nor
his practice. But he was one of the fortunate ones who by
taking pains can produce an effect of easiness; who can recast
and recast a sentence, and in the end leave it looking as if it
had dropped from a running pen. One of the fortunates, we say;
for an expression of innocent unconsciousness is as becoming
in a sentence as in a face. . . .

Thoreau believed in well-packed sentences, each expres-
sive of its own thought, rememberable and quotable. Of the
beauties of a flowing style he had heard something too much.
In practice, nevertheless, whether through design or by some
natural felicity, he steered a middle course. The sentences
might be complete in themselves, detachable, able to stand
alone, but the paragraph never lacked a logical or even a formal
cohesion. It was not a collection of "infinitely repellent particles," nor even a "basket of nuts." A great share of the writer's
art, as he taught it, lay in leaving out the unessential,—the getting in of the essential having first been taken for granted. As
for readers, in his more exalted moods he wished to write so
well that there would be few to appreciate him; sometimes, indeed, he seemed to desire no readers at all. He speaks with stern
disapproval of such as trouble themselves upon that point and
"would fain have one reader before they die." A lamentable
weakness, truly.

In his present estate, however, let us hope that he carries
himself a shade less haughtily, and is not above an innocent
pleasure in the spread of his earthly fame, in new readers and
new editions, and such choicely limited popularity as befits a
classic. Even in his lifetime, as Emerson tells the story, he
once tried to believe that something in his lecture might interest a little girl who told him she was going to hear it if it
wasn't to be one of those old philosophical things that she did
not care about; and this although he had just been maintaining,

characteristically, that whatever succeeded with an audience must be bad. He speaks somewhere against luxurious books, with superfluous paper and marginal embellishments. His taste was Spartan in those days. But he was never a stickler for consistency, and we may indulge a comfortable assurance that he takes no offense now at the sight of his Cape Cod journey— in which he worked so hard on that soft, leg-tiring Back-Side beach to get the ocean into him—decked out in colors and set forth sumptuously in two volumes. It is a very modest author who fears that his text will be outshone by any pictures, no matter how splendid. But who would have thought it, fifty years ago,—a book by the hermit of Walden in an *édition de luxe*, to lie on parlor tables! If only his father and his brother John could have seen it!

Thoreau believed in himself and in the soundness of his work. He coveted readers, and believed that he should have them. Without question he wrote for the future, and foresaw himself safe from oblivion. Emerson regretted Henry's want of ambition, we are told. He might have spared himself. "Show me a man who consults his genius," said Thoreau, "and you have shown me a man who cannot be advised." And he was the man. He was following an ambition of his own. If he did not keep step with his companions, it was because he "heard a different drummer." His ambition and what seemed his wayward singularity have been justified by the event. His "strange, self-centred, solitary figure, unique in the annals of literature," is in no danger of being forgotten. But what is most cheering about his present increasing vogue, especially in England, is that it arises from the very quality that Thoreau himself most prized, the innermost thing in him,—the loftiness and purity of his thought. Simplicity, faith, devotion to the essential and the permanent,—these were never more needed than now. These he taught, and, by a happy fate, he linked them with those natural themes that change not with time, and so can never become obsolete.

BARRETT WENDELL (1855-1921) was Professor of English at Harvard from 1880 to 1917 and a pioneer in the teaching of American literature. He published studies of Cotton Mather and of Shakespeare, as well as his influential *A Literary History of America* (1900). Wendell believed that Thoreau's "constant intrusion of his personality ranges him in a lower rank" than Emerson.

Thoreau

BARRETT WENDELL

A Literary History of America (New York: Charles Scribner's Sons, 1900), pp. 332-37.

If Alcott is rapidly being forgotten, the case is different with Thoreau. For whatever the quality of Thoreau's philosophy, the man was in his own way a literary artist of unusual merit. He was born in 1817, of a Connecticut family, not long emigrated from France. On his mother's side he had Yankee blood, but not of the socially distinguished kind. What little record remains of his kin would seem to show that, like many New England folks of the farming class, they had a kind of doggedly self-assertive temper which inclined them to habits of personal isolation. Thoreau graduated at Harvard College in 1837. While a student he gained some little distinction as a writer of English; his themes, as undergraduate compositions are still called at Harvard, though commonplace in substance, are sensitively good in technical form. After graduation, he lived mostly at Concord. Though not of pure Yankee descent, he had true Yankee versatility; he was a tolerable farmer, a good surveyor, and a skilful maker of lead-pencils. In one way or another, then, he was able by the work of comparatively few weeks in the year to provide the simple necessities of his vegetarian life. So he early determined to work no more than was needful for self-support, and to spend the rest of his time in high thinking.

In the general course which his thinking and conduct took, one feels a trace of his French origin. Human beings, the French philosophy of the eighteenth century had strenuously held, are born good; evil, then, must obviously spring from the

distorting influences of society. Accepted by the earlier Transcendentalists, this line of thought had led to such experimental
communities as Brook Farm and the still more fleeting Fruitlands. Thoreau was Frenchman enough to reason out individualism to its logical extreme. The reform of society must be
accomplished, if at all, by the reform of the individuals who
compose it. Communities, after all, are only microcosmic
societies, wherein must lurk all the germs of social evil. Let individuals look to themselves, then; under no other circumstances can human nature unobstructedly develop its inherent
excellence. So for twenty-five years Thoreau, living at Concord, steadily tried to keep himself free from complications
with other people. Incidentally he had the good sense not to
marry; and as nobody was dependent on him for support, his
method of life could do no harm.

His best-known experiment was his residence for about
two years in the woods near Concord, where he built himself
a little cabin, supported himself by cultivating land enough
to provide for his immediate wants, and devoted his considerable leisure to philosophic thought. The fruit of this experiment was his well-known book, "Walden;" published in
1854, it remains a vital bit of literature for any one who loves
to read about Nature.

Of course Thoreau was eccentric, but his eccentricity was
not misanthropic. Inclined by temperament and philosophy
alike to this life of protestant solitude, he seems to have regarded his course as an experimental example. He was not
disposed to quarrel with people who disagreed with him. All
he asked was to be let alone. If his life turned out well, others
would ultimately imitate him; if it turned out ill, nobody else
would be the worse. Though his philosophising often seems
unpractically individual, then, it never exhales such unwhole-
someness as underlay Alcott's self-esteem. What is more, there
can be no question that his speculations have appealed to some
very sensible minds. All the same, if he had confined himself
to ruminating on the eternities and human nature, with which
his sympathy was at best limited, his position in literary
history would hardly be important. What gave him lasting
power was his unusually sympathetic observation of Nature. A

natural vein of indolence, to be sure, prevented him from observing either precociously or systematically; but when, as was more and more the case, he found himself alone with woods and fields and waters, he had true delight in the little sights which met his eyes, in the little sounds which came to his ears, in all the constant, inconspicuous beauties which the prosaic toilsomeness of Yankee life had hitherto failed to perceive.

Nature, as every one knows, had been a favourite theme of that romantic revival in England whose leader was Wordsworth. In one aspect, then, Thoreau's writing often seems little more than an American evidence of a temper which had declared itself in the old world a generation before. Nothing, however, can alter the fact that the Nature he delighted in was characteristically American. First of all men, Thoreau brought that revolutionary temper which recoils from the artificialities of civilisation face to face with the rugged fields, the pine woods and the apple orchards, the lonely ponds and the crystalline skies of eastern New England. His travels occasionally ranged so far as the Merrimac River, Cape Cod, or even beyond Maine into Canada; but pleasant as the books are in which he recorded these wanderings, as exceptional as were Cotton Mather's infrequent excursions through the bear-haunted wilds to Andover, we could spare them far better than "Walden," or than the journals in which for years he set down his daily observations in the single town of Concord. Thoreau's individuality is often so assertive as to repel a sympathy which it happens not instantly to attract; but that sympathy must be unwholesomely sluggish which would willingly resist the appeal of his communion with Nature. If your lot be ever cast in some remote region of our simple country, he can do you, when you will, a rare service, stimulating your eye to see, and your ear to hear, in all the little commonplaces about you, those endlessly changing details which make life everywhere so unfathomably, immeasurably wondrous. For Nature is truly a miracle; and he who will regard her lovingly shall never lack that inspiration which miracles breathe into the spirit of mankind.

Nor is Thoreau's vitality in literature a matter only of his observation. Open his works almost anywhere,—there are ten volumes of them now,—and even in the philosophic passages you will find loving precision of touch. He was no immortal maker of phrases. Amid bewildering obscurities, Emerson now and again flashed out utterances which may last as long as our language. Thoreau had no such power; but he did possess in higher degree than Emerson himself the power of making sentences and paragraphs artistically beautiful. Read him aloud, and you will find in his work a trait like that which we remarked in the cadences of Brockden Brown and of Poe; the emphasis of your voice is bound to fall where meaning demands. An effect like this is attainable only through delicate sensitiveness to rhythm. So when you come to Thoreau's pictures of Nature you have an almost inexhaustible series of verbal sketches in which every touch has the grace of precision. On a large scale, to be sure, his composition falls to pieces; he never troubled himself about a systematically made book, or even a systematic chapter. In mere choice of words, too, he is generally so simple as to seem almost commonplace. But his sentences and paragraphs are often models of art so fine as to seem artless. Take, for example, this well-known passage from "Walden":—

"Early in May, the oaks, hickories, maples, and other trees, just putting out amidst the pine woods around the pond, imparted a brightness like sunshine to the landscape, especially in cloudy days, as if the sun were breaking through mists and shining faintly on the hillsides here and there. On the third or fourth of May I saw a loon in the pond, and during the first week of the month I heard the whippoorwill, the brown thrasher, the veery, the woodpewee, the chewink, and other birds. I had heard the wood-thrush long before. The phebe had already come once more and looked in at my door and window, to see if my house were cavern-like enough for her, sustaining herself on humming wings with clinched talons, as if she held by the air, while she surveyed the premises. The sulphur-like pollen of the pitch-pine soon covered the pond and the stones and the rotten wood along the shore, so that you could have collected a barrelful. This is the 'sul-

phur showers' we hear of. Even in Calidas' drama of Sa-
contala, we read of 'rills dyed yellow with the golden dust
of the lotus.' And so the seasons went rolling on into summer, as one rambles into higher and higher grass."

The more you read work like that, the more admirable you will
find its artistic form.

With Thoreau's philosophising the case is different. Among
Emerson's chief traits was the fact that when he scrutinised
the eternities in search of ideal truth, his whole energy was devoted to the act of scrutiny. Vague, then, and bewildering as
his phrases may often seem, we are sensible of a feeling that
this Emerson is actually contemplating the immensities; and
these are so unspeakably vaster than all mankind—not to speak
of the single human being who for the moment is striving
to point our eyes toward them—that our thoughts again and
again concern themselves rather with the truths thus dimly
seen than with anything concerning the seer. The glass through
which Emerson contemplated the mysteries is achromatic.
Now, Thoreau's philosophic speculations so surely appeal to
powerful minds who find them sympathetic that we may well
admit them to involve more than they instantly reveal to minds
not disposed to sympathise. Even their admirers, however, must
admit them to be coloured throughout by the unflagging self-
consciousness involved in Thoreau's eccentric, harmless life.
Perhaps, like Emerson, Thoreau had the true gift of vision; but
surely he could never report his visions in terms which may
suffer us to forget himself. The glass which he offers to our eyes
is always tinctured with his own disturbing individuality. In
spite, then, of the fact that Thoreau was a more conscientious
artist than Emerson, this constant obtrusion of his personality
ranges him in a lower rank, just as surely as his loving sense of
nature ranges him far above the half-foolish egotism of Bronson
Alcott. More and more the emergence of Emerson from his surroundings grows distinct. Like truly great men, whether he was
truly great or not, he possessed the gift of such common-sense
as saves men from the perversities of eccentricity.

PAUL ELMER MORE (1864-1937), one of the leaders of the New Humanist movement, taught classical literature at Harvard, Bryn Mawr, and Princeton, edited *The Nation* from 1909-14, and wrote numerous books, among them the *Shelburne Essays* (14 vols., 1904-35). "Thoreau," More wrote, "was preeminently the poet and philosopher of his school."

A Hermit's Notes on Thoreau

PAUL ELMER MORE

Atlantic Monthly, Vol. 87 (June, 1901), 857-64. More's personal introductory observations are deleted.

Thoreau's work was distinguished from that of his American predecessors and imitators by just these qualities of awe and wonder which we, in our communings with Nature, so often cast away. Mere description, though it may at times have a scientific value, is after all a very cheap form of literature; and, as I have already intimated, too much curiosity of detail is likely to exert a deadening influence on the philosophic and poetic contemplation of Nature. Such an influence is, as I believe, specially noticeable at the present time, and even Thoreau was not entirely free from its baneful effect. Much of his writing, perhaps the greater part, is the mere record of observation and classification, and has not the slightest claim on our remembrance,—unless, indeed, it possesses some scientific value, which I doubt. Certainly the parts of his work having permanent interest are just those chapters where he is less the minute observer, and more the contemplative philosopher. Despite the width and exactness of his information, he was far from having the truly scientific spirit; the acquisition of knowledge, with him, was in the end quite subordinate to his interest in the moral significance of Nature, and the words he read in her obscure scroll were a language of strange mysteries, oftentimes of awe. It is a constant reproach to the prying, self-satisfied habits of small minds to see the reverence of this greathearted observer before the supreme goddess he so loved and studied.

Much of this contemplative spirit of Thoreau is due to the soul of the man himself, to that personal force which no analy-

sis of character can explain. But, besides this, it has always
seemed to me that, more than any other descriptive writer of
the country, his mind is the natural outgrowth, and his essays
the natural expression, of a feeling deep-rooted in the historical
beginnings of New England; and this foundation in the past
gives a strength and convincing force to his words that lesser
writers utterly lack. Consider the new life of the Puritan colonists in the strange surroundings of their desert home. Consider the case of the adventurous Pilgrims sailing from the
comfortable city of Leyden to the unknown wilderness over
the sea. As Governor Bradford wrote, "the place they had
thoughts on was some of those vast & unpeopled countries of
America, which are frutfull & fitt for habitation, being de-
voyd of all civill inhabitants, wher ther are only salvage &
brutish men, which range up and downe, little otherwise than
ye wild beasts of the same." In these vast and unpeopled countries, where beast and bird were strange to the eye, and where
"salvage" men abounded,—men who did not always make the
land so "fitt" for new inhabitants as Bradford might have desired,—it was inevitable that the mind should be turned to explore and report on natural phenomena and on savage life. It
is a fact that some of the descriptions of sea and land made
by wanderers to Virginia and Massachusetts have a directness
and graphic power, touched occasionally with an element of
wildness, that render them even to-day agreeable reading. This
was before the time of Rousseau, and before Gray had discovered the beauty of wild mountain scenery; inevitably the
early American writers were chiefly interested in Nature as
the home of future colonists, and their books are for the most
part semi-scientific accounts of what they studied from a utilitarian point of view.

But the dryness of detailed description in the New World
was from the first modified and lighted up by the wondering
awe of men set down in the midst of the strange and often
threatening forces of an untried wilderness; and this sense of
awful aloofness, which to a certain extent lay dormant in the
earlier writers, did nevertheless sink deep into the heart of
New England, and when, in the lapse of time, the country
entered into its intellectual renaissance, and the genius came

who was destined to give full expression to the thoughts of his people before the face of Nature, it was inevitable that his works should be dominated by just this sense of poetic mystery.

It is this New World inheritance, moreover,—joined, of course, with his own inexplicable personality, which must not be left out of account,—that makes Thoreau's attitude toward Nature something quite distinct from that of the great poets who just preceded him. There was in him none of the fiery spirit of the revolution which caused Byron to mingle hatred of men with enthusiasm for the Alpine solitudes. There was none of the passion for beauty and voluptuous self-abandonment of Keats; these were not in the atmosphere he breathed at Concord. He was not touched with Shelley's unearthly mysticism, nor had he ever fed

> "on the aerial kisses
> Of shapes that haunt thought's wildernesses;"

his moral sinews were too stark and strong for that form of mental dissipation. Least of all did he, after the manner of Wordsworth, hear in the voice of Nature any compassionate plea for the weakness and sorrow of the downtrodden. Philanthropy and humanitarian sympathies were to him a desolation and a woe. "Philanthropy is almost the only virtue which is sufficiently appreciated by mankind. Nay, it is greatly overrated; and it is our selfishness which overrates it," he writes. And again: "The philanthropist too often surrounds mankind with the remembrance of his own cast-off griefs as an atmosphere, and calls it sympathy." Similarly his reliance on the human will was too sturdy to be much perturbed by the inequalities and sufferings of mankind, and his faith in the individual was too unshaken to be led into humanitarian interest in the masses. "Alas! this is the crying sin of the age," he declares, "this want of faith in the prevalence of a man."

But the deepest and most essential difference is the lack of pantheistic reverie in Thoreau. It is this brooding over the universal spirit embodied in the material world which almost always marks the return of sympathy with Nature, and which is particularly noticeable in the poets of the present century. So Lord Byron, wracked and broken by his social catastrophes, turns for relief to the fair scenes of Lake Leman, and finds in the high mountains and placid waters a consoling spirit akin to his own.

> "Are not the mountains, waves, and skies, a part
> Of me and of my soul, as I of them?"

he asks; and in the bitterness of his human disappointment he would "be alone, and love Earth only for its earthly sake." Shelley, too, "mixed awful talk" with the "Great Parent," and heard in her voice an answer to all his vague dreams of the soul of universal love. No one, so far as I know, has yet studied the relation between Wordsworth's pantheism and his humanitarian sympathies, but we need only glance at his Lines on Tintern Abbey to see how closely the two feelings were interknit in his mind. It was because he felt this

> "sense sublime
> Of something far more deeply interfused,
> Whose dwelling is the light of setting suns,
> And the round ocean, and the living air,
> And the blue sky, and in the mind of man;"

it was because the distinctions of the human will and the consequent perception of individual responsibility were largely absorbed in this dream of the universal spirit, that he heard in Nature "the still, sad music of humanity," and reproduced it so sympathetically in his own song. Of all this pantheism, whether attended with revolt from responsibility or languid reverie or humanitarian dreams, there is hardly a trace in Thoreau. The memory of man's struggle with the primeval woods and fields was not so lost in antiquity that Nature had grown into an indistinguishable part of human life. Governor Bradford wrote his story of the Pilgrims, "that their children may see with what difficulties their fathers wrastled in going throug these things in their first beginnings," and the lesson had not been lost. If Nature smiled upon Thoreau at times, she was still an alien creature who only succumbed to his force and tenderness, as she had before given her bounty, though reluc-

tantly, to the Pilgrim Fathers. A certain companionship he had
with the plants and wild beasts of the field, a certain intimacy
with the dumb earth; but he did not seek to merge his personality in their impersonal life, or to look to them for a response to
his own inner moods; he associated with them as the soul associates with the body.

More characteristic is his sense of awe, even of dread, toward the great unsubdued forces of the world. The loneliness
of the mountains such as they appeared to the early adventurers
in a strange, unexplored country; the repellent loneliness of the
barren heights frowning down inhospitably upon the pioneer
who scratched the soil at their base; the loneliness and terror of
the dark, untrodden forests, where the wanderer might stray
away and be lost forever, where savage men were more feared
than the wild animals, and where superstition saw the haunt of
the Black Man and of all uncleanness,—all this tradition of
sombre solitude made Nature to Thoreau something very
different from the hills and valleys of Old England. "We have
not seen pure Nature," he says, "unless we have seen her thus
vast and drear and inhuman. . . . Man was not to be associated
with it. It was Matter, vast, terrific,—not his Mother Earth that
we have heard of, not for him to tread on, or be buried in,—
no, it were being too familiar even to let his bones lie there,—
the home, this, of Necessity and Fate." After reading Byron's
invocation to the Alps as the palaces of Nature; or the ethereal
mountain scenes in Shelley's Alastor, where all the sternness of
the everlasting hills is dissolved into rainbow hues of shifting
light as dainty as the poet's own soul; or Wordsworth's familiar
musings in the vale of Grasmere,—if, after these, we turn to
Thoreau's account of the ascent of Mount Katahdin, we seem
at once to be in the home of another tradition. I am tempted
to quote a few sentences of that account to emphasize the
point. On the mountain heights, he says of the beholder: "He is
more lone than you can imagine. There is less of substantial
thought and fair understanding in him than in the plains where
men inhabit. His reason is dispersed and shadowy, more thin
and subtile, like the air. Vast, Titanic, inhuman Nature has
got him at disadvantage, caught him alone, and pilfers him of
some of his divine faculty. She does not smile on him as in

the plains. She seems to say sternly, Why came ye here before your time? This ground is not prepared for you. It is not enough that I smile in the valleys? I have never made this soil for thy feet, this air for thy breathing, these rocks for thy neighbors. I cannot pity nor fondle thee here, but forever relentlessly drive thee hence to where I *am* kind."

I do not mean to present the work of Thoreau as equal in value to the achievement of the great poets with whom I have compared him, but wish merely in this way to bring out more definitely his characteristic traits. Yet if his creative genius is less than theirs, I cannot but think his attitude toward Nature is in many respects truer and more wholesome. Pantheism, whether on the banks of the Ganges or of the Thames, seems to bring with it a spreading taint of effeminacy; and from this the mental attitude of our Concord naturalist was eminently free. There is something tonic and bracing in his intercourse with the rude forces of the forest; he went to Walden Pond because he had "private business to transact," not for relaxation and mystical reverie. "To be a philosopher," he said, "is not merely to have subtle thoughts, nor even to found a school, but so to love wisdom as to live according to its dictates, a life of simplicity, independence, magnanimity, and trust;" and by recurring to the solitudes of Nature he thought he could best develop in himself just these manly virtues. Nature was to him a discipline of the will as much as a stimulant to the imagination. He would, if it were possible, "combine the hardiness of the savages with the intellectualness of the civilized man;" and in this method of working out the philosophical life we see again the influence of long and deep-rooted tradition. To the first settlers, the red man was as much an object of curiosity and demanded as much study as the earth they came to cultivate; their books are full of graphic pictures of savage life, and it would seem as if now in Thoreau this inherited interest had received at last its ripest expression. When he traveled in the wilderness of Maine, he was as much absorbed in learning the habits of his Indian guides as in exploring the woods. He had some innate sympathy or perception which taught him to find relics of old Indian life where others would pass them by, and there is a well-known story of his answer to one who asked him where such relics could be discovered: he merely stooped down and picked an arrowhead from the ground.

And withal his stoic virtues never dulled his sense of awe, and his long years of observation never lessened his feeling of strangeness in the presence of solitary Nature. If at times his writing descends into the cataloguing style of the ordinary naturalist, yet the old tradition of wonder was too strong in him to be more than temporarily obscured. Unfortunately, his occasional faults have become in some of his recent imitators the staple of their talent; but Thoreau was preëminently the poet and philosopher of his school, and I cannot do better than close these desultory notes with the quotation of a passage which seems to me to convey most vividly his sensitiveness to the solemn mystery of the deep forest.

"We heard," he writes in his Chesuncook, "come faintly echoing, or creeping from afar, through the moss-clad aisles, a dull, dry, rushing sound, with a solid core to it, yet as if half smothered under the grasp of the luxuriant and fungus-like forest, like the shutting of a door in some distant entry of the damp and shaggy wilderness. If we had not been there, no mortal had heard it. When we asked Joe [the Indian guide] in a whisper what it was, he answered,—'Tree fall.' "

GILBERT P. COLEMAN (1866-1941?), as late as 1906, argued that any survey of the critics of Thoreau should be devoted in major part to Lowell. Coleman's sympathetic essay, however, reflects a close reading of S. A. Jones' *Pertaining to Thoreau*, and most of the other criticism of the preceding twenty years as well.

Thoreau and His Critics

GILBERT P. COLEMAN

The Dial, Vol. 40 (June, 1906), 352-56.

Probably no writer in America can lay claim to a sounder foundation for fame than Thoreau. He has earned every inch of the way he has gained. There has been no boom for him. He has had few helping hands, and has had to contend against

a singular combination of misunderstanding, lack of appreciation, ignorance, and, in one case at least, of misrepresentation
that is said to have been inspired by personal prejudice.

It is amusing, and occasionally startling, to observe the
infinite variety of criticism that has been stirred up by Thoreau's life and works. Many writers, for example, are agreed
in describing his temperament as ascetic. Robert Louis Stevenson, however, is not alone in holding the opposite view. "He
was not ascetic," says Stevenson ("Familiar Studies"), "rather
an Epicurean of the nobler sort." Professor Nichols, in his little
work on American Literature, apparently is satisfied with middle ground, when he applies to Thoreau the classification,
"lethargic, self-complacently defiant, too nearly a stoico-epi-
curean adiaphorist to discompose himself in party or even in
national strifes." Nearly all the critics are agreed that Thoreau
was a humorist, though they are by no means agreed as to
the quality of his humor. Another school, headed by Lowell, is
quite certain that he possessed no humor whatever. One writer
speaks of him as "repellent, cold, and unamiable," while another declares that "in all social relations he was guided by a
fine instinct of courtesy," and Emerson, who knew him nearly
as well as anybody ever did, says that "he was really fond of
sympathy"; a highly appreciative essayist speaks of the "fine
resonant quality of his emotional side," and finds that he was
"always thoroughly kindly and sympathetic."

"Thoreau is dry, priggish, and selfish," again announces
Stevenson, in one of his most oracular moods; and a writer in
the "Church Quarterly Review" says that he was "thoroughly
selfish, quite out of sympathy with men and their sufferings,
barbaric if not animal in his tastes, and needlessly profane."
On the other hand, Mr. John Weiss, who was a fellow-collegian
with Thoreau and has written an essay dealing almost entirely
with his personality, takes a somewhat different view when
he says that "no writer to-day is more religious"; and according to Mr. William Sloane Kennedy, "the influence of his ragged
energy, his fine idealism, the purity and honesty and manliness
of his life, shall for generations breathe through the literature
and the life of America like a strengthening breeze." Emerson,
in the familiar biographical sketch prefaced to the "Excursions,"

after paying a loving tribute to his departed friend, sums up his life as a practical failure: "Instead of engineering for all America, he was the captain of a huckleberry-party. Pounding beans is good to the end of pounding empires one of these days; but if, at the end of years, it is still beans!" Mr. Kennedy, however, at once applies the antidote: "He excites envy by his success. His life is a rebuke which is felt and resented"; and Mr. Higginson backs this up in his "Short Studies," when he says, "It is common to speak of his life as a failure, but to me it seems, with all its drawbacks, to have been a great and eminent success."

A writer in the "Knickerbocker Magazine" regarded Thoreau as a "rural humbug"; whereas Emerson has conferred upon him the degree of Bachelor of Nature, and Mr. Torrey has elevated him to that of Master of the Art of Living. One school would have him a "skulker," "imperfect, unfinished, inartistic, parochial," "a mixture of misanthropy and self-conceit"; while others have said that he was "sincerity itself, and might fortify the convictions of prophets in the ethical laws by his holy living." He is often called a "thrifty Yankee," yet the same "Knickerbocker" reviewer is of the opinion that "Walden" is "a book needed where the philosophy of thrift is too prevalent." "He attempts no flights," says one. "For the moment Thoreau soars the empyrean with eagle sweep," says another. Again, it was said by a reviewer writing in 1891, that "upon the whole, there seems to be no reason for concluding that Thoreau can maintain his present prominence among American writers, or that his place in literature, if permanent, will be a high one." In opposition to this, we have the prophecy of many, as indicated by Mr. Sanborn, that Thoreau is likely to occupy a higher place in American literature than Emerson himself. "He lived some time by the sea," writes another, "and often visited its shore; yet, so far as we may judge from his writings, he was not much affected by the wondrous beauty and majesty of old ocean." To offset this is "Cape Cod" with its now famous descriptions of old ocean, quoted by such a discriminating artist as Thomas Bailey Aldrich; and also the confession of Thoreau himself, who admits that the ocean was, after all, a bigger and a more inspiring thing than even his beloved Concord and Lincoln Pond.

The same delightful variety of criticism extends, more impersonally, to Thoreau's books. "Cape Cod," for example, is "dry reading," according to Mr. Kennedy. A reviewer in "Frazer's Magazine," however, finds it "a curious and valuable work." "The volume on Cape Cod is deliberately formless in style," is the judgment of Thoreau's sympathetic biographer, Mr. H. S. Salt. "Of all his books, 'Cape Cod' has the most finished and sustained style," is the somewhat contrary view of Mr. Weiss. "He inflicts his full quantity [of dulness] in such books as 'Cape Cod,' or 'The Yankee in Canada,'" solemnly declares Stevenson; whereas Mr. Weiss observes that "the pages of 'Cape Cod' bear the reader along without conscious effort," and others are equally certain that it is the most human, connected, and interesting of all of Thoreau's writings. One writer, however, insists that the book is "juiceless, uninspired, perishable, a third-rate work,"—an opinion that is not corroborated by a reviewer in the contemporaneous "Dial," who prescribes the volume as a cure for the blues. In speaking of "Walden," one critic observes that very few will be able to read the book a second time. Mr. Higginson thinks it is "one of the few books in all literature that may be read with pleasure once a year."

Of those opinions of Thoreau which have evidently been based on insufficient information, the most incomplete, unsatisfactory, inadequate, though possibly the cleverest and most brilliant, is that of Robert Louis Stevenson. He has presumed to reveal Thoreau's character and opinions fortified only by a perusal of the published letters, of "Walden," of Emerson's biographical sketch, and by a scrutiny of a badly executed wood-cut. He thinks he sees a rude nobility, like that of a barbarian king, in the unshaken confidence which Thoreau has in himself, and in his indifference to the wants, thoughts, or sufferings of others; and he quotes, as illustrating this point, "If ever I *did* any good in their [men's] sense, of course it was something exceptional and insignificant compared with the good or evil I am constantly doing by being what I *am*." But in what respect does this show indifference to the wants, thoughts, or sufferings of others? To indulge in a little paradox on our own account, right here lies the very unselfishness of Thoreau's selfishness. The poet-naturalist, as he was constituted, was better able to help his fellow-man by living his own life as perfectly as possible than by mere commonplace acts of charity. "Walden" was the foundation for Stevenson's screed; yet it is plain that the pages on "Philanthropy" must have been skipped, for there Thoreau says, "I would not subtract anything from the praise that is due to philanthropy, but merely demand justice for all who by their lives and works are a blessing to mankind."

It appears that after Stevenson had published his little essay in the "Cornhill Magazine," it met the eye of Thoreau's Scotch disciple, Dr. A. H. Japp; and the latter gentleman immediately took the reviewer to task. Therefore, when the essay was presented in book form in the collection entitled "Familiar Studies of Men and Books," Stevenson wrote his "preface by way of criticism," in which he is kind enough to retract a number of the harsh things he had said about the poet-naturalist, attributing them to a "too earnest reflection on imperfect facts." The preface is highly entertaining, and shows with what unerring aim two Scotchmen, shooting at long range, can miss the bull's-eye of fact, and the circumadjacent rings of easily deduced inference. After this illumination from Dr. Japp, Stevenson learns that if Thoreau were content to dwell on Walden Pond it was not merely with designs of self-improvement, but in order to serve mankind in the highest sense. "Hither [to Walden] came the fleeing slave; thence was he despatched along the road to freedom. That shanty in the woods was a station in the great Underground Railroad." Of course we all know how the underground railroad story originated,—how Thoreau once received a fleeing slave under his protection, and, at the cost of infinite discomfort and considerable risk to himself, had him sent safely to Canada. But that this was his practice, and that the retreat to Walden was undertaken for this purpose, cannot be believed by anyone who has an adequate acquaintance with the facts.

It is said that Lowell entertained a prejudice against Thoreau, occasioned by a certain matter that affected the latter's pride and hurt the former's editorial dignity. Even if this prejudice existed, we do not believe that it inspired the mistaken and unjust criticism of Thoreau in "My Study Windows." The criticism was the result, we believe, of a lack of sympathy, and of constitutional inability, on Lowell's part, to comprehend the point of view of the poet-naturalist. Indeed, never were two men more widely, more hopelessly apart. On the one hand is Lowell, the polished gentleman, the future Minister to the Court of St. James, the genial poet and accomplished scholar, the college professor of *belles-lettres*, the affable companion, full of grace, courtesy, sparkling wit and crackling humor, with well-trimmed whiskers and perfectly fitting clothes. On the other hand we have Thoreau,—a man of the woods, a rustic, who avoided the society of women because he felt ill at ease, was hardly affable even to his most intimate friends, but was congenial to woodsmen and woodchucks, jumping fences to make a short cut, walking the backbone of Cape Cod with a brown paper parcel and an umbrella, sitting by the roadside in order to study the configuration of a skunk, writing of himself ("A Yankee in Canada"), "I had for all head-covering a thin palmleaf hat without lining, that cost twenty-five cents, and over my coat one of those unspeakably cheap, as well as thin, brown linen sacks of the Oak Hall pattern, which every summer appear all over New England, thick as the leaves upon the trees. It was a thoroughly Yankee costume, which some of my fellow-travellers wore in the cars to save their coats a dusting. I wore mine at first because it looked better than the coat it covered, and last because two coats are warmer than one, though one is thin and dirty."

In one of those singularly apt figures for which Lowell is noted, he shows, to the satisfaction of many readers (judging from the approbation which his essay has received), that Thoreau is an imitator of Emerson. Thoreau has "picked his strawberries from Emerson's garden. . . . He is a pistillate plant kindled to fruitage by the Emersonian pollen. . . . He has stolen the windfall apples from Emerson's orchard," and so on. That there was a certain resemblance between Thoreau and Emerson, cannot be denied. It appears to be generally agreed by all those who were personally acquainted with both that the philosopher made his influence felt on the poet-naturalist. Some writers assert with confidence that all of Thoreau's philosophy was inspired by Emerson's lecture on "Nature," although there are certain awkward objections to this, the principal of which is that Thoreau was not acquainted with "Nature" until after he had done considerable philosophizing independent of a tutor. Others have maintained that Thoreau was not only unconsciously affected by the magnetic power of his friend and townsman, but that he deliberately set himself to work to copy him in manner, in speech, in mode of walk, in the fashion of wearing his beard, and (but perhaps this was less deliberate) in the shape of his nose.

There can, of course, be no doubt that Emerson exerted a very subtle and irresistible influence on all who came into contact with him. Indeed, many pilgrims visited him in order that they might come within this influence. His was without question the most powerfully æsthetic, the most originally transcendental mind in America at the time when Thoreau lived, and this powerful and original mind was united with a personality singularly sweet and engaging. Thoreau, a young man some sixteen years the junior of his patron, was greatly indebted to Emerson,—more so, probably, than appears in any of the biographical records. No doubt he was in a measure influenced by Emerson's thought. In our view, whatever there was in Thoreau of professed transcendentalism was due largely to the influence of Emerson. But that he was a mere imitator, —that his work, his thoughts, his philosophy, is a mere reflection of the great light shed by his brilliant contemporary,—it is impossible to believe. Though the two were alike in many superficial aspects, they were poles apart in many essentials. Emerson himself has warmly resented the idea that Thoreau was only a disciple, and as stoutly maintained that his friend was an original genius. And Emerson's son, in "Emerson in Concord," says: "The charge of imitating Emerson, too often made against Thoreau, is idle and untenable, though unfortunately it has received some degree of sanction in high quarters. . . . Thoreau was incapable of conscious imitation. His faults, if any, lay in exactly the opposite direction." And Dr. Holmes, in his "Life of Emerson" says: "Thoreau lent him [Emerson] a new set of organs of sense of wonderful delicacy.

Emerson looked at nature as a poet, and his natural history, if left to himself, would have been as vague as that of Polonius. . . . Emerson's long intimacy with him taught him to give an outline to many natural objects which would have been poetic nebulæ to him but for this companionship."

Lowell again says: "He looked with utter contempt on the august drama of destiny of which his country was the scene, and on which the curtain had already risen." It is difficult to understand how these lines could have been written by anyone who had the slightest acquaintance with Thoreau's views and activity in regard to the great political question that agitated the country during his later years. None of the animadversions on Thoreau has appeared to be more unjust than this. Is it possible that Lowell was ignorant of Thoreau's attitude toward slavery? of his incarceration for refusal to pay a tax, and the reason he gave therefor? of his addresses concerning John Brown? It is true that Thoreau abhorred politics, and, in his exaggerated way, never spared an opportunity to give vent to those views which were regarded by his neighbors as stamping him an oddity. But to say that he looked with contempt on the "august drama of destiny" of which his country was the scene, is surely erroneous. For not only did he *not* look with contempt on this drama, but he was an actor in it, and an actor of great spirit and earnestness. Lowell, indeed, has given us his clever "Biglow Papers," and may therefore be said to have been more than a mere spectator at that memorable performance; but while he was composing congenial drolleries in the cosy solitude of his library, while the North was seeking compromise, while many even of the most pronounced Abolitionists were playing only thinking parts, it was Thoreau, the hermit, the skulker, the selfish recluse who had no concern for the sufferings of his fellows, who boldly came to the front and championed John Brown—John Brown, the crazy man who was so foolish as to "lose his life for a few niggers." "What avail all your scholarly accomplishments and learning," said Thoreau on that historic occasion when he addressed the citizens of Concord, "compared with wisdom and manhood? To omit his [Brown's] other behavior, see what a work this comparatively unread and unlettered man wrote within six weeks! Where is our professor of *belles-lettres,* or of logic and rhetoric, who can write so well?" Did this stray shaft lodge in Lowell's library?

Lowell further says: "Thoreau's shanty life was a mere impossibility, as far as his own conception of it goes, of an entire independency of mankind," and he goes on to say that his experiment actually presupposed all that complicated civilization which is practically abjured, and triumphantly points out that Thoreau squatted on another man's land, borrowed still another man's axe, and obtained from society his boards, his nails, his bricks, his lamp, his fishhooks, his plow, his hoe. But would Lowell have Thoreau purchase his land? That would involve bargain and sale, the transfer of money, the registration of deeds, and other incidentals more nearly "presupposing all that complicated civilization" than mere squatting. And would Lowell insist that Thoreau make his own axe, mix his own mortar, bake his own bricks, forge his own plough, and write his own library, before he retires to the woods for a little contemplation? It strikes us that the genial Lowell is here a little severe on "the adroit and philosophic solitaire." It is true that the latter wrote by far the larger part of his own library, which he playfully says consisted of nearly nine hundred volumes, over seven hundred of which he wrote himself; but it is manifestly too exacting to demand of any reasonable anchorite, no matter how profound his abjuration of society, that he should return to the condition of Adam, and construct his shanty without nails, bricks, axe, or mortar. Possibly Lowell would insist on the fig-leaf. Other critics, like him, disturbed by Thoreau's shanty life, insisted that he should return to a state of savagery if he would camp out on the pine-clad shore of Walden. The axe that he borrowed of Bronson Alcott becomes a formidable weapon in their hands, with which they would demolish at a blow the "shanty" and the whole fanciful structure of domestic economy and idealistic philosophy. Thoreau with an axe is a humbug. He should return to the stone age, and burrow in the earth like a muskrat; nothing less will satisfy the demands of those who would have him live up to the very letter of what they conceive to be his self-banishment from society. And here is how Thoreau, in an anticipative mood, answers these cavillers: "It is difficult to begin without borrowing, but perhaps it is the most generous course to permit your fellow-man to have an interest in your enterprise."

It is natural that this retreat to Walden should stand out as the most conspicuous feature of Thoreau's career. It was something new; the reasons he gave for it were novel and stimulating; it threw an atmosphere of picturesque romance about a figure already sufficiently odd and perplexing. The book that he wrote there has an attractive title, and its contents are such as to invite many shades of criticism. Most of the conflicting judgments of Thoreau's life and work may be traced to a false conception of the Walden episode. The real purpose of this episode, it seems to us, is that Thoreau might have leisure and opportunity for his reading, his study of nature, his writing,—and a general good time in the bargain. "I went into the woods to transact some private business," he writes; and that might well end the matter.

The chief error of many of Thoreau's critics is that they fail to detect his humor, his fondness for extravagance of statement, his hyperbole. They accept him literally. Thoreau should be read through his life as well as through his books. Much that he writes is written in the effort at paradox. He is a confessed exaggerator. There is about him, on the surface, a great deal of charming and innocent boasting. But it belongs to the surface only. Underneath, we find the loving friend, the often true philosopher, the preacher, the moralist, the narrator, and, above all and saving all, the humorist. As for his writings, some persons have compared them to the freshness of an ocean breeze. They are more. They are like an electric current in a live wire. You are liable to be shocked at any moment. But it is a stimulating, an inspiring shock. You need not read him consecutively,—you need not worry about the paradoxes, the exaggerations, the boasting, the self-complacency, the false economy. They may all be safely taken for the sake of the tonic that goes with them. But his humor is the essential thing for his critics to perceive. No man can be said to be a recluse, to be a misanthrope, to be really in earnest in his hyperbolic and paradoxical desire to demolish society, who possesses a humor such as Thoreau's. This is his supremely genuine quality, and it is the quality in him that makes him most human and most persuasive. Those who do not find this quality in him, read his books in vain.

Thoreau is too valuable a possession, not only to American literature but to all literature, to be dealt with in an inappreciative or superficial manner by any critic, however witty or brilliant. His is a complex nature, not readily understood, and it is sometimes difficult to see with his vision. It is for this reason that those who would approach him in a critical spirit should approach him with caution and with sympathy. His is one of the rare cases known in literature where a noble spirit, a witty and inspiring mind, and a moral force of great value and attraction, have been brought together in one man. Thoreau inspires, charms, and elevates. The reader who comes to Thoreau's books in a sympathetic and appreciative spirit will leave them a better man. He will hear sermons without dulness, he will hear music without discord, and there will be revealed to him a religion that insists on no dogmas or creeds, and is wide enough to embrace all sects. "To live rightly and never to swerve, and to believe that we have in ourselves a drop of the Original Goodness besides the well-known deluge of original sin,—these strains sing through Thoreau's writings." We would not wish every man a Thoreau. Civilization has not reached that ideal stage of development when it would be other than awkward for all able-bodied men to sit, rapt in reverie on the shore of a Walden pond, speculating on the character of mists or on the immortality of the pine. But we would wish a part of Thoreau for every man.

JOHN ALBERT MACY (1877-1932), scholar of American literature, was for a time a member of the staff of *The Nation*. In addition to *The Spirit of American Literature* (1908) he published *Socialism in America* (1916) and edited *American Writers on American Literature* (1931). He still feels it necessary in 1908 to rebut the charge that Thoreau was a "skulker." As to the "General Characteristics" of American literature, Macy observes in *The Spirit of American Literature* (p. 11): "American literature is on the whole idealistic, sweet, delicate, nicely finished. There is little of it which might not have been approved in *The Youth's Companion*. The notable exceptions are our most stalwart men of genius, Thoreau, Whitman, and Mark Twain."

Thoreau

JOHN ALBERT MACY

The Spirit of American Literature (New York: Doubleday, Page and Co., 1908), pp. 171-88.

When Thoreau died, Emerson wrote: "The country knows not yet, or in the least part how great a son it has lost." In fifty years the country, the world, has learned more of this great son. Friends and editors have assembled one by one the eleven volumes of the standard edition; and the recent publication of his complete journal indicates that there are readers who regard the least of his notes as worthy of preservation. The growing cult of the open air, the increasing host of amateur prodigals returning to nature, have given fresh vogue to his sketches of woods and waters. But, for all that, the man is not yet fully understood. Lowell's unsympathetic essay, product of a mind from which poetry and youth had evaporated, and of a social outlook grown conventionally decorous, has carried inevitable authority. Like Macaulay's essay on Bacon and Jeffrey's blundering miscomprehension of Wordsworth, it is an example of how one great reputation may for a period smother and distort another. Stevenson's popular essay, written in his half dramatic attitude of athletic good-cheer and arm-in-arm sympathy with a hooray-boy world, is based on a misconception of Thoreau's character and his message as a whole. It overemphasizes the gentle reservation with which Emerson tempers his praise. Emerson in a few words sets forth the rounded integrity of Thoreau's work and personality; in one place he makes a comment upon his fellow-philosopher's proneness to negation and opposition. The comment, in its place, is just to Thoreau and expresses Emerson's more inclusive amiability. Stevenson singles out from Emerson's total estimate the negative characteristic, and stiffens it into an anti-social asceticism which is not foreign to Thoreau's nature but is by no means its dominant quality.

That original minds stand above the comprehension of mediocre minds of their own period and of later times is a fact observable everywhere in the history of the human intellect. More than that, some minds are not merely above the common herd; they are in advance of the best culture of their day and must await the intelligence of later generations to give them full recognition. Emerson and Holmes were as comprehensible to their generation as to ours. Whitman and Thoreau were trail-blazers; they went before to survey regions where later comers find a broad highway. Thoreau's vision shot beyond the horizon which bounded and still bounds the sight even of that part of the world which fancies itself liberal and emancipated.

"I am," says Thoreau, "a poet, a mystic and a transcendentalist." He was all that, and, moreover, he was an anarchist. He was the one anarchist of great literary power in a nation of slavish conformity to legalism, where obedience to statute and maintenance of "order" are assiduously inculcated as patriotic virtues by the social powers which profit from other peoples' docility. "Walden" and "A Week on the Concord and Merrimac Rivers" have been accepted as classics. The essays on "Forest Trees" and "Wild Apples" were to be found in a school reader twenty-five years ago. But the ringing revolt of the essay on "Civil Disobedience" is still silenced under the thick respectability of our times. The ideas in it could not today be printed in the magazine which was for years owned by the publishers of Thoreau's complete works. Boston Back Bay would shiver! It would not do, really, to utter aloud Thoreau's ideas in a society whose leading university, Thoreau's alma mater, has recently ruled, "that the halls of the university shall not be open for persistent or systematic propaganda on contentious questions of contemporaneous social, economic, political or religious interests." That is, let the university offer fifty courses in philosophy, history and literature which is dead enough not to be dangerous to vested authority, but let it not take any part in philosophy, history, or literature which is in the making! The application of Thoreau's principles to the injustices of our present political and industrial life would be condemned as disloyally "un-American" in the community where he lived and which is now owned, body and soul, factory and college, by State Street. Thoreau's intellectual kinsmen are not there. For an adequate recognition of the value of Thoreau's challenge to authority one turns to no living New Englander, but to that other solitary and indignant moralist, Tolstoy.

On the right of the individual to withhold his sanction of word and deed from a government by any minority or majority which is engaged in dishonest practices and enforces brutal laws, the American and the Russian philosopher are mainly in accord. Each says to government: "You may take me and break me because you are physically strong, but willing party to your legalized system of plunder and murder I will not be." The government against which Tolstoy rebelled is melodramatically barbarous, so that liberal minds all over the world find themselves in sympathy with him. It is easy to protest against tyranny on the other side of the planet. Thoreau's government (which is so like the present government of the United States that the change of a word or two, the insertion of modern instances, makes his essay as pertinent as if written yesterday)—Thoreau's government skulks behind the pacific mask of democracy; it deforms children, kills men and ruins women by common consent and not by the cossack forces of a picturesquely tyrannous Czar. The prosperous and so-called cultivated classes who manage for us our industrial, educational, literary and religious affairs, hold up horrified hands at Russia, but naturally have no quarrel with the system of government at home which leaves them in peace and offers them a career of ease. Therefore in the gallery of ideas through which admiring American youth is conducted, Thoreau's portrait of government is discreetly turned to the wall. His nature books, his poetic notes on the seasons, are recommended to an ever-growing number of readers. The flaming eloquence of his social philosophy, the significance, the conclusion of his experiment in individualism, is ignored. We praise Tolstoy, even in cultivated Boston, but we remain unacquainted with our own spiritual liberator.

One difference between Tolstoy and Thoreau is vital, a difference in personal circumstances. Tolstoy was born a landed aristocrat. He struggled in vain to bring the conduct of his life into accord with his beliefs. He desired to be a workman, but could only dabble in manual toil. In spite of his attempt to renounce copyright, his world-famous fictions brought money to his family. Circumstances enmeshed him, and his titanic struggle to extricate himself entangled him more and more, and made him a tragic figure. His life came to an impotent conclusion; only death, as in some Greek tragedy, could restore dignity and moral consistency. Thoreau, on the other hand, was born poor; he remained a bachelor; he earned his living by productive labour; and thus he had the good fortune to be able to practise his philosophy. He was not directly, nor by any economic indirection, dependent for his bread on another man. Tolstoy, an agonized prisoner in a wealth which he thought polluted him, may well have envied the Yankee pencil-whittler and land surveyor, a jack-of-all-trades and master of several, who did his honest day's work beside the common labourers of the world. The leisure which he spent in the company of sages, poets, and prophets, whose peer he was, he earned with his hands. He was spared the humiliation of writing sermons on freedom in time won at the expense of some other man's freedom.

"If I devote myself to other pursuits and contemplations," he says, "I must first see, at least, that I do not pursue them sitting upon another man's shoulders. I must get off him first, that he may pursue his contemplations, too."

One other difference between Tolstoy and Thoreau is essential; it springs from that primary difference in their social stations. Tolstoy groaned beneath the agony of a suffering world; he took upon himself the sins of his class. His long cry of pain, which the work of his last twenty years hurls at the dull ears of humanity, is unrelieved except by a sad, half-rationalized Christianity, confessedly unconsoling. He tortured himself with an almost morbid sense of responsibility for evils remote from his private duties, evils which he could not help. Thoreau, on the contrary, enjoyed life. "I came into this world," he says, "not chiefly to make this a good place to live in, but to live in it, be it good or bad." When they put him in jail for refusing on principle to pay his poll tax (he had nothing on which to impose a property tax), he did not make a martyr of himself, but with his mouth slightly awry wrote five dryly humorous pages about "My Prisons," in which legal contrivances are made to look not merely oppressive but ridiculous. He laughs at the jailer and official, his neighbours in their attitudes as policeman and soldier. A man of humour, one might think, would be ashamed to appear on a street in Thoreau's town in blue uniform with a star on his breast, lest Thoreau emerge suddenly from the woods and contemplate the insignia of authority with a faintly acid smile.

Thoreau is not a theorist who argues himself into anarchism by the routes of bookish reasoning. The philosophy of anarchism was not in his lifetime so highly developed, codified and rationalized as it is now; and it is doubtful if Thoreau would have had much patience with its elaborately systematic arguments in support of an unsystematic conduct of life. "To speak practically and as a citizen," he says, "unlike those who call themselves no-government men, I ask for, not at once no government, but at once a better government." He was no selfish opponent of the inconveniences of society. The state might have his money if it used it for useful, or at worst, harmless enterprises, such as building roads. He was willing to conform with any peaceful nonsense or extravagance. "One cannot be too much on his guard . . . lest his action be biased by obstinacy or an undue regard for the opinions of men." He simply asked not to be made accessory to legalized crime. He had no disposition to reform the world, though he joined the abolitionists, like all decent New Englanders of all creeds and political principles. "The government does not concern me much, and I shall bestow the fewest possible thoughts on it."

That was a fair and a practical attitude for a freeman in an agricultural nation like America sixty years ago, where he who had skill to work could get a living somehow. A complexly organized industrial system has since grown up in America, all the good land is occupied, or at least fenced with titles, and to-day even so capable a man as Thoreau would find it difficult to support himself in decency with a half day's work. Thoreau's views fitted his time and his community. Tolstoy, holding the same views, fifty years later, was trying to hark back to conditions that the world of production had outlived even in Russia. What Thoreau, the maker of pencils, would say to a modern pencil-factory where he, like other workmen, would have to apply for a job, or make no pencils, we can only guess, Yankee-wise. We guess that he would have understood it shrewdly and inspected its machinery with the eye of a born mechanic, and not have protested against it as his epigone, Tolstoy, protested against the advance of modern industry.

With the great changes that have come in the relations between a workman and his tools, some of Thoreau's single-handed individualism has grown obsolete. So far forth as it concerns those practices of government and habits of society which have not appreciably altered or improved, it remains a much-needed word of rebellion. "How does it become a man to behave toward this American government to-day? I cannot for an instant recognize that political organization as my government which is the slave's government also." For "black slave," which he means, substitute "white slave" or "child labourer" and the sentence stands vividly pertinent to the blessed year 1912. "This people," he said, "must cease to make war on Mexico, though it cost them their existence as a people." Substitute "Philippines" for "Mexico," and the sentence is part of many an honest man's belief this morning. "The standing army," says Thoreau, "is only an arm of the standing government. The government itself, which is only the mode which the people have chosen to execute their will, is equally liable to be abused and perverted before the people can act through it. Witness the present Mexican War, the work of comparatively few individuals using the standing army as their tool." Was that written yesterday when, under pretence of preserving law and order on the Mexican frontier, the financial powers in control of these United States, investors in Mexican "securities," sent an army of freeborn American soldiers to the Rio Grande?

The entire essay on "Civil Disobedience" should be read by us timorous moderns to renerve us in time of abuse. We have, it seems, lost the art of speaking so eloquently and courageously, but we can make the most of a man who spoke for us sixty years ago and whose work it is respectable to quote, for he is an established New England classic.

Thoreau was not concerned primarily with government, because he was so situated that he could turn his back on it and not suffer. In his time an independent man could enjoy liberty of utterance and occupation. Thoreau asked to be let alone, and he was let alone. Non-interference between him and the government was mutual and friendly, except when the tax-collector reached his official hand into the Concord woods and seized that distinguished poll, enumerated as H. D. Thoreau, occupation, surveyor.

Thoreau's work is a long notebook of "surveyor's" jottings, a continuous journal, all autobiographic, some sections of which are assembled into essays.

His first book, "A Week on the Concord and Merrimac Rivers," consists of seven discursive essays on a multitude of subjects. There is rather more reflection upon literature and life in general than narrative of the week's experiences. This insurgent and original man, who lives near the heart of nature, who, like Whitman, regards a woodchuck's hole as a cosmic fact, is a critic of literature, a reader of Elizabethan poets. In a later book, "Cape Cod," he recites the sonorities of Homer on the Yankee sands. In his first book he recites the beauties of nature reclining on the bosom of oriental religion and British poetry.

On Saturday he paddles out on the river. The purling of the water, the echoes of civilization on the banks are vividly realized. But by Sunday morning the little stream has flowed into the vasty deeps of Hindoo and Greek philosophy, and when the Sabbath evening comes we have added nothing to our knowledge of local geography but have listened to one of the very best essays on books. The paragraphs on style form one of the most melodious of all discourses on the art of expression; Thoreau exemplifies the art he is explaining. Whoever enjoys the inconsistency of man may note that for ten pages, in the skilful cadences of a practised "scholar," Thoreau dwells on the merit of the brief word, the eloquence of unlettered men, the farmer's call to his team and other primitive, manly modes of speech. He pays his warmest tribute, however, not to the style of the Concord farmer, but to—Sir Walter Raleigh.

"Sir Walter Raleigh might well be studied, if only for the excellence of his style, for he is remarkable in the midst of so many masters. There is a natural emphasis in his style, like a man's tread, and a breathing space between the sentences, which the best of modern writing does not furnish. His chapters are like English parks, or say rather like a Western forest, where the larger growth keeps down the underwood, and one may ride on horseback through the openings. All the distinguished writers of that period possess a greater vigor and naturalness than the more modern—for it is allowed to slander our own time—and when we read a quotation from one of them in the midst of a modern author, we seem to have come suddenly upon a greener ground, a greater depth and strength of soil. It is as if a green bough were laid across the page, and we are refreshed as by the sight of fresh grass in midwinter or early spring. You have constantly the warrant of life and experience in what you read. The little that is said is eked out by the implication of the much that was done. . . . The word which is best said came nearest to not being spoken at all, for it is cousin to a deed which the speaker could have better done. Nay, almost it must have taken the place of a deed by some urgent necessity, even by some misfortune, so that the truest writer will be some captive knight, after all. And perhaps the Fates had some such design, when, having stored Raleigh so richly with the substance of life and experience, they made him a fast prisoner, and compelled him to make his words his deeds and transfer to his expression the emphasis and sincerity of his action."

Beautiful, fluent, and suggestive! But meanwhile what has become of our village anarchist, whom even the tax collector cannot make a captive knight, but who is paddling idly on a New England river—for a week?

On Tuesday a fine description of daybreak from a mountain, an experience not of this week but of another year; on Wednesday a fine sermon on friendship; on Thursday the story of Hannah Dustan and her justifiably murderous exploit among the Indians, accompanied by a discourse on epic stories and history. On Friday "the wind blew steadily downstream, so that we kept our sails set, and lost not a moment of the forenoon by delays, but from early morning until noon were continually dropping downward. With our hands on the steering paddle, which was thrust deep into the river, or bending to the oar, which indeed we rarely relinquished, we felt each palpitation in the veins of our steed, and each impulse of the wings which drew us above. The current of our thoughts made as sudden bends as the river"—and so he steers into a fine discussion of Ossian. He returns into the current to glide past Tyngsboro and Chelmsford, "holding in one hand half a tart country apple pie"—thence back into a beautiful eddy of thought about poetry, and the week is ended—a leisurely week covering ages of human thought.*

Of this interesting book, full of exquisite reflections and of as deep wisdom as ever came out of the universe by way of Concord, the author sold two hundred copies; the rest he took back from the printer and stored in a garret, a transaction which he records with unresentful dry humour.

His next book, the only other which he lived to see in print, is "Walden," his masterpiece, a greater book than the "Week," of the same tone and texture, but informed by a more explicit unifying philosophy of life. It records his actual experiment in individualism. It is alive with the reality of daily doings and is rounded to a higher reality, to one man's complete view of the life worth living and the destiny of the race. Emerson, paying his frugal way by lecturing and writing, makes many observations about society and solitude, the place of the individual in nature, but he lives among men and does

---

* Alcott said that this book was "Virgil, White of Selbourne and Izaak Walton and Yankee settler all in one." This is intended as high praise and does express the varied wealth of the book. But Alcott could not turn a lofty intention into words without getting something wrong. There is about as much of Virgil in Thoreau as there is of Seneca!

not know from experience the effect of abiding sole and self-dependent in the midst of an unpopulated wood. Thoreau, investigator and surveyor, tries solitude for two years, makes nature a laboratory, and brings back the record of his experiment. "Walden" is one of those whole, profound books in which the best of an author is distilled. In his two years by the pond Thoreau observed sharply what he could do with nature and what nature did to him; he pondered at leisure over what it all meant and made, not a collection of random jottings, but a summarized report.

Thoreau does not, as some people imagine, argue the case for the wilderness as against the town; on the contrary he loves best the cultivated land with people on it. He merely uses the wilderness to try himself in; he goes where the nature ingredients are unmixed with other things, as an experimenter in dietetics isolates his "food-squad" to increase human knowledge, not to please their palates. Thoreau tells what he lived for, how he lived, and thereby throws light on what humanity lives for. His attitude is neither modest nor magisterial; it is sometimes rather disdainful, his reflections on the life that his neighbours led are often coolly contemptuous. But for the most part he is setting forth *his* life and makes *his* conclusions clear, without urging them upon the reader's acceptance. He probes into the economies of an unthinking prosperity like other radical philosophers; but whereas the satiric dissections of a Carlyle leave the world a ruin and the pieces not worth picking up, Thoreau builds a courageous and cheerfully re-modelled life, practical for him at least, and though not to be foisted on the world like a reformer's nostrum, valuable to any neighbour who will read intelligently. "So I lived," he seems to say; "so I believed; so I found out and realized *my* sense of life. Take it or leave it. My experience taught me that to build a fine house to live in is less important than to build a good man to live in it. If that is not a practical ideal, please examine my bean account and see if by your own dull bread-winning, cake-stealing standards of life, I did not prove myself a competent husbandman."

Thoreau does not turn his back on responsibilities nor flaunt his idleness in the sweaty face of humanity; he is a conscientiously busy man, busy about his life and needs, and not unmindful of the needs of others; he holds his head up honestly, the equal of the thoughtless driven toiler, and is much his superior in the satisfaction of man's need for high meditation. The philosophy of "Walden" is near to the selfish self-culture of the unsocial Greek. States cannot be built on it any more than they can be built on Epictetus or on Plato's "Republic," but like them Thoreau stimulates the individual to examine himself and see where he stands in the midst of the solar system, to inquire what his activities amount to and what is the motive of them.

There is more in "Walden" than philosophy and unsocial experiment in the business of making a living. It is full of the poetry of the open world, an "hypaethral" book, unroofed to the skies. The birds fly and sing and the trees bud. Sometimes they have their technical names, for Thoreau is too clever to know less about a thing he sees than does some commonplace naturalist of the schools; but a naturalist he avowedly is not. He says in his Journal that the Secretary of the Association for the Advancement of Science asked him to fill in the blanks of a circular letter by way of answering certain questions, "among which the most important one was, what branch of science I was especially interested in. . . . I felt that it would be to make myself a laughing stock of the scientific community to describe to them that branch of science which especially interests me, inasmuch as they do not believe in a science which deals with the higher law. . . . How absurd that though I probably stand as near to Nature as any of them, and am by constitution as good an observer as most, yet a true account of my relation to Nature should excite their ridicule only." Again he writes in the Journal: "Man cannot afford to be a naturalist, to look at Nature directly, but with only the side of his eye. He must look through and beyond her. To look at her is as fatal as to look at the head of Medusa. It turns the man of science to stone." Thoreau is, as he prayed to be, a "hunter of the beautiful." He is in league with the stones of the field, and the beasts of the field are at peace with him. He is a better naturalist than most men of literary imagination, and he has more imagination than most naturalists.

There are two kinds of mystics. One shrouds himself in his cloudy dreams, mistaking his murky vision for fact. The other, open-eyed and cheerful amid the sunlit world, feels himself near the heart of living things. The one is a theologian; the other is a poet. For all his interest in the hazier transcendentalists and his admiration for the stupendous absurdities of Swedenborg, Thoreau is less near to the religious mystic than to the nature poet of all times, and especially to Wordsworth. Thoreau's spirit is that of a poet, though his verses are not good, for he was wanting in "the decisive gift of lyrical expression," as Emerson says of Plato and might have said of himself. Like his contemporaries, Thoreau misreads Nature as a collection of moral lessons, but he is not blind to her naked loveliness, and he finds her lessons not austere, but consoling. "Not by constraint or severity shall you have access to true wisdom, but by abandonment and childlike mirthfulness. If you would know aught, be gay before it."

Mystic and transcendentalist, he is not a foggy-minded dreamer with his head lost in vacant unrealities. He lived not ascetically, but heartily, and could have said on his deathbed like Hazlitt that he had had a happy life. He did not shrink from facts like some other poets who have fled stricken to the shadowy woods. He looked upon things courageously. But he had his private criteria of what was worth looking at. His quarrel with politicians is characteristic. He is contemptuous of them, not because they are engaged in sordid matters, not because they are "practical" (the sentimentalist's charge against them), but because they are not earnestly busy at the tasks they pretend to engage in. They are poor politicians. "They who have been bred in the school of politics fail now and always to face the facts," he says.

In his wonderful essay, "Life Without Principle," he says: "I have often been surprised when one has with confidence proposed to me, a grown man, to embark in some enterprise of his, as if I had absolutely nothing to do, my life having been a complete failure hitherto. . . . No, no! I am not without employment at this stage of the voyage. To tell the truth, I saw an advertisement for able-bodied seamen, when I was a boy, sauntering in my native port, and as soon as I came of age, I embarked." So he sailed, a clear-eyed steersman, content and confident as in the canoe which he paddled on Concord River, to that morrow—the concluding words of "Walden"— "which mere lapse of time can never make to dawn. The light which puts out our eyes is darkness to us. Only that day dawns to which we are awake. There is more day to dawn. The sun is but a morning-star."

The Rise to Fame
1917-41

Rather than love, than money, than fame, give me truth.
"Conclusion," *Walden*

MARK VAN DOREN (1894-   ) has been a professor of English at Columbia University, literary editor of the *Nation,* and has written novels, critical biographies, and poetry. For his *Collected Poems* (1939) he was awarded the Pulitzer Prize.

Position

MARK VAN DOREN

Henry David Thoreau, A Critical Study (Boston: 1916; New York: Russell and Russell, 1961), pp. 109-28.

Thoreau's permanent, best qualities—his sly and edged excellence, his leavening power—come into fuller recognition as his less essential qualities are subtracted and retreat. He is properly discounted only as his readers grow civilized and distrust the exposition of the elementary; he will come fully into his own when there is no one left who takes him literally and recommends his audacity as either profound or ultimate. The by-products of his living and his thinking—the excellences of the "Week" and "Walden," and whatever he prepared for print —are more essential than their central product, the extravagances of the Journal. His theory of life, so neatly conceived, so skillfully and variously expressed, so pointedly reinforced by reading and quotation, comes ultimately to seem futile and somewhat less than adequate; while the very neatness of conception, the very skill and variety and flavor of expression, the very quotations, endure. That Thoreau's main product was nothing, and his main effort vain, his own Journal best betrays. Emerson thought "he had exhausted all the capabilities of life in this world." The many pages of the Journal which uncover his private sense of bewilderment and pain when friends disappeared and confess his growing impotence in expansion, are the flattest denial that Thoreau died with any such conviction in his heart.

Yet the Journal is also the best witness that it was indeed Thoreau's ambition to exhaust all the capabilities of life in this world. Better still, the Journal reveals why he had to fail. It is the Journal which gives the best clue to the character of Thoreau's thinking, which gives to understand that Thoreau's

187

whole philosophical significance is involved in the fact that he thought in a vacuum.

It is very specifically that Thoreau says he inhabits a vacuum, and it is very adroitly that he defends his choice of habitation; it is perhaps in spite of himself that he proves better than almost any other theorizer the ultimate futility of all living in a vacuum. At any rate, his very clear remarks upon the subject, and his most relentless pursuit of its essence, make him a very satisfactory figure in which to observe its bearings and its consequences. Within his vacuum Thoreau was to become perfect with the least difficulty, was to be reborn into the Universe with the slightest travail. He was to be all that Man can be, at once and forever. He was to find Reality and keep it for a companion. By taking thought he was to achieve absolute glory. And all would be very easy. "The brave man braves nothing," he boasted in "The Service." "What a hero one can be without moving a finger!" "Not having anything to do, to do something." To be a real man—how extremely easy, if only one has courage to slough real responsibilities! Intellectual perfection was quite within reach. "One may have many thoughts and not decide anything," decided Thoreau. He had only to knock the bottom out of his consciousness to know how unfathomably profound he was. He had only to withdraw into a dark corner to witness how pure white was the flame of his thought. Moral perfection was even a simpler matter *in vacuo*. Emerson had thrown out the disconcerting statement in "The Transcendentalist" that "We have yet no man who has leaned entirely upon his character." Thoreau could do that easily enough. All he needed to do was to "rise above the necessity of virtue," so that his vices would "necessarily trail behind," and to facilitate the operation of the will by removing all the occasions for exercising it. He could not but be perfect when he was above having to be tested. He could solve any problem in his vacuum absolutely to his satisfaction. He proposed, for instance, to

> "Find out heaven
> By not knowing hell."

Complete æsthetic and spiritual satisfaction also came easily in the vacuum. The humming of a telegraph-wire could supply the first; the second was inherent in a life of vacuous expansion. "Simplify, simplify!" cried Thoreau like a Rousseau in "Walden." In his vacuum he simplified the meaning of exaltation of soul until it became equivalent to the sensation of expansion, equivalent to the reminder (from anywhere) "that there were higher, infinitely higher, planes of life which it behooved me never to forget."[1] That sensation and that reminder he demanded infinite room to indulge and hearken for. No other mortal could be near; only the universe, the equivalent of self, was to attend. A real spiritual existence was at stake. The duty of the self was to comprehend reality; reality was to be found only in the whole—the universe; therefore the duty of the individual was to betake himself where the universe in reality was. But the self by its own nature was fitted not only for comprehending the universe, but for being the universe as well; so that to be one's self was the only legitimate aspiration of man. To magnify the self, to have sensations of infinitude, to thrum with the excitement of the universe, was the ambition of the man who went to Walden Pond.

Thoreau speaks in the Journal some thirty times of the excitement which the humming of a telegraph-wire caused within him. "He thought the best of music was in single strains," said Emerson; a single strain of music was for him that "finest strain that a human ear can hear." "The laws of Nature break the rules of Art"; the telegraph-wire told him more about himself—brought the universe closer around him—than the noblest symphony. For symphonies, being civilized, presuppose rules and intelligence, while the telegraph-wire—"When we listen to it we are so wise that we need not to know."[2]

The telegraph-wire, which Thoreau does not mention after 1854 (probably because he thought he had exhausted its meaning), had been significant to him because it had seemed intensely spiritual. It had concentrated into a single strain the meaning of the universe, had furnished him at no expense (at no cost of "life") the entire spiritual stock which it is possible

---

[1] *Journal*, II, 497.
[2] *The Service*, 13.

for man to accumulate. If Thoreau lost faith in the telegraph-wire, he never ceased to believe what Emerson had spent his life preaching: that "spirit" is a single fact, that the soul has a single voice, that all spiritual values are indistinguishably blended in one experience—Inspiration. Any source of inspiration suffices; the exaltation is the thing; man should be ready to be anything, in the ecstasy of being stimulated. Thoreau never lost faith, as Emerson never did, in this Inspiration, this facile monopoly of spiritual privileges. When he found the world unsatisfactory, he scarcely knew why—and blamed the world. He scarcely suspected that his intensity was distilling the essence out of a vacuum, and not out of life.

Such men, complained Pascal, "inspire notions of simple greatness, and that is not the state of man." Thoreau's spiritual existence was more than easy; it was hopelessly, fatally easy. Assure himself as he might that his own will was the will of the universe, that thought and feeling are indistinguishable, that soul and body are one, that necessity is sweet, that good and evil are phantoms easy to dissolve, yet he never succeeded in stepping entirely out of his little private darkness. Perhaps he read George Herbert's exhortation, in "The Church Porch," to self-scrutiny:—

> "By all means use sometimes to be alone.
>   Salute thy self, see what thy soul doth wear.
>   Dare to look in thy chest, for 't is thine own,
>   And tumble up and down what thou find'st there."

But if he read it, he read it wrong, read it without the "sometimes"; took it literally and absolutely. And so doing, he fell into the error which Bacon describes as proceeding "from too great a reverence, and a kind of adoration of the mind and understanding of man; by means whereof men have withdrawn themselves too much from the contemplation of nature, and the observations of experience, and have tumbled up and down in their own reason and conceits. Upon these intellectualists," Bacon goes on to say, "which are notwithstanding commonly taken for the most sublime and divine philosophers, Heraclitus gave a just censure, saying, *Men sought truth in their own little worlds, and not in the great and common world;* for they disdain to spell, and so by degrees to read in the volume of God's works; and contrariwise by continual meditation and agitation of wit do urge and as it were invocate their own spirits to divine and give oracles unto them, whereby they are deservedly deluded."

Thoreau deluded himself, not because he was introspective, but because he was introspective in a certain mistaken, fruitless way. His speculations and experiences, intellectual, moral, æsthetic, yielded no important results, not because they were private, but because their privacy was their sole end and aim. Plato and Shakespeare were introspective, and learned to know the world in private; but the world they learned to know was large and important, the "great and common world." They studied themselves along with the rest of the world— Plato his opinions with the opinions of other men, Shakespeare his impressions with the impressions of other men; Thoreau studied himself alone—his opinions and his impressions by themselves. Shakespeare and Plato, like all men who are versed in the arts of comparison or dialectic, studied themselves as members of the universe; Thoreau studied himself as the universe. Shakespeare and Plato sought to learn their bearings in the world; Thoreau lost sight of bearings, and sought to be the world itself. Thoreau deluded himself precisely in proportion as he refused to keep the very delicate balance which it is necessary for a great and good man to keep between his private and his public lives, between his own personality and the whole outside universe of personalities. Thoreau's introspection was sterile in so far as it was a brooding reverie of self-contemplation rather than an effort to measure and correct and check himself by reference to things beyond himself. His counsel of perfection is meaningless to others in so far as it is intended to be realized in a vacuum, apart from contacts or comparisons; it was useless to him in that it did not permit of friction with other perfections, did not provide for that jostling and settling into place which the seasoned philosophy of life has undergone. It is clear that Thoreau could not see the bearings of his vacuous and expansive effort: "Is it all my fault?" he asked in the Journal.[1] "Have I no heart? Am I incapable of

[1] *Journal,* IV, 314.

expansion and generosity? I shall accuse myself of everything else sooner." It is clear enough that he was incapable of distinguishing between fruitless and fruitful expansion—the expansion which merely distends the self at the present stage of its ignorance, and the expansion which really enlarges the self by thrusting it out into play with surrounding selves. Stevenson suggests that "the world's heroes have room for all positive qualities, even those which are disreputable, in the capacious theaters of their dispositions. Such can live many lives, while Thoreau can live but one, and that with continual foresight." Thoreau refused pretty consistently to believe that there was any other life besides his own. "You think," he addressed an imaginary critic in the later Journal,[1] "that I am impoverishing myself by withdrawing from men, but in my solitude I have woven for myself a silken web or *chrysalis*, and, nymph-like, shall ere long burst forth a more perfect creature, fitted for a higher society." A very brave hope, but unrealized anywhere in his career, if the Journal is to be believed.

If it is asked what led Thoreau into his error, what led him to believe he could find out all things by and in himself, perhaps Matthew Arnold gives the keenest answer: "The blundering to be found in the world," says Arnold, "comes from some people fancying that some idea is a definite and ascertained thing, like the idea of a triangle, when it is not." The difficulty with Thoreau, as with many a philosopher during the nineteenth century, was that he had hypostatized an abstraction and seen his own reflection in it. During that century, the seedtime of the modern social soul, when the sun withheld its warmth and mankind suffered growing-pains, abstractions seemed blessed beyond all other commodities because they held out most promise of nourishment, of hope for the solution of the secret of life. When nine tenths of life seemed flowing away, men were wont to seek refuge on the island of an abstraction. When mind and heart and soul were being explained away, men doggedly identified themselves with certain functions of their minds and hearts and souls and demanded immunity. "Elsewhere the world may change, but oh! not

[1] *Ibid.*, IX, 246.

here!" they cried. Hallowing abstractions in the face of doubt, clutching at phenomena of consciousness in the face of science, they preached and lived vehemently all their lives what right reason condemns as inadequate and provincial. "Work," "Art," "Happiness," "Beauty," "Inspiration," "Reality" rode the century relentlessly. Belief was adequate if sincere and passionate. Men lived fully enough if they represented some quality or aspect of human nature to the consistent exclusion of other aspects and qualities; if they were gripped and warped by a concept or stamped in an attitude, and forgot all else. Men of that time are not so much men as faculties—not so much individual human beings as individual forces. Carlyle is a whole universe in miniature, "creaking, groaning, tortuous." Coleridge, says Sir Walter Scott, is "a lump of coal rich with gas, which lies expending itself in puffs and gleams, unless some shrewd body will clap it into a cast-iron box, and compel the compressed element to do itself justice." Byron is an angry, glowing cheek. Keats is an odor hanging heavily close to the earth. Shelley is a mad bird who would fly higher than is possible. Wordsworth is a column of white mist moving among the hills. Ruskin is a swift, fevered river. Emerson is an electric wire snapping and emitting brilliant, cold sparks. Thoreau is a pard-like hunter, moving quietly whither he likes and refusing to be touched.

Thoreau is one of the most deliberate of all hypostatizers. Born into a philosophical school whose ideas were already well formed, younger by ten years than most of its adherents, and with a craftman's mind for visualizing details, it is no wonder that he, most scrupulously of all men in America or Europe, should have assumed to be real, and attempted to live, the generalizations of Goethe and the abstractions of the transcendental philosophy. Nor is it surprising that, with his passion for the specific, he should have hypostatized a little more strenuously than he did such abstractions as Character, Will, Spirit, Moral Nature of Man, Life, Self, the Present,—that he should have hypostatized more strenuously than he did those abstractions, the quality of "Reality." It is not surprising that a man so quixotically practical should have asserted, when he heard his contemporaries complaining that life had lost its realities, that Reality did exist, and that he would go out and capture it. The hypostatizing of Reality is the simplest of everyday occurrences. Children believe that grown-ups are realler than themselves, and countrymen fancy that real life is to be had for the seeking in cities. The man who went out wolfishly to "live deep and suck out all the marrow of life, to cut a broad swath and shave close, to drive life into a corner, and reduce it to its lowest terms, and, if it proved to be mean, why, then to get the whole and genuine meanness of it, and publish its meanness to the world," leaves no one doubting that the monster which pursued him was Reality hypostatized into life and turned loose upon him. Reality and its pard-like hunter —these make up "the Thoreau." Thoreau's whole life was a search for embodied Reality, and his whole contention on paper is that Reality is accessible. "How to live, how to get the most out of life, how to extract the honey from the flower of the world. That is my every-day business. I am as busy as a bee about it," is not the only passage of its kind in the Journal. "Be it life or death," he adds, "we crave only reality." He is confident that "there is a solid bottom everywhere" if we only have the courage to sink to it. "Let us settle ourselves and work and wedge our feet downward through the mud and slush of opinion and prejudice and tradition, and delusion, and appearance, . . . to a hard bottom and rock in place—which we can call reality."

When Thoreau says he is seeking "what was always and always must be because it really is now," the temptation is irresistible to speculate upon the probability of his success. It is easy to guess that he will look nowhere outside himself for "what really is now." If he finds his self, he finds reality. If he finds reality, he has found the universe. "It is only he," said Confucius, "in the world, who possesses absolute truth who can get to the bottom of the law of his being. He who is able to get to the bottom of the law of his being will be able to get to the bottom of the law of being of other men. He who is able to get to the bottom of the law of being of men will be able to get to the bottom of the laws of physical nature. He who is able to get to the bottom of the laws of physical nature will be able to influence the forces of creation of the Universe. He who can influence the forces of creation of the Universe is one with the Powers of the Universe." Thoreau never gets to the bottom of the law of his being because he fails to keep the other men in mind, because he loses his bearings, because he does not recognize his individual being as in any way distinguishable from universal being. He probes for the bottom of his being in Walden Pond, before he has taken the trouble to be anything among other beings away from Walden Pond. He hopes to find what his self is like absolutely apart from relationships. He hypostatizes "self," sees nothing else, loses its bearings, and so loses it. Like the secret of harmony, it "always retreats as I advance"; and all he can do is to follow helplessly —a nothing in search of a something; a nothing perpetually dividing itself into a something and getting infinity. The problem of self, like the problem of love, is his sore affliction. "There is no remedy for love but to love more," said he. So with being; there is no remedy for being but to be infinitely more—of nothing.

But it is as much of a mistake, on the whole, for Thoreau's critic to take him literally, as it was for Thoreau to take himself so seriously; few other persons besides the critic are going to do it. Thoreau's example in society need not be worried about. The instinct of self-preservation in humanity and the common capacity for humor bring it about, of course, that "Walden" is in general not taken literally. It is easy enough to point out that Thoreau's main effort came to nothing; but the likelihood remains that Thoreau will always count for something among sophisticated persons who take him with the sufficient allowance of salt. That something, though it be only a by-product, and though it represent only a fraction of the man—"I speak out of the best part of myself," said Thoreau in another connection—is permanent, and of the first importance.

The best there is in Thoreau is not the naturalist part of him. Emerson predicted that the example of his usefulness would lead to the creation of a "profession" of naturalist: "I think we must have one day a naturalist in each village as invariably as a lawyer or doctor . . . all questions answered for stipulated fees." But Thoreau the philosopher of human relationships, talking of friendship and charity and solitude, will be remembered when Thoreau the visitor of wild flowers will beg for notice.

Philosophically considered, the best of Thoreau is not his extreme transcendental gospel, the darkest corner of his little private darkness; is not his urging of the elementary; is not his association with a very provincial school which did not know enough in general. If read as scripture, as some of his friends read him, or as madman, as Lowell read him, he will yield nothing. He cannot be taken literally any more than a wild odor can be seized and kept. "I am permitted to be rash," he said in the "Week." It is his temper which is needed and felt, and not his vagaries that need be worshiped or excused. He is a good hater and refuser, and the world likes that now and then. Men like to be pricked; men demand to be made mad on occasions. Men like Thoreau's temper in the atmosphere as much as they like the flavor of his wild apples in their memories. "These apples," he says, "have hung in the wind and frost and rain until they have absorbed the qualities of the weather or season, and thus are highly *seasoned,* and they *pierce* and *sting* and *permeate* us with their spirit"; if his philosophical offering misses richness, it is highly enough spiced. His sting is far from venomous; "I would give up most other things to be so good a man as Thoreau," wrote Stevenson to one of the biographers. No philosophical attack on Thoreau's individualism can take the tonic out of his pages or the temper out of his independence. It can be shown that he was unreasonable, and hypostatized "self"; but in "Walden" (if not in the Journal) he still stands alone, halfway enviable in his loneliness. Whittier thought "Walden" "very wicked and heathenish"— but "capital reading." The "Good heart, weak head" of Emerson furnishes a perpetual text for Thoreau. The steadfast air of the pages on philanthropy in "Walden" should alone preserve Thoreau's name. An extreme example of self-satisfaction can do no harm in the twentieth or any century. If Thoreau seems "all improved and sharpened to a point," his example nevertheless remains delicious. As long as individual excellence is prized by however slight a minority, his books will be instructive, says Lowell, "as showing how considerable a crop may be raised on a comparatively narrow range of mind, and how much a man may make of his life if he will assiduously follow it, though perhaps never really finding it at last."

Thoreau will be found a very satisfactory spokesman for one who feels driven into a position somewhat analogous to his position in 1840. Not only is he a wholesome shocking force in the lives of young people who have been brought up too exclusively on positivistic or humanitarian principles; he stands pretty staunchly back of one when one desires to strike at the confident and benevolent leveler, with his wash of sociality and sentiment, and when one desires to cry, "I do not believe you! Man is great!" "Do not seek so anxiously to be developed," warns Thoreau, "to subject yourself to so many influences, to be played upon. It is all dissipation." The greatest apostle of Leisure in his century, he put to flight Folly's sociological brood, and only asked for leisure to be good. That his reaction was unreasonable, and that his refuge was in an instinct ("immemorial custom" and "transcendent law") as objectionable as the socialistic instinct, does not cripple his support when it is necessary that one be unreasonable. One can be as combative and as assertive now and then as Thoreau was always; one still "finds it difficult to make a sufficiently moderate statement"; one still wants to bristle with indignant hyperbole and paradox in the humanitarian, scientific, reformatory, or pragmatic presence. If Thoreau loses in the broadest sense by being terribly single-minded, he is valuable in a narrower sense by virtue of his very singleness—valuable as a protestant, valuable as an antidotal flavor.

Thoreau, finally, is an American classic. He will always appeal to the "confirmed city-men" he affected to pity. For the same reason that "Robinson Crusoe" appeals most to land folk, "Walden" will appeal more and more to the men and women of "institutions," to men in studies and clubs, to boys by the fireside in winter. Thoreau is eminently a citizen in the republic of letters, and continues some excellent traditions. "Even his love of Nature seems of the intellectual order," Whitman thought, "—the bookish, library, fireside—rather than smacking of out of doors. . . . I often find myself catching a literary scent off his phrases." The readers of "Walden" will not distrust it because it is literary; they will treasure it—one cannot say how long—because it is literary, because it is a classic, because it furnishes definite delight. A substantial critic thought "Walden" in 1879 "the only book yet written in America that bears an annual perusal," and remarked that for his own part, with "Walden" in his hands, he could wish "that every other author in America might try the experiment of two years in a shanty." As almost every one has been ambitious to be a second Crusoe, so a few spirits (perhaps more than confess it) will always be furtively suspecting that by two years in the woods they could do themselves some service. "Crusoe" and "Walden," classics of solitude, people do not want to do without.

"No truer American existed than Thoreau," said Emerson. At least no more plain-spoken representative of transcendental New England could be asked for, it seems safe to say. There can be little doubt that the spirit of "Walden" has pervaded the American consciousness, stiffened the American lip, steadied the American nerve, in a ponderable degree. By creating a classic image of the cynic hermit in ideal solitude Thoreau has demonstrated some of the meannesses of the demands of Time and Matter, and furnished the spirit and will for social criticism; he has made men acute critics, if not sensible shepherds, of their own sentiments.

ARCHIBALD MACMECHAN (1862-1933), Canadian scholar and essayist, was George Munro Professor of the English Language and Literature in Dalhousie University when he contributed the essay on Thoreau to the *Cambridge History of American Literature*. MacMechan was not disposed to quarrel with Emerson's or Lowell's interpretation of Thoreau: Thoreau could be explained, he believed, as a "village rebel" who had attempted "to stand aloof from his kind."

Thoreau

ARCHIBALD MACMECHAN

The Cambridge History of American Literature, Vol. 2 ([1917]; New York: The Macmillan Company, 1944), 1-15.

The life of a village community is not seldom enriched by the inclusion of a rebel, an original who refuses obstinately to conform to type, and succeeds in following out his idea, in contrast to the humdrum routine of his fellows. When the community happens to be Concord, the picturesque and historic village where the Revolution began, the Weimar of American literature, and when the rebel happens to be an American faun, the conjunction must result in no ordinary enrichment. There on 12 July, 1817, just after the second war with Britain, David Henry Thoreau was born to a small farmer and artisan who kept a shop and painted signs. The French-looking surname came by way of the Channel Islands, for the author's grandfather was born in Jersey, and, in spite of his British origin, had served as a sailor in a Continental privateer. Thoreau passed his life in the village of his birth, and now his name is indissolubly associated with it.

For a generation which plumes itself upon its "breadth," no slight effort is needed to picture the life of a typical New England village before the Transcendental movement had broken up the hard old Puritanic crust. It was a rigid and limited life made up of work, thrift, duty, and meetings. Caricatured and ridiculed though it be, that old stern life moulded men and women of the toughest moral and intellectual fibre. Puritanism was an intellectual creed, and led directly to the cultivation of the intellect. The minister and the schoolmaster were twin ruling powers. None questioned the value of education; it was almost a fetish. So as a child in a Puritan community, Henry Thoreau followed the regular routine of the common school until he was ripe for the university.

Thoreau became a man of letters, but he was also a wild man, a faun; he became Emerson's man, and—although it is rather difficult to fit into the picture—he was a Harvard man. He went up at sixteen and took his degree at twenty. His portrait at this time shows a smooth, grave face dominated by a Roman nose and overhung by a bush of fine brown hair. What benefit he derived from his college years is a matter both of record and of inference. "What I was learning in college was chiefly, I think, to express myself," he writes five years after leaving Harvard. Perhaps the most significant memorial of his college career is the Latin letter he wrote to his sister Helen, in 1840. It gave him pleasure to use the language of

Virgil and Cicero, for one of the many paradoxes in Thoreau's life was the union of true American contempt for tradition with an unaffected love of the classics. After a diatribe against the narrow religiosity of New England, he draws breath to praise, "the Ionian father of the rest," with the enthusiasm of Keats.

> There are few books which deserve to be remembered in our wisest hours, but the Iliad is brightest in the serenest days, and embodies still all the sunlight that fell in Asia Minor. No modern joy or ecstasy of ours can lower its height, or dim its lustre, but there it lies in the east of literature, as it were the earliest and latest production of the mind.

From the wildwood simplicity of Walden, he startles the reader with deliverances which might have come from the Bodleian.

> Those who have not learned to read the ancient classics in the language in which they were written must have a very imperfect knowledge of the history of the human race. . . . Homer has never been printed in English, nor Æschylus, nor Virgil even,—works as refined, as solidly done, as beautiful almost as the morning itself; for later writers, say what we will of their genius, have rarely if ever equalled the elaborate beauty and finish and the life-long and heroic literary labours of the ancients.

Thoreau translated the *Prometheus Vinctus* and tried his hand at Pindar. His pages are sown with classical allusions and quotations. The sunset at Cape Cod brings a line of Homer into his memory "with a rush," as the shining torch of the sun falls into the ocean. He has words of just appreciation for Anacreon. His odes

> charm us by their serenity and freedom from exaggeration and passion, and by a certain flower-like beauty, which does not propose itself, but must be approached and studied like a natural object.

Such genuine admiration for Greek genius is rare at any time, and certainly not many American hands could have been busy translating Æschylus, Pindar, and Anacreon in the hurried forties and fifties of the nineteenth century. This large and solid academic basis for Thoreau's culture is not generally observed. His devotion to the Greeks rings truer than his various utterances on Indian literature and philosophy. Besides, he was well seen in the English classics from Chaucer downwards. A few pages of *A Week* yield quotations from Emerson, Ovid, Quarles, Channing, *Relations des Jesuits,* Gower, Lydgate, Virgil, Tennyson, Percy's *Reliques,* Byron, Milton, Shakespeare, Spenser, Simonides. As Lowell remarks, "His literature was extensive and recondite." The truth is, Thoreau was a man of letters, whose great ambition was to study and to write books.

During and after his college career, Thoreau taught school, like the hero of *Elsie Venner.* He is quite frank about this episode. "As I did not teach for the good of my fellow-men, but simply for a livelihood, this was a failure." Brief as was his apprenticeship to the schoolmaster trade, one might possibly conjecture that it left some mark upon him. The many citations of recondite literature do not escape the suspicion of parade and pedantry. There is a certain gusto with which he inserts the botanical name of a plant after the picturesque vernacular, and distinguishes between *Rana palustris* and *Rana pipiens.* In general, the tone he adopts towards the world is that of the pedagogue dealing habitually with inferior minds.

After his college days comes an episode which his biographers seem inclined to slur over, perhaps from a false sense of the dignity of biography, and that is the two years, from 25 April, 1841, to May, 1843, which Thoreau spent under Emerson's roof. By the time Thoreau left Harvard, Emerson had become a power in the spiritual life of America. His brief career as a Unitarian minister was already far behind him; he had made his pilgrimage to Europe; he had penetrated the wilds of Scotland to Craigenputtock because one Thomas Carlyle, another unrecognized genius, lived there. He had given in Boston those lectures on *Great Men* and *The Philosophy of History* which foreshadow the great address commonly called the declaration of independence for American literature. He had brought out his Scottish friend's odd book, *Sartor Resartus,* a publication which accelerated the Transcendental movement. Emerson discovered the youth Thoreau as a true poet, and communicated the discovery in a letter to Carlyle. Thoreau became a member of Emerson's household, apparently as general "help," a relationship which all Americans will understand but which will be the despair of Europeans.

> The most practical and handy person in all matters of every day life, a good mechanic and gardener, methodical in his habits, observant and kindly in the domestic world,

is the character Emerson gives him. There must have been a cash nexus, but the essence of the relationship was the tie uniting master and pupil, sage and disciple. This long and close association with the great literary force of that time had no slight effect in moulding Thoreau's character and determining his bent.

> His biographer, who knew him personally, says that he imitated Emerson's tones and manners so that it was annoying to listen to him.

The imitation of Emerson in Thoreau's writing is equally apparent. Lowell saw and condemned it in his criticism of *A Week.* In prose there is the sentence which reads like an oracle. It may be the profoundest wisdom, or it may be the merest matter of moonshine. When Thoreau writes "Ancient history has an air of antiquity," or, "Give me a sentence which no intelligence can understand," the critic can only fall back on the Gilbertian comment upon the young man who "expresses himself in terms too deep for me." The imitation of Emerson's poetry is even more marked and results in what Lowell calls Thoreau's "worsification." He had no candid friend to tell him what Dryden told "Cousin Swift." There was, on the other hand, no little benefit in mere contact with such a personality as Emerson, much more in continual and close intercourse with him. The stimulus to thought must have been most potent, and Emerson's influence could not but stiffen Thoreau in his natural independence and confirm him in his design of living his own life.

The village rebel who will not conform rebels first against the local religion. It is the obvious thing to rebel against. What Thoreau dissented from was New England Puritanism, as is plainly shown in "Sunday" of *A Week*. The atmosphere of that lost religion hangs about the letter of his roommate at Harvard, who became a minister in due course. One thinks of the letters young Mr. Tennyson of Trinity was exchanging with other Cambridge "Apostles" about the same time. The salutation is "Friend Thoreau," which seems to have been the accepted convention at the time. Perhaps the most significant sentence in it runs:

> I hear that you are comfortably located in your native town, as the guardian of its children, in the immediate vicinity, I suppose, of one of our most distinguished apostles of the future, R. W. Emerson, and situated under the ministry of our old friend Reverend Barzillai Frost, to whom please make my remembrances.

It does not appear that Thoreau after reaching manhood was ever "situated under the ministry" of the Reverend Barzillai Frost. In "Civil Disobedience," he writes:

> Some years ago, the State met me on behalf of the Church and commanded me to pay a certain sum toward the support of a clergyman, whose preaching my father attended, but never I myself. "Pay" it said, "or be locked up in jail." I declined to pay. But unfortunately, another man saw fit to pay it.

The recusant even rendered the authorities a reason in writing for his recusancy.

> Know all men by these presents that I Henry Thoreau do not wish to be regarded as a member of any incorporated society which I have not joined.

Opposition to the State followed naturally on opposition to the Church. To his honour, Thoreau took a stand against slavery when it was anything but popular to do so, even in the State of Massachusetts. In all his words on this theme there is a fire not to be found elsewhere. What roused him was the spectacle of fugitive slaves escaping to the free North, and, through the action of Northern courts, dragged back into slavery. The State was clearly in the wrong; Thoreau, in his own phrase, "declared war on the State," by refusing to pay his poll-tax. He believed that such passive-resistance by a number of taxpayers would bring about the abolition of slavery. He was therefore quite consistent with himself when he stood forth from the crowd as the champion of John Brown in his history-making raid on Harper's Ferry. Public opinion, North and South, condemned the raid as the outrage of a fanatic attempting to kindle a servile war. Thoreau was of the remnant who saw its true bearing.

It was in the first year of his Walden hermitage that Thoreau was arrested and lodged in jail for refusing to pay his poll-tax. He tells how he was going to the cobbler's, with a shoe to be mended, when the Law laid hold of him, how he spent the evening very pleasantly with the other inmates of the lock-up, how he was released next morning, and immediately started off with a berry-picking party. This "grand refusal" struck the imagination of Stevenson, who considers it the most significant act of Thoreau, and more important than his retreat in Walden. A parallel might be found in Stevenson's account of his brief incarceration in a French prison in the epilogue to *An Inland Voyage*. Again, some friend paid Thoreau's poll-tax for him, but he never wavered in his reasoned policy of passive resistance to an unjust, slavery-supporting State. At the same time, he never refused to pay the highway tax, because, "I am as desirous of being a good neighbour as I am of being a bad subject." "I simply wish," he continues, "to refuse allegiance to the State, to withdraw and stand aloof from it effectually."

His next step was a more remote withdrawal, an attempt to stand aloof from his kind. It was an attempt to live by himself and to himself, in fact, to turn modern hermit. Apparently the idea had long been germinating in his mind. On that far-off Harvard commencement of 1837, he took part in a "conference," an obsolete academic exercise resembling a medieval "disputation." He took one side of an argument and a fellow-student, afterwards a judge, maintained the opposite. The subject debated was "The Commercial Spirit." In his set speech, the grave, shock-headed graduate from Concord suggested that

> the order of things should be somewhat reversed; the seventh should be man's day of toil, wherein to earn his living by the sweat of his brow; and the other six his Sabbath of the affections and the soul—in which to range this widespread garden, and drink in the soft influences and sublime revelations of Nature.

The young collegian's division of time may have provoked a smile, but the day was to come when he was to make the actual experiment. Thoreau had turned against the Church, he had turned against the State, and now he turned against organized society. He perceived that man was bound to the wheel of circumstance, he was the passive, unquestioning slave of a vain and sordid routine. One man at least would wrench himself free from the mill at which he saw his fellows ceaselessly toiling. He would carry out his boyhood's dream, and, by reorganization of his life, obtain freedom for the things that matter. By making life more simple, he would cheat circumstance and really begin to live.

> I dream of looking abroad summer and winter, with free gaze from some mountainside, while my eyes revolve in an Egyptian slime of health—I to be nature looking into nature with such easy sympathy as the blue-eyed grass in the meadow looks in the face of the sky. From such recess, I would put forth sublime thoughts daily, as the plant puts forth leaves.

It only remained to choose his "recess."

Apparently the suggestion as to the particular recess came from his friend, Channing, who writes,

> I see nothing for you in this earth but that field which I once christened "Briars"; go out upon that, build yourself a hut, and there begin the grand process of devouring yourself alive.

Thoreau was a natural ascetic. He ate little flesh meat, but subsisted almost entirely on vegetable food; he drank nothing but water; he never married. He refers in a letter to a nameless lady who wished to marry *him*, and he calls the inverted courtship "tragic." In the Age of Faith he would have fled to the wilderness for the same reason that he built his hut by Walden pond, in order to save his soul. Salvation for him meant escape from endless labour for the acquisition of useless things. By another paradox of his career, he freed himself from New England thrift by being still more thrifty. By denying himself and faring more scantily than his neighbours, he secured leisure for pursuits they could not comprehend. Thoreau is a prophet of the simple life, perhaps the first in America. He uses the very term.

> I do believe in simplicity. When the mathematician would solve a difficult problem, he first frees the equation from all encumbrances, and reduces it to its simplest terms. So simplify the problem of life, distinguish the necessary and the real.

He was preaching to his friend Blake what he had already practised. He had felled the pines with his borrowed axe, and dug his cellar, and built his

> tight shingled and plastered house, ten feet wide by fifteen long, and eight feet posts, with a garret and a closet, a large window on each side, two trap-doors, one door at the end, and a brick fireplace opposite.

It was a little smaller than the room he occupied at Harvard. The materials cost less than twenty-nine dollars; and by cultivating beans and other vegetables he was able to support himself at an annual expense of a little more than eight dollars.

This was removing the encumbrances from the equation, with a vengeance, but Thoreau could make a "dinner" of berries. The experiment lasted from March, 1845, until September, 1847, and then having satisfied himself that the thing could be done, he gave it up.

Two years later, Thoreau published his first book, *A Week on the Concord and Merrimack Rivers.* The actual voyage was performed by the two brothers Henry and John in the late summer of 1839 in a boat of their own making, "painted green below with a border of blue, with reference to the two elements in which it was to spend its existence." During his Walden retirement, Thoreau worked over the original record of his pleasant outing, expanding it greatly by the inclusion of very various material, and had it published at his own risk by Monroe in 1849. It was the year of the Argonauts, of the gold-rush to California, and such literary treasure as the odd book contained was not much regarded. Though favourably reviewed by Ripley and by Lowell, it did not please the public, and over seven hundred copies out of an impression of one thousand were thrown back on the author's hands. It is another of the paradoxes of Thoreau's career that since his death, this failure has been edited with almost benedictine care.

Lowell's praise of *A Week* can hardly be termed excessive. After dwelling on its weak points, its lack of unity, its imitation of Emerson, its dolorous verse, he continues,

> the prose work is done conscientiously and neatly. The style is compact and the language has an antique purity like wine grown colourless with age.

The truth is that Thoreau with all his genuine appreciation of the classics never learned their lessons of proportion, restraint, "nothing too much." Nor was the example of his master Emerson likely to correct his own tendency to formlessness. The principle of selection is absent. The week's excursion is only an excuse for including Emersonian essays on friendship and chastity, or dissertations on the Laws of Menu, or translations of Anacreon, till the reader asks resentfully what they are doing in this dory-modelled *galère,* painted green below with a border of blue, on the Merrimack and Concord, lucid streams. If he had possessed the artistic instinct of Stevenson, or had undergone Stevenson's rigid self-imposed discipline in the writer's craft, he might have made *A Week* as complete a little masterpiece as *An Inland Voyage. A Week* fails on account of its scattering aim. It is neither a record of a week's excursion, nor a book of essays, but a jumble of the two. Thoreau's American contempt for tradition accounts for the artistic failure.

Where Thoreau is not the transcendental essayist, but the first-hand observer of nature, he is delightful. When discoursing on such a theme as the common sunfish, the reader wishes he would never end.

> The breams are so careful of their charge that you may stand close by in the water and examine them at your leisure. I have stood over them half an hour at a time, and stroked them familiarly without frightening them, suffering them to nibble my fingers harmlessly, and seen them erect their dorsal fins in anger when my hand approached their ova, and have even gently taken them out of the water with my hand. . . . As you stand thus stooping over the bream in its nest, the edges of the dorsal and caudal fins have a singular dusty golden reflection, and its eyes, which stand out from its head, are transparent and colourless. Seen in its native element, it is a very beautiful and compact fish, perfect in all its parts, and looks like a brilliant coin fresh from the mint.

If the whole book had been of this texture, it would be a classic. Another element in the book which Thoreau valued slightly—those incidental glimpses of a vanished America—will be prized by later generations. His accounts of the mountain people he discovered, of the girl combing her black hair, of his surly host, Rice, and his strange inn, of the old farmer praying in the dim morning pasture, of the canal boatmen, of the lockmen's house, and the small-voiced but sincere hospitality of the Yankee housewife offering the obsolete refreshment of "molasses and ginger," read like pages Irving forgot to put into *The Sketch Book.* These things are seen with the naturalist's clear grave eyes and recorded in plain words with no attempt at oracular profundity. For the sake of more such true pictures of reality, how gladly would the modern reader forego the disquisitions on Persius and Ossian.

The next year, 1850, Thoreau and his friend Channing made a brief raid across the border into Quebec, though the record of his experience was not published until 1866, with the title *A Yankee in Canada.* Stevenson found the book dull. Still, it has an interest of its own for the light it sheds on Thoreau's peculiar temperament, and particularly on his robust Americanism, a sentiment based on traditional dislike of Britain and on contempt for monarchy as an effete institution. Patriotism is a curious passion. It does not seem possible to love one's own country except by hating some other country. Emerson defines Thoreau almost in these terms:

> No truer American existed than Thoreau. His preference of his country and condition was genuine, and his aversation from English and European manners and tastes almost reached contempt.

With no great love for the institutions of his own land, he showed his instinctive preference for them during his one brief sojourn under an alien flag. His attitude throughout is one of consistent patronage to all he sees and hears. The redcoats in the citadel at Quebec have the manhood drilled out of them. Britain, he believes, is "red in the knuckles" with holding on to the Canadas, and must soon relax her grasp. Towards the great mystery of historical Christianity, he is equally contemptuous. The devout worshippers in the Cathedral at Montreal, absorbed in prayer and regardless of gazing strangers, suggest the parallel of his fellow Yankees going to meeting on a week-day, after the cattle-fair. The Sisters of Charity whom he saw in the street looked as if they had cried their eyes out, "insulting the daylight with their presence." That the soldier and the religious had something valuable to which he was a stranger, never occurred to him. In other words, he was

blind to the romance of war and the poetry of faith. Even the
natural courtesy of the *habitants* seems to him mere servility.
For the American of Thoreau's generation, history began with
the musketry of the embattled farmers at Concord bridge.
Before that day, there was only a dark welter of wicked kings
and mad tories. These limitations prevented him from realizing,
as Parkman did, the epic struggle which ended on the Plains
of Abraham. He indeed transcribes the inscription on the monument to Wolfe and Montcalm, but the splendour and pathos of
their fate leave him unmoved. Still, this rigid and narrow
provincialism gives salt to his books and explains his revolt
against convention. It was his Americanism which drove Thoreau to realize himself in his own way.

In 1854, Thoreau published the book by which he will
always be best known, *Walden, or Life in the Woods*. It is
by far the deepest, richest, and most closely jointed of his
books. It shows Thoreau at his best, and contains all that he
had to say to the world. In fact, he is a man of one book, and
that book is *Walden*. In plan, it is open to the same objection
as *A Week*, and might almost plead guilty to the charge of
obtaining a hearing under false pretences. "Life in the woods"
suggests the atmosphere of *As You Like It* and the Robin Hood
ballads, but not moralizings on economy and the duty of being
yourself. The reader who takes up the book with the idea
that he is going to enjoy another *Robinson Crusoe* will not be
pleased to find that every now and then he will have to listen
to a lay sermon, or a lyceum lecture.

Still it is the adventurous, *Robinson Crusoe* part that is
imperishable. How a man resolved to live in a new way,
how he borrowed an axe and began felling pines on the ground
that sloped southward to a wonderful pond, how he trimmed
his rafters, dug his cellar, bought an Irish labourer's shanty,
transported the materials to a new site and raised the frame,
appeal to the open-air instinct of every man. Even how he
maintained the fire on the hearth, and grubbed out the fat
pine roots to feed it, are matters of absorbing interest. His
struggle with the weeds and poor soil of the two-acre patch on
which he raised his beans and potatoes, every item of his various accounts, his food, his daily routine, his house-cleaning,

have the fascination of a narrative by Defoe. The reader follows
the solitary in his swim across the lake, or through the wood to
the village, or about the hut, or along the rows of beans, with a
zest he can hardly explain to himself. The reason is that Henry
Thoreau in Walden wood is the same as the mariner of York
on the Island of Desolation; he represents once more the struggle of primitive man to obtain food and shelter, in fact the epic
of civilization. The interest of the theme is perennial.

Walden is also the memorial of an American faun, of a
wild man who lived in the woods, who carried an umbrella
like Robinson Crusoe, to weatherfend his head, and used a
microscope to study insects with. About the same time, just
after leaving Harvard, Thoreau found his first arrowhead and
began his first journal, and the two streams of tendency ran
side by side in his nature till the end. Intercourse with nature
was even more necessary to Thoreau than intercourse with
books. Intercourse with human beings he thought he did not
need, but he was always tramping off to the village for a chat.
He was not a real solitary, for visitors were always coming
to view the progress of the odd experiment in living. Still
Thoreau differed widely from the ordinary gregarious man in
that he could manage to be alone for long periods with the
woods and the sky. A friend called him a poet-naturalist; but
the description is not exact. He hardly views nature as a
poet, and he is surpassed by not a few observers of nature, who
have had the stimulus of Darwin. The merely pictorial in
nature does not much interest him, probably because he had
seen no pictures. To Thoreau nature is no divinity as she is
to Wordsworth; she is simply the pleasantest of companions, or
rather the pleasantest environment for a natural man. In a
house, in a town, he is like a creature caged. It is characteristic
that after swimming across the lake, he would sit in his doorway all morning, "in a wise passiveness," as Wordsworth would
term it. So wild creatures live in the wild, when not hunger-
driven. The wild things found him to be of their own kind;
a mouse made friends with him, a hen partridge led her brood
about his hut, he could take a fish out of the water in his hand.
Thoreau is perhaps the first to suggest the pleasure of hunting
animals without a gun, of learning about them without any

desire to kill. He was not influenced by Darwin, or such a conception as the struggle for existence. Nature to him was not red in tooth and claw with ravin; it was a gentle, friendly, peaceful alternative to the mean greed and futile toil of man. The atmosphere of Walden is always serene and free from cloud or storm. Rain and winter come in their season; but they never seem to touch him; the rain does not wet, and the winter does not chill. There may be a thousand nooks in New England more beautiful than Walden, but they remain unknown, while the pine-clad slope which this strange being discovered and haunted for two years is charted as a permanent addition to the world-wide map of Romance.

Thoreau has two styles, the oracular and the simple; and in *Walden* the simple prevails. Like the water of the pond, it is clear, colourless and wholesome. Thoreau is a careful writer, with an instinct for the right word which was developed and strengthened by a lifelong devotion to the best books. His love of the classics must have tended to purify his style and increase its natural dignity. *Walden* is generally free from oracular phrases and grotesque locutions like "eyes revolve in an Egyptian slime of health." It must always retain the deep unfailing value of all autobiography, personal memoirs, "confessions." The record of a life will never fail of an audience. When a man declares, "Thus I did, thus I thought, thus I felt," other men are always eager to attend his tale.

The Walden experiment was not unlike the other Transcendental experiment of Brook Farm. Both were declarations of independence; both were attempts to place life on a new basis; both broke down. The Greek dog-sage in his tub, the English Quaker in his suit of leather, the Yankee land-surveyor in his wooden hut are three object lessons to the world of the ancient truth that "a man's life consisteth not in the abundance of the things that he possesseth." The Walden experiment is open to all the criticism of Lowell: "it presupposed all the complicated civilization which it theoretically abjured." Even for Thoreau it was not a success. In the first year, his Homer lay open on the table, but he was so busy that he could only read it by snatches; in the second year, he was forced to set up a prosaic stove in the place of the romantic fire-place.

Thoreau's ideal of a world of book men, or contemplatives, is a dream. Still, the experience of the ascetic always shames the grossness of the worldly wiseman. If a man can live for a year for eight dollars, we certainly spend too much on things we could do without. Thoreau's experiment will always have its appeal to hot, ambitious spirits on their first awakening to the intricacy of life. The hero of *Locksley Hall* longs to escape from civilization to summer isles of Eden. At least one American man of letters has followed Thoreau's example by going into retreat.

After living in his hut for two years, Thoreau supported himself for three more by cultivating his garden, like Candide. Thus he obtained the freedoms he desired, the leisure to think, and to read, and to write, and to be himself. Then he went back to his land-surveying, his communing with the spirits of the wild, and the compilation of his voluminous journals. From the latter, several volumes have been quarried for the definitive edition of his works. They must always be of more interest to the admirer of Thoreau and the student of literature than to the general reader.

Then came the break-down of his health. It was the irony of fate that the man who lived according to nature, who obeyed the dictates of spare temperance, who never seemed to tire, should die of tuberculosis, the scourge of civilized life. His latest portrait, a daguerreotype taken in New Bedford, seven months before his death, shows a hairy, innocent, pathetic face; the eyes have the mute appeal of the consumptive. In 1861, the stricken man made a trip to the West, in the vain hope of restoration to health by change of air. He died in his birthplace, Concord, on 2 May, 1862, in the second year of the Civil War. He has been blamed for expressing his sense of detachment from that terrible conflict, but if, like Mercutio, he cries, "A plague on both your houses!" it must be remembered that, like Mercutio, he was a dying man. His last letter, dictated to his sister, concludes, "I am enjoying existence as much as ever, and regret nothing."

Emerson has written an appreciation of Thoreau with intimate knowledge and tender humanity. To that estimate, little can be added, or taken away. Lowell and Stevenson have appraised his character and his work, none too gently. Of himself he said, "I am a mystic, a Transcendentalist, and a natural philosopher."

NORMAN FOERSTER (1887-   ) has served on the faculties of the University of North Carolina and the University of Iowa. During the 1920's, along with Irving Babbitt and Paul Elmer More, he was one of the leaders of the New Humanism. Among his many books are *Nature in American Literature* (1923), which contains a long critique on Thoreau, *American Criticism* (1928), and *Toward Standards* (1930). Professor Foerster believed, one hundred years after Thoreau's birth, that the task of the critic of Thoreau was still "in the main one of discovery."

The Humanism of Thoreau

NORMAN FOERSTER

Nation, Vol. 105 (July 5, 1917), 9-12.

One hundred years from his birth and some fifty years from his death, Thoreau has come into his own, perhaps more than his own. Obscure and contentedly "unsuccessful" while his friend Emerson was the anointed leader of a spiritual, social, and literary movement, he has since his death steadily advanced in popular and critical favor, until now he stands almost side by side with the shining leader himself. During his lifetime the author of two books, he has now to his credit no less than twenty volumes. The first edition of his "Week on the Concord and Merrimac Rivers," a copy of which recently sold at about one hundred dollars at auction, was so dismal a failure that the publisher returned the greater part of the edition, and the author found the growth of his library very suddenly accelerated: "I have now," he reported, "a library of nearly nine hundred volumes, over seven hundred of which I wrote myself."

But the interpretation of Thoreau and his writing has been even more unsettled than his reputation. His personality is so pronounced and at the same time so subtle and various that he is inevitably many things to many people. He has been regarded as an American Diogenes and a rural Barnum; as a narrow Puritan, a rebel against Puritanism, and a German-Puritan romanticist; as a poet-naturalist; as a sentimentalist; as a hermit; as a loafer; as a poser; as a prig and skulker; as a cynic; as a stoic; as an epicurean. Certainly he is not all of these; possibly he is several of them, or none of them—something else, rather. The one encouraging fact is that he is, permanently, what he is. Our task, therefore, a century after his birth, is still in the main one of discovery.

I

It has been shown often enough that Thoreau was not fundamentally a scientist, not even a field naturalist, despite his addiction to the observation and recording of natural appearances and phenomena. It was not to study the fauna and flora of Middlesex County that he spent his life in roaming daily over his familiar native countryside, though that was clearly one of his purposes; nor was it to view the ever-changing landscape with the charmed eye of the artist, though that too was clearly one of his purposes. How, then, are we to account for these two facts: first, that he devoted himself so ardently to nature, and, secondly, that he held himself aloof from the life of men? The two facts have been neatly, but not convincingly, related by Thoreau's latest critic, who, finding that Thoreau failed to derive from his human friendships that "complete sympathy and toleration" which his ideal demanded, "went *therefore* to Nature, and was satisfied with her companionship."*
We may be sure, for one thing, that Thoreau was attracted to nature, not for a single reason, but for several reasons, as other people are. After all, he was something of a naturalist, and he was more of an artist than has been generally recognized. But what more than anything else brought him out in all weathers —rain, snow, sleet, fog—alone or with a more than superfluous companion, ever and again to the old forest shrines and hillcrest temples, was the mystic's hope of detecting "some trace of the Ineffable." "If by patience, if by watching, I can secure one ray of light, can feel myself elevated for an instant upon Pisgah, the world which was dead prose to me become living and divine, shall I not watch ever? Shall I not be a watchman

* Mark Van Doren, *Henry David Thoreau: A Critical Study*, p. 87.

henceforth? If by watching a whole year on the city's walls I may obtain a communication from heaven, shall I not do well to shut up my shop and turn a watchman?" So he sold his mornings to the Philistines, and, shutting up his shop, dedicated his afternoons to the gods. Far afield he wandered, to shaggy wildernesses inhabited by apparitions of the red Indian, to kindly valleys basking in light, now seeking the alien comradeship of the muskrat and the great blue heron, and again the

> "Jest and youthful jollity"

of the bobolink and the buttercups; or, less often, in the village itself he would study the habits of men, "as curious to me as if they had been prairie-dogs." His life was a quest of the Holy Grail, undertaken in all purity of body and mind and soul, and in the fulness of faith and devotion. "We always seem to be living," he felt, "just on the brink of a pure and lofty intercourse," and he would live so alertly as to be ever ready for the slightest relentings of the austere gods of the universe. "No man knoweth," he wrote, "in what hour his life may come."

The hint might issue from any source. "It needs but a few wisps of straw in the sun, or some small word dropped, or that has long lain silent in some book." It might be in the strains of a sparrow, or in the expression of Indian grass, *Sorghum nutans,* which, on one occasion, haunted him for a week "like the glance of an eye," or in an

> Unrecorded beam slanted across
> Some upland pasture where the Johnswort grew,

or in the sudden vision of fresh water above the station on returning to Concord after a trip, or even in the cosmical hum of a mosquito. To one who ranged over the countryside in this conviction, nature could indeed have no monotony; this Izaak Walton of the soul demanded no captured fish, but would be content with faint nibbles or none, for reminiscence and expectation could fill many a dull hour and landscape with golden visions.

Far from holding intercourse with nature easy—to be had whenever he chose to paralyze mind and will so that his sensuous life might mingle with that of nature unhindered—Thoreau was fully aware of the actual elusiveness of nature. "Nature is so reserved!" he exclaims in a mood all too rare in these days of facile intercourse. "She always retreats as I advance." "A momentous silence reigns always in the woods, and their meaning seems just ripening into expression. But alas! they make no haste." This is the open secret of nature. He professes no esoteric initiation; he is no priest of nature, but, like all human beings, a mere layman, absolutely devoted, now and then rewarded with a glimpse of the holy of holies, but a glimpse of a thing so rare, so strange, so perfect, that when it is over it leaves no distinct image. Nature did not hold aloof, he felt, without good reason. If she seemed to bend over him with sympathy, he might as well spare himself the delirium of proximity, for perfect knowledge of her she would never grant.

II

Was not the thing he sought, after all, not out there in nature, in the pine groves and upland grasses, but within his own mind and heart? Steadily conscious as he is of his love of the outward, in his profounder hours Thoreau remembers happily the supremacy of the inward. Man, not nature, is foremost in his view, despite the all but universal impression to the contrary in Thoreau's "public" to-day.

For one thing, it is easily shown that the idealism which, in a crude, sketchy form, served him as a working philosophy, offered every encouragement for a preference of man to nature; "man is all in all, Nature nothing, but as she draws him out and reflects him." He would fain get a side view, he says, a suggestive glimpse of a thing, rather than stare it in the face deliberately, because what really concerns him is not there, but consists in his relation to it. The thing itself is "a mere reflecting surface." All harks back to the spiritual universe within man, all points to the inferiority of the actual. Stirred by the dramatic drowning of Margaret Fuller, he is perplexed at the "singular prominence and importance" commonly attached to the "stream of events which we consent to call actual," and concludes brusquely enough, "I do not think much of the actual. . . . It is a sort of vomit in which the unclean love to wallow." Far more real is "that other mightier stream which carries us along with it." On the one stream our bodies float; on the other, our spirits. That dualistic division is unquestionably Thoreau's normal view. Once, and I think once only, he expressed himself as having faith in the senses because, if we only perfected them, we might see God. "Are we to be put off and amused in this life, as it were with a mere allegory? Is not Nature, rightly read, that of which she is commonly taken to be the symbol merely?" This exaltation of the Flux, dictated by impatience, reminds us of the mood of pantheistic revery which Thoreau now and then indulged. But the conception is even rarer than the mood, and does not count in comparison with the innumerable references to nature as a symbol of spirit.

A familiar statement occurs in the attractive poem entitled "The Inward Morning," of which the first two stanzas read:

> Packed in my mind lie all the clothes
> Which outward nature wears,
> And in its fashion's hourly change
> It all things else repairs.
>
> In vain I look for change abroad,
> And can no difference find,
> Till some new ray of peace uncalled
> Illumes my inmost mind.

Day would not dawn, he says, were it not for this inward morning. In the mind is all; there lie packed all the clothes of nature ("like a young lady's trunk going to Mount Desert," says the lively Channing), and what the mind chooses to wear, or is inspired to wear, determines what the aspect of nature is. "This earth which is spread out like a map around me is but the lining of my inmost soul exposed." "The seasons and all their changes are in me. . . . Almost I believe the Concord would not rise and overflow its banks again, were I not here. After a while I learn what my moods and seasons are. . . . The perfect correspondence of Nature to man, so that he is at home in her!" "Our thoughts and sentiments answer to the revolutions of the seasons, as two cog-wheels fit into each other. A year is made up of a certain series and number of sensations and thoughts which have their language in nature." If I am excited by the roar of a cataract, I may well remember that there is "a waterfall which corresponds even to Niagara somewhere within" me. If I would see my own mind, I look at the sky. Even the smallest things in nature are the counterpart of a spiritual substance within us—"Each humblest plant, or weed, as we call it, stands there to express some thought or mood of ours." "Now I am ice, now I am sorrel," so deftly do we fit each other.

> I am the autumnal sun,
>
> .   .   .   .
>
> I am all sere and yellow,
> And to core mellow.
> The mast is dropping within my woods,
> The winter is lurking within my moods.

Time and space are but forms of thought. "I am time and the world. . . . In me are summer and winter, village life and commercial routine, pestilence and famine and refreshing breezes, joy and sadness, life and death." And he concludes by asking a question that must have taken him a long way—"Why did I invent time but to destroy it?"

Thus, as Thoreau roamed over his Concord countryside, he was, as he knew at bottom, becoming acquainted with himself, with the spiritual universe latent in him as in every man, and not simply with outward nature. This spiritual universe he looked upon as static, fixed for all time, as in Plato, so that his task was to come to know it, rather than, as in the contemporary German philosophy, to create it for himself. He could write, in the German way, "This world is but a canvas to our imaginations"; yet his was no world-positing ego—instinctively, if he had understood Fichte and his followers, he would have shunned that invitation to excess, to infinite longing, to indulgence in the nauseating delights of the lower ranges of human emotion. The idea of correspondence, indeed, meant in his case a veritable discipline. Nature will not reveal man to himself unless he fits himself to perceive the correspondence. He is to rely, not on the outer world of nature, but on his own inner nature—"the pond will not seem like a mountain tarn, but a low pool, a silent muddy water, a place for fishermen." He knew that he could not get the better of nature, drive a shrewd Yankee bargain with such as she: here, as in political economy, he says, supply answers to demand. "Nature does not cast pearls before swine. There is just as much beauty visible to us in the landscape as we are prepared to appreciate —not a grain more." He proceeds to explain this by reminding us of the familiar truth that different persons see different objects in nature, that you see mainly what you are looking for, that when you have once become familiar with the idea, or image, of a plant, for example, you can hardly see anything else. Nature's supply depends on your demand, your fitness to receive. This view accounts, in part, for the discipline of the will and mind to which Thoreau made himself submit.

Depreciating the actual, he asserts roundly that "our thoughts are the epochs in our lives: all else is but as a journal of the winds that blew while we were here." The truly rich man, he says, is he who finds delight in his own thoughts. Such were the Hindus, with their perpetual contemplation. Such was he himself, when the gods were kind. "If I am visited by a thought, I chew that cud each successive morning, as long as there is any flavor in it. Until my keepers shake down some fresh fodder." His life at Walden offered a perfect opportunity for reflection, and well did he use it. Some of his pleasantest hours there, he tells us, were during the interminable rainstorms of spring and autumn, when, confined to his hut, he enjoyed a long evening memorable in its soothing roar of the elements and its sense of solitude, "in which many thoughts had time to take root and unfold themselves." No doubt his thinking assumed various forms: more often syllogistic than Emerson's, it was also more fanciful, and, if not so elevated, was perhaps more flexible. Not often was it idle, inchoate dreaming. There was a backbone in his mind, so to speak, that would bend but not yield completely. Though clothed in images, his thoughts were not the disordered dream of the nerveless sen-

timentalist, but shone before him bright as the world of the
Greek. His mind had clarity, delicacy, grasp, penetration, mas-
culine energy, as his books show. The man who wrote "Walden"
was not given to empty revery, but to genuine reflection and
contemplation.

Wittingly beset by the tyranny of observation, Thoreau
welcomed occasions that encouraged thinking. Walking by
night had at least this advantage, he found, that moonlight
is more favorable to reflection than sunlight. "The intense light
of the sun unfits me for meditation, makes me wander in my
thought; my life is too diffuse and dissipated." Again, he liked
certain unseasonable days in midsummer, when "the coolness
concentrated your thought." Solitude, again, invited fruitful
brooding, as society did not, and he was therefore glad to
spend most of his days apart from men. Observation and reflection together succeeded in worsting the hobgoblin of solitude—a miserable loneliness; for only once in the Walden solitude did Thoreau experience an unpleasant sense of being
alone, and then but "for an hour." The solitude of winter he
rejoiced in, the "dear privacy and retirement and solitude
which winter makes possible"! That was his favorite season, if
he had one, and first of all it stood for the inward life, as his
italics suggest: "Winter, with its *inwardness*, is upon us. A man
is constrained to sit down, and to think." Far from needing a
rich, glowing landscape, he was deeply satisfied with the cold
and barren splendors of winter and of autumn—for "November
Eat-heart" was also very dear to him. He relished a November
day such "as will almost oblige a man to eat his own heart. . . .
Ah, but is not this a glorious time for your deep inward
fires?" He liked to assert that his inward wealth was in steadfast proportion to the outward poverty and dreariness, and
doubtless we may believe him. But, after all, there is an occasion for reflection superior to any of those already mentioned. Thinking he viewed sometimes as the clearing-house
for impressions, or "influences," more or less unconsciously
gathered in his converse with the outer world; and he was
wise enough to recognize that the best place for this clarifica-
tion was within doors. "Out of doors," he confesses, "my
thought is commonly drowned, as it were, and shrunken,

pressed down by stupendous piles of light ethereal influences, for the pressure of the atmosphere is still fifteen pounds to a square inch. I can do little more than preserve my equilibrium and resist the pressure of the atmosphere. I can only nod like the rye-heads in the breeze. I expand more surely in my chamber, as far as expression goes, as if that pressure were taken off; but here outdoors is the place to store influences." His expression expands, he means, of course, because his mind contracts, concentrates. If expansive, partly obedient to the currents of nature, when out of doors, he concentrated within doors, allying himself with that greater stream of the eternities —"The stream I love unbounded flows," to use the phrase of his friend Emerson. In the presence of nature, he prized sounds; in his chamber, silence, "the communing of a conscious soul with itself." Sound, he remarks, is when we hear outwardly, silence when we hear inwardly. Silence, like nearly everything that he rated highly, is thus of man, not of nature: "It takes a man to make a room silent," or, he might have added, to make nature silent.

Despite all his observation, despite the acuteness of his perceptive faculties, he was an ardent votary of what he termed "a kind of Brahminical, Artesian, Inner Temple life." It pleased him to contrast his own piety with the brazen triviality of his fellow-men, who toiled and chattered and bargained and cheated and wallowed in the actual, while he found joy, peace, and certainty in the unchanging real. While they sent forth their "confused *tintinnabulum*," he hearkened to the still voices of Silence and Solitude, and came to his bearings. He was a *Doppelgänger* with a difference, for the part of him that, as he says, was spectator to the rest, ironically forming its own opinions and uttering them, was the universal spirit, "no more I than it is you." Instead of being "wholly involved in Nature," he was subservient to the spirit within. This, and not nature, was the inspirer that he referred to when he suggested that, if he did not keep pace with his companions, it was because he heard a different drummer.

His was no gospel of loafing and inviting the soul. Instead of merely inviting the soul, he would go to bring her, and instead of loafing, he would work unceasingly. *This* was his gospel, rather: "Many of our days should be spent, not in vague expectations and lying on our oars, but in carrying out deliberately and faithfully the hundred little purposes which every man's genius must have suggested to him." There was a grim deliberation and an inflexible faithfulness about everything that Thoreau did; he did not lie on his oars and drift with the current, but sat stiffly at the helm, directing his course with, if anything, an excess of concentration. He knew, if no one else did, where he was going, and in his mastery had a lively contempt for the sentimental mode of life, which, as he puts it, does not set a goal before itself and "cannot build a causeway to its objects," but idly "sits on a bank looking over a bog, singing its desires." The tormenting desires of European romanticism—the sighs, the aching void, the meltings, the sweet abandon, the infinite weariness—were more remote from him than was the common-sense of the eighteenth century. Whatever romantic traits he had were held in check by an intellectual attitude that reminds one of the deists, and an emotional attitude that reminds one of the Puritans.

"All wisdom is the reward of a discipline, conscious or unconscious"; "That aim in life is highest which requires the highest and finest discipline"—in such remarks do we come very close to the essential Thoreau. The straight and narrow way of right living is indicated by one's "genius," or inner light. Obey your genius—obey it fully—and you have submitted to the sternest of taskmasters. Thoreau, at least, did not ask, "What do I desire?" but "What *ought* I to desire—what does that heart of flame within me, unconcerned, disinterested as a judge, demand of me?" So soon as he saw his goal, he proceeded thitherward without rest or deviation.

The goal, of course, was always an inward one. While the sentimentalist tried to escape from his self—losing his sense of separateness by immersion in outward nature, or in the life of a past time, or in the rapt harmony of music, Thoreau unflinchingly stared his self in the face, and studied it. "The art of life! . . . By what disciplines to secure the most life, with what care to watch our thoughts. To observe what transpires, not in the street, but in the mind and heart of me!" Never, in one sense, has there been a more introspective writer than

Thoreau. He watched his mind as a cat watches a mouse hole; and when the thought or feeling ventured forth, he pounced upon it with a skill born of long practice, and recorded it in his journal that night, and there it reposed, one more bit of real life won from chaos. He cared little, as I have said, for the factual world—events, even the largest, if they "transpired" outside his private universe, were insignificant. It did not occur to him that he might inhabit a double universe by bringing "the street" into his private universe and making fast friends of them. People in general committed the error of living in the street, and therefore, it seems, he would see what might be learned by living in his own "mind and heart." If he was not great enough to live wisely in both, he at least lived most thoroughly, most "intensively," in his chosen world. And this world was boundless. He was rarely introspective in the sense that he was solicitous of the welfare and the personal phenomena of Henry David Thoreau; when he looked within, it was to study spirit, soul, mind, the divinity in man. He was often quite indifferent as to Henry David Thoreau, in his absorption in the fragment of the general soul that chanced to dwell in that personality. Whoever can hold his faculties to this high enterprise may be called provincial or narrow in a most limited sense, for the self that is studied is essentially the self of everybody—the universal self.

III

If we apply Sainte-Beuve's method to Thoreau by studying him through his disciples, we shall be brought to the conclusion that he was an anchorless poetic soul drifting in the life of Nature and embracing divinity at will; fervidly worshipping Nature "for her own sake" (whatever that may mean), and spurning everything that is distinctively human. Nothing could be further from the truth. It has been the ill fortune of Thoreau to be most seriously misunderstood by those who have most needed to understand him—those who have sought to imitate or emulate him. Huxley remarked of Newman that one could extract from his writings a veritable book of infidelity; similarly, one could find in Thoreau's work good reason for regarding him primarily as a misanthrope or a "Nature-lover" or almost anything else. But he was more nearly an exponent of humanism than of naturalism. More in the flux than Emerson, and committed, like Emerson, to the romantic doctrine of individualism, he nevertheless shared with Emerson an abiding sense of the universal in man, and, owing to his love of the classics as well as to the Puritan tradition, he had a conception of the spiritual life that perhaps transcends in profundity and elevation (but not in expression) anything to be found in the European romantic movement, including Wordsworth. In comparison with Emerson, moreover, it may be said of him that, if he did not habitually dwell in that high plateau region in which Emerson was ever at home, he yet had a feeling for dialectic that renders him more pungent than Emerson and an instinct for discipline that we do not find in the one genuinely "beautiful soul" of Concord. He is for those who would live in the spirit without ceasing to live in the concrete show world. "Time is but the stream I go a-fishing in. I drink at it; but while I drink I see the sandy bottom and detect how shallow it is. Its thin current slides away, but eternity remains."

The Centenary of Thoreau

ANONYMOUS

Outlook, Vol. 117 (September, 1917), 44.

One hundred years ago Henry David Thoreau was born in Concord, Massachusetts. It is interesting to speculate as to how much of our present understanding and appreciation of nature and of the virtues of simple living can be traced to the influence of this philosopher, who was also a man. No American writer has had a greater influence in helping his countrymen to an appreciation of the proper relation between man and nature, a relationship which since the eighteenth century has had many curious developments.

From the urban civilization of the eighteenth century, through the romantic sentimentalism of those who imagined that they were protesting against the artificialities of the age in which they lived, to the vital friendship between Thoreau and the wild life of Walden Pond is a long journey indeed. The artificial grotto of Pope, the sentimentality of Rousseau, or the mawkish enthusiasm for the simplicity of savage life of Bernardin de Saint-Pierre—even perhaps Thomson's love of nature or Gray's appreciation of the wild beauty of the Alps— belong in a very different world from that which has been made familiar to us and a part of our daily lives through the message of Thoreau. The dividing line between these two worlds is not a difficult one to draw.

On the one hand there is imitation, insincerity, sentimentality, and, at the best, little more than the appreciation of an outsider who observes with pleasure a phenomenon apart from his own life. On the other side of the line there is originality, sincerity, sentiment, and an appreciation of the fundamental unity of man and nature—a unity which demands neither the renunciation of nature for the sake of civilization nor a renunciation of civilization for the sake of nature.

Thoreau was never guilty of proclaiming a savage state better than a state of civilization, but he harbored a clear understanding of the deficiencies of the civilization of his time and a tremendous longing to bring within its limits the boundless advantages which come to those who free themselves from the dictates of materialism and who place a true value upon the cultivation of the imagination.

Thoreau played a part in the warfare against low public ideals, and a still more important part in proving by his private life the possibility of putting those ideals within the reach of the average conscience.

As the inevitable charges of "peculiarity" which always attend the progress of a man of genius have died out of the public discussion of the message of Thoreau, he stands forth as one of the greatest and most inviting figures in our literary history. It is not too much to say of Thoreau, as did Emerson: "Here is a Damascus blade of a man such as you may search through nature in vain to parallel."

NEWELL CONVERS WYETH (1882-1945), American painter, provided the illustrations for *Men of Concord and Some Others, As Portrayed in the Journal of Henry David Thoreau,* ed. Francis H. Allen (1936). Many of the originals for this volume are now preserved in the Concord Free Public Library. Dislike for Thoreau in 1919, Wyeth contended, rested on persistent misapprehensions about him.

Thoreau, His Critics, and the Public

N. C. WYETH

The Thoreau Society Bulletin, No. 37 (October, 1951). Though this essay was written in 1919, it remained unpublished until it was read by Mr. Anton Kamp at the annual meeting of the Thoreau Society in 1951. A section composed largely of quotations from Thoreau has been deleted.

I have been an enthusiastic student of Thoreau for twelve or fourteen years, which of course is not an impressively long period, but of sufficient length in which to have learned how comparatively few people read him and how superficially and falsely the large majority of these few accept him.

To so many Thoreau is merely interesting. His personal singularities or eccentricities, so called, furnishing not much more than amusement—his marvelous clarity of thought and expression so astonishingly pertinent to this levelling and tragical age is passed over almost casually.

Perhaps I am too severe, but after considerable seeking and observation, I can come to no milder conclusions.

On the other hand, I have noted with the deepest satisfaction that the few serious students of his works with whom I have chanced to talk are invariably and tremendously impressed by the extraordinary amount of foundation truth, the wealth of inspirational appeal and the exquisite and vigorous beauty they find in his writings.

It is an old, old story, that many of the masters in art have suffered unutterably for the lack of appreciation and understanding, their labors to prevail only years after they die; but seldom has an author suffered the calumny of such bitter criticism from powerful and influential contemporaries; and added to this the persistent and hidebound misrepresentation by his publishers, a force which continues unabated to this day. Of this last I shall speak later.

Thoreau's bitterest contemporary, James Russell Lowell, in his well-known and oft-quoted critical essay, declared the sage of Walden Pond a "charlatan," his constant seeking for solitude a "theatricalet" and his shanty life in the Walden Woods a "pastoral masquerade." And this within five years after Thoreau's death!

One cannot suppress the feeling that Lowell in this critique betrayed certain of his own limitations, if not, then there certainly are in it traces of malignant misconception.

The perfect revealment of the complete Thoreau is now before the world in the fourteen volumes of his JOURNALS, published in 1906, and these constitute an unanswerable denial of Lowell's disastrous comments.

It was Mr. John Galsworthy I think who called this particular essay "one of the most pitiful ineptitudes in literature" and the same can almost be repeated of Stevenson's "Thoreau" which appeared in the popular series called FAMILIAR STUDIES in which he creates of his subject a man of iron coldness, a forbidding companion in the fields or in his books. He called Thoreau "dry, priggish and selfish who has none of that large unconscious geniality of the world's heroes." From the point of view of diverting sociability (in which Stevenson excelled) this may be a just judgment, but in Thoreau's expansion of *self* he meant business—the magnificent results in his books are unimpeachable testimony to his rightness. . . .

No, Thoreau was not "dry and priggish," and his "selfishness" so-called, was highly justified as an all-important factor in the complete unfolding of his particular genius.

Stevenson all but scoffs at the paltry number of half a dozen books, which at that time was all to represent Thoreau's twenty-five years or more of literary endeavor. But one can readily account for this comment from the prolific Scot. The fact that Thoreau's greatest works (what became the fourteen volumes of his JOURNALS) were not published until later gives one a certain delicious satisfaction in the light of Stevenson's little thrust. One cannot resist drawing certain comparative symbols from this incident on contrasting the two men.

So, in a great measure, these two, Lowell and Stevenson, are responsible for the barrier that stands between Thoreau and the large reading public. Lowell's voice is perhaps the most influential American voice in the cultured circles of England today and it has been so for fifty years—consequently he is deeply regarded here; and Stevenson's attractive, blind writing on almost any topic reaches every one. They constitute a powerful tandem of opposition which will take years and years to overcome; but one feels encouraged indeed when THE LONDON SPECTATOR vouchsafes that "the influential value and intrinsic beauty of Thoreau is steadily ascending, threatening, ever so soon, to eclipse that of his famous contemporary, Emerson."

But no author living or dead is known to his contemporaries. The spirit eludes and even now the felicitous last word is still to be said. It is this fascination of expectancy that gives to the proper study of the author's life, character, and opinions its special charm of lastingness.

To the genuine student the discrepancies and contradictions of criticisms will drive him from the critics to the author himself, but almost all the prominent criticisms of Thoreau have in them a sort of fatal animadversion that leaves its subject withered and dead.

There was super-courageousness in Thoreau which seemed to get on the nerves of his fellow writers; even Emerson shuddered and made a face when the pungency of his young neighbor's virility of *words plus action*—assailed the serenity of his study. And one finds a clue to this genial man's uneasiness by an admission in his diary wherein he commends Thoreau the Naturalist because he practiced what Emerson the Philosopher preached! . . .

The other serious misrepresentation of Thoreau to the public, created and fostered by the publishers, to which I referred in opening this paper, is, in my mind a more insidious interruption to the public's reading and understanding of his message than any of the others referred to.

Boston, during that remarkable period of intellectual brilliancy and literary productivity was really dependent to a large degree upon the stimulus that radiated from Concord. No debates, conferences, or dinners were complete without representatives from this town; and it is said that owing to the non-existence of midnight trains to Concord, all functions of any special intellectual significance provided a waiting carriage as a matter of course, to convey the distinguished guests back to their homes.

It was not long before literary Boston got down on all fours to their neighbors in the north, and a glamour, almost a legendary glamour seemed to fall upon the little town like a veil.

Emerson of course was the very hub of the Transcendental wheel—even more, one commentator called all the other celebrities of Concord "pistillate plants kindled to fruitage by the Emerson pollen." They treated Emerson as though all the gods of Olympus had put on clean linen when he was moulded —an admiration that dwindled into adulation.

Particularly were the Boston publishers affected in this way, and the smaller lights, "the hangers on," broke into profuse print, writing endless newspaper articles, pamphlets, and magazine editorials upon one or the other of these men and women. Margaret Fuller, Bronson Alcott—the hero of Fruitlands, Hawthorne, Ephraim Bull, Channing, Judge Hoar—and also Wendell Phillips, Garrison, Agassiz, Longfellow and Holmes, although these latter were not strictly of Concord they became so identified with its atmosphere as to be considered of that charmed circle, and lastly Thoreau.

These men and women were soon classified and pigeonholed in the local public's mind—Emerson, Philosopher—Hawthorne, Novelist—Bull, Horticulturist—Hoar, Jurist, etc. with a sort of transcendental nimbus hovering over all of them. Thoreau they relegated to the naturalist class with a little of the "stoic" thrown in for good measure. Emerson constantly told absurd tales to Agassiz of Thoreau's superlative powers of observation; and of miracles, miracles which never happened! Of fishes that would swim to Thoreau's submerged hand and rest within it—in a sort of communion I suppose; of birds that followed him through the woods, of pines that caressed him with their lips. Emerson must have believed these stories for some of them appear in his otherwise delightful essay on his neighbor and friend.

And so Thoreau was stamped as the *Naturalist*.

Years ago when I asked my grandfather, who was a prominent Swiss Horticulturist in Massachusetts and who had associated with Louis Agassiz and Ephraim Bull during the propagation of the now famous Concord Grape, what he had thought of Thoreau, he answered, absently, with that shrug of the shoulders so typical of the foreigner—"Oh—Amateur Naturalist!" My grandfather had in all probability talked with Thoreau, but doubtless Thoreau listened mostly and gave out little clue to his deeper interests.

In all forewords and prefaces that appear in the various editions of his books, this *Naturalist* idea dominates almost to the complete exclusion of Thoreau the poet. And particularly of that which he stands for first, last, and always—philosophy— *pertinent, practical* and *profound.* Even the last handsome edition of his complete works, which contains a long introductory article by Bradford Torrey, is devoted in great part to a veritable cross-examination of the sage of Walden as an ornithologist. Even our valuable John Burroughs is constantly harping upon the mistakes of his bird observations, and can never seem to grasp the comparative insignificance of this phase of Thoreau's study. Mark Van Doren in his splendid critical study of Thoreau says of Mr. Burroughs, "He has never been quite able to understand what Thoreau was doing and has been content to observe that 'he put the whole of Nature between himself and his fellows!' "

The effect of all this upon the public (and particularly upon that very important part of the public, the younger generation in their formative period) has been utterly discouraging, for if there is anything more dry, dusty and more unattractive than the categorical notes of a scientific observer of birds, flowers and trees, I don't know it.

I grew up under the shade of Concord and consequently heard a great deal of the celebrities who had lived there, but I was made to feel a strong distaste for Thoreau, and had mental visions of a rusty, crusty old hack wandering about the fields and woods with a green specimen can on his back, professional spectacles on his face, and a pair of bird glasses forever in his hand. But Thoreau, as he lay on his back watching a soaring hawk, revelling in the celestial beauty of its movements against the white clouds, had exclaimed—"Why should I want to know the length of its entrails!" Contrary to the impressions I carried for years and which I find are common to many, his real warmth when the fire burns is irresistible. Listen, for instance, to this sentence, characteristically combining his ornithological interests with his poetic instincts—"The song sparrow is heard in fields and pastures, setting the midsummer to music: —as if it were the music of a mossy rail or fence-post." To him soaring hawks were "kites without strings" and when he and his companion are traveling across country, keeping out of the sight of houses, yet compelled to traverse here and there a farmer's field, they "shut every window with an apple tree." Gems like these lie thick upon his counter.

But there are more useful things than jewels to be found in Thoreau's stock, there are real tonics to brace a man when he is weary, to cleanse his vision until he sees the heights again —and there are blisters and plasters in great variety and of warranted strength to make a man repent the lowness of his aims and the vulgarity of his satisfactions.

In Thoreau we find, preeminently, moral wisdom, the foundation source of the arts in general, especially the art of life.

ODELL SHEPARD (1884-1967), biographer, critic, editor, poet, was from 1917 to 1946 Goodwin Professor of English at Trinity College. He is the author of many books, among them *Pedlar's Progress; The Life of Bronson Alcott* (1937). "Two things must be done for Thoreau before he can take his due place as one of the three or four most original men of letters America has produced," Shepard observed in 1920: first, "get him out of the Emerson shadow," and second, "make it clear that he was not a naturalist."

The Paradox of Thoreau

ODELL SHEPARD

Scribner's Magazine, Vol. 68 (September, 1920), 335-42.

Among the belongings of Henry David Thoreau which are shown to the visitor in Concord—his bed, his chair and writing-desk, his quill, and the buckskin suit given him by an Indian friend—is a curious walking-stick which was cut from a cherry-tree seventy years ago by a man who knew how to use a jack-knife. There are few pieces of dead wood that one would give more to possess. It has gone walking with Emerson and Hawthorne; it has "travelled much in Concord," as also in Sudbury, Lincoln, Acton, and Billerica; it may have climbed Monadnock or tapped its way through the Tuckerman Ravine; it has been intimate with a man who allowed few intimacies, and that in his best moments, when he was alone in swamp or forest or out with the moon at midnight listening to the baying of dogs in distant farmsteads.

Despite these noble memories, however, it is a very ordinary walking-stick except in the particular that it has been whittled flat along one side and notched to the length of twenty-four inches. Here, indeed, is a peculiarity. Usually, when one takes his walking-stick from the corner, he slams the door on mathematics and cuts across lots, content to measure distances by simple fatigue and hunger and thirst. But here is a stick which combines rambling with routine. It can measure a mountain or a field-mouse. It can either ignore boundaries or make them. In short, it is a most self-contradictory, paradoxical stick, and a perfect representative, therefore, of the vagabond-surveyor who cut and carried it.

What were the gods about when they condemned this dreamer, this leaper of fences, this scorner of property, to earn his living by surveying other men's woodlots? Hear the man whose name is set down on one of the best maps of Concord as "H. D. Thoreau, Civ. Engr." sighing for "a people who would burn the fences and let the forest stand"! And yet, although the fact has not been recognized by those who can see in him only a misanthropic lover of the wild, Thoreau was quite as much interested in fences as in forests. It was no condemnation of the gods, but just the conflict of two deadly opposites deep-rooted in his mind, which drove him from forests to fences, from dreams to mathematics, from walking-sticks to measuring-rods, and back again. Finally he learned to combine the two. In that strange combination lies the secret of his genius.

All that may be charged against the gods in the case of

Thoreau is that they confined a Yogee and a Yankee, a mystic and a mathematician, a seer and a surveyor, in one human skin —and then prepared themselves for amusement. Undoubtedly there was something grandly humorous in the combination—

> "Yet half a beast is the great god Pan
> To laugh as he sits by the river,
> Making a poet out of a man"!

Up from the struggle thus foreordained in Thoreau rose the bubbles of his perennial paradox. Thence came his weather-cock moods and fancies. All his life long the surveyor kept up with the seer in him an endless colloquy, of which the twenty volumes of his published works are a stenographic report. Thoreau the seer rambled about all his life long with a walking-stick, but Thoreau the surveyor used it as a measuring-rod.

How much can be done with a measuring-rod two feet in length depends upon the man who carries it. Holding his at arm's length, Thoreau saw that it seemed taller than Monad-nock and longer than the Milky Way. Thus he learned perspec-tive. What was near at hand always bulked huge and momen-tous to him, but the distances dwindled swiftly to a point. He sedulously kept this naïve innocence of the eye, allowing no intrusion of the abstract intelligence to correct its simple ver-dict. The central and most remarkable thing about him, indeed, was a sort of inspired frugality, an ability to make a very little go a great way, to make what he had suffice. New England thrift found in this man whose "greatest wealth was to want but little" its most shining example. No man ever scanned his pennyworth more narrowly, no man ever drove a shrewder Yankee bargain with the world, no man was ever framed to get better service out of a two-foot measure than he.

Concord itself was a two-foot measuring-rod, as Thoreau well enough knew, but he held it up against Babylon and Rome and dwarfed them to a speck. Thus he became the very apothe-osis of the provincial. All his triangulations were calculated with the main street of his village as a base; the centre of all his circles was just the village spire. This meant, at the least, that in the midst of a nomadic and deracinated generation

Thoreau *had* a centre, and that his triangles had one fixed and certain term. His provincialism was not without elements of humor and whim, but it had much of wisdom also. Concord was a small enough part of the world for one to learn something about it in a lifetime, but it was typical of all the rest. The man who had studied religion in its meeting-house, law in its town hall, commerce on the Musketaquid, trade on Main Street, and society in its parlors, had not much to learn from wider travels. He had seen the elements. The great world could offer him nothing but repetition.

Thoreau made such use of his opportunities that nothing Concordian, at last, was alien to him. In order to become a true citizen of the world, then, he had only to learn that nothing was alien to Concord, whether it happened in Main Street or Texas, at Walden Pond or on the Congo. It may fairly be said that he did learn this. The John Brown episode and the ever increasing pressure of the slave question taught him that even the tiny creek on which he lived must feel the tides of the sea. So long as the influence of slavery came no nearer than Boston he was not much concerned; for Boston, fifteen miles away, had always been a semi-foreign city to him, concerning which he was cheerfully prepared to believe the worst. But when he saw that his own town could not escape this evil thing, he was instantly on the alert. Despite his hatred of newspapers, he suddenly found that no man can afford to neglect *The Times* in favor of the Eternities, for the reason that there is no clear division between the two. Despite his hatred of politics, he astonished the townsfolk with two of the most passionate political speeches that came out of the war—"Civil Disobedience" and "Slavery in Massachusetts." These speeches reveal a mind suddenly made aware that no little town liveth unto itself alone and show how expansile a true provincialism may be at need. Provincial they are, however, for all their wide purview, illustrating a phase of patriotic feeling in comparison with which our present federalism and our incipient internationalism are in their infancy. In the last analysis, they urge nothing less than the secession of Concord from the Union. But if Concord would not secede, Thoreau would—and did. It is worthy of note that when he went to jail rather than pay a small tax to the

national government which he thought was supporting slavery, he cheerfully paid a larger one for the maintenance of town roads.

Thoreau's boastful provincialism and professed contempt for travel may seem to some readers a mere crying of sour grapes. From Lowell's essay on Thoreau—which some one has called, a bit too harshly, "the work of an extraordinarily brilliant snob"—one gets the idea that the man's limitations were first imposed upon him and then glorified by his egotism. Lowell states the view, plausible enough in Boston, which assumes that all men really want the same things and that every man must be bitterly chagrined who does not get these things. But this has never been the Concord view, and it was not Thoreau's. What all men are supposed to want he was unusually well equipped to get, had he not thought the price too high. "It takes a man of genius," he says, "to travel in his own country, in his native village—to make progress between his door and his gate. But such a traveller will make the distances which Hanno and Marco Polo and Cook and Ledyard went over seem ridiculous." Always thus, with a courageous and admiring eye upon his own limitations, he makes them shine with the lustre of special advantages. Nothing in Fate's quiver can harm such a man.

Thoreau was armed in triple bronze by the stern delight he took in the very meagreness of his resources. In his lucid intervals, which were frequent enough, he must have seen that Concord was not in fact exceptionally favored by the gods. "But what a faculty must that be," he says, "which can paint the most barren landscape and humblest life in glorious colors! It is pure invigorated senses reacting upon a sound and strong imagination. Is not that the poet's case?" Precisely. And was it not his own? The less there was of promise in his raw material, the greater was the challenge of the artist's passion in him —to that passion which always strives to achieve maximum results with the minimum of means. Thus he strove to find each day a new significance and beauty in that which he saw for the millionth time, setting himself to such severe ascetic training that he became, in the dew-clear delicacy of his five senses, a sort of Spartan Keats.

No one need hope to understand Thoreau who does not see that his limitations were, for the most part, self-imposed. How cheerfully, at all events, he speaks of them! "The old coat that I wear is Concord," he writes to a friend. "It is my morning robe and study gown, my working dress and suit of ceremony. And it will be my nightgown after all." In the case of so complete a devotion it was natural that the environment should powerfully mould the man, and there is, in fact, scarcely any major quality of Thoreau's thought or style which is not referable, at least remotely, to the fact of his lifelong residence in a New England village. Of this man who might so easily have been a dull philosopher, Concord made almost a poet by teaching him the uses and beauty of the actual, by providing a firm soil of the concrete for the anchors of his transcendentalism to grapple in. His desire to make a complete inventory of the town's resources may have been antecedent even to that passion for Nature for which he is chiefly known—and this may be the reason why he "spoke of Nature as though she had been born and brought up in Concord." Firm grip upon reality was what the transcendentalists most needed. The fact that Thoreau had it seems due in no small degree to the influence of his native town. He begs his friend Ricketson, who is writing a history of New Bedford, to "let it be a local and villageous book. That is the good old-fashioned way of writing, as if you actually lived where you wrote." Working on this sound theory, Thoreau himself often makes us hear almost the very throb of his pulse. He writes in his Journal: "I am living this 27th of June, 1847—a dull cloudy day and no sun shining. The clink of the smith's hammer sounds feebly over the roofs, and the wind is sighing gently. The farmer is ploughing in yonder fields, craftsmen are busy in the shops, the trader stands up in the counter, and all works go steadily forward." Is there not a startling actuality in these words, as though the dead man were whispering in one's ear? Such sentences, like a few in Samuel Pepys, seem to crumple time and space.

Concord did other important things for Thoreau. Consider, for example, his persistent trick, amounting almost to a vice, of likening small things to great and great to small. It is not fanciful to attribute even this, his habitual exaggeration, to the influence of his village life. If you live in a microcosm, you will have to exaggerate enormously to make others see what it means to you. If you survey the universe with a two-foot rod, you will have to use it as though it were a slide-rule. Thus every trifle became tremendous to Thoreau. For the almost pathetic poverty of his materials he made himself a rich amends in the gorgeous uses he put them to. Extraordinarily frugal in other matters, he was a spend-thrift in his thought and style, reminding one of Carlyle's remark: "Sense can support herself handsomely for eighteen-pence a day; but for Fantasy planets and solar systems will not suffice." The minute changes of scene noticeable in dropping down the Musketaquid from Concord to Lowell were to Thoreau's eyes like a panorama of foreign lands. He speaks of the men of Bedford and Billerica, two or three miles over the hills from where he sits writing, as of strange and unaccountable dwellers in Ultima Thule. Thus he gets his romantic distances, both of space and time, on remarkably cheap terms, making a little go a great way. The results of this magnifying habit of mind often border the grotesque, as where he speaks of the raindrop which struck the right slope of his nose and ran down the ravine there, remarking: "Such is the origin of rivers." But this is the source, too, of some of his best things: "Ever and anon the lightning filled the damp air with light, like some vast glow-worm in the fields of ether, opening its wings"—a simile which it would be hard to better, except for the negligible detail that the glow-worm has no wings.

It is still the general impression that Thoreau made next to nothing of the fact that the little town in which he spent his life was inhabited by human beings. Mr. John Burroughs, in his essay on "Thoreau's Wildness," says that he appears to have been as stoical and indifferent and unsympathetic as a veritable Indian. This is the view which was given currency by Emerson's essay and which his selection of Thoreau's letters seemed to corroborate. It was unhesitatingly accepted by Robert Louis Stevenson and was spread broadcast by his paper on Thoreau. Nevertheless, this opinion will not stand against the almost universal testimony of those who knew the man best—and it is worthy of notice that he had through-out his life an unusual number of close friends. It is stag-gered by his essays on Friendship and on Love, in comparison with which those of Emerson seem cold and formal. It be-comes grotesque in the light of certain letters—say those to Mrs. Lydian Emerson—which were published by Mr. Frank Sanborn.

Undoubtedly there was too much ego in Thoreau's cos-mos. He liked to think himself the sole spectator for whom Nature's pictures were painted, and he would have understood the sharp twinge of jealousy with which Wordsworth always heard any other person make mention of mountains. If his neighbors had obeyed his denunciatory exhortations and taken to living in the woods and fields, that, if anything, would have made him leave Concord. Yet he had by no means the qualities necessary to a successful hermit. The source of his chronic ir-ritation at mankind was not misanthropy. It was, perhaps, even the reverse. He had hoped more from human nature than it could give, habitually forgetting our frame that we are dust. He was always on the lookout for better bread than is made of good wheat flour, having in his mind's eye some Platonic loaf which had soured, for him, all others. Ten miles down the river, he could think most lovingly of his fellows, but in the parlor at Emerson's house the demon of negation so ruled his mem-bers that even the master of that house once said, with well-nigh paternal forbearance: "Henry is with difficulty sweet." The perfect motto for Thoreau would have been *Noli me tangere.* Both for better and for worse, he never learned to say "Yes."

Toward the world outside of Concord and the whole ques-tion of his social duty, also, Thoreau seemed indifferent, but was not. He had been in that breathless audience which heard Emerson's address on the "American Scholar" at Harvard in the year of Thoreau's graduation—one of those young men who listened "as if a prophet were proclaiming to them 'Thus saith the Lord,'" and who resolved that they too should be, in the noble phrase of the speaker, "delegated minds." No man went from that room, not even the speaker himself, who adhered more closely in later life to the spirit and letter of the address than did Thoreau. While the merchants of Concord bought and sold, while the farmers ploughed and reaped, he sat in the doorway of his cabin, thinking. Diogenes in his tub personified no more exasperating challenge and rebuke. In that very place where, as it is written, a prophet is without honor, there Thoreau deliberately sat down and stayed—"in his own country, and among his own kin, and in his own house." The moral courage, the hardening of purpose, the stiffening of character, which this involved must be evident enough. Not ten men in America could have fully understood what he was about, and not even many women. Margaret Fuller damned his manuscripts with faint praise, Elizabeth Hoar edged the scalpel of her wit upon him, the grocers of Concord sent him on errands. It was very hard to explain to a world which had not felt the need of such a thing that he was a "delegated mind." He made no explanations whatever, but went on thinking at the rate of a volume of Journal notes per year, keeping in the midst of the crowd, although not with perfect sweetness, the independence of solitude.

What did it all come to in the end, this experiment of Thoreau's in vigorous independence and intensive self-culture, these forty-five years of devotion to lofty ideals, of high thinking, of living "as delicately as one plucks a flower"? He gave up in his pursuit of happiness nearly all that other men cared for —wealth, fame, ease, and pleasure. The crucial question is: Was he happy? Now, although he asserts that he was so with almost damnable iteration, one cannot finally stifle a doubt. One wishes that the high color which he always wears were more certainly the glow of health. He often felt the rare joy of mere passive being, he had his "ecstatic moments" and his hours of transfiguration, but one fears that he seldom knew the sober and durable pleasure that comes of pulling one's full weight in the world's united effort. Moreover, he was a reformer without a programme, a worshipper of the deed who never began to act. Here, one would say, is a formula for misery. But when we conclude that a given man cannot be anything but miserable, we are likely to overlook the prevalence of hope. As a matter of fact, Thoreau came near to a steady radiance of joy through his invincible expectation of better things. He always felt it possible that to-morrow's dawn might broaden over paradise, and all that he ever said of the actual grovelling of men is atoned for by his hopes of what men might become. He loved to think that the life in us, like the water in the river, might rise higher this year than ever before, and drown out all the muskrats. "Give me the old familiar walk," he said, "post-office and all—and this ever-new self, this infinite expectation and faith which does not know when it is beaten." With this one weapon of hope he fended off unweariedly "that defeat which the present always seems," and it was only this which made him able to say that he loved his fate to the very core and rind. Concerning his final success in life we have his own words, perhaps the most memorable that he ever penned: "If the day and the night are such that you greet them with joy, and life emits a fragrance like flowers and sweet-scented herbs, is more elastic, more starry, more immortal—that is your success."

Two things must be done for Thoreau before he can take his due place as one of the three or four most original men of letters America has produced. The first of these is to get him out of the Emersonian shadow. Superficial readers, learning that both the Concord writers were "transcendentalists," but that Emerson was in some vague way the American leader of the school, remembering that Thoreau was Emerson's junior by fourteen years, that he lived some time in Emerson's house, and built his Walden cabin on Emerson's land, that in his youth he resembled Emerson even in voice and manner, have drawn the natural conclusion that Thoreau shone with only a lunar light. It is as impossible to confute as it is to justify this specious conclusion on *a priori* grounds. The two men read the same books, walked the same streets, talked to the same persons, for many years—and that at a time when Concord practised a sort of communism in the realm of ideas. Moreover, the two men talked interminably with each other. Who can say that Emerson was less likely to appropriate a flashing thought or sentence from the younger man, whose agile and germinal intelligence he greatly admired, than Thoreau was to give the lie to all his proud boast of independence by servile imitation of the master? The fact is, as Moncure Conway says

in his absorbing "Autobiography," that "Thoreau was an imitator of no mortal." But the minds of critics and of the public
are now so finally made up on this subject that perhaps no
mere statement of facts can change them. We have here simply
another example of that injustice whereby the towering protagonist of epic or romance slowly gathers into his own cycle
all the exploits of lesser heroes. "To him that hath shall be
given."

Turning to the writings of the two men, one finds, amid
much similarity of thought and expression which is easily ex-
plicable as the result of common influences playing upon them
both, a difference in philosophy which is radical and wide-
spreading. "Trust the instinct to the end," says Emerson,
"though you can render no reason." This is strongly countered
by Thoreau's sentence: "Man's life consists not in his obedience
but in his opposition to his instincts." Says Emerson: "Place
yourself in the middle of the stream of power and wisdom
which animates all whom it floats, and you are without effort
impelled to truth and right, and to a perfect contentment."
Thoreau's words on the same general topic have not the sound
of a feeble echolalia: "I cannot afford to relax discipline because God is on my side, for He is on the side of discipline."
Even in these contrasted quotations we catch a glimpse of one
good reason for the fact that while Emerson has been widely
popular for eighty years, Thoreau, in his deeper and more significant pages, has scarcely been read. Thoreau does not flatter
the sluggard in us. He could not float with any stream. Wherever he found a current, he began to swim against it. As Emerson
wistfully pointed out, he had *muscle*—mental and moral muscle
as well as physical. Emerson seems to have lived upon celestial
capital stored for him by the supererogatory virtue of his ancestors. Thoreau earned his way. He laid an uncomfortable and
unpopular emphasis upon practice, being chiefly remarkable
among the Concord philosophers for the fact that he lived his
philosophy. "To be a philosopher," he says, voicing a truth
which has been largely forgotten since the time of Socrates,
"is to solve some of the problems of life not only theoretically
but practically." That was a significant scene which was enacted
one morning at Concord jail, in which Thoreau had spent the

night after refusing to pay his poll-tax. Deeply shocked and grieved, Emerson peered through the bars and said: "Henry, why are you here?" Instantly came back the Yankee reply: "Waldo, why are you *not* here?"

It is hard to do full justice to Thoreau without some appearance of injustice to the man who was unquestionably, in almost all respects, his superior. If it seems that Thoreau was in some ways a better exponent of Emersonianism than Emerson was himself, that may be due to the fact that he travelled with lighter luggage. The simple fact is that Emerson rendered Thoreau the highest service any teacher can give by setting the young man free—to go his own way. For this, and for the lifelong stimulus of Emerson's presence, Thoreau gave his friend the loving reverence which all men gave, and which was inevitable. "One needs must love the highest when one sees it."

The second thing to be done for Thoreau is to make it clear that he was not a naturalist, and did not even wish to be one. He was afraid that the scientist in him might starve out the poet, that the fences might overcome the forest. "I fear," he says, "that my knowledge is from year to year becoming more exact and scientific; that, in exchange for views as wide as heaven's cope, I am being narrowed down to the microscope." There is nothing here of that self-immolating devotion of the scientist which enabled Charles Darwin to sit quietly by and watch the slow atrophy of one whole side of his nature. Neither is there anything resembling the method of the modern scientist in Thoreau's choice of field. He seems to have been about equally interested in birds and fishes, turtles and lichens, flowers and rocks, weather and ants, mountains and woodchucks. The very range of his study, most of which was necessarily superficial, shows that his heart was not in that patient accumulation of fact by which science was in his time plodding toward its unknown goal. He would be more in sympathy with the biology of our own day, which more and more subordinates description and classification of species to the quest of ultimate laws and principles. When he was asked by a certain society what branch of science he was especially interested in, he wrote in his Journal: "I felt that it would be to make myself a laughing-stock to describe to them that branch which especially interests me, inasmuch as they do believe in a science which deals with the higher law. . . . How absurd that though I probably stand as near to Nature as any of them, and am by constitution as good an observer as most, yet a true account of my relation to Nature should excite their ridicule only."

What, then, was his real relation to Nature? Fundamentally, it was a religious one. He saw the material world more clearly than the mystics, but far more imaginatively, also, and under a holier light, than the ordinary scientist. Nature was to him chiefly "a means and a symbol." It was less a scientific than a religious impulse which kept him pressing on, chiefly by the way of intuition, toward the final Mystery of Things and the innermost Holy of Holies. He was always on the trail of his famous Horse and Hound.

In roving tirelessly about the woods and fields on this high quest, he picked up large stores of information and misinformation concerning matters to which scarcely any one in America had paid any attention. It was natural that his woodcraft and powers of observation should be exaggerated by the bookish persons about him who had neither the one nor the other, and that a legend should grow about his name in this way which could not sustain the attacks of those who have followed precisely the trails he blazed. His instruments were few and poor, he had no guides and few competitors, he had never known what we understand by scientific training. The result has been no little innocent amusement to professional and amateur scientists in correcting his many blunders and in wondering that he did not know this and that. But they attack a straw man. The real Thoreau wrote in his Journal: "Man cannot afford to be a naturalist, to look at Nature directly, but only with the side of his eye. He must look through and beyond her."

Doubtless Thoreau would have been glad to solve the mystery of his "night-warbler." Once he had done so, however, he would have moved on at once into some other parish of the Infinite. His ignorance was really more useful to him than his knowledge. One can imagine him smiling benignly at the ladies and gentlemen who scramble through thicket and swamp, opera-glass in hand, and complacently set down in their field-books at the end of a weary chase: "*Siurus auricapillus,* un-known to Thoreau." One can almost hear him murmur those helpful words of his friend's:-"When me they fly, I am the wings."

But if Thoreau was not a naturalist, then what was he? He was a practical philosopher, constantly asking and trying to answer the most important question of all: how to live. This fact, patent enough to one who reads him without prepos-session, has been neglected in our idle gossip about his knowl-edge or ignorance of Nature. It has been obscured by the ma-lign sarcasms of Lowell's essay. Even in the brilliant biographi-cal sketch which Emerson wrote shortly after Thoreau's death we see the man already fading swiftly into myth. The result is that certain words of that sketch are as true to-day, and in a double sense, as they were when written: "The country knows not yet, or in the least part, how great a son it has lost."

Thoreau is still lost to us. We have been bemused these sixty years by a mere legend about him. The country has yet to learn that it had in him not merely an amusing eccentric, not merely a shining target for the arrows of critical wit, but one of the few primary thinkers and teachers we have pro-duced. For here was a man who stood with his head in the clouds, perhaps, but with his feet firmly planted on actual rubble and grit. He was "true to the kindred points of Heaven and Home." Here was a mind with a most unusual combination of accuracy with range, of audacious fancy with severe fidel-ity to fact—a mind that brought telescopic findings to bear upon the most microscopic field and took soundings of the In-finite from a cockboat. Here was a life in which the physical daring of our earlier frontiersmen turned inward and became a sort of spiritual pioneering. Of this man and mind and life we have made chiefly a spectacle and a laughing-stock, ignor-ing the fact that Thoreau's eminently practical thought was really concerned, in the last analysis, solely with definite hu-man problems. The major question, how to live, was at the end of all his vistas. He learned something about the woods and fields and something about books, becoming probably the best read man in Concord at a time when that was a distinction; but these studies were always ancillary to his study of man's life. And when he turns upon the human animal those eyes which have grown so keen in watching woodchucks, he can see mankind to the quick with his searching sidelong gaze. It is when he forgets the woodchuck, concerning which others now know more than he did, and begins to speak of men, that it behooves us to listen. We have talked and written more than enough about his misanthropy, his wildness, his solitude, his egoism. The real man, in whom these qualities were superficial and secondary, the man Thoreau whose main business was the application of shrewd common sense to the actual facts of life, has been very generally ignored. For who does not prefer amusement to instruction and, still more, to admonition? Too clearly for our comfort Thoreau saw what ails us, and he prescribed a cure which still seems worse than the disease. Accordingly, we have crunched the mere husk of him and thrown away the kernel.

Much of the blame, however, for the fact that we still regard Thoreau as a mere transcendental wild man must be borne by the man himself. It cannot be denied that he was deliberately "queer," or that, in the midst of solitude, he adjusted his pose with a keen eye for the picturesque, thereby reminding even his admirers of what was said of Châteaubriand, that he "would have liked to live in a hermit's hut upon a public stage." Thoreau never learned, moreover, that self-expression is a social act. He wrote for an audience of one, taking little pains to be clear and still less to be ingratiating. The "celestial homespun" of his style, accordingly, shows many a woful patch and thrum. In a strict sense, he never learned to write, but only to exclaim—his genius, as Emerson said, being better than his talent. If he could always have chosen definite and manageable subjects, as he did in that crisp, compact, and witty paper on "The Landlord," of which Stevenson would have been proud; if he could have taken as models the great French masters of style instead of Hindu visionaries and Teutonizing Englishmen; if he could have made his sentences flow more like a river and less like a moraine of boulders—then he might have been not only a great writer but a *good* one as well.

Even such as he was, with all his faults and foibles upon

him, this odd-chores-man of Concord looms higher year by
year on the horizon of our literature, and is "still loftier than
the world suspects." We may yet learn that he was neither a
naturalist nor an Emersonian echo; he may yet teach us something regarding the sources of a sound and enduring patriotism, something about economy, something about contentment;
but even to-day, imperfectly understood as he still is, he must
be considered as rather more than a picturesque figure. That
ancient warfare of forests and fences, which is all the past of
America, is brought to a vivid and powerful focus in him. He
draws the mystery of the wilderness about our very doors. In
the rude boat which he has made with his own hands he drops
quietly down the River of Commonplace which flows through
our own tame little town, he doubles strange cliffs which are
after all only over the hill, and brings back shining wares from
the next township as though from foreign and almost fabulous
lands. He helps us to be content with what we have by making
us see the glory of the near and familiar. He shows us what
can be done with even a two-foot measuring-rod when it is
carved on a walking-stick.

LEWIS MUMFORD (1895-   ) has interpreted the culture and thought of
America in terms of architecture and literature. He has written a number
of influential books, among them, *Sticks and Stones* (1924), *The Brown
Decades* (1931), and *The Culture of Cities* (1938). "Taking America
as it was," Mumford wrote in 1926, "Thoreau conceived a form, a habitat,
which would retain what was unique in the American contact with the
virgin forest, the cultivated soil, and the renewed institutions of the New
England town."

The Dawn

LEWIS MUMFORD

The Golden Day (New York: Norton, 1926), pp. 107-20.

The pioneer who broke the trail westward left scarcely a trace
of his adventure in the mind: what remains are the tags of pioneer customs, and mere souvenirs of the past, like the Pitts-
burg stogy, which is our living connection to-day with the

Conestoga wagon, whose drivers used to roll cigars as the first covered wagons plodded over the Alleghenies.

What the pioneer felt, if he felt anything, in the midst of these new solitudes; what he dreamt, if he dreamt anything; all these things we must surmise from a few snatches of song, from the commonplace reports issued as the trail was nearing its end, by the generation of Mark Twain and Hamlin Garland, or by the reflections of their sons and daughters, romantically eager, like John G. Neihardt's, critically reflective, like Susan Glaspell's, or wistfully sordid, like Edgar Lee Masters' Anthology. Those who really faced the wilderness, and sought to make something out of it, remained in the East; in their reflection, one sees the reality that might have been. Henry David Thoreau was perhaps the only man who paused to give a report of the full experience. In a period when men were on the move, he remained still; when men were on the make, he remained poor; when civil disobedience broke out in the lawlessness of the cattle thief and the mining town rowdy, by sheer neglect, Thoreau practiced civil disobedience as a principle, in protest against the Mexican War, the Fugitive Slave Law, and slavery itself. Thoreau in his life and letters shows what the pioneer movement might have come to if this great migration had sought culture rather than material conquest, and an intensity of life, rather than mere extension over the continent.

Born in Concord about half a generation after Emerson, Thoreau found himself without the preliminary searchings and reachings of the young clergyman. He started from the point that his fellow-townsman, Emerson, had reached; and where he first cleared out of his mind every idea that made no direct connections with his personal experience, Thoreau cleared out of his life itself every custom or physical apparatus, to boot, which could not stand up and justify its existence. "A native of the United States," De Tocqueville had observed, "clings to the world's goods as if he were certain never to die; and he is so hasty at grasping at all within his reach, that one would suppose he was constantly afraid of not living long enough to enjoy them. He clutches everything, he holds nothing fast, but soon loosens his grasp to pursue fresh gratifications." Thoreau completely reversed this process: it was because he wanted to live fully that he turned away from everything that did not serve towards this end. He prized the minutes for what they brought, and would not exercise his citizenship at the town meeting, if a spring day by Walden Pond had greater promise; nor would he fill his hours with gainful practices, as a maker of pencils or a surveyor, beyond what was needed for the bare business of keeping his bodily self warm and active.

Thoreau seized the opportunity to consider what in its essentials a truly human life was; he sought, in Walden, to find out what degree of food, clothing, shelter, labor was necessary to sustain it. It was not animal hardihood or a merely tough physical regimen he was after; nor did he fancy, for all that he wrote in contempt of current civilization, that the condition of the woodcutter, the hunter, or the American Indian was in itself to be preferred. What he discovered was that people are so eager to get the ostentatious "necessaries" of a civil life that they lose the opportunity to profit by civilization itself: while their physical wants are complicated, their lives, culturally, are not enriched in proportion, but are rather pauperized and bleached.

Thoreau was completely oblivious to the dominant myths that had been bequeathed by the Seventeenth Century. Indifferent to the illusion of magnitude, he felt that Walden Pond, rightly viewed, was as vast as the ocean, and the woods and fields and swamps of Concord were as inexhaustible as the Dark Continent. In his study of Nature, he had recourse on occasion to the scientific botanists and zoölogists; but he himself had possession of a method that they were slow to arrive at; and it is easier for us to-day to understand the metaphysical distinction of Thoreau's kind of nature study than it would have been for Gray or Agassiz. Like Wordsworth before him, like Bergson after him, he realized that in current science "we murder to dissect," and he passed beyond the artful dismemberments of contemporary science to the flower and the bird and the habitat themselves. "Not a single scientific term or distinction," he wrote once in his notebook, "is the least to the purpose. You would fain perceive something and you must approach the object totally unprejudiced. You must be aware that nothing is what you take it to be. . . . Your greatest success will be simply to perceive that such things are, and you will have no communication to make to the Royal Society." In other words, Thoreau sought in nature all the manifold qualities of being; he was not merely in search of those likenesses or distinctions which help to create classified indexes and build up a system. The aesthetic qualities of a fern were as important for his mode of apprehension as the number of spores on a frond; it was not that he disdained science, but that, like the old herbalists and naturalists he admired, he would not let the practical offices of science, its classification, its measurements, its numerations, take precedence over other forms of under-standing. Science, practiced in this fashion, is truly part of a humane life, and a Darwin dancing for joy over a slide in his microscope, or a Pupin, finding the path to physics through his contemplation of the stars he watched as a herdboy through the night, are not poorer scientists but richer ones for these joys and delights: they merely bow to the bias of utilitarianism when they leave these things out of their reports. In his attitude toward scientific truth Thoreau was perhaps a prophetic figure; and a new age may do honor to his metaphysics as well as to his humanity.

The resolute acceptance of his immediate milieu as equal to the utmost that the earth could offer stood by Thoreau in his other activities, too. He captained huckleberry parties as he might have led a battle, and was just as much the leader in one as he would have been in the other. His courage he re-served for better occasions than the battlefield, for he was ready to go to jail for his principles, and to mock Emerson for remaining outside. As for his country, he loved the land too well to confuse it with the shifting territorial boundaries of the National State. In this, he had that vital regional consciousness which every New Englander shared: Hawthorne himself had said that New England was as large a piece of territory as could claim his allegiance. Thoreau was not deceived by the rascality of politicians, who were ready to wage war for a coveted patch of Mexico's land; nor did he side with those who, for the sake of the Union, were ready to give up the principles that alone had made the Union valuable. What he loved was the land-scape, his friends, and his companions in the spirit: when the

Political State presumed to exercise a brass counter-claim on these loyalties it might go to the devil.

Thoreau's attitude toward the State, one must note, was just the opposite to that of the progressive pioneer. The latter did not care what sort of landscape he "located" in, so long as he could salute the flag of his country and cast his vote: Thoreau, on the contrary, was far too religious a man to commit the idolatry of saluting a symbol of secular power; and he realized that the affairs controlled by the vote represented only a small fraction of an interesting life, while so far from being indifferent to the land itself, he absorbed it, as men have absorbed legends, and guarded it, as men preserve ceremonies. The things which his contemporaries took for the supreme realities of life, matter, money, and political rights, had only an instrumental use for Thoreau: they might contribute a little to the arrangement of a good life, but the good life itself was not contained, was not even implied in them. One might spend one's life pursuing them without having lived. "There is not one of my readers," he exclaimed, "who has yet lived a whole human life."

In Thoreau's time, industrialism had begun to puff itself up over its multiplication of goods and the increase of wants that it fostered, in order to provide the machine with an outlet for its ever-too-plentiful supply. Thoreau simply asked: "Shall we always study to obtain more of these things, and not sometimes be content with less?" "If we do not get our sleepers and forge rails and devote long days and nights to work," he observed ironically, "but go tinkering with our lives to improve *them*, who will build the railroads?" Thoreau was not a penurious fanatic, who sought to practice bare living merely as a moral exercise: he wanted to obey Emerson's dictum to save on the low levels and spend on the high ones. It is this that distinguishes him from the tedious people whose whole existence is absorbed in the practice of living on beans, or breathing deeply, or wearing clothes of a vegetable origin: simplification did not lead in Thoreau to the cult of simplicity: it led to a higher civilization.

What drove Thoreau to the solitude of the woods was no cynical contempt for the things beyond his reach. "Before we can adorn our houses with beautiful objects, the walls must be stripped, and our lives must be stripped, and beautiful house-keeping and beautiful living be laid for a foundation: now, a taste for the beautiful is most cultivated out of doors, where there is no house, and no housekeeper." The primeval woods were a favorable beginning for the search; but Thoreau did not think they could be the end of it. The land itself, however, did stir his imagination; he wrote:

> All things invite this earth's inhabitants
> To rear their lives to an unheard of height,
> And meet the expectation of the land.

"The expectation of the land!" One comes upon that phrase, or its equivalent, in almost every valid piece of early American thought. One thinks of moorland pastures by the sea, dark with bayberries and sweet fern, breaking out among the lichened rocks; and the tidal rivers bringing their weedy tang to the low meadows, wide and open in the sun; the purple pine groves, where the needles, bedded deep, hum to the wind, or the knotted New England hills, where the mountain laurel in June seems like upland snow, left over, or where the marble breaks through into clusters of perpetual laurel and everlasting; one sees mountain lakes, giant aquamarines, sapphires, topazes, and upland pastures where the blue, purple, lavender and green of the huckleberry bushes give way in autumn to the fringe of sumach by the roadside, volcanoes of reds and crimsons; the yellow of September cornfields, with intenser pumpkins lying between the shocks, or the naked breasts and flanks of the autumn landscape, quivering in uneasy sleep before the white blanket puts it to rest. To smell this, taste this, and feel and climb and walk over this landscape, once untouched, like an unopened letter or a lover unkissed—who would not rise to meet the expectation of the land? Partly, it was the challenge of babyhood: how will it grow up and what will become of it? Partly, it was the charm of innocence; or again, it was the sense of the mighty variety that the whole continent gives, as if between the two oceans every possible human habitat might be built, and every conceivable variety of experience fathomed.

What the aboriginal Indian had absorbed from the young earth, Thoreau absorbed; what the new settlers had given her, the combing of the plow, the cincture of the stone fence or the row of planted elms, these things he absorbed too; for Thoreau, having tasted the settled life of Concord, knew that the wilderness was not a permanent home for man: one might go there for fortification, for a quickening of the senses, for a tightening of all the muscles; but that, like any retreat, is a special exercise and wants a special occasion: one returned to Nature in order to become, in a deeper sense, more cultivated and civilized, not in order to return to crudities that men had already discarded. Looking ahead, Thoreau saw what was needed to preserve the valuable heritage of the American wilderness. He wrote:

> The kings of England formerly had their forests to hold the king's game, for sport or food, sometimes destroying villages to create and extend them; and I think that they were impelled by a true instinct. Why should not we, who have renounced the king's authority, have our national preserves, where no villages need be destroyed, in which the bear and panther, and some even of the hunter race, may still exist, and not be "civilized off the face of the earth,"—our own forests, not to hold the king's game merely, but to hold and preserve the king himself also, the lord of creation,—and not in idle sport of food, but for inspiration and our own true recreation? or shall we, like the villains, grub them all up, poaching on our own national domain?

These pregnant suggestions of Thoreau, which were to be embodied only after two generations in our National and State Parks, and in projects like Mr. Benton MacKaye's great conception of the Appalachian Trail, make the comments of those who see in him only an arch-individualist, half-Diogenes, half-Rousseau, seem a little beside the point. The individualism of an Emerson or a Thoreau was the necessary complement of the thoroughly socialized existence of the New England town; it was what prevented these towns from becoming collections of yes men, with never an opinion or an emotion that differed from their neighbors. He wrote for his fellow-townsmen; and his notion of the good life was one that should carry to a higher pitch the existing polity and culture of Concord itself.

> As the nobleman of cultivated taste surrounds himself with whatever conduces to his culture—genius—learning—wit —books—paintings—statuary—music—philosophical instruments, and the like; so let the village do—not stop short at a pedagogue, a parson, a sexton, a parish library, and three selectmen, because our pilgrim forefathers got through a cold winter once on a bleak rock with these. To act collectively is according to the spirit of our institutions; and I am confident that our circumstances are more flourishing, our means are greater than the nobleman's.

Do not these sentences alter a little our stereotype of homespun New England, of Individualistic America?

Just as Thoreau sought Nature, in order to arrive at a higher state of culture, so he practiced individualism, in order to create a better order of society. Taking America as it was, Thoreau conceived a form, a habitat, which would retain what was unique in the American contact with the virgin forest, the cultivated soil, and the renewed institutions of the New England town. He understood the precise thing that the pioneer lacked. The pioneer had exhausted himself in a senseless external activity, which answered no inner demands except those for oblivion. In his experiment at Walden Pond, Thoreau "learned this, at least . . . that if one advances confidently in the direction of his dreams, and endeavors to live the life which he has imagined, he will meet with success unexpected in the common hours. . . . In proportion as he simplifies his life, the laws of the universe will appear less complex, and solitude will not be solitude, nor poverty poverty, nor weakness weakness. If you have built castles in the air, your work need not be lost; that is where they should be. Now put the foundations under them."

In short, Thoreau lived in his desires; in rational and beautiful things that he imagined worth doing, and did. The pioneer lived only in extraneous necessities; and he vanished with their satisfaction: filling all the conditions of his environment, he never fulfilled himself. With the same common ground between them in their feeling towards Nature, Thoreau and the pioneer stood at opposite corners of the field. What Thoreau left behind is still precious; men may still go out and make over America in the image of Thoreau. What the pioneer left behind, alas! was only the burden of a vacant life.

VERNON LOUIS PARRINGTON (1871-1929), a professor at the University of Washington from 1908 to 1929, wrote studies of the Connecticut Wits and of Sinclair Lewis. He is best known, however, for his *Main Currents in American Thought*, a history of American ideas from the point of view of the Jeffersonian liberal as they are refracted through American literature.

Henry Thoreau
Transcendental Economist

VERNON LOUIS PARRINGTON

Main Currents in American Thought (3 vols., New York: Harcourt, Brace and Company, 1927-30), Vol. 2, 400-413. Several long quotations from Thoreau are deleted.

"Wisdom crieth in the streets and no man regardeth her"; yet "she teacheth temperance and forethought, justice and fortitude; than which men can have in their life nothing more profitable."

The single business of Henry Thoreau, during forty-odd years of eager activity, was to discover an economy calculated to provide a satisfying life. His one concern, that gave to his ramblings in Concord fields a value as of high adventure, was to explore the true meaning of wealth. Honest, fearless, curiously inquisitive—a masterless man who would give no hostages to fortune—he proved his right to be called a philosopher by seeking wisdom as a daily counselor and friend, and following such paths only as wisdom suggested. Out of his own experience, tested in the clear light of the Greeks, he wrote a transcendental declaration of independence that may be taken

as the final word of the Concord school touching the great is-
sues of practical living. *Walden* is the handbook of an economy
that endeavors to refute Adam Smith and transform the round
of daily life into something nobler than a mean gospel of plus
and minus.

It was the common opinion of his neighbors that Henry
Thoreau was a queer fellow who had somehow got all his values
topsy-turvy. And yet the more thoughtfully one considers him,
the more doubtful it appears whether the queerness lay with
him or with his critics. Unfortunately a wholly honest and
original man is so rare as to fall under common suspicion. To
the inmates of Bedlam a sane man will appear queer. In a
society of serfs a masterless man will be accounted an outlaw.
To the Concord farmers Thoreau appeared strange only because he applied in his daily life a truth they assented to on
the Sabbath. The principle that life is more than the meat and
the body than raiment was familiar enough to the Sunday doctrines of Concord; but that a man should seriously apply it on
week-days; that he should propose to regulate his mid-week
activities by the economy of the Sermon on the Mount, passed
the comprehension of practical Yankees who followed quite
another economy. It was Thoreau's conduct that perplexed
them, rather than his philosophy.

From first to last that conduct was serenely logical. To
this disciple of the ancient wisdom, Sabbath and week-day
were one, and in seeking to square his daily life with the ancient precept, Thoreau became the arch-rebel of his group, the
most individual amongst the "lunatic fringe" of the transcendental movement, the one who escapes elusively from the grip
of an adjective. He slips out of all phrases devised to imprison
him. "A bachelor of nature," Emerson, with his gift for cryptic
phrase, called him; "poet-naturalist," Ellery Channing who
knew him intimately, chose to call him. "I am a poet, a mystic,
and a transcendentalist," Thoreau said of himself, disregarding
his nature writings. Yet none of these phrases, true as they are,
quite adequately sums him up. At the risk of committing a
fresh futility, one may perhaps suggest that he was a Greek
turned transcendental economist. His life seems to have been
a persistent experiment in values. A philosopher of the open

air who kept his mind clear and his nerves robust by daily contact with wind and weather; a mystic who pried curiously into
the meaning of nature and was familiar with Hellenic and
Oriental systems of thought; a Yankee, skilled in various
homely crafts, yet rather interested in proving for himself
what things were excellent and taking nothing on hearsay—
Thoreau's chief business would seem to have been with life
itself, and how it might best be lived by Henry Thoreau; how
a rational being, in short, might enjoy the faculties God has
given him, following the higher economy and not enslaving
himself to the lower, so that when he came to die he might
honestly say, I have lived.

Amongst the members of the transcendental school Thoreau was the one Concord man, born and bred there, literally
of the soil and loving the things of the soil. His tireless rovings
were commonly bounded by the familiar Concord horizons. His
life had taken deep root in the Concord fields, and he refused
to join the restless multitude of the *déracinés*, who seek novel
experiences in a succession of transplantings. No English peas-
ant ever clung to the home-acres with more loving tenacity.
He was a countryman in instinct, distrusting the great city
twenty miles away that disseminated its virus through the out-
lying villages and farms. The city was wedded to the economy
of industrialism and exploitation. But as a child of Jean Jacques,
Thoreau chose to believe that the road to heaven ran through
the fields and not over the cobblestones of Boston; he discovered an honest integrity of character oftener in the country
than in Lowell mills, yet none too often there. It was easier
to be free there, yet even in Concord village the herd mind was
always laying springes to catch the unwary; and Thoreau
would not be caught. He was poet and philosopher as well as
countryman, and he weighed his own life and the life of his
neighbors in the scales of Hellenic thought. He was surveyor
of broader fields than his neighbor's wood-lot; was acquainted
with other mysteries than the mystery of pencil-making. He
desired other ends than those his shopkeeping, farm-tending
neighbors served; he would not be encumbered as they were.
He could not carry such gross impedimenta in his pack and be
a free man; the pack was too heavy; and he proceeded to

lighten it with a thoroughness that startled Concord. He "signed off" from Dr. Ripley's church; with Alcott, he refused to pay his poll tax: he severed his allegiance to the Commonwealth of Massachusetts and the Federal government; he rid himself of all concern at what Concord thought of his ways; he spoke out his honest convictions in the village Lyceum—convictions about John Brown and slavery and Massachusetts' part in sending negroes back to their masters—quite careless of the disapproval of Judge Hoar and other Concord dignitaries. Such a man had never before walked the village streets, and the spectacle filled his neighbors with amazement.

With so much useless luggage got rid of, Thoreau was ready to set about the high business of living. To outward appearance a somewhat angular Yankee, practical and capable, he was at heart a Greek, with the delight in the simple round of the seasons and a responsiveness to natural beauty that belonged to the older civilization. Brought up under the "pale negations" of Dr. Ripley's theology, he emerged a pagan. He was the most widely read in Greek literature of the Concord transcendentalists; had translated *Prometheus Bound,* and much of Pindar; and was completely at home in the clear Greek atmosphere. Who but a Hellenist could utter such words as these which serve as his apology for the Walden experiment?

> I went to the woods because I wished to live deliberately, to front only the essential facts of life, and to see if I could learn what it had to teach, and not, when I came to die, discover that I had not lived. I did not wish to live what was not life, living is so dear; nor did I wish to practice resignation, unless it was quite necessary. I wanted to live deep and suck out all the marrow of life, to live so sturdily and Spartan-like as to put to rout all that was not life, to cut a broad swath and shave close, to drive life into a corner, and reduce it to its lowest terms, and, if it proved to be mean, why then to get the whole and genuine meanness of it, and publish its meanness to the world; or if it were sublime, to know it by experience, and be able to give a true account of it in my next excursion. (*Walden,* "What I Lived For.")

To seek Pan in a tired world and recover joys that have long been forgotten is a business that only a romantic will engage in; yet Thoreau set out on the quest with a clear-eyed purpose:

> . . . My Good Genius seemed to say,—Go fish and hunt far and wide day by day,—farther and wider,—and rest thee by many brooks and hearth-sides without misgiving. Remember thy Creator in the days of thy youth. Rise free from care before the dawn, and seek adventures. Let the noon find thee by other lakes, and the night overtake thee everywhere at home. There are no larger fields than these, no worthier games than may here be played. Grow wild according to thy nature, like those sedges and brakes, which will never become English hay. Let the thunder rumble; what if it threaten ruin to farmer's crops? that is not its errand to thee. Take shelter under the cloud, while they flee to carts and sheds. Let not to get a living be thy trade, but thy sport. Enjoy the land, but own it not. Through want of enterprise and faith men are where they are, buying and selling, and spending their lives like serfs. (*Ibid.*, "Baker Farm.")

> If the day and the night are such that you greet them with joy, and life emits a fragrance like flowers and sweet-scented herbs, is more elastic, more starry, more immortal,—that is your success. All nature is your congratulation, and you have cause momentarily to bless yourself. . . . The true harvest of my daily life is somewhat as intangible and indiscernible as the tints of morning or evening. It is a little star-dust caught, a segment of the rainbow which I have clutched. (*Ibid.*, "Higher Laws.")

To save one's soul has always been accounted in New England a matter worthy of a man's best effort, and Thoreau's days were given over to it with a single-heartedness without parallel even in New England. The Puritan, he believed, had suffered his high spiritual mission to be sacrificed to the economic; he would recover that mission by sacrificing the economic to the spiritual; but he would interpret the spiritual as a Hellenist rather than a Hebraist. The Christian otherworldliness seemed to him unduly regardless of the loveliness of this world. "Christianity," he says in the *Week*, "only hopes. It has hung its harp on the willows, and cannot sing a song in a strange land. It has dreamed a sad dream, and does not yet welcome the morning with joy."

> I am not sure but I should betake myself in extremities to the liberal divinities of Greece, rather than to my country's God. . . . In my Pantheon, Pan still reigns in his pristine glory, with his ruddy face, his flowing beard, and his shaggy body, his pipe and his crook, his nymph Echo, and his chosen daughter Iambe; for the great God Pan is not dead, as was rumored. Perhaps of all the gods of New England and of ancient Greece, I am most constant at his shrine. (*The Week*, "Sunday.")

His extraordinarily frank evaluation of the New Testament, and of Calvinistic New England that had too long chewed the cud of conscience—"they did not know when to swallow their cud, and their lives of course yielded no milk"—is the work of a pagan from whom all creeds slip easily. Few more searching sermons have been preached in Massachusetts than the sermon that composed itself as Thoreau's boat floated down the Concord River, past the Billerica meeting-house where the honest villagers were worshiping the God of New England—a sermon that with fine irony summons minister and congregation to consider the deeper teachings of their sacred book. . . .

As Thoreau understood the problem of economics there were three possible solutions open to him: to exploit himself, to exploit his fellows, or to reduce the problem to its lowest denominator. The first was quite impossible—to imprison oneself in a treadmill when the morning called to great adventure, to burden oneself with useless fardels when the pack must be kept light, was the folly of a slave mind. He had observed his neighbors closely and found little good in their way of self-exploitation.

> I have travelled a good deal in Concord; and everywhere, in shops, and offices, and field, the inhabitants have

appeared to me to be doing penance in a thousand remarkable ways. . . . How many a poor immortal soul have I met well-nigh crushed and smothered under its load, creeping down the road of life, pushing before it a barn seventy-five feet by forty, its Augean stables never cleansed, and one hundred acres of land, tillage, mowing, pasture and woodlot. . . . The better part of the man is soon ploughed into the soil for compost. (*Walden,* "Economy.")

To exploit one's fellows seemed to Thoreau's sensitive social conscience an even grosser infidelity. The leisure of a slave driver, got by imprisoning his fellows in a treadmill, was an ignoble leisure from which came the empty vulgarity of modern life. "If I devote myself to other pursuits and contemplations," he said, "I must first see, at least, that I do not pursue them sitting upon another man's shoulders. I must get off him first, that he may pursue his contemplations, too." Freedom with abstinence seemed to him better than serfdom with material well-being, for he was only giving up the lesser to enjoy the greater, as was the privilege of the philosopher.

To be a philosopher is not merely to have subtle thoughts, nor even to found a school, but so to love wisdom as to live according to its dictates, a life of simplicity, independence, magnanimity, and trust. It is to solve some of the problems of life, not only theoretically, but practically. . . . When he has obtained those things which are necessary to life, there is another alternative than to obtain the superfluities; and that is, to adventure on life now, his vacation from humbler toil having commenced. (*Walden,* "Economy.")

It was the reply of the arch-individualist to the tyrannous complexities of society, and it set him apart even in the world of transcendentalism. Other members of the group professed to have found a better way out of the dilemma—the way of Brook Farm and Fruitland; a richer life was to be achieved not by espousing poverty but by coöperation. But Thoreau could not adopt the coöperative solution; he must either accept society as it was or remove. Convinced that it was not worth accepting—that one made a foolish bargain in selling oneself to it—he was content to remove to Walden Pond. "I came into this world," he said, "not chiefly to make this a good place to live in, but to live in it, be it good or bad." "I desire to speak impartially on this point, and as one not interested in the success or failure of the present economical and social arrangement." He did not advocate that other men should build cabins and live isolated. He had no wish to dogmatize concerning the best mode of living—each must settle that matter for himself. But that a satisfying life should be lived, that the fox should somehow get free even though he left his tail in the trap, he was vitally concerned about. "The youth may build or plant or sail, only let him not be hindered from doing that which he tells me he would like to do." Let him at least rid himself of the false gospel of creature comforts, which men pay too high a price for.

The story of Thoreau's emancipation from the lower economics is the one romance of his life, and *Walden* is his great book. More restrained than the *Week* and lacking the exuberant beauty of the latter—its noble talk and scathing criticism—it is "informed by a more explicit unifying philosophy." It is a book in praise of life rather than of Nature, a record of calculating economies that studied saving in order to spend more largely. But it is a book of social criticism as well, in spite of its explicit denial of such a purpose, and in its speculations much of Carlyle and Ruskin and William Morris crops out. In considering the true nature of economy he concluded, with Ruskin, that "the cost of a thing is the amount of what I call life which is required to be exchanged for it, immediately or in the long run." Conceive of life as cheap, a poor thing to be exploited, and the factory system becomes the logical economic order; but conceive of it as dear, and the common happiness the great objective of society, and quite another sort of industrialism will emerge. Thoreau did not look with approval on the rising city of Lowell, with its multiplying spindles and increasing proletariat, and he did not understand why Americans should boast of a system that provided vulgar leisure for the masters at the cost of serfdom for the workers.

> Where is this division of labor to end? [he asks] and what object does it finally serve? I cannot believe that our factory system is the best mode by which men may get clothing. The condition of the operatives is becoming every day more like that of the English; and it cannot be wondered at, since, as far as I have heard or observed, the principal object is, not that mankind may be well and honestly clad, but, unquestionably, that the corporations may be enriched. (*Walden,* "Economy.")

The whole middle-class philosophy of exploitation was hateful to him, the middleman equally with the manufacturer. "Trade curses everything it touches; and though you trade in messages from heaven, the whole curse of trade attaches to the business." Men have been deceived by a false economy—lured by the bog lights away from the open fields to flounder in the miasmic marshes. While Ruskin was still pottering over Turner, Thoreau was elaborating in *Walden* the text: The only wealth is life. . . .

At Walden Pond and on the Merrimac River Thoreau's mind was serene as the open spaces; but this Greek serenity was rudely disturbed when he returned to Concord village and found his neighbors drilling for the Mexican War, and when authority in the person of the constable came to him with the demand that he pay a due share to the public funds. The war to him was a hateful thing, stupid and unjust, waged for the extension of the obscene system of negro slavery; and Thoreau was brought sharply to consider his relations to the political state that presumed to demand his allegiance, willing or unwilling, to its acts. Under the stress of such an emergency the transcendentalist was driven to examine the whole theory of the relation of the individual to the state. He was not political-minded; he had concerned himself little with political theory; he would gladly let the government alone if government would let him alone; he was even prepared to make excuses for government. But he would not compromise with his conscience; and when the state applied the principle of coercion, he applied the counter principle of passive resistance. It was while he was domiciled in Walden cabin that the hand of the law seized him and thrust him into Concord jail. He went with the constable quietly, but there was dangerous contempt in his heart. It seemed absurd that a man could not go to the cobbler's for a pair of mended boots, but he must be interfered with by a neighbor playing the rôle of constable. Constable, jailer, the magistrate on the bench, all the elaborate machinery of the law, Thoreau contemplated quizzically and judged his neighbors fools to have exchanged their freedom for such masquerades. Those who got anything from such instruments—lawyers and propertied men—might think well of them, but they were a mere impertinence to Thoreau who wanted to go huckleberrying. When they let him out he went quietly after his berries, and discovered there was "no state in sight among the berry bushes." "I saw," he remarked casually, "that the state was half-witted, that it was as timid as a lone woman with her silver spoons, and that it did not know its friends from its foes, and I lost all my remaining respect for it and pitied it."

But Thoreau was not done with the comedy. It set him upon thinking, and the result was the essay, *Civil Disobedience*. Taken by itself alone, it is a somewhat astonishing performance. This Yankee transcendentalist quite evidently has turned philosophical anarchist. But read in the light of Emerson's *Journals*, or in the light of Godwin's *Political Justice*, it is easily comprehensible. It is no more than transcendental individualism translated into politics, with all comfortable compromises swept away. Its sources run straight back to eighteenth-century liberalism with its doctrine of the minimized state—a state that must lose its coercive sovereignty in the measure that the laws of society function freely. Very likely Thoreau had never read Godwin, yet his political philosophy was implicit in *Political Justice*. In Godwin's thinking the problem of man in society is the problem of a voluntary adjustment of the individual to the state; and it is only by establishing economics and politics on morality, that political justice is possible. The moral law is the fundamental law, superior to statutes and constitutions; and to it the citizen is bound to render allegiance. "The object of the present state of society is to multiply labor," asserted Godwin; "in another state it will be to simplify it." "The only adequate apology of government is necessity." "Government however reformed" is "little capable of affording solid benefit to mankind." "Give us equality and justice but no constitution. Suffer us to follow without restraint the dictates of our own judgment, and to change our forms of social order as fast as we improve the dictates of our own judgment." "The pretense of collective wisdom is the most palpable of all impostures." "The true reason why the mass of mankind has so often been the dupe of knaves, has been the mysterious and complicated nature of the social system. Once annihilate the quackery of government, and the most home-spun understanding will be prepared to scorn the artifices of the state juggler that would mislead him."

By his own path Thoreau came to identical conclusions. There is little in *Civil Disobedience* that is not in *Political Justice*. To neither thinker is there an abstract state, society or nation—only individuals; and to both, the fundamental law is the law of morality. Political expediency and the law of morality frequently clash, and in such event it is the duty of the individual citizen to follow the higher law. Thoreau went even further, and asserted the doctrine of individual compact, which in turn implied the doctrine of individual nullification; no government, he said, can have any "pure right over my person or property but what I concede to it". . . .

Such a man quite evidently would go for Nullification as fiercely as Garrison. Even though he might wash his hands of society, the cries of those who suffered injustice followed him, and when the Fugitive Slave Law passed, it robbed him of his peace, destroying his pleasure in wonted things. The slave hunters were in Boston streets, and justice in the person of Commissioner Loring was sending Anthony Burns back to slavery. As he contemplated the spectacle his wrath against a coercive government flamed up. "My thoughts are murder to the state," he complained bitterly, "and involuntarily go plotting against her."

I would remind my countrymen that they are to be men first, and Americans only at a late and convenient hour. . . . I hear a good deal said about trampling this law under foot. Why, one need not go out of his way to do that. This law rises not to the level of the head or the reason; its natural habitat is in the dirt. It was born and bred, and has its life, only in the dust and mire, on a level with the feet; and he who walks with freedom, and does not with Hindoo mercy avoid treading on every venomous reptile, will inevitably tread on it, and so trample it under foot,— and Webster, its maker, like the dirt-bug and its ball. ("Slavery in Massachusetts," in *Works*, Vol. X.)

The law will never make men free; it is men who have got to make the law free. They are the lovers of law and order who observe the law when the government breaks it.

Thoreau was a stern judge, and he held his age in low esteem. His Concord neighbors seemed to him poor fellows with too little spirit to be free men; they were the raw material of standing armies, militia, jailors, constables, and the *posse comitatus*. And then one day into the field of his vision came a plain Yankee, primitive and heroic, John Brown of Ossawatomie. In the contemplation of his life and death Thoreau felt a shock of new faith run like an electric current through his veins. The age was no longer dead to him, for it had bred a man. "I rejoice that I live in this age," he exclaimed, "that I am his contemporary." He had found his hero—not in past times as Carlyle and Emerson had done, but in the present among his own Yankee kind. He had talked with John Brown in Concord and recognized him as a primitive idealist of rugged mold, a stern moralist who set justice above the law. That this man should be so grossly misunderstood by lesser men, so foully slandered, filled him with sorrow and with wrath also. "When a noble deed is done, who is likely to appreciate it? They who are noble themselves. I was not surprised that certain of my neighbors spoke of John Brown as an ordinary felon, for who are they? They have either much flesh, or much office, or much coarseness of some kind" ("The Last Days of John Brown," in *Works*, Vol. X, p. 241). His trial and conviction Thoreau regarded as a judgment, not on John Brown, but upon America; the lawyers and editors and politicians who judged him were only convicting themselves.

His company was small indeed, because few could be found worthy to pass muster. Each one who there laid

down his life for the poor and oppressed was a picked man,
culled out of many thousands, if not millions; apparently a
man of principle, of rare courage, and devoted humanity;
ready to sacrifice his life at any moment for the benefit of
his fellow-man. It may be doubted if there were so many
more their equals in these respects in all the country,—I
speak of his followers only,—for their leader, no doubt,
scoured the land far and wide, seeking to swell his troop.
These alone were ready to step between the oppressor and
the oppressed. Surely they were the very best men you
could select to be hung. That was the best compliment
this country could pay them. They were ripe for her gallows. She has tried a long time, she has hung a good many,
but never found the right one before.

I do not believe in lawyers, in that mode of attacking
or defending a man, because you descend to meet the
judge on his own ground, and, in cases of the highest importance, it is of no consequence whether a man breaks a
human law or not. Let lawyers decide trivial cases. Business men may arrange that among themselves. If they were
the interpreters of the everlasting laws which rightfully
bind man, that would be another thing. A counterfeiting
law-factory, standing half in a slave land and half in a free!
What kind of laws for free men can you expect from that?
("A Plea for Captain John Brown," in *Works*, Vol. X, p.
197.)

In Thoreau the eighteenth-century philosophy of individualism, the potent liberalisms let loose on the world by Jean
Jacques, came to fullest expression in New England. He was the
completest embodiment of the *laissez-faire* reaction against a
regimented social order, the severest critic of the lower economics that frustrate the dreams of human freedom. He was
fortunate in dying before the age of exploitation had choked
his river with its weeds; fortunate in not foreseeing how remote is that future of free men on which his hopes were fixed:

The life in us is like the water in the river. It may rise
this year higher than man has ever known it, and flood the
parched uplands; even this may be the eventful year,

> which will drown out all the muskrats . . . such is the char-
> acter of that morrow which mere lapse of time can never
> make to dawn. The light which puts out our eyes is dark-
> ness to us. There is more day to dawn. The sun is but a
> morning-star. (*Walden.*)

With the dawning of that day perhaps men will sit once
more at the feet of the ancient wisdom and fashion their lives
upon the principle that the soul is more than the meat and
the body than raiment. Perhaps they may even shape for themselves new heroes—"above and after all, the Man of the Age,
come to be called workingman." He and his deeds are looked
down upon in our time—"It is obvious that none yet speaks to
his condition, for the speaker is not yet in his condition."
"Literature speaks how much still to the past, how little to
the future; how much to the East, how little to the West"
("Thomas Carlyle and his Works," in *Works*, Vol. X, p. 118).
One of the great names in American literature is the name of
Henry Thoreau. Yet only after sixty years is he slowly coming
into his own.

GILBERT VIVIAN SELDES (1893-   ), journalist, drama critic, and editor,
has written several books on American popular culture, among them *The
Seven Lively Arts* (1924). Seldes refuted the interpretation that Thoreau
was "a series of paradoxes," "a split personality," and found him instead
to be "homogeneous and complete."

Thoreau

GILBERT SELDES

American Writers on American Literature, ed. John Macy (New York: Live-
right, 1931), pp. 164-76.

The first step in the rescue of Thoreau's reputation has, fortunately, been made. It is already common knowledge, and in
the course of fifty years it may penetrate to the primary text-
books on American literature, that Thoreau was not a naturalist.
The text-books will be at some pains to explain that he was indeed a nature lover, but they will never again dismiss the burning energy of a comet in the terms of a skyrocket.

The second step has still to be taken. It is the re-combining
of the elements in Thoreau, or, to put it otherwise, the annihilation of a series of paradoxes. From Emerson to Parrington,
every writer on Thoreau has found a phrase in which one word
is the enemy of the next: "Bachelor of Nature," "Yankee-Greek,"
"Poet-Naturalist," "Transcendentalist-Economist"; even his style
has to be described as "celestial-homespun." No one has said
that Thoreau was a varied man, even a versatile man; every one
has said, or implied, that he was two men. The idea of the war-
ring souls in a single body comes down to us from the romantic
era and is peculiarly sympathetic to some forms of contemporary psychology. We make our deep divisions between the life of
action and the life of contemplation, between the affirmer and
the denier, between the voluptuary and the ascetic. We insist
that Thoreau is interesting because he has a split personality.
Yet the one simple, natural name which comes to us at the
thought of Thoreau gives the lie to these intellectual fancies
and actually points to his great significance for us. He was an
individualist because he was an individual—one of those who
are not divided. He was not destroyed by an internal conflict
between the transcendentalist and the surveyor, between the
Yankee and the Greek; he was made, he was created, because
he was both. Two rivers, channeled far apart, met in him. If he
had been a perfect man, we should never have known that they
rose from separate sources. He was not perfect, but he was
homogeneous and complete. His diaries are frank and copious;
they record unfulfilled ambitions, longings, doubts and disappointments. They say nothing more to us than that he was human and suffered the destiny of human kind. Fundamentally
he did what he wanted to do to a greater degree, and probably
with more satisfaction, than most people of his temper; he
found more than most of those who search.

This is to me the central truth of Thoreau and it sets into
new relations almost everything he did. It corresponds to the
central episode in his life and in his literature: the exploration of Walden Pond. I call it exploration because it was Thoreau's entrance into life and not his withdrawal from it. He
may have been mistaken in believing that life lay on the shores
of Walden, but he was going forward "to encounter the reality

of experience"; he was not retreating. He knew definitely that for him life was not to be found as a New England surveyor or pencil-maker. The rest of his world was moving westward, but Thoreau was never more Yankee than when he turned his back on the Yankees and pushed his way through the forest to make a clearing where he could live. He has said it all himself in his most famous passage, as noble and as wise a paragraph as American literature has ever produced.

"I went to the woods because I wished to live deliberately, to front only the essential facts of life, and see if I could not learn what it had to teach, and not, when I came to die, discover that I had not lived. I did not wish to live what was not life, living is so dear; nor did I wish to practice resignation, unless it was quite necessary. I wanted to live deep and suck out all the marrow of life, to live so sturdily and Spartan-like as to put to rout all that was not life, to cut a broad swath and shave close, to drive life into a corner, and reduce it to its lowest terms, and, if it proved to be mean, why then to get the whole and genuine meanness of it, and publish its meanness to the world; or if it were sublime, to know it by experience, and be able to give a true account of it in my next excursion. For most men, it appears to me, are in a strange uncertainty about it, whether it is of the devil or of God, and have *somewhat hastily* concluded that it is the chief end of man here to 'glorify God and enjoy Him forever.' . . ."

I cut the quotation at this point because Thoreau's purpose is one thing and his method another. Behind the purpose there is a faith; behind the method, skepticism. The faith is not that life is necessarily good, only that it is our single wealth. "I came into this world," he says elsewhere, "not chiefly to make this a good place to live in, but to live in it, be it good or bad." He stands, therefore, opposed to the moralist and to the esthete. Most of the people who clamber out of the bog on either side, of morality or estheticism, are carried so far by their impetus that they land in the other. Thoreau stood on high, solid and fertile ground.

I am skeptical of the method he chose; coming back to the long paragraph I have just quoted, I recall the rapture—it is the only accurate word—which I experienced when I read it at the age of fifteen, and because I know now that "to drive life into a corner" is more than an adolescent's ideal, because I experience a more profound, a less faithful, excitement, I am moved to postpone the criticism I have to make. The significant thing is Thoreau's intention. Perhaps it would be right to say that it is significant because he was one of the last men to whom that purpose seemed both necessary and noble. If the modern world runs to disaster, it is not because a hundred bungalows and radios and outboard motors infest Walden Pond, but because no one would go to Walden Pond if they did not. "There is a lake in every man's heart," says George Moore. But it is not a lake by the shores of which we may be content to sit; we are under compulsion to cross it. We are all convinced "somewhat hastily" of the genuine meanness of life, not because we have thought about it, but because we refuse to think. We will not go to the heart and center; we spend our time devising wry tunes to accompany our retreat.

Thoreau was centripetal. His doubts of culture and education were based on a fear lest "all cultivation [be] necessarily superficial, and its roots may not even be directed toward the center of being," and the next entry in his *Journal* is: "Find out as soon as possible what are the best things in your composition, and then shape the rest to fit them. The former will be the mid-rib and veins of the leaf." It is not so soft a doctrine as it appears, for one does not arrive easily or instinctively at this knowledge. "What is peculiar in the life of a man," he warns us, "consists not in his obedience, but his opposition, to his instincts." This is not the iron string of self-reliance, although there is more metal in it than in Emerson's "Trust thyself." Once again Thoreau specifies: "I cannot afford to relax discipline because God is on my side, for he is on the side of discipline."

There is no circumference without a center and Thoreau made Concord his center because he had to have a place to stand so that like Archimedes he could measure and move the world. Thoreau hugged the little territory he knew and judged all life by it—but not before he had taken its own measure with supreme accuracy. "I have traveled a good deal in Concord," he says gravely, because it was for him possible to travel in a

village, or in a cabin, or in an hour. Stay with him for as long
as the first day of his week on the Concord River and "you
shall see men you have never heard of before, whose names
you don't know . . . on bleak, wintry distant shores . . . and
many other wild and noble sights . . . such as they who sit in
parlors never dream of. You shall see rude and sturdy, experienced and wise men . . . greater men than Homer, or Chaucer,
or Shakespeare, only . . . they never took to the way of writing
. . . or what have they not written on the face of the earth
already?" This is genuine; it is not literature to make a book
seem more important, and it is central to Thoreau's thought. By
profound experience he knew far more of the actual world
than the Lowells, who had been ambassadors abroad, and the
Peales and the Storeys, who had fled to Rome because America
offered them no background. He was, among the New England
writers, perhaps the best informed on the two great civilizations
of Greece and India and he had some insight into the meaning
of Confucius. But he believed seriously that if he displaced himself by a mile, he learned new things, and just as seriously that
if he stayed where he was he absorbed a civilization. As he says,
he was "at home."

"I love that the rocks should appear to have some spots of
blood on them, Indian blood at least; to be convinced that the
earth has been crowded with men, living, enjoying, suffering,
that races passed away have stained the rocks with their blood,
that the mold I tread on has been animated, aye, humanized. I
am the more at home. I farm the dust of my ancestors, though
the chemist's analysis may not detect it. I go forth to redeem
the meadows they have become. I compel them to take refuge
in turnips." And when he eats a white oak acorn, he says, "To
have discovered this palatableness in this neglected nut, the
whole world is to me the sweeter for it. I am related again to
the first man."

The rocks, the trees, the huckleberry and the muskrat, the
rivers and the snow, are so much evidence brought by Thoreau
to the unity of nature, which is not only a spiritual unity; it
exists as a physical fact for him, and as a fact in time. The completeness of his life could be achieved in Concord because he

felt himself the descendant of the first man and the ancestor of the last one. Continuity implies order and order, discipline.

I do not intend to force this, the least familiar of Thoreau's ideas, nor to insist that everything else in him is necessarily in harmony with his central thought. He was, in other phases, a good transcendentalist, a disciple of Emerson, an enemy of society, a kind of philosophic anarchist. Accustomed to wandering in the woods, he took any path, broke through any brush, with the serene confidence that he would come into the open at the end. Naturally, he had often to retrace his steps. It remains primary that he knew where he was going and was willing to endure hardship to get there. Mr. Lewis Mumford, commenting on *Walden*, has placed Thoreau justly: "Thoreau was not a penurious fanatic, who sought to practice bare living merely as a moral exercise: he wanted to obey Emerson's dictum to save on the low levels and spend on the high ones. It is this that distinguishes him from the tedious people whose whole existence is absorbed in the practice of living on beans, or breathing deeply, or wearing clothes of a vegetable origin: simplification did not lead in Thoreau to the cult of simplicity; it led to a higher civilization."

A higher civilization meant, for Thoreau, a higher degree of self-development; it meant also a better life than the life of the mill-owner, the Forty-niner, the slaveholder, the shopkeeper, the politician. It pleases us that Thoreau was against the spirit of his age because we feel ourselves betrayed by our ancestors; yet if that were all, if Thoreau had not also been opposed to the enemies of his age, he would not be half so important to us. The middle of the century was not only the time of expansion and mobility, of restless energy which seemed always to lead to profits; it was the age of religious hysteria, of moral excitement, of the Practical Christian Republic at Hopedale and the despair of Fruitlands and the serio-comic phalansteries and Brook Farm. Thoreau seemed to divine the ultimate issue of "reform," which was, although we hardly know it, uplift and repression.

He was, in a word, skeptical of goodness. The violence of the revival spirit naturally offended him and he said, "repentance is not a free and fair high-way to God." (Parenthetically, how different this is from the skepticism of to-day which also rejects repentance, because there is no God.) "A wise man will dispense with repentance. It is shocking and passionate. God prefers that you approach him thoughtful, not penitent. . . ." The equally urgent, quiet forms of goodness are as objectionable; he complains of farmers that conversation with them is unprofitable because of their moralizing and says that loafers are better company: "for society a man must not be too *good* or well-disposed, to spoil his natural disposition." The mania for doing good which swept over New England frightened Thoreau; it is tainted goodness, which he calls carrion, and he will run for his life if he hears that any one is coming to his house with the conscious design of doing him good. And then, in one of those astounding flashes (like Emerson's dictum that God forgives everything but bad manners), he says, "Our manners have been corrupted by communication with the saints."

This is true anarchism; it is more important, more individual than the antinomianism which brought Thoreau to a village jail for failure to pay taxes and more profound than the Godwinian morality which appeared in the lecture on Civil Disobedience. Thoreau had a profound sense of the community; he objected to the State because the State was an evil-doer; in this he was the precise counterpart of the Perfectionist John Humphrey Noyes. Noyes renounced all allegiance to the government of the United States in "an instrument similar to the Declaration of '76," and Thoreau declared that no government could have any "pure right over my person or property but what I concede to it." The covenant of Perfectionism, however, released Noyes from moral obligation; Thoreau's withdrawal from the social state is entirely a matter of morals: "If the law is of such a nature that it requires you to be an agent of injustice to another, then, I say, break the law." It is natural enough for Thoreau to speak so and to act so; nevertheless, it was accidental. In most of his contacts with the law, his withers were unwrung and he said with some acerbity, let the galled jade wince; he had other business in life, business more interesting than the destruction of the State to which he was, for the most part, not hostile, but indifferent.

Thoreau did not usually build general laws on the foun-

dation of his impulses. Society, which annoyed him far more
than the State ever did, he despised not because it interfered
so much with his own life, as because it defeated its own purpose; it diminished life for its votaries, where it should have
given abundance. Since he lived in a community, he had to
resist pressure, but he loved his own power to resist; he did
not grow sour. He wished to write his *Journals* in blank books
and found those he bought at the store already marked off with
a red line near the margin, for dollars and cents, as if his philosophical economy must be reduced to commerce. He notes the
circumstance; but what saddens him is the effect of the ledger
on those who live by the ledger. "There is no glory so bright
but the veil of business can hide it effectually," he says; "with
most men life is postponed to some trivial business." It is the
criticism of a man who has suffered no postponement.

What was the glory he sought? It had almost nothing to do
with other human beings ("I rarely look people in their faces,"
he writes) and the great Nature of which he was a worshiper
was largely a means to the self-discovery, the self-development
to which he devoted his life. He wanted liberty and knew that
no other liberty was worth having if it was bought at the price
of freedom and peace in our minds. He wanted to be himself
and despised audiences (and society entire) because "they
want all of a man but his truth and independence and manhood." There does not seem to have been in the world any
occupation (except that of being a poet, a thinker, a diarist)
which he wanted for himself; the profession roughly ascribed
to him, that of scientific naturalist, he grew more and more to
distrust, with the example of Darwin before him and with the
natural tendency in himself to let dissection interfere with observation and enjoyment. He wanted to make a living, not a
dying, by work, and reproached society because it had never
solved the problem, for itself and so for him.

He wanted independence and depth. It is amusing to discover in his *Journals* passages which seem to have been written
sixty days, and not sixty years ago. There is this, on the Yes-man
of American business: "Men are very generally spoiled by being
so civil and well-disposed. You can have no profitable conversation with them, they are so conciliatory, determined to agree

with you. . . . The thousand and one gentlemen whom I meet, I meet despairingly, and but to part from them, for I am not cheered by the hope of any rudeness from them." (The Yankee rustic is there, craving a rough surface to rub him the wrong way.) And again, as if he foresaw the day when the air would be choked with broadcasting, he says, "We are in great haste to construct a magnetic telegraph from Maine to Texas: but Maine and Texas, it may be, have nothing important to communicate. . . . As if the main object were to talk fast, and not to talk sensibly. . . . We are eager to tunnel under the Atlantic . . . but perchance the first news that will leak through into the broad, flapping American ear will be that the Princess Adelaide has the whooping cough."

I have said that he escaped from a dainty estheticism and from fanatical morality, yet it is clear that the whole effort to move always at a higher level is fundamentally a moral one and the beauty he discovered in the world shows that he had an extraordinary sensibility. The first did not lead him into crusades, the second did not corrupt action. One way to the heights is by completeness; he would not have his senses dulled, and his *Journals* are eyes and finger-tips, tongue and nose, above everything, ears of extraordinary accuracy. They are his instruments of precision, his testing chemicals—and at the same time they are manifestations of the completeness with which he lived. This life of his senses is removed from estheticism because it is never offended; he seems incapable of taking offense at whatever exists in nature, and even the sensuality which he does not understand, does not outrage him.

I think the happiest illustration of his sense, his wisdom, his power to see the good and the evil, without being overwhelmed by either, lies in two passages he wrote about the railroad. It was the time when Ruskin was lifting his voice in a shrill curse against the violator of the virgin earth. Thoreau has none of this bitterness; the railroad offends him only when he sees it mastering man: "We do not ride on the railroad; it rides upon us. Did you ever think what those sleepers are that underlie the railroad? Each one is a man, an Irishman, or a Yankee man. The rails are laid on them, and they are covered with sand, and the cars run smoothly over them. They are sound sleepers, I assure you. And every few years a new lot is laid down and run over; so that if some have the pleasure of riding on a rail, others have the misfortune to be ridden upon. And when they run over a man that is walking in his sleep, a supernumerary sleeper in the wrong position, and wake him up, they suddenly stop the cars, and make a hue and cry about it, as if this were an exception."

And he is willing to forget even this when the whistle of the locomotive penetrates to Walden Pond and he thinks: "Have not men improved somewhat in punctuality since the railroad was invented? Do they not talk and think faster in the depot than they did in the stage office? There is something electrifying in the atmosphere of the former place. I have been astonished at the miracles it has wrought; and some of my neighbors, who, I should have prophesied, once for all, would never get to Boston by so prompt a conveyance, are on hand when the bell rings. . . . We have constructed a fate, an *Atropos*, that never turns aside. . . .

"What recommends commerce to me is its enterprise and bravery. It does not clasp its hands and pray to Jupiter. I see these men every day go about their business with more or less courage and content, doing more even than they suspect, and perchance better employed than they could have consciously devised.

"Commerce is unexpectedly confident and serene, alert, adventurous, and unwearied. It is very natural in its methods, withal, far more so than many fantastic enterprises and sentimental experiments, and hence its singular success. I am refreshed and expanded when the freight train rattles past me, and I smell the stores which go dispensing their odors all the way from Long Wharf to Lake Champlain, reminding me of foreign parts, of coral reefs, and Indian oceans, and tropical climes, and the extent of the globe." (It is worth noting that this, which is part of a long and brilliant description of the railroad train, comes in the chapter on Sound. Throughout the *Journals* one other contemporary invention lifts Thoreau's heart: the telegraph. In the humming of its wires he hears the Æolian harp, and rejoices.)

There is no inner quarrel between these two passages,

and they indicate, as clearly as need be, the purity of Thoreau's thought. Some one (possibly Emerson) said of him, "Henry is with difficulty sweet," but this was an illusion to his party manners; in his private life he was and remained sweet, with the sweetness of fresh spring water, because his spirit was never poisoned by any excess of longing, any excessive sacrifices. Mr. I. A. Richards has analyzed the making of a fanatic in a brief paragraph: "When any desire is denied for the sake of another," he says, "the approved and accepted activity takes on additional value; it is coveted and pursued all the more for what it cost. Thus the spectacle of other people enjoying both activities without difficulty, thanks to some not very obvious adjustment, is peculiarly distressing, and such people are usually regarded as especially depraved."

This is what Thoreau escaped. What he surrendered, he did not much regret.

Something, however, escaped him, something precious was dissipated without his knowledge. I do not mean his capacity for sexual love. Of that he tells us almost nothing, has no criticism, no loftiness of feeling to communicate. (It is only remarkable that he does not list it among the trifling businesses which keep man too busy to live.) If he never experienced this love and fled from those who loved him, the stigmata of his crucifixion are not visible to us. Oddly, it is a kind of innocence whose passing he mourns—he, who appears to us to have kept his freshness and purity to the last day. When he was thirty-four he wrote: "I think that no experience which I have to-day comes up to, or is comparable with, the experiences of my boyhood. . . . My life was ecstasy. In youth, before I lost any of my senses, I can remember that I was all alive, and inhabited my body with inexpressible satisfaction; both its weariness and its refreshment were sweet to me. This earth was the most glorious instrument, and I was audience to its strains. To have such sweet impressions made on us, such ecstasies begotten of the breezes! I can remember how I was astonished. . . . For years I marched as to a music in comparison with which the military music of the streets is noise and discord. I was daily intoxicated, and yet no man could call me intemperate."

Thoreau feels that "our most glorious experiences are a kind of regret. Our regret is so sublime that we may mistake it for triumph." He has some use for maturity, since a man must be saturated with truth before he can report it, and "what was enthusiasm in the young man must become temperament in the mature man," but the unhappiness lingers; "the youth gets together his materials to build a bridge to the moon . . . and at length the middle-aged man concludes to build a woodshed with them."

That Thoreau did not cross the bridge to the moon is only common fate; that he refused to build woodsheds is his singular merit. But the nostalgia for his youth is disturbing, his sense of the greater richness of immature life is a positive weakness. It makes weak the last years of his life: he was twenty-two when he made his great voyage, by thirty he was done with Walden Pond, and although the records of these two adventures were long worked over and not published for many years, Thoreau did not grow wiser, did not see more clearly, did not grow by accretion and development. The last few years of the *Journals* are less meaty ("nutty" was his own word, but it has the wrong flavor now); they are perceptibly sadder. He was not disappointed in what the world brought him, for he had turned "a face of bronze to expectations"; he was disappointed in what he brought to the world. One thinks of his favorite legend, the story of Apollo in servitude to Admetus. But for what crime?

He began by studying himself, valuing himself. In typical transcendental style he writes: "Let us wander where we will, the universe is built about us, and we are central still." (This is after Copernicus, but before Darwin.) Some ten years later, when he was thirty-four years old, he cries out, with perhaps some fear: "May I love and revere myself above all the gods that men have ever invented. May I never let the vestal fire go out in my recesses." He is afraid of dissipating his strength; he is saving up. One can suspect that the divine event for which he was saving himself did not occur, that he began to doubt, in the end, whether he was indeed "central still." Because he falls into the pit of egocentricity and says, with humorous exaggeration, but quite naturally, that the Concord

River might not overflow its banks if he were not there to see. This is called solipsism or madness, and it is the penalty which always hangs over the head of the self-centered man.

I do not think that the profound and beautiful thing Thoreau had to say and do in the world could have been said and done by him in any other way. My single doubt is whether simplification is the only method. If you read ten further lines in the noble passage I have quoted from *Walden*, you find that this surveyor of humanity used only two of the primary processes of mathematics: subtract, he cries, and divide; never add, never multiply. "Instead of a million, count half a dozen . . . let your affairs be as two or three . . . instead of a hundred dishes, five. . . . Simplify, simplify! Simplicity, simplicity, simplicity!"

It appears to us that we live in a world a thousand times more complicated than his; we know, without doubt, that an organized pressure exists to make us always add and multiply, and always the items in these gross mathematics are trivial, secondary—they are things. We do not know, because no man has yet shown us, how to extract life out of things and—again somewhat hastily—assume that things must kill the soul. The natural result for most of us is to take refuge in flight either from things or from the soul; we deny the importance of one or the existence of the other. The whole preoccupation of Thoreau becomes negligible to us if we lose his natural sense of value, his fixed idea that there is a level higher than sheer animalism upon which man can live. His importance to us then is in the assertion that wisdom, nobility, the things of the spirit exist to gratify man and make him truly complete and happy. His proof is the simple one that, without them, life is too mean and too trivial to be lived. But he leaves us still in doubt because he was unwilling to struggle against the multitudinous, the ever-changing and ever-multiplying. He was sympathetic enough with the wisdom of the East to correct the excesses of the West; he was too sympathetic to be the Western man in his ideal proportions.

Mid-Century Insights and
Appraisals: 1941 to the Present

Authors are a natural and irresistible aristocracy in every society, and, more than kings or emperors, exert an influence on mankind.
"Reading," *Walden*

Henry David Thoreau *by Malvina Hoffman*
The Hall of Fame for Great Americans at New York University

FRANCIS O. MATTHIESSEN (1902-50), biographer and critic, was professor of English at Harvard. Though he wrote influential critical studies of T. S. Eliot, Henry James, and Theodore Dreiser, Matthiessen's *American Renaissance*, with its preoccupation with myth and tragedy, elicited far greater interest in the two decades following its publication than any of his other books.

Thinking in Images

FRANCIS O. MATTHIESSEN

American Renaissance (New York: Oxford University Press, 1941), pp. 92-99.

> 'Her pure, and eloquent blood
> Spoke in her cheeks, and so distinctly wrought
> That one might almost say, her body thought.'
> —DONNE

In spite of his keenness in scrutinizing the reports of his senses, Thoreau remained wholly the child of his age in regarding the material world as a symbol of the spiritual. He who held that 'the poet writes the history of his body' declared in another mood that 'poetry is the mysticism of mankind.' He could even contradict his enunciation that it was not the subject but the roundness of treatment that mattered, by saying that 'a higher truth, though only dimly hinted at, thrills us more than a lower expressed.' He stated early and kept repeating that he was ever in pursuit of the ineffable: 'The other world is all my art; my pencils will draw no other; my jack-knife will cut nothing else; I do not use it as a means.'

Yet even in that affirmation of faith Thoreau does not disappear into the usual transcendental vapor.[1] He gives us the

[1] Consider by contrast the record of one of Alcott's periods of illumination: 'And this seems to be our Apotheosis. Shall we name fitlier by another name what we see and feel as Ourselves? For now the mysterious meters and scales and planes are opened to us, and we view wonderingly the Crimson Tablets and report of them all the day long. It is no longer Many but One with us . . . I am drawn on by enchantment, and seem taking the leaves of the tree of life there plucked for me, and to sojourn I know not whither through regions of spirit—some Atlantides, perhaps, of the Mind and Seats of the Blessed . . .' Alcott's words betray themselves at once by their stock 'literary' echoes, by the looseness and abstractness that fail to convey the impression of a thing clearly seen or wholly experienced. In mystical literature, no less

sense that he is a man whose grip remains firm on this world as well, whose hand can manage both his knife and his pencil. In fact, Thoreau's success as an artist is exactly in proportion to such balance between means and end. On the occasions when he attempts a direct approach to his end, when, that is to say, he voices his bare thoughts, as in his pages on ideal friendship, his mind is revealed as much less capacious and less elastic than Emerson's. On the other hand, when he simply heaps up facts, as in the later volumes of his journal, he himself recognizes that facts so stated are parched, that they 'must be the vehicle of some humanity in order to interest us,' that they 'must be warm, moist, incarnated—have been breathed on at least. A man has not seen a thing who has not felt it.' This is to remark again that Thoreau was not specially equipped either for abstract theorizing or for strictly scientific observation. But when he could base theory on his own sturdy practice, as in 'Life Without Principle' or 'Civil Disobedience,' the impact of his humanity was dynamic. And when, as a writer, he could fuse his thought and his observation by means of a symbol, which was not just suggested but designed in sharp detail, he was able, in Coleridge's phrase, to 'elicit truth as at a flash.'

Thoreau's own description of his most fertile process, in the chapter 'What I lived for,' is that 'we are able to apprehend at all what is sublime and noble only by the perpetual instilling and drenching of the reality that surrounds us.' The gerunds are characteristic, drawn from verbs of touch that penetrate to his inner being. They show the kind of fusion he could make by training into his writing the alertness of his senses. A passage from the *Week* will instance this fusion further, and will reveal the degree to which he could practice his theory. He introduced some entries from the account book of an old Concord fisherman, whose occupation was gone when the shad were

---

than in other types, the manner of writing is organically dependent upon the strength and lucidity of the vision. The concrete firmness of an Edwards or a Woolman even in communicating what lies beyond the senses is one indication of what the transcendentalist lost by giving up the modes of traditional piety in order to assert the divineness of himself. One thing that saved Thoreau was his awareness of the shift in the object of his worship. As he said in his Sunday morning service on the Concord, 'of all the gods of New England and of ancient Greece,' he was perhaps most constant at the shrine of Pan.

blocked out by the factory dams. These entries ran mostly to the daily purchase of 'rum and sugar, sugar and rum, N.E. and W.I., "one cod line," "one brown mug," and "a line for the seine,"; rum and sugar, sugar and rum . . . Rather a preponderance of the fluid elements; but such is the fisherman's nature. I can faintly remember to have seen this same fisher in my earliest youth, still as near the river as he could get, with uncertain, undulatory step, after so many things had gone down-stream, swinging a scythe in the meadow, his bottle like a serpent hid in the grass; himself as yet not cut down by the Great Mower.'

The rhythm is a clear instance of what Thoreau meant by saying that it was not so much the music as the marching to the music that he felt. For here, as in many other typical passages, his eye is reinforced not by varied sounds so much as by impressions of movement and of muscular pressure. He catches the step of the fisher in unison with the sweep of his scythe, though the word 'undulatory' blends too with the flow of the river, merging the old man as closely as possible with the source of his former pleasures. In that fashion Thoreau projected his conception of the harmonious interaction between man and nature, without which he did not believe that man could be adequately described.

But the river in which so many things have gone down stream is also that of the fisherman's throat, of his drunken life, the disintegration of which Thoreau conveys entirely in concrete terms, each suggesting a significance beyond itself. The snake that the old man might encounter while mowing is likewise that of his temptation; and his own figure with its scythe calls up that of Time. The final metaphor may seem too literary, the romantic stock-in-trade. Along with Thoreau's fondness for his whimsical pun on 'fluid,' it may be the kind of thing Carlyle objected to when he called the *Week* 'too Jean Paulish.' However, 'the Great Mower' saves itself, at least to a degree that most of Richter's self-conscious fancies do not, by the fact that it has not been lugged in arbitrarily. It has grown integrally out of the context, and that lends some freshness to it.

The organic structure of Thoreau's symbols became more marked in *Walden*, as in the laconic: 'Having each some shingles of thought well dried, we sat and whittled them, trying our knives, and admiring the clear yellowish grain of the pumpkin pine.' The deft telescoping of sense impression and thought allows full play to both. We can share in the relish of what he has seen, since his delicate skill has evoked the very look of the wood at the moment of being cut into. But the desultory act of whittling becomes also the appropriate image for conversation between Alcott and Thoreau around the winter hearth in Thoreau's hut. The single sentence gives a condensed dramatic scene, the very way these two friends appeared while trying their minds on thoughts 'well dried' by use; and, in this case, Thoreau's double meaning is pungent, since it frees the air of the suspicion of solemnness that might be there without it.

A more extended example of thinking in images is the best-known passage in the book, the core of his declaration of purpose:

> I went to the woods because I wished to live deliberately, to front only the essential facts of life, and see if I could not learn what it had to teach, and not, when I came to die, discover that I had not lived. I did not wish to live what was not life, living is so dear; nor did I wish to practise resignation, unless it was quite necessary. I wanted to live deep and suck out all the marrow of life, to live so sturdily and Spartan-like as to put to rout all that was not life, to cut a broad swath and shave close, to drive life into a corner, and reduce it to its lowest terms, and, if it proved to be mean, why then to get the whole and genuine meanness of it, and publish its meanness to the world; or if it were sublime, to know it by experience, and be able to give a true account of it in my next excursion.

The measured pace seems in exact correspondence with his carefully measured thoughts, and serves, as effective rhythm always does, to direct the fullest attention to the most important words. The satisfaction that we have seen him taking in the feel of syllables in the muscles of his mouth and throat is carried across to us by the placing of 'deliberately': as the first long word in the sentence, followed by a marked pause, it compels us to speak it as slowly as possible, and thus to take in its full weight: deliberate = *de + librare,* to weigh. A kindred desire to bring out the closest possible relation between the sense of a word and its sound seems to operate in his placing of 'resignation,' for again the pause emphasizes its heavy finality. A clearer instance of his 'philological' interest is the pun on 'dear,' which is not distracting since its basic sense of 'beloved' is no less relevant than its transferred sense of 'expensive.' Hence it encompasses something of what Coleridge praised in the puns of the Elizabethans, a compressed and thereby heightened variety.

But the chief source of power here seems to lie in the verbs of action: 'front,' barer than the more usual 'confront,' is also more muscular. Behind Thoreau's use of it is his conviction that the only frontier is where a man fronts a fact. The extension of its range is reserved for the third sentence, where his metaphors shift rapidly but not in a way to interfere with one another, not until each has released its condensed charge. For the primitive act of sucking out the marrow is not incompatible with the military image, appropriate to this Spartan intensity, of putting to rout life's adversaries. And as the campaign returns from the enemy to the pursuit of the essence, both the range and pressure of Thoreau's desire are given fuller statement by the widened image of harvesting and the contracted image of closing in on a hunted quarry. With that final dramatic concentration, we are able to feel what it would really mean to reduce life to its lowest terms. The phrase is no longer a conventional counter since we have arrived at it through a succession of severe and exhilarating kinesthetic tensions. After which a characteristic turn for Thoreau is not to leave the impression of anything grim, but, by mentioning his 'next excursion,' to suggest its relaxed pleasure.

By this method of presenting an experience instead of stating an abstraction, Thoreau himself has elucidated both the meaning and the value of his long preoccupation with 'wholeness.' From the time he announced in 'The Service' that 'the exploit of a brave life consists in its momentary completeness,' he continued to make brief definitions of that quality, and of how it might be gained. These have direct bearing on the skill he had mastered in such passages as have just been discussed. The year after 'The Service' he developed his sentence further: 'The best and bravest deed is that which the whole man—heart, lungs, hands, fingers, and toes—at any time prompts . . . This is the meaning of integrity; this is to be an integer, and not a fraction.' He subsequently shifted his symbols to correspond to his own mode of existence, and grouped them not around the warrior hero but around the scholar, who, if he is wise, 'will confine the observations of his mind as closely as possible to the experience or life of his senses. His thought must live with and be inspired with the life of the body . . . Dwell as near as possible to the channel in which your life flows.' In this respect more than in any other was the practice of Thoreau's scholar more thoroughgoing than Emerson's. He never wavered in his belief that 'steady labor with the hands, which engrosses the attention also, is unquestionably the best method of removing palaver and sentimentality out of one's style, both of speaking and writing.' Emerson also advocated work in the garden as a sanative balance for the thinker, but neither his temperament nor muscles were geared to it, as his small son observed when he shouted, 'Papa, I am afraid you will dig your leg.' Nor did these efforts serve to steady and release his skill in writing; like Hawthorne at Brook Farm, he merely found his energies exhausted by them.

But for Thoreau, as for Robert Frost, this gospel was a living act. The root of his hatred of the division of labor was that it destroyed the potential balance of his agrarian world, one of the main ideals of which was the union of labor and culture. As Dr. Channing said, 'I wish to see labor honored and united with the free development of the intellect and heart. Mr. Alcott, hiring himself out for day labor, and at the same time living in a region of high thought, is perhaps the most interesting object in our commonwealth. I do not care much for Orpheus in *The Dial*, but Orpheus at the plow is after my own heart.' Although Channing's enthusiasm might have cooled if he had watched Orpheus neglect the plow for conversations at Fruitlands,[2] his general position was subscribed to on every hand. As Julian Hawthorne said of the world to which his father and mother had belonged, 'The seed of democracy was bearing its first and (so far) its sweetest and most delicate fruit. Men and women of high refinement, education, and sensibilities thought it no derogation, not only to work for their living, but to tend a counter, sweep a room, or labor in the field.' But what might be accepted as a sensible necessity by some and degenerate into a monotonous routine for others was hailed by Thoreau. He always insisted that 'men should not labor foolishly like brutes, but the brain and the body should always, or as much as possible, work and rest together.' That doctrine merges with what he wanted his rhythm to possess, the concentration that rises out of repose. Only by such unity of experience might his speech be 'vascular.' He developed his physiological analogy when, playing with the old notion of the bowels as the seat of compassion and tenderness, he said that poetry must not pass through them alone lest it become 'mere diarrhoea.' The poet 'must have something pass his brain and heart and bowels, too, it may be, all together.'

Such a violent analogy was necessary to startle his contemporaries out of their complacent dreaminess. Ellery Channing, irritated that Thoreau jotted down notes on their walks, said petulantly, '*I* am universal; I have nothing to do with the particular and definite.' But Thoreau's answer was that he also wanted to record something beside details: 'Facts which the mind perceived, thoughts which the body thought,—with these I deal.' There could hardly be a better definition of the way whereby he spanned the gap between the idea and the object. This power to unite thought with sense impression, the immediate feeling with the reflection upon it, is what Eliot

---

[2] Yet to be fair to Alcott it should be added that however perversely his actual ventures might turn out, he still believed, when sixty, that it was his good fortune to have been 'born in the country and brought up in the arts of husbandry under the eye of a skillful farmer, who gave me early to my hands and the uses of tools, so that from a child I have known what to do with them . . . I came as naturally to the spade, the plow, the scythe and sickle as to book and pen.' That early training may have been the reason why he was a pioneer in education through his insistence that it was necessary to develop children's bodies as well as their minds.

has discerned to be the distinguishing attribute of the English metaphysical poets, and has called—in a term now somewhat worn by his followers but still indispensable for its accuracy —their 'unified sensibility.' One of the analogies by which he defined this quality is as explosively physical as Thoreau's. The seventeenth-century writers knew that it was not enough to 'look in your heart and write.' 'Donne looked into a good deal more than the heart. One must look into the cerebral cortex, the nervous system, and the digestive tracts.'

There are not many points of contact between Thoreau and Eliot. But it belongs to the New England heritage of both to insist upon integrity; and each found one of the strongest reinforcements of his own aims in the seventeenth-century strain. Thoreau's most cogent application of Donne was when he rounded again (1859) upon his perennial theme: 'A man thinks as well through his legs and arms as his brain . . . The poet's words are, "You would almost say the body thought!" I quite say it.'

By following the course of Thoreau's own observations on language and rhythm in relation to sense experience, I have tried to define the distinctive qualities of his style. But these raise wider questions. His kinship with the seventeenth century is not a coincidence. His repeated affirmation of the organic correspondence between art and nature is not an analogy peculiar to Emerson and himself. By investigating the reasons why not only Thoreau but Melville felt as close to the work of Sir Thomas Browne as to that of their own contemporaries, we can hope to understand better the sources from which our mid-century renaissance sprang, and also to understand why we have felt again to-day the vitality of the seventeenth-century tradition. By examining 'the organic principle' as it was understood by Coleridge, we can apprehend a major theory of art, the theory that conditioned *Leaves of Grass* no less than *Walden*, and that leads directly into modern functionalism. In the next two chapters, therefore, we shall be engaged in related experiments. In the first of these we shall be concerned with appraising the art of Emerson's day through what its writers valued most in the art of the past. In the second we shall examine what these writers meant by the correspondence of art to nature, and why they found such a stimulus for fresh art in their rediscovery of this fundamental relationship. The first should throw most light on Thoreau and Melville and the twentieth-century rebirth of metaphysical poetry; the second, on Thoreau and Whitman and recent developments in our architecture and the arts of design. In both chapters Emerson will be found to have played a crucial role through his consciousness of the values involved.

REGINALD LANSING COOK (1903-   ) is Charles A. Dana Professor of English and American Literature at Middlebury College, and was director of the Bread Loaf School of English from 1946-64. A recent president of The Thoreau Society, he has published, among other books, *Walden Revisited* (1945) and *Passage to Walden* (1949). "In attaining a correspondence between natural phenomena and his inner moods," Professor Cook has written of Thoreau, "he released the possibility of inward growth, not alone for himself, but for all men."

From
The Sinews of *Walden*

REGINALD L. COOK

Passage to Walden (Boston: Houghton Mifflin Company, 1949), pp. 231-38.

The kind of work Thoreau wanted to do—"A book of the seasons, each page of which should be written in its own season and out-of-doors, or in its own locality wherever it may be"— he achieved in the *Journal*, and more, he succeeded in giving us the natural history of a whole township. After conquering the wilderness of Concord, he extended his horizon to include the wilderness reaches of the Maine woods and the seaward reach of Cape Cod. His general theme was the outdoors, and his writing amplified his subject-matter, for in the essay he discovered a form through which to communicate natural beauty latent in such commonplaces of life as a wayside ditch or a fallow field. His selection of themes was constitutional. Outdoors meant health and well-being to him; indoors meant sluggishness and sickness. He contended that a great part of our trouble was attributable to our indoor way of living. He thought he might undertake a crusade against houses, and in a way his books represent just such a crusade. In his writings he tried for what he called a hypaethral character, "to use," as he explained, "an epithet applied to those Egyptian temples which are open to the heavens above, under the *ether.*" He didn't want his books to smell of the study or library, but rather of the fields and woods. He wanted them to be unroofed—hypaethral. Considerably more hypaethral than *A Week* are *Walden* and the *Journal.* They are resinous and earthy enough, and almost entirely unroofed. Surely they are as permeated with the outdoors as a sugar maple with streaming sap in March.

Reading Thoreau's writings inspires a reserved but sterling admiration that advances steadily a degree at a time. They draw us quietly but insistently outdoors, into the fields and wood paths, along the country brooks, toward upland vistas. There is a tang to the writing like that of wild apples in late autumn—the tang of the natural life in the open air. The fruit of his mind—those hardy, well-ripened thoughts—were seasoned in the wind and frost and rain and sunshine, until they absorbed the qualities of their natural environment. In the field and woods they are spirited and racy; indoors they might be found harsh and crabbed to the delicate, house-bred palate. They represent his essential qualities—tanginess and tartness.

In the history of letters his contribution consists in the fact that he gave the relationship of man to nature, already firmly embodied in literature, clearer definition and a fresher and more vigorous expression. As a prose craftsman he possessed the ability to communicate with poetic imagination his sensitive response to nature's essential beauty, disclosing to us the seclusive life of the creatures of nature, like the old pout and her fry, or like the nascent life forming in a clutch of turtle eggs, or like the bream which when raised from its nest keeps up a sculling motion, "for unlike ours, the element in which they live is a stream which must be constantly resisted." His prose is, in effect, the product of a vigorous if somewhat perversely independent thinker, who seasoned his individualistic thought in contemplation, who unsheathed his emotions reservedly, and who loosed his conviction with defiance. One criterion by which one judges good prose writing is whether or not, when simply and clearly recorded, it takes hold by its own energy. By such a token Thoreau's writing excels. It represents muscularity of thought and a constitutional earthiness. The energy of the earth is in all that he had to say.

He was essentially a poetic proseman, if we accept his definition of poetry as "a true account of the actual," for whom living was the reception and communication of thoughts. This he says was his salient: to communicate those parts of his life which he would gladly live again. No wonder his writings are tonic and enheartening to the crippled or wounded spirit and invigorating to those who stand in need of inspiration. The natural vigor which emanates from his writings is as refreshing "as if a green bough were laid across the page." His record imparts courage and well-being.

He thought there was no more Herculean task than to think a thought about this life and then get it expressed. This was what he lived for, why he walked and talked and used his hands in manual labor, why he disciplined his senses, and why he practised with such patience and determination the arduous craft of writing. His writing does represent the fusion of an independent way of seeing life with an idiomatic way of expressing himself. His skill is shown in the degree to which he successfully mastered thought and feeling so that he neither blurred the clarity of the one nor diminished the intensity of the other through facile and inexact use of words. It is apparent also that he avoided overintensification of the personal pressure in expression which results only in mannered writing. Because the substance of his thought is rooted in a way of life with which he was intimately familiar, the reader is constantly reassured by "the warrant of life and experience" in what he reads.

His books, like his sentences, were the result of a long probation. It took seven years for the experience at Walden Pond and ten years for the voyage on the Concord and Merrimack Rivers to settle. Both *Walden* and *A Week* represent the crystallization of multiple experience, but *Walden* represents greater concentration of energy; each chapter is compounded experience. Its effect is linear; the effect of *A Week* is less so because it is less selective and orderly. The former has the Indian feel of nature; the latter is filled with unfolding vistas as of a boatman on a winding stream. There is a deliberate tread in the prose rhythm of each book, a pinch of the east wind in the expression, and a telling restraint.

It is in what his writings show of man's relationship to the New World environment that the significance of the experience chiefly inheres. The land is our heritage, and the basic desire of the American has been to realize in relationship to it a greater freedom for the human spirit. It is precisely because Thoreau's writings show under what conditions and on what terms the human spirit can most completely fulfil itself in the new world that he is one of our most influential writers. In the detailed record of a passionate attachment to his environment Thoreau shows us what it means to be naturalized in the New World. Nothing native was alien to him. Through a sensitive and imaginative sympathy he assimilated and he contained the naturistic tradition. He succeeded also in renewing it through the male energy of his prose.

Walden, more organic in structure and more compelling in its thought than *A Week,* is well established as the most indigenous nature classic in American literature. It is one of America's indispensable books. Its auroral atmosphere—"Rise free from care before the dawn, and seek adventures"—is like a morning song. Its content is affirmative, tangy, and surcharged. Its essence consists partly in the superb articulation of Thoreau's correspondence with nature, partly in the vindication of solitude and contemplation, partly in the exaltation of individualism, but mainly its essence consists in the galvanizing challenge of Thoreau's personal "awakeness" to those who have not yet learned how to emancipate their lives from material possessions. A challenge to conventional existence, *Walden* reflects its author's brag—a brag, by the way, for humanity and not alone for himself. "If I seem to boast more than is becoming," he said, "my excuse is that I brag for humanity rather than for myself; and my shortcomings and inconsistencies do not affect the truth of my statement."

❀   ❀   ❀   ❀

His passion for nature was very strong, as vigorous certainly as Whitman's passion for democracy, and as intense as Poe's passion for supernal beauty, but because his imagination was practical it restrained the powerful emotional surge to earthways. In Emerson's *Journals*, Thoreau is quoted as saying, "I wish so to live as to derive my satisfactions and inspirations from the commonest events, so that what my senses hourly perceive, my daily walk, the conversation of my neighbors, may inspire me, and I may dream of no heaven but that which lies about me." His interest in the concrete was only the focus of his experience. What did he see? What vision of reality had he? He made no notable discovery, like blind Huber's, that some species of ants practise slavery. Nor did he, like Swammerdam, fix the identity of the Queen Bee. He devised no scheme similar to Linnaeus' classification of plants in the *Systema Naturae*, (which, in spite of obvious limitations, was at least a scientific handle), nor did he originate a way of systematizing nature as Lamarck did by differentiating between the animals that were vertebrate and those that were invertebrate. Nor did he compose detailed studies such as Fabre painstakingly produced in his *Souvenirs entomologiques*. Thoreau did none of these things, yet his accomplishment and contribution to literature and philosophy, if not to science, was equally significant. In attaining a correspondence between natural phenomena and his inner moods, he released the possibility of inward growth, not alone for himself, but for all men, and a continual renewal of the intellectuality of civilization through a harmony of the human spirit with untamed nature. Civilized men he thought should never alienate themselves from nature, the original source of their physical, moral, and intellectual health. One of the main Thoreauvian emphases is the realization of joy and power originating in the organic functional relationship of a man with his natural environment.

To realize the wisdom of the natural ways, Thoreau did not reject the arts, techniques, and contributions of civilization. He did not advocate a return to the primitive way of life. Such an attitude he would have considered as irrational and obscurantist. He did not, like D. H. Lawrence, renounce the domination of the intellect and concomitantly proclaim the doctrine of the free, uninhabited action of the primal, intuitive forces in our blood-stream. He would have given an emphatic negative to the inquiry in *Women in Love*: "Isn't the mind . . . our death? Doesn't it destroy all our spontaneity, all our instincts? Are not the young people growing up to-day, really dead before they have a chance to live?" He did not believe in the surrender of the conscious will to primitive impulse. He did not believe that intellect negated spontaneity of natural response. What he did believe was that there were plenty of champions of the civilized life. He wished only "to speak a word for Nature, for absolute freedom and wildness, as contrasted with a freedom and culture merely civil." This is his statement. It is direct and clear enough. It does not exclude or reject civilization; it speaks only for the other side.

Thoreau's writings celebrate neither the primitive nor the sophisticated, but the simple life. To the sociologist they are an interesting reflection of the mutually harmonious relationship of the organism and its environment. In order to share what Thoreau experienced, one must be able to imagine what he lived, because his writings are the condensation of his mental and physical experience. Among those writings which originate in the experience of the American people and which reflect the acclimatizing of the American in his environment, Thoreau's are foremost. Our country will be completely the homeland of the American people when each region is as cherishable and rewarding spiritually as Concord was for Thoreau. For generations European stock transported to the New World had taken possession of America, but it was not until Thoreau speaks out that one has the sense of an American's passionate attachment to his region. He represents a stake-in-nature. There is a natural authority in what he says by right of being on the ground. He had lived here long enough for his foundations to settle; they rested on the security of the American earth.

What Henry Thoreau assures the enlightened citizens of the western world is the certainty that nature quickens and renews the human spirit through sympathetic relationship. By discovering and recording his association with the chief phases of nature in the progression of its seasonal cycles, he indicated a way for Americans to become naturalized in the American environment. His acquaintance with New England drift boulders, cattle fairs, meeting-houses, thin sandy soil, scrub oak, sweet fern, lilacs, swamp pinks, northeasters, huckleberries, hermit thrushes, bobolinks, rather than with skylarks and fieldfares, redstarts and meadow pipits, downs and coombes, heather and furze, billberries and haws of Old England, make his contribution as redolent of the New World as buckeyes are indigenous to Ohio or burr oaks to Illinois or redwoods to California. Though Concord only happened to be his meeting-place with nature, nevertheless he readily identified himself with it and sprang up like a natural shoot in its generous soil. It was his victory to be naturalized without succumbing to domestication. In a sense he was committed, yet free. He was committed to the regional spirit of place, but he was elemental like the prevailing wind. He was, in the true sense of the word, an elemental saunterer in Concord, and the world of nature was resonant in his ears, sensitive to his touch, graphic to his eye, pungent to his nostrils, savory on his tongue. "Of thee, O earth, are my bone and sinew made. . . . Here have I my habitat. I am of thee."

JOSEPH WOOD KRUTCH (1893-   ) has served on the editorial staff of *The Nation* and as Professor of English at Columbia and the New School for Social Research. In addition to his biography of Thoreau (1948), he has written biographies of Poe and Samuel Johnson, along with influential analyses of contemporary life such as *The Modern Temper* (1929). The reason Thoreau continues to be popular may simply be, Professor Krutch suggests, "that he is so stimulating a thinker and so extraordinarily fine a writer."

The Steady
Fascination of Thoreau

JOSEPH WOOD KRUTCH

The New York Times Book Review (May 20, 1951), pp. 1, 28.

During his life Henry David Thoreau was able to publish only two volumes. The first, issued at his own expense, sold less than 300 copies, the remaining 700-odd resting permanently on his own shelves. The second was "Walden," which did somewhat better, but not well enough to get a second printing before he died. Thoreau probably suffered less than most from failure. Nevertheless he would be pleased, as well as surprised, to know that "Walden" has been translated into most civilized languages and that Houghton Mifflin has just issued, for the second time, the journal of nearly 7,000 printed pages in which he collected the raw materials for books he never wrote because no one wanted to read them.

Popular opinion notwithstanding, this sort of exclusively posthumous fame is not very common. Most enduringly popular writers achieve a considerable measure of celebrity in their own time. Moreover, if Thoreau failed to do so, it was not because what he wrote seems at first sight remote from the interests of his contemporaries. After all, he was at least a kind of Transcendentalist in the very heyday of Transcendentalism; at least a kind of abolitionist at the height of the abolition movement; and he was, above all, a celebrator of nature in that New England which all but invented "nature walk." Yet that same New England which gave Emerson international as well as local popularity barely tolerated Thoreau.

Obviously there was something about his tone or his "slant" that irritated his contemporaries as much as it has stimulated readers of a later time—some roughness or acidity which we contrast favorably and they contrasted unfavorably with the blandness of Emerson. Was it the fierce nonconformity that made it impossible for him to agree even with other nonconformists and forced him to insist upon being both a Transcendentalist and an abolitionist with a difference? Was it the fact that his attitude toward nature was more nearly scientific and less suavely moralistic than the fashionable one?

Or was it even, perhaps, that he was, as Emerson was not, a good hater as well as a great lover? He wanted, so he said, to make his Journal a record of his loves not of his hates, but he did not wholly succeed. Read in it, for example, his account of the visit of the three oily "reformers." It is almost as venomous as anything in Swift.

Even today Thoreau enjoys two reputations which remain

more or less separate. In his own mind his criticism of that
life of quiet desperation, which he thought most men led,
was always to be considered in contrast with that happy,
healthy life "of nature" which they might be leading. One
group of twentieth-century readers goes to him to discover
what he meant by that last phrase and to read his account of
how joyfully he pursued his career as "Inspector of Snow
Storms." Another, interested chiefly in his criticism of existing
society, draws from it destructive arguments, while it remains
unconvinced by his defense of a simple life unencumbered with
superfluous "things."

Some of the founders of the British Labor party acknowledged him as one of their major prophets, but they certainly
did not propose a civilization dominated by what they would
call the very low "standard of living" which Thoreau advocated, and they certainly did not anticipate that leisure to
observe nature would be the principal reward of the worker in
a Socialist society.

Neither, for that matter, was either Gandhi or Tolstoy
what he himself would have recognized as a Thoreauist. Indeed,
Thoreau himself had no desire for disciples and said that he
should prefer to have in the world as many different kinds of
people as possible.

In a sense, then, one might argue that—since even today
the majority of Thoreau's readers are no more than half convinced—the reason why he continues to be popular is simply
that he is so stimulating a thinker and so extraordinarily fine
a writer. That he is both is as clear from the Journals as it is
from "Walden" itself. From the earlier portions of that Journal
a good deal of "Walden" was assembled, and in the later
portions there are—besides a number of rougher notes and a
not inconsiderable amount of routine record—page after page as
freshly felt and as brilliantly phrased as the best of "Walden."

An anthologist is compelled to take as much from these
Journal writings (which Thoreau never saw in print) as from
his one famous book. Passages of description like that of the
snowstorm, or any one of the dozens dealing with his encount-
ers with wild animals or with his thoughts upon the destructive-
ness of man, are like nothing ever written before. And they are

better than anything which any of the scores who have taken him as their model have been able to achieve since. Along with these passages are others like that outburst concerning the Gold Rush and the whole philosophy of men who would "live by luck—without contributing any value to society." "The hog that roots his living, and so makes manure," he says, "would be ashamed of such company."

If such things explain Thoreau's present fame, they do not explain why his contemporaries recognized so slowly his greatness, even as a mere writer. Yet the reasons are not really so very obscure. So far as his attitude toward nature is concerned, it was something he had to teach others before they could share it.

They were prepared for the sentimental-picturesque and for Emerson's somewhat fanciful method that enabled him to find soothing moral lessons in all natural phenomena. They were not prepared for Thoreau's special sort of pantheism —some, indeed, thought it blasphemous—nor for that intimate fellow-feeling for all living creatures, which many "nature writers" have since tried to express and which one will find today so conspicuous in the works of Albert Schweitzer. Thoreau also had a "reverence for life" that most readers were not prepared to understand.

For the increased comprehension of his social criticism there is a grimmer reason. He was in a sense a prophet of doom. Whereas he wrote in an age of optimism, when growing greatness seemed the manifest destiny of America, he is read in an age when the gloomiest see a future darker than he did and even the more optimistic are beset by doubts and fears.

It is not that there are many willing even now to accept his program. Very few—even the severest critics of our industrial society—believe, as he did, not merely that the distribution of goods is equitable but that a superabundance of such goods, no matter how well distributed, is no sign of a healthy or a happy civilization. There are, nevertheless, a great many more now than there once were who are willing to consider sympathetically his negative criticism, his insistence that the pursuit of wealth and the actual achievement of wealth have not produced the results hoped for.

He lived at the beginning of the great era of invention and of industrial expansion. He predicted the failure of a great experiment that was just being tried. We are living at the disillusioned end of at least one epoch of expansion, and what must have seemed to most of his contemporaries mere crankiness and perversity seems less obviously that today.

Who in his day could have thought his choice of railroad building as a symbol of the futility of mechanical complexity other than absurd? We, on the other hand, are better prepared to see the wry humor of his remarks on that subject. "When the smoke is blown away and the vapor condensed it will be perceived that a few are riding but the rest are run over." Whether justified or not, it is certainly a very common opinion in our time that modern invention has indeed managed to run over many of the persons it was supposed to benefit.

RAYMOND ADAMS (1898-   ), bibliographer, critic, and for many years a professor of English at the University of North Carolina, was an organizer of The Thoreau Society and its first president. He has been an editor of the *Thoreau Society Bulletin*, and has written numerous articles on Thoreau and on nineteenth-century American literature.

Thoreau's Mock-Heroics and The American Natural History Writers

RAYMOND ADAMS

Studies in Philology, Vol. 52 (1955), 86-97. An address delivered before The Grolier Club, New York City, March 16, 1954, in connection with an exhibit marking the centennial of the publication of *Walden*.

There was a time, and not so very long ago, when the *Walden* passage about the grim battle of the red and black ants was the only thing by Henry Thoreau most Americans had read. That was in the school readers as the sole representation of all his writings. I suppose it was put there because it was a short narrative, very simple, and easily taken from its context, for it is an episode that hardly has so much as a context. Thus it fitted the demands of an anthologist very well. Besides, it was a safe passage, something that could hardly be said of every passage of *Walden*. Moreover, it contained some allusion to Concord Fight and thus might reënforce a history lesson; and it contained still more allusion to the *Iliad* and to Greek warfare and thus might reënforce other lessons, for at that time American school children studied ancient history and read Bryant's *Iliad*.

In Thoreau's own day, of course, neither Bryant's *Iliad*, nor Pope's *Iliad*, nor anybody's *Iliad* except the original Greek poem was studied in the academies that prepared boys for college, and Thoreau could be reasonably sure that an allusion to Achilles, Priam, or Andromache would not fall into an uncomprehending mind—at least among the formally educated. Girls did not so often read Greek in the original; but from the casual way in which references to the classics were dropped into the general literature of the day, it is evident that a decent acquaintance with Homer was nothing but decent. By the close of the nineteenth century the "deliterating" process in secondary education had gone so far that one could get into college with no more knowledge of Homer than would be gained from studying Bryant's translation. Even then a freshman would have heard of Achilles and Priam. It is only now that we have freshmen and even sophomores who are completely "disallusioned."

Nothing by Thoreau was a college entrance requirement in those days. Nor would anything by Thoreau normally then be read in college. So the elementary reading books included the battle of the ants more as a gesture toward natural history literature than as a gesture toward Thoreau. It was a prose passage to stand alongside Emerson's

> The mountain and the squirrel
> Had a quarrel,

—to compare one battle with another.

Yet, the instinct of the early anthologist was right, I think. By accident he had selected from a great book a passage that represented its author at his best in one particular. Surely it did not seem a very important particular at the time, and it has not seemed a *very* important particular since. But I wonder if we may not put this mock-heroic device of Thoreau's—never better practiced by him than in the account of the ant battle—into place as one of the keys that will help unlock his mystery.

There is, to begin with, no doubt about Thoreau's knowledge of the classics and particularly no doubt about his admiration of Homer's epics. Early in his long association with the Concord Lyceum, six years out of college, his third lecture before that lyceum (November 29, 1843) was on "Ancient Poets" and concerned itself with Homer along with Ossian and Chaucer. It was a lecture he liked well enough to print as an essay in the January, 1844, *Dial* and to use again five years later as part of *A Week on the Concord and Merrimack Rivers*. Moreover, the early volumes of his journal and the books he prepared for the press are peppered with Homer allusions—*peppered* is a carefully chosen word here, for a phrase from Homer is the spice of many a page. But we need not labor Thoreau's knowledge of the classics. He could not have escaped them if he would; and it is clear that he had literary perception enough not to want to escape them but to like them even when they were still textbook tasks from day to day. Nor do we read far in his notes before we are aware that he knew and liked epics, from Homer and Virgil to Dante and Milton, and (because it was the romantic period) those curious epics MacPherson's *Ossian* and Bailey's *Festus*. But Homer remained his favorite.

All this classical influence on Thoreau is the subject of Miss Ethel Seybold's recent book, *Thoreau, The Quest and the Classics*,[1] an index of his entire knowledge of Greek and Roman literature and an essay on his seeking throughout his life for what she calls "Homeric simplicity of life and thought." We need now only be reminded of what everyone knows: that Thoreau was a reader and to a degree a scholar of Latin and Greek writings, that Homer held first place among them, and that thus he knew the epic at its fountainhead. He knew it so well, indeed, that his imagination seems to have turned to it naturally. And his fancy turned to it too in the way that marks all mock-heroic—a fanciful analogy, an interpretation of the small in terms of the large, an examination of the inconsiderable under such a microscope of real or implied epic comparison

[1] New Haven: Yale University Press, 1951.

that it becomes considerable and rises to significance and dignity.

There is an example (for it is time to see some examples) early in *Walden*. Thoreau, in the "Where I Lived and What I Lived For" second chapter of the book, is writing his great hymn to morning and is thinking of course of Homer. He writes, "Morning brings back the heroic ages." Then without pausing he picks up within his airy little house among the pines the merest morning incident,

> I was as much affected by the faint hum of a mosquito making its invisible and unimaginable tour through my apartment at earliest dawn, when I was sitting with door and windows open, as I could be by any trumpet that ever sang of fame. It was Homer's requiem; itself an Iliad and Odyssey in the air, singing its own wrath and wanderings.[2]

Little anopheles takes on heroic proportions; he very genuinely affects Thoreau, who now sees the room in the proportions it must assume during the auroral flight of a buzzing wandering insect, but an insect endowed with the greatest human traits, an embodied Iliad and Odyssey both, at once a wrathful Achilles *and* a wandering Ulysses. That one invisible matutinal buzz should be two Homeric heroes rolled into one and should do his (or their) own singing of wrath and wanderings must give Thoreau's mosquito some kind of an All-American mock-epic rating.

So it is when we look more closely at the great battle of the ants:

> . . . It was not a *duellum,* but a *bellum,* a war between two races of ants, the red always pitted against the black, and frequently two red ones to one black. The legions of these Myrmidons covered all the hills and vales in my woodyard, and the ground was already strewn with the dead and dying, both red and black. It was the only battle which

[2] *The Writings of Henry David Thoreau* (20 vols.; Boston, 1906), II, 98-99. This work will hereafter be referred to as *Writings.*

I have ever witnessed, the only battlefield I ever trod while the battle was raging; internecine war; the red republicans on the one hand, and the black imperialists on the other. . . . It was evident that their battle-cry was "Conquer or die." In the meanwhile there came along a single red ant on the hill-side of this valley, evidently full of excitement, who either had despatched his foe, or had not yet taken part in the battle; probably the latter, for he had lost none of his limbs; whose mother had charged him to return with his shield or upon it. Or perchance he was some Achilles, who had nourished his wrath apart, and had now come to avenge or rescue his Patroclus. . . . I should not have wondered by this time to find that they had their respective musical bands stationed on some eminent chip, and playing their national airs the while, to excite the slow and cheer the dying combatants. I was myself excited somewhat even as if they had been men. The more you think of it, the less the difference. And certainly there is not the fight recorded in Concord history, at least, if in the history of America, that will bear a moment's comparison with this, whether for the numbers engaged in it, or for the patriotism and heroism displayed. For numbers and for carnage it was an Austerlitz or Dresden. Concord Fight! Two killed on the patriot's side, and Luther Blanchard wounded! Why here every ant was a Buttrick,—"Fire! for God's sake fire!"—and thousands shared the fate of Davis and Hosmer. There was not one hireling there. I have no doubt that it was a principle they fought for, as much as our ancestors, and not to avoid a three-penny tax on their tea; and the results of this battle will be as important and memorable to those whom it concerns as those of the battle of Bunker Hill at least.[3]

When one talks about the hills and vales of a woodyard, a sunny valley and an eminent chip, the battle cry of an ant, the shield of an emmet whose Spartan mother sent him into battle, and the wrath of a pismire Achilles, one is using the method of

[3] *Writings*, II, 253-55.

the mock-epic—and in the present instance using it very well, it seems to me.

The mosquito's flight was all classical. But this battle of the ants gets local and dwarfs Concord's very own battle. The neighbors might not mind a mocking of the seige of Troy; but it is quite another thing to mock in Concord itself the fight at North Bridge. And this formicidal conflict is presented as much more important than the fight on the Nineteenth of April; it is as vast, as principled, and as consequential as Bunker Hill. Thus satire appears. The first example merely created a sense of wonder by raising to epic proportions a mosquito's wanderings through a little room. This raises embattled insects to the importance of men in order to reduce men to the level of insects. That partakes of Swift as well as Homer. Quite unwittingly, we may be sure, the early anthologist even while he sought a harmless passage from *Walden* let a seed of Thoreau's satire and social criticism fall into his book. Of course, he could hardly quote at all from *Walden* and keep out social comment, for it is latent in every paragraph.

Epic similes appear all through Thoreau's writings. It is not something peculiar to *Walden*. And it is not a device restricted to insects. For instance, there is the great skunk-cabbage of the October 31, 1857, journal:

> If you are afflicted with melancholy at this season, go to the swamp and see the brave spears of skunk-cabbage buds already advanced toward a new year. Their gravestones are not bespoken yet. Who shall be sexton to them? Is it the winter of their discontent? Do they seem to have lain down to die, despairing of skunk-cabbagedom? "Up and at 'em," "Give it to 'em," "Excelsior," "Put it through,"— these are their mottoes. Mortal human creatures must take a little respite in this fall of the year; their spirits do flag a little. There is a little questioning of destiny, and thinking to go like cowards to where the "weary shall be at rest." But not so with the skunk-cabbage. Its withered leaves fall and are transfixed by a rising bud. Winter and death are ignored; the circle of life is complete. Are these false prophets? Is it a lie or a vain boast underneath the skunk-

cabbage bud, pushing it upward and lifting the dead leaves with it? They rest with spears advanced; they rest to shoot!

I say it is good for me to be here, slumping in the mud, a trap covered with withered leaves. See these green cabbage buds lifting the dry leaves in that watery and muddy place. There is no can't nor cant to them. They see over the brow of winter's hill. They see another summer ahead.[4]

The vegetable has something heroic here. It behaves like a dauntless knight, however unlike a knight it may smell. It is endowed with courage that puts to shame our human fear. It will not even think of dying; and so it burgeons life.

Yet if death come, we may still be shamed into better burials by the mock-heroic of the leaves in the last two paragraphs about "fallen leaves" in "Autumnal Tints":

> It is pleasant to walk over the beds of these fresh, crisp, and rustling leaves. How beautifully they go to their graves! how gently lay themselves down and turn to mould!—painted of a thousand hues, and fit to make the beds of us living. So they troop to their last resting-place, light and frisky. They put on no weeds, but merrily they go scampering over the earth, selecting the spot, choosing a lot, ordering no iron fence, whispering all through the woods about it,—some choosing the spot where the bodies of men are mouldering beneath, and meeting them halfway. . . . They teach us how to die. One wonders if the time will ever come when men, with their boasted faith in immortality, will lie down as gracefully and as ripe,—with such an Indian-summer serenity will shed their bodies, as they do their hair and nails.
>
> When the leaves fall the whole earth is a cemetery pleasant to walk in. I love to wander and muse over them in their graves. Here are no lying nor vain epitaphs. What though you own no lot at Mount Auburn? Your lot is surely cast somewhere in this vast cemetery, which has been consecrated from of old. You need attend no auction to secure a place. There is room enough here. The loose strife shall

4 *Writings*, XVI, 150-51.

bloom and the huckleberry-bird sing over your bones. The woodman and hunter shall be your sextons, and the children shall tread upon the borders as much as they will. Let us walk in the cemetery of the leaves; this is your true Greenwood Cemetery.[5]

The satire is more bitter here. The skunk-cabbage but shamed us out of our fears; the death of leaves may shame us out of vanities, our sepulchral trappings. But Thoreau's method is still that of mock-epic: the minikins of nature are superior to the magnificoes of men, equal to the creations of poets.

But Thoreau's mock-heroic trait need not be bitter nor satiric. It can illustrate itself in gentler ways. To the insects and leaves we must add the fish; and to the heroic morning of wrath and wandering we must add the evening peace at the close of the "Sunday" chapter of *A Week*:

The Scene-shifter saw fit here to close the drama of this day, without regard to any unities which we mortals prize. Whether it might have proved tragedy, or comedy, or tragi-comedy, or pastoral, we cannot tell. This Sunday ended by the going down of the sun, leaving us still on the waves. But they who are on the water enjoy a longer and brighter twilight than they who are on the land, for here the water, as well as the atmosphere, absorbs and reflects the light, and some of the day seems to have sunk down into the waves. The light gradually forsook the deep water, as well as the deeper air, and the gloaming came to the fishes as well as to us, and more dim and gloomy to them, whose day is a perpetual twilight, though sufficiently bright for their weak and watery eyes. Vespers had already rung in many a dim and watery chapel down below, where the shadows of the weeds were expanded in length over the sandy floor. The vespertinal pout had already begun to flit on leathern fin, and the finny gossips withdrew from the fluvial street to creeks and coves, and other private haunts, excepting a few of stronger fin, which anchored in the stream, stemming the tide even in their dreams. Mean-

5 *Writings*, V, 269-70.

while, like a dark evening cloud, we were wafted over the cope of their sky, deepening the shadows in their deluged fields.[6]

This lilliputian city of the fish is seen from street level, eye to eye with the gossips staying late. Chapel bells ring, shadows lengthen, saturated fields lie on either side, and overhead, like a waterfowl, a pout pursues his solitary way. And then, far above, like some huge cloud of doom, deeper darkness drifts. And this deep, dark thing is but the bottom of a rowboat. It startles one, for the little city of the fish had been magnified until the reader himself had accepted the illusion of size.

When the Sunday sun went down and dimness overtook the little city under the water, Thoreau says he and his brother were left "still on the waves." What waves were these beating against a ship sailing like an ominous evening cloud over a city in the sea? They were the waves of the Merrimack River, no great rollers in fact! Nor is the ship a galleon. It is the awkward rowboat of the Thoreau brothers, and they are its two-man crew. They are sailing and rowing the boat down sluggish Concord River and up the Merrimack across the New Hampshire line. Then, after a ten-day overland excursion, the brothers will return to the boat, retrace the route through the two rivers until one evening by starlight they will pass under the rude bridge that arched the flood, will enter Sudbury River at Egg Rock, and after seven days on the water will feel the boat "grating against the bulrushes of its native port."

Thoreau went to Walden Pond to write a book. And his book is the Odyssey of that river trip. It is a small Odyssey, to be sure, a one-week voyage across a state line, never more than a stone's throw from land, never meeting great dangers, never running any risks. Yet in the book it is always called a "voyage," and the two brothers are called "sailors," and each town seen from the water is a foreign place filled with strangeness and wonder, and the return is to a "port."

A Week is itself a mock-epic, mild and fluvial. Those people who have hunted vainly for the source of its plan in travel books and even in Dubartas have forgotten that on his shelf at

[6] *Writings*, I, 118.

Walden while he prepared the story of these wanderings stood the great original of travel books, the record of wanderings back from Troy. People have missed it because, like the tribute Henry Thoreau is paying throughout the book to his brother John, the Odyssean quality is so delicate. The mock-epic quality of the battle of the ants is obvious. Line upon line Thoreau follows the pattern of an epic battle, and there is enough satire of war in the account to make it recognizable for the mock-epic that it is. Are the unyielding insects displaying the bravery of the greatest legendary heroes? Or do men in human battles behave like insects? It is not entirely clear, and it was not intended to be clear.

However, in *A Week* there is no hint that man is trivial. The book as a whole is pastoral rather than epic. Its structure is a voyage that is reminiscent of Homer, but its material is the material of a romantic essayist. The magnification contributed by raising a little boat trip to the proportions of a voyage and a little venture to the proportions of an adventure succeeds in giving to the book the feeling of strangeness and wonder about neighborhood things that nature writers try so often to achieve and that few before Thoreau had achieved. Thoreau succeeded because he ran but a thread of the mock-epic through his first book; he did not push his fancy until it interfered with the greater imagination of the book. It is an artist who refrains from pushing a fanciful conceit beyond its delicate safe limit. There are flaws in *A Week*: it runs the risk of being a compilation of youthful journal entries, and it has essays like "Friendship" planted in it so loosely that they fairly invite the separate printing they have so often had. Yet the book is great because flowing through it as unnoticed as the slow current of Concord River itself is the mood put there by a mild mock-epic device that did raise an incident to an adventure and widened a riverbank in a neighboring New England town into a foreign shore.

Having played with an Odyssey, Thoreau must have been tempted after he left the solitude of the Pond to write an Iliad as well. His attitude at Walden had never been, of course, that of an Achilles sulking in his tent, withdrawn from battle. That alone may have dissuaded him. His life at Walden bore few if any resemblances to the events of the Iliad. It is true, as Miss

Seybold suggests, that he may have thought of his going to the Pond as a Homeric quest for values as essential and primitive as those in Homer; but it was simply not possible to think of his activities at Walden in epic terms such as he had so easily applied in the Odyssean parallel in the river voyage.

Walden is a comment out of solitude on society, so it lent itself to short mock-heroic passages like those about the mosquito or the ants. But the book as a whole could hardly be cast in any epic pattern, unless we regard the condensing of the action of two years into one as a gesture toward epic unity. A record of inner growth in solitude is not the stuff epics, or mock-epics, are made of.

Yet there is one trait. The little region of the pond provides ample room for his imagination. The pond itself is a fair sea, its shores are continent enough. Commerce is there as well as wildness; history and legends are there around the old cellar holes and the footpath around the pond, but a frontier is there too with its solitude and its horizons suggesting not only the prairies of the west but, as he said, the steppes of Tartary. There are in *Walden* surprisingly many references to the history of the place and to old settlers dead and gone. Thus an illusion of antiquity is cast over the place. And in such a setting elemental men pass through the woods, timeless hunters, fishers, woodcutters whose primitive occupations return the shores of the pond to nature. Concord village is over the rise to the north and is hardly out of sight of our consciousness for a minute, the railway is physically in sight across the water; both are ready to serve, and do serve, as subjects for satire. But in spite of village and train, Thoreau's art has given to Walden Pond and its woods a remoteness in time and place that make them a microcosm.

We can drop the phrase mock-heroic now in favor of the word microcosm. One of Thoreau's great contributions to natural history writing is his mastery of the microcosm figure. The mock-epic device raises the small to heroic proportions; but always, as its name suggests, it mocks some epic or other, has the taint of bookishness about it. It lends itself better to social criticism than to nature writing. So too the microcosm device raises the small to heroic proportions, not by drawing the parallel with some book or legend, but by drawing the parallel with great nature itself. The single little object obeys a cosmic law, so it is itself a little cosmos. How Emerson must have helped Thoreau to this idea: "A leaf, a drop, a crystal, a moment of time, is related to the whole, and partakes of the perfection of the whole. . . . Each creature is only a modification of the other; the likeness in them is more than the difference, and their radical law is one and the same."[7] The little time at Walden and the little place become in the book a microcosm of time and place. This is one (among many others, to be sure) of the qualities of greatness in the book.

As *Walden* viewed merely as a piece of natural history writing is an unprecedented book, teaching Richard Jefferies and John Burroughs and Wilson Flagg and John Muir, Packard and Pike, Torrey and Teale, so perhaps the microcosm method from transcendentalism by way of Emerson became in Thoreau, and especially in *Walden*, the precedent from which the naturalists have learned. The literary naturalist has a special problem. He cannot be the objective zoölogist or botanist. He must raise nature to the level of man's sympathy; but he cannot be the sentimentalist either and indulge in the pathetic fallacy, that error which ascribes human feelings to all things. Isn't the solution often found by naturalists in this very microcosm method whereby the small obeys such an overpassing law that it and man share in something beyond them both?

Perhaps we can see this ability of literary naturalists best if we go back to Thoreau once more for our examples—use him, as it were, as a microcosm of the microcosm method. There is a necessity sometimes to magnify physically, to show the radical analogies by expanding the small until it looms large enough to show the laws of its nature, to be measured in larger terms. "A day," said Thoreau in *Walden*, "is an epitome of the year. The night is the winter, the morning and evening are the spring and fall, and the noon is the summer."[8] Sure enough the laws of the seasons can be applied to a day, but not until the day has been seen in calendar terms. There can be sheer physical magnification as when he said, "Nature will bear the closest in-

[7] *The Complete Works of Ralph Waldo Emerson*, "Concord Edition" (12 vols.; Boston: cop. 1903), I, 43-44.

[8] *Writings*, II, 332.

spection. She invites us to lay our eye level with her smallest leaf, and take an insect view of its plain."[9] Here is the transcendentalist's law of perfection in nature, easily seen in gross examples but now to be seen also in the smallest leaf. Thinking as so often of the classics, Thoreau writes,

> Would it not be a luxury to stand up to one's chin in some retired swamp for a whole summer's day, scenting the sweet-fern and bilberry blows, and lulled by the minstrelsy of gnats and mosquitoes? A day passed in the society of those Greek sages, such as described in the "Banquet" of Xenophon, would not be comparable with the dry wit of decayed cranberry vines, and the fresh Attic salt of the moss beds. Say twelve hours of genial and familiar converse with the leopard frog. The sun to rise behind alder and dogwood, and climb buoyantly to her meridian of three hands' breadth, and finally sink to rest behind some bold western hummock. To hear the evening chant of the mosquito from a thousand green chapels, and the bittern begin to boom from his concealed fort like a sunset gun! Surely, one may as profitably be soaked in the juices of a marsh for one day, as pick his way dry-shod over sand. Cold and damp,—are they not as rich experience as warmth and dryness?[10]

One is reminded of the close-up photography of present day naturalists. Close-ups can be done with pen as well as with camera, and either way the object is not science and not sentimentality but appreciation, that prime object of the literary naturalist.

Another microcosm is the seeing of leaves floating near the banks of a river in the fall as if each leaf were a ship in harbor:

> Perchance, in the afternoon of such a day, when the water is perfectly calm and full of reflections, I paddle gently down the main stream, and, turning up the Assabet, reach a quiet cove, where I unexpectedly find myself sur-

[9] *Writings,* VII, 92.

[10] *Ibid.,* 141-42.

rounded by myriads of leaves, like fellow-voyagers, which seem to have the same purpose, or want of purpose, with myself. See this great fleet of scattered leaf-boats which we paddle amid, in this smooth river-bay, each one curled up on every side by the sun's skill, each nerve a stiff spruce knee,—like boats of hide, and of all patterns,— Charon's boat probably among the rest,—and some with lofty prows and poops, like the stately vessels of the ancients, scarcely moving in the sluggish current,—like the great fleets, the dense Chinese cities of boats, with which you mingle on entering some great mart, some New York or Canton, which we are all steadily approaching together. How gently each has been deposited on the water! No violence has been used toward them yet, though, perchance, palpitating hearts were present at the launching. And painted ducks, too, the splendid wood duck among the rest, often come to sail and float amid the painted leaves,—barks of a nobler model still![11]

What an innumerable fleet! What graceful "Nicean barks"! Has anyone else so well conveyed the dryness and lightness of fallen leaves? It was the artist in Thoreau that suggested dryness by floating the leaves on *water*.

Lastly, we must notice the social microcosm. We need not detail more, for we have already seen ants raised to organized armies and fish spending an evening on Water Street just below the Strand. Thoreau sees flocks of snow buntings, and he magnifies their flight into one that covered Maine and New Hampshire and settled at last on Massachusetts as a good place to get breakfast. "They have the pleasure of society at their feasts, a hundred dining at once, busily talking while eating, remembering what happened in Grinnell Land."[12] Or he sees forty or fifty water bugs roused by a warm spell in January, spinning and gyrating in a bay of Nut Meadow Brook. "I would like to know what it is they communicate to one another, they who appear to value each other's society so much. How many water bugs make a quorum? How many hundreds

11 *Writings*, V, 267-68.

12 *Writings*, XV, 229.

does their Fourier think it takes to make a complete bug?"[13]

Perhaps after all there is not much difference between mock-heroic episodes and microcosmic imaginings. For a century now our American literature has been enriched by the application of both methods to natural history until we have a literature of nature such as had not existed before. It scarcely could have existed prior to romanticism; but even after romanticism it hardly did exist before *Walden*. John Ray and Gilbert White were of a different school, so were Kirby and Spence, so too in America were the Bartrams, Alexander Wilson, and even John James Audubon. *Walden's* greatness may not be entirely nor even primarily in its qualities as a book of natural history. But it has those qualities too. They are the qualities of lightness and imagination, keenness and universality in the treatment of nature. Our literature of nature has those qualities now because *Walden* had them, and perhaps because Thoreau continued to use them in his writings that followed on the heels of *Walden*. We must remember that it was the success of *Walden* that gave us the shelf full of Thoreau books published during the fifty years between *Walden* and the great set of his journal in 1906. Because of Thoreau's art the rich array of our American literature of nature is by far the richer. If *Walden*, which did so much more, had done only that for us, its centennial would be memorable.

WALTER HARDING (1917-   ) has been secretary of the Thoreau Society since its founding in 1941. He has done extensive biographical research on Thoreau, and is author, among other books, of *The Days of Henry Thoreau* (1967) and *A Thoreau Handbook* (1959). Professor Harding is editor-in-chief of the forthcoming definitive edition of Thoreau's works sponsored by the Center for American Editions.

Thoreau's Fame Abroad

WALTER HARDING

Boston Public Library Quarterly, Vol. 11 (April, 1959), 94-101.

Henry David Thoreau was generally neglected by the American literary critics and historians of his lifetime and, in fact, through-

13 *Writings*, XVI, 256.

out the nineteenth century. He was "a prophet without honor in his own country" until fairly recent years. Now there is rarely a protesting voice when he is rated as one of our most outstanding authors. Turning to England one finds a somewhat different pattern. As has so often been the case, British critics were much quicker to recognize Thoreau's genius, although often there were dissenters there too.

In 1849, when it was published in Boston, a few copies of *A Week* were sent to the firm of John Chapman in London for distribution. The book received only two reviews. The *Athenaeum* termed it one of the "worst offshoots of Carlyle and Emerson." But the *Westminster Review* commented, "Notwithstanding occasional attempts at fine writing, and some rather long-winded disquisitions upon religion, literature, and other matters, —sometimes naturally arising from the incidents of the voyage, sometimes lugged in apparently without rhyme or reason, —the book is an agreeable book." Thoreau had complimentary copies sent to a few prominent Englishmen, and one, James Anthony Froude, wrote to him in thanks, "In your book . . . I see hope for the coming world."

In 1854, when *Walden* was published, again a few copies were sent to England. George Eliot gave it a brief but favorable notice in the *Westminster Review* and six months later wrote her friend Miss Sara Hennell, "I thought 'Walden' . . . a charming book, from its freshness and sincerity, as well as for its bits of description." *Chamber's Journal* printed an unfavorable notice almost entirely cribbed from the American reviews in *Putnam's* and the *Knickerbocker*, but adding, "The natural sights and sounds of the woods, as described by Mr. Thoreau, form much pleasanter reading than his vague and scarcely comprehensible social theories." The anonymous article "An American Rousseau" in the *Saturday Review* is an excellent example of the ability of the British to understand and appreciate Thoreau long before his own countrymen did. Reviewing the first edition of *Excursions*, it analyzes the essays therein, recognizing the scientific value of "The Succession of Forest Trees" and pointing out that in such pieces as "Autumnal Tints" Thoreau is not "seeing sermons in stones" but suggesting a "significant parallelism between the mind and heart of man and the economy of nature."

Mabel Collins, writing on "Thoreau, Hermit and Thinker" thought "some of his works are better worth studying than the more elaborate works of the popular professors of philosophy." But Robert Louis Stevenson, in his notorious "Henry David Thoreau: His Character and Opinions" declared, "In one word, Thoreau was a skulker." Some years later Gilbert P. Coleman remarked in the American *Dial*, "Of those opinions of Thoreau which have evidently been based on insufficient information, the most incomplete, unsatisfactory, inadequate, though possibly the cleverest and most brilliant, is that of Robert Louis Stevenson." A. H. Japp, the British biographer of Thoreau, made haste to suggest to Stevenson that he had misunderstood Thoreau's character. In a later preface to his essay, Stevenson retracted much that he had said, commenting, "Here is an admirable instance of the 'point of view' forced throughout, and of too earnest reflection on imperfect facts . . . I have scarce written ten sentences since I was introduced to him, but his influence might be somewhere detected by a close observer." But it was the earlier essay which won the wider hearing.

Although the British publishers imported American editions of Thoreau's works for many years, in 1886 the first true English edition of *Walden* appeared in Camelot Classics. Other volumes followed rapidly, so that by 1900 there were at least twenty editions of Thoreau's books in the British Isles. Typical of comments of the period are Havelock Ellis's "Thoreau has heightened for us the wildness of Nature"; W. H. Hudson's "*Walden* . . . I should be inclined to regard as the one golden book in any century of best books"; and Will H. Dircks's "Thoreau's is a rare and remarkable spirit."

It was, however, the Fabians and early Labour Party members who really popularized Thoreau in England. Robert Blatchford, whose *Merrie England* with a sale of two million copies was the first Labour Party best-seller, began his book with the injunction that if his readers first read *Walden* they would more easily understand his book, and confessed that he slept with *Walden* under his pillow. Many of the local units of the Labour Party were called Walden Clubs. Inexpensive paperbound editions of *Walden* and *Civil Disobedience* were distributed with the party's blessing. William Archer, the translator of Ibsen, lived from 1890 to 1895 at a cottage near Ockham in Surrey which he called "Walden." Edward Carpenter confessed that *Walden* served "to make me uncomfortable for some years," and frequently quoted from it in his *Towards Democracy*.

The Eagle and the Serpent, a "little magazine" published in London from 1898 to 1902, was "dedicated to the philosophy of life enunciated by Nietzsche, Emerson, Stirner, Thoreau and Goethe." In Ireland, inspired by his father's reading of *Walden*, William Butler Yeats wrote one of his most beloved poems "The Lake Isle of Innisfree." But Arthur Rickett in *The Vagabond in Literature* thought that Thoreau's reputation was being harmed by the over-zealous attempts of his followers to defend him from any and all charges of wrong-doing.

The centenary of Thoreau's birth was celebrated in London in 1917 at a public meeting at which W. H. Hudson proclaimed that "when the bicentenary comes around . . . he will be regarded as . . . one without master or mate . . . and who was in the foremost ranks of the prophets." The London *Bookman* devoted a whole issue to Thoreau, including a long reminiscent essay by Ralph Waldo Emerson's son Edward.

In the 1920's H. W. Nevinson thought *Walden* "the most beautiful product that ever sprang from American soil," and H. M. Tomlinson confessed, "I suppose Thoreau has done as much as any other writer to give my mind a cast . . . There have been reviewers who have hinted at origins for my books, but not one of them has ever noticed that I must have brooded long on Walden Pond." But Llewellyn Powys dismissed Thoreau as "neither a profound thinker nor a great writer."

More recent comments on Thoreau include Somerset Maugham's, "The interest of Walden must depend on the taste of the reader. For my part, I read it without boredom, but without exhilaration"; Cartwright Timms thought Thoreau has a pertinent message for us "in this age, when so many people are content to live their lives at second-hand"; Charles Morgan, the novelist, regarded Thoreau as "a man completely undaunted by the pressure of collectivism, in the highest sense an Uncommon Man, whose teaching is even more closely applicable to our age than it was to his"; Hubert Woodford maintained, "The Philosophy of Thoreau may be regarded as a corrective and a tonic for much of the artificiality of average human life"; and for Holbrook Jackson, "He becomes what many men entangled in the world would like to be, but which, lacking even his negative courage, they can never be."

Perhaps the outstanding fact in any consideration of Thoreau's influence outside of England is that it is primarily a twentieth-century phenomenon—even chiefly a phenomenon of the period since World War II. This is especially true of Latin America. To be sure, Joe Marti, the late nineteenth-century Cuban radical, was familiar with Thoreau's writings and mentioned him occasionally in his essays, but he stirred up no widespread interest in Thoreau among his countrymen. *Walden* was first translated into Spanish by Julio Melina y Vedia in Buenos Aires in 1945. A much more adequate version by Justo Garate appeared in Buenos Aires in 1949 and was sufficiently popular to require a second, revised edition before the year was out. Previously a selection from Thoreau's journal and essays, translated by Horacio E. Roque, had appeared in Buenos Aires in 1937. And a translation by Ernesto Montenegro of "Civil Disobedience" was published in Santiago, Chile, in 1949. A Portuguese translation of *Walden* by E. C. Caldas was printed in Rio de Janeiro in 1953. No editions of Thoreau's works seem to have appeared in either Spain or Portugal, and there have been no book-length critical studies or biographies in either language.

Walden was translated into French by L. Fabulet in Paris in 1922. It has remained in print consistently since that date and is now in its seventh edition. Regis Michaud translated a volume of selections in 1930. Léon Bazalgette published a fictionized biography of Thoreau in 1924, and in 1929 Andrée Bruel published her doctoral dissertation *Emerson et Thoreau*, one of the most detailed studies of the relationship of the two men.

There are indications of an earlier interest in Thoreau in

France. On September 15, 1887, Th. Bentzon published an article "Le Naturalisme aux États-Unis" in the *Revue des Deux Mondes,* stating that if *Walden* were to be translated into French it would be sufficient "to establish his reputation in France as a writer and thinker." In 1904 Marcel Proust wrote to the Comtesse de Noailles, "Read . . . the admirable pages of *Walden.* It seems as if one had read them out of one's self, they issue so much from the depth of our intimate experience." And André Gide has written, "I remember the day when Fabulet met me in the Place de la Madeleine and told me about his discovery [of *Walden*]. 'An extraordinary book,' he said, 'and one that nobody in France has heard about.' It happened that I had a copy of 'Walden' in my pocket."

As has so frequently been the case with American writers, Thoreau has received marked attention in Germany. *Walden* was first translated into German by Emma Emmerich in 1897. It has since been translated by Wilhelm Nobbe in 1905, by Frz. Reuss in 1914, by F. Meyer in 1922, by Siegried Lang in 1945, by Augusta V. Bronner in 1947 (a condensed version), by Anneliese Dangel in 1949, and by Fritz Krokel in 1950 (another condensed version). H. G. O. Blake's selections from the journals entitled *Winter* had been translated by Emma Emmerich in 1900.

In 1895, A. Prinzinger published a small pamphlet biography, *Henry D. Thoreau, Ein Amerikanischer Naturschilderer,* and in 1899, Karl Knortz, Whitman's friend and translator, another, *Ein Amerikanischer Diogenes.* There have been numerous critical essays on Thoreau in various German periodicals and books.

Frederik van Eeden (1860-1932), a Dutch short story writer and a socialist, was chiefly responsible for the interest in Thoreau in Holland. In 1897 he set about establishing a utopian community at Bussum, near Amsterdam, which he named Walden in honor of Thoreau. In 1902, Miss Suze de Jongh van Damwoude translated *Walden* into Dutch with a foreword by van Eeden; the binding and endpapers were designed by members of the community.

Interest in Thoreau in Denmark reached a high point during World War II, when leaders of the Danish resistance movement looked upon "Civil Disobedience" as a manual of arms. Soon after the war Martin Ashfield, one of the resisters, began a translation of *Walden*, but abandoned it when a version by Ole Jacobsen appeared in 1949. According to A. Ejvind Larson, the publisher, the edition was a great and totally unexpected success. When he commissioned the translation, he "hoped it would be possible to make the Danish public realize how great Thoreau was." But the first edition was exhausted in seventeen days, and a new edition was printed immediately. In 1951 Ole Jacobsen translated a pamphlet edition of "Walking" and "A Winter Walk."

In 1947 Frans B. Bengtsson translated *Walden* into Swedish in an edition beautifully illustrated by Stig Asberg. And in 1953 the work appeared in the Norwegian of Andreas Eriksen.

In 1901 Tolstoy wrote "A Message to the American People," in which he stated: "If I had to address the American people, I should like to thank them for the great help I have received from their writers who flourished about the 'fifties. I would mention Garrison, Parker, Emerson, Ballou, and Thoreau, not as the greatest, but as those who, I think, specially influenced me . . . And I should like to ask the American people why they do not pay more attention to these voices (hardly to be replaced by those of financial and industrial millionaires, or successful generals and admirals), and continue the good work in which they made such hopeful progress." The great Russian novelist includes many selections from Thoreau in his anthology *A Circle of Reading*. Gandhi and Tolstoy found a common interest in Thoreau in their extended correspondence. *Walden* was translated into Russian by P. A. Bulanizke in 1910, but no new version seems to have appeared since the revolution.

Walden was first translated into Czechoslovakian in 1924, and again in 1933 and in 1950. But this third edition, before it could be published, was seized by the Russians, "pending ideological investigation into its contents," and, to this writer's knowledge, it was never released.

Walden was translated into Italian by Guido Ferrando in 1920, and reissued in 1928. In 1954, Biancamaria Tedeschini

Lalli published a biographical study, *Henry David Thoreau,* based apparently chiefly on Henry Seidel Canby's biography.

"Civil Disobedience" was turned into Yiddish in New York in 1907 and again in Los Angeles in 1950. There have been frequent articles on Thoreau in Yiddish newspapers around the world. Supposedly *Walden* is now being translated into Hebrew in Israel.

Walden was first published in Japan in English, with notes in Japanese, in 1922. It was translated into Japanese in 1925 by Imai. A volume of English selections appeared in 1929. A new translation by Kodate Seitare was made in 1933, and the 1925 translation was reissued in 1934. A version by Emai Kisei as well as selections from *Walden* translated by Toru Okamoto appeared in 1948. In 1950 the book was translated by Hoitsu Miyanishi; in 1951, by Saburo Kanki; and in 1953, by Akira Tomita. Nor has Japanese publication been limited to *Walden.* In 1949 R. H. Blyth edited some selections from Thoreau's *Journal* and later a shortened version of *A Week.*

Apparently Thoreau has never been translated into Chinese. But Lin Yutang, in his *Importance of Living,* asserts: "Thoreau is the most Chinese of all American authors in his entire view of life . . . I could translate passages of Thoreau into my own language and pass them off as original writing by a Chinese poet, without raising any suspicion." Brooks Atkinson has told the writer that when he was a New York *Times* correspondent in China, during World War II, his copy of *Walden* disappeared. He learned later that his house-boy had started reading it, and was so entranced that he began to translate it into Chinese.

However, the most notable example of Thoreau's impact upon the modern world was Mahatma Gandhi's use of "Civil Disobedience." Gandhi went to England as a young man to study law. Through his vegetarian habits he became acquainted with Henry Salt, the British editor and biographer of Thoreau, who was also a vegetarian. Later, in 1906 or 1907, when he was fighting for the rights of Indians in South Africa, he received a copy of "Civil Disobedience" from a friend. "His [Thoreau's] ideas influenced me greatly," Gandhi told Webb

Miller. "I adopted some of them and recommended the study of Thoreau to all my friends who were helping me in the cause of Indian independence. Why, I actually took the name of my movement from Thoreau's essay, 'On the Duty of Civil Disobedience' . . . Until I read that essay I never found a suitable English translation for my Indian word *Satyagraha* . . . There is no doubt that Thoreau's ideas greatly influenced my movement in India."

Gandhi printed copious extracts from "Civil Disobedience" in his South African newspaper *Indian Opinion* for October 26, 1907, reprinting them later in pamphlet form for distribution among his followers. Roger Baldwin, then director of the American Civil Liberties Union, meeting Gandhi in France in 1931 on his way to the London conference, noted that he carried a copy of "Civil Disobedience" with him. It has been recorded that Gandhi always had a copy with him during his imprisonment. Nor was he unacquainted with Thoreau's other writings. In 1929 he wrote Henry Salt, "I felt the need of knowing more of Thoreau, and I came across your Life of him, his 'Walden,' and other shorter essays, all of which I read with great pleasure and equal profit." Like many other followers of Thoreau, he found "Life without Principle" another major document, publishing long portions of it in his *Indian Opinion* for June 10 and July 22, 1911.

That interest in Thoreau in India has continued since Gandhi's death is reflected in the recent publication of an anonymous pamphlet biography, *Henry David Thoreau: The Man Who Moulded the Mahatma's Mind*, in Delhi. In the summer of 1956 the Indian government announced that it was sponsoring the publication of *Walden* in all the major Indian languages. Thus Thoreau, who fed upon the literature of the Orient, returned in kind to the Orient full measure. The "hermit of Walden Pond," looked upon by his contemporaries as a second-rate imitator of Emerson, has become not only one of the principal literary figures of his nation, but of the world.

JOHN BRODERICK (1926-   ) is presently Acting Chief of the Manuscript Division of the Library of Congress and Adjunct Professor of English at George Washington University. He has taught also at the University of Texas, the University of Virginia, the University of North Carolina, and Wake Forest University. He has published widely in scholarly journals, among them *American Literature, Studies in Philology, Nineteenth-Century Fiction,* University of Texas *Studies in English, American Quarterly,* and *College English.*

The Movement
of Thoreau's Prose

JOHN BRODERICK

American Literature, Vol. 33 (May, 1961), 133-42.

> Our voyaging is only great-circle sailing.
> *Walden*

> Our expeditions are but tours, and come round
> again at evening to the old hearth-side from which
> we set out. Half the walk is but retracing our steps.
> "Walking"

Although Henry David Thoreau clearly aimed such barbs as these at the unadventurous sojourner in life, the quotations fairly describe the pattern of his own walks, the history of his life, and even—I venture to suggest—the pattern of his most characteristic prose and the structure of some of his controlling ideas.

I

A geometric design of the life of Thoreau would run to loops and curlicues. Concord was home base for a series of forays into the larger, more or less alien world. These began as practical *ad hoc* ventures: a pencil-selling trip to New York, interim teaching in Canton, Massachusetts, the four-year Harvard enterprise itself, designed to fit him for the great world and thus perhaps to disqualify him for Concord. That Henry—and not his brother John—should have been the beneficiary of family sacrifices is curious, and Thoreau himself is reported to have said that his education was not worth its cost. Whatever the family hopes and whatever his own evaluation, Harvard did not entirely "take" with Thoreau. During his freshman year, he walked home from Cambridge, the last two miles in his stocking feet. And when at the end of four years he returned to Concord, better shod and clutching the diploma a misinformed posterity has sought to deny him, he was—though he may not have realized it then—home to stay.

He may not have realized it, for the young graduate busily set out his trotlines for employment, and one who knew him well said that he would have gone to Alexandria, Virginia, to teach "if accepted." Nevertheless, there soon appeared a nagging, if only partly conscious, reluctance to leave his native town for more than a short excursion. Shortly before he left college Mrs. Thoreau had advised her son to "roam abroad to seek your fortune." His eyes filled with tears, but his sister Helen kissed him and spoke comfortingly, "No, Henry. You shall not go. You shall stay at home and live with us."[1] And so he did. His longest subsequent absence from Concord occurred in 1843 during his perfunctory and unhappy assault on the literary capital of New York at the urging of his patron, Emerson. It was conspicuously unsuccessful, and perhaps made Thoreau the readier the next year to decline a friend's invitation to visit Europe.

The outings made memorable for literature had begun in 1839 when Henry and John Thoreau spent a week on the Concord and Merrimac rivers. Others followed: to Wachusett, to Cape Cod, to Maine, to Canada, most memorably to Walden Pond. The river voyage initiated the pulsations of departure and return prominent especially in the years after Walden. Thoreau made the excursions of the 1850's with his eye on the periodical market, no doubt, but an excursion to Maine was an excursion merely, defined by return to Concord, whereas the ambitious venture to Staten Island had threatened to become linear, not circular. Concord, "the most estimable place

---

[1] The anecdote is told by William Ellery Channing in *Thoreau the Poet-Naturalist* (Boston, 1902), p. 18.

in all the world," was his locus of value, periodic departures from which were followed by symmetrical returns.

The Concord he loved was, of course, not the tiny village but the spacious "town." When the restless 1840's ended with the failure of his first book, Thoreau settled into a routine of daily existence, the high moment of which was the afternoon walk to Conantum, to White Pond, to Walden. "Set out at 3 P.M. for Nine-Acre Corner Bridge *via* Hubbard's Bridge and Conantum, returning *via* Dashing Brook, rear of Baker's, and railroad at 6:30 P.M."[2] So goes a representative passage in Thoreau's *Journal*, the literary monument of the normal life of the 1850's. Excursions outside the township supplied the travel books; daily excursions within it supplied the *Journal*. It is said that the amount of his daily writing in his *Journal* was equivalent to the length of his daily walk.

As for the longer excursions, only at Walden and on the rivers did Thoreau achieve ideal rapport between physical and spiritual. The river voyage was mental as well as literal, but, as study of Thoreau's revisions has shown, speculation was rooted in the sheer hard facts of the 1839 voyage. At Walden Thoreau soared because he first came "to know beans." The walk or the successful excursion was thus the factual grounding, the means of spiritual release, and often the literary symbol for their fusion.

II

Thoreau's writings, like *Leaves of Grass*, are full of movement, are on the go. The "walk" supplies structural thread for "Walking," "A Walk to Wachusett," "A Winter Walk," and *Cape Cod*. The extended walk or "journey" serves for *The Maine Woods*, *A Week on the Concord and Merrimack Rivers*, a "water walk" with occasional scrambling along the bank. Even "Civil Disobedience" records what its author calls "a long journey," the result of "traveling into a far country," and the dislocations of life arraigned in "Slavery in Massachusetts" symbolically culminate in this: "The remembrance of my country spoils my walk." (The surprisingly optimistic conclusion of the latter es-

---

[2] Henry David Thoreau, *Writings*, Walden Ed. (Boston and New York, 1906), VIII, 307.

say is occasioned by a white water-lily, "the emblem of purity," discovered on a walk.) *Walden* itself might be regarded as a year-long walk, for as in his daily walk Thoreau moved away from the mundane world of the village toward one of heightened awareness and potentiality, only to return spiritually reinvigorated, so *Walden* records an adventuring on life which structurally starts from and returns to the world of quiet desperation.

Thoreau has rarely received credit for such compositional excellence in large matters. James Russell Lowell spoke of his inability to sustain a work "to the serene balance of completeness" while praising his "exquisite mechanical skill" in the sentence or the paragraph.[3] The distinction has remained viable, despite considerable recent interest in Thoreau's structures. His writing is still likely to be described by friendly critics as a "mosaic" or "montage." One of the best, while comparing the writing to "an Indian's quiet tread, covering ground, making distance," nonetheless considers Thoreau "essentially an aphorist whose unit of writing was the epigrammatic sentence."[4] Thoreau's best paragraphs, however, do not depend entirely on "the personality of the writer" for their unity. Instead, they move as Thoreau did and as his books do—from the mundane known to the transcendent knowable and back again. By various stylistic means he involves the reader in an intense spiritual experience, only to set him down again in the world from which he has been removed, presumably with more abundant resources for living.

A fairly simple example of such writing is the first paragraph of *Walden:*

> When I wrote the following pages, or rather the bulk of them, I lived alone, in the woods, a mile from any neighbor, in a house which I had built myself, on the shore of Walden Pond, in Concord, Massachusetts, and earned my living by the labor of my hands only. I lived there two

[3] James Russell Lowell, *Writings*, Riverside Ed. (Boston and New York, 1892), I, 370.

[4] Reginald L. Cook, *Passage to Walden* (Boston, 1949), pp. 220-225.

years and two months. At present I am a sojourner in
civilized life again.[5]

The paragraph begins deceptively, especially since the disarm-
ing qualification, "or rather the bulk of them," suggests a
characteristic fastidiousness about fact which authenticates
Walden as a whole. But the remainder of the first sentence
comprises a series of short phrasal units, all but one of which
("in Concord, Massachusetts") puts the "I" at greater and
greater remoteness from the world of the ordinary reader,
removed by solitude, by locality, by personal construction of
his dwelling, and by activity—manual labor. The last two sentences of the paragraph mark the return. The second sentence
suggests that the distancing experience had temporal limits (a
suggestion implicit in the first three words of the paragraph;
we have also been reassured by "Concord, Massachusetts").
The last sentence "places" the "I," but there is ambiguity in
the word "sojourner," suggesting that his return may be only
temporary, that like Melville's Bulkington he may soon ship on
another voyage, that he has not passively renewed ordinary
obligations. The paragraph, in short, is a miniature of *Walden*
as a whole.

In its "out-and-back" movement the paragraph is typical,
but in its simplicity of means it is less so. Many of Thoreau's
paragraphs have the same movement but employ more complicated devices. Such paragraphs often begin with deceptively
simple, largely monosyllabic utterances which are succeeded
by poetic, allusive, metaphorical enrichment before the return.
But the closing sentence—often humorous—serves two functions: it completes the release, but it also recalls the journey
just completed. Meanwhile, during the journey Thoreau has
kept his reader aware of starting point and destination. Puns,
irony, quirky quotations and allusions, careful etymologies—
these are a few of his devices to relieve some of the tension of
the journey and forecast release from its spiritual intensity.

The most concentrated example of such writing may be an
amusing, rather trivial paragraph near the end of "Economy"
in *Walden:*

5 *Writings,* II, 3.

Not long since I was present at the auction of a dea-
con's effects, for his life had not been ineffectual:—
"The evil that men do lives after them."
As usual, a great proportion was trumpery which had begun to accumulate in his father's day. Among the rest
was a dried tapeworm. And now, after lying half a century in his garret and other dust holes, these things were
not burned; instead of a *bonfire,* or purifying destruction of
them, there was an *auction,* or increasing of them. The
neighbors eagerly collected to view them, bought them all,
and carefully transported them to their garrets and dust
holes, to lie there till their estates are settled, when they
will start again. When a man dies he kicks the dust.[6]

The spiritual exhortation of the paragraph is slight, emerging
chiefly from the negative examples of "desperation" concerning
furnishings. But almost all the devices are here: the pun ("ineffectual"), the familiar quotation eccentrically used, the ety-
mologically exact play on *auction* and *bonfire.* The sheer
ingenuity of these words and phrases prompts a double response, in which amusement softens the ardors of the better
life and actually secures these ardors a hearing. But the most
effective sentence is the last, in which the familiar folk remark
cuts two ways. Its familiarity is reassuring (even the low-keyed
demands of this paragraph are ultimately impracticable). But
its metaphoric aptness ("dust" is a favorite term of Thoreau's
for what is wrong with life) sets up reverberations which echo
the demands for a life of sanity and principle, even at the
moment of release from absolute insistence upon it.

One of the most justly famous passages in *Walden* is that
sublime apologia for life in the woods.

I went to the woods because I wished to live deliberately, to front only the essential facts of life, and see if I
could not learn what it had to teach, and not, when I came
to die, discover that I had not lived. I did not wish to
live what was not life, living is so dear; nor did I wish
to practise resignation, unless it was quite necessary. I
wanted to live deep and suck out all the marrow of life, to

6 *Writings,* II, 75.

live so sturdily and Spartanlike as to put to rout all that
was not life, to cut a broad swath and shave close, to drive
life into a corner, and reduce it to its lowest terms, and,
if it proved to be mean, why then to get the whole and
genuine meanness of it, and publish its meanness to the
world; or if it were sublime, to know it by experience, and
be able to give a true account of it in my next excursion.
For most men, it appears to me, are in a strange uncertainty about it, whether it is of the devil or of God, and
have *somewhat hastily* concluded that it is the chief end
of man here to "glorify God and enjoy him forever."[7]

An intense paragraph like this provides little comfort for the
man unwilling to accept the most strenuous demands of the
moral life; but there is some. The first sentence, like its author,
begins deliberately, then mounts and mounts—to an ironic
climax. The ultimate distinction of the idealist between "life"
and "not life" is nonetheless presented in a verbally playful
way. The slightly humorous qualifications of the next sentence
("living is so dear" and "unless it was quite necessary") provide
additional momentary relief before we are confronted with
that remarkable series of metaphors for life at its best. We have
passed Conantum and Nine-Acre Corner now; we are at
Walden itself. The language which records the author's fronting of life at "its lowest terms" (really the highest) has forced
the reader to a similar fronting. The excitement, the challenge,
the appeal are almost unbearable. But we cannot live at Walden
forever. To perpetuate such godlike moments would require
transfiguration of the human condition. Mercifully, the author
initiates a return by the parallel qualifications, "if it proved to
be . . .or if it were. . . ." The jocularity of "my next excursion"
distances both author and reader from the epiphany only
recently shared. The joke continues with the powerful extravagance of the next sentence (ironically balanced by the modest
"it appears to me"), but the last words of the paragraph are
"glorify God and enjoy him forever," words almost meaningless in their reassuring familiarity. The sojourner through this

[7] *Writings*, II, 100-101.

paragraph, however, has had a glimpse of the glory itself, and for him life (and the stale quotation) can never be exactly the same as before he entered the woods.

The long paragraph following this one in *Walden* reveals other stylistic means of departure and safe return: playful allusions to classical myth and fable (ants and men, pygmies and cranes) and the straight-faced drollery connected with the extended pun on "sleepers." Between these is the almost strident recommendation of "simplicity." In such a passage as that on simplicity, Thoreau loses some of the aesthetic detachment which he elsewhere maintains, but his functional stylistic devices enable the reader, at least, to enter and leave the paragraph with profit and without embarrassment. The companion passage in "Conclusion" in *Walden* ("I left the woods . . ." and the paragraph following) has roughly the same movement, out and back, culminating: "If you have built castles in the air, your work need not be lost; that is where they should be. Now put the foundations under them." Here we emerge almost with a blueprint for approximating in ordinary life the glimpsed reality in art of Romantic idealism.

And there are similar passages: such familiar paragraphs in *Walden* as those beginning "The mass of men lead lives of quiet desperation" ("Economy") and "With thinking we may be beside ourselves in a sane sense" ("Solitude"); that in *A Week* beginning "The New Testament is an invaluable book" ("Sunday"); the paragraph in "Walking" from which the epigraph is taken; and others. Thoreau's highly charged polemical writing ("Civil Disobedience," "Slavery in Massachusetts," and "A Plea for Captain John Brown"), on the other hand, has many paragraphs in which the author provides a journey without a return, working instead toward a more conventional climax. And, needless to say, a great many paragraphs do not reveal this kind of movement at all. But a surprising amount of Thoreau's best remembered and most effective writing through analysis displays its stylistic kinship to the well-loved walk.

Walden as a whole has recently surrendered its dynamic structural secret, in which the movement of the book is associated with the rhythm of the seasons. Still obscure, however, is the nature of some subordinate "movements," embracing several chapters. For example, after explaining where "I" lived and what "I" lived for, Thoreau treats first "Reading," an activity closely associated with civilized life, moves next to "Sounds," many of which still remind him of the village but which progressively and inexorably lead him (and us) further and further into the intense, distancing experience available in "Solitude," which culminates in the account of mystical visits from "the old settler and original proprietor," God himself. An almost too startling return from this high moment begins in the next chapter, "Visitors," the first paragraph of which incongruously, we almost feel *irreverently*, associates the saintly hero of *Walden* with a "bar-room." And the return is completed two chapters later in "The Village," a momentary return (the shortest chapter in *Walden*) before renewing the memorable journey.

At the very center of *Walden* is a troublesome but important chapter called "Higher Laws," which re-echoes some of the objectionable stridency of earlier passages. It nevertheless clearly contains a very intense spiritual exhortation in which fishing is associated with the primitive or wild and the renunciation of animal food with the spiritual or higher nature. The next chapter, "Brute Neighbors," commences with a comic, ironic dialogue between Poet and Hermit, in which the hermit must choose between going "to heaven or a-fishing." He eventually casts for the latter, sure that there "never is but one opportunity of a kind." Astute readers have recognized here some kind of descent, but this particular descent is merely one more example of the Thoreauvian "return" since the ironic dialogue is a comic version of the dualism so stridently insisted on in "Higher Laws." The function of the irony of self-disparagement here and elsewhere is to relax the tensions of the earlier chapter and enable the reader to return, chastened and invigorated but not left in the air of the inhuman abstraction of an impossible dualism.

It is of some interest that these two patterned side trips off the main itinerary of *Walden* cannot be discovered in the first prospectus, the earliest version of the book as reconstructed by J. Lyndon Shanley.[8] That first version lacks also "Conclu-

---

[8] *The Making of Walden* (Chicago, 1957).

sion" and thus lacks the ultimate return from Walden with its poignant admission: "I do not say that John or Jonathan will realize all this." In fact, almost none of the specimen passages cited above appear in the "first" *Walden*. Their absence suggests that whatever else Thoreau did with his masterpiece between 1847 and 1854, he discovered the possibilities of a pulsating, dynamic style which would engage the reader, secure his willing suspension of inertia, and involve him in a series of literary journeys seemingly of the greatest import, but not journeys without end.

In style as well as structure, in language as well as idea, then, Thoreau recapitulates the archetypal Romantic theme of rebirth. His significant contribution to the theme is his recognition that the moment of spiritual rebirth is not infinite, that the walk cannot be prolonged indefinitely, that return is inevitable. To death and re-birth, he adds re-entry. In a way, readers of Thoreau have always sensed this characteristic, seeking, however, to define it in philosophical or ethical terms, "the poet-naturalist," for example. But Thoreau, we must remember, is a literary artist, whose service to philosophy and ethics is to provide a fresh literary experience of perhaps old ideas and values. At its best his writing renews the vitality of a life of principle by providing the reader vicarious participation in a compelling version. His rhetorically extreme and seemingly intransigent claims for such a life, however, carry their own ironic qualification and thus make it available as ideal reality, if not as normal actuality.

Thoreau the man had his forbidding rigidities and intransigencies, of course, and Thoreau the almost priggish letter-writer even more. Such static intransigency does pop up now and then in the writing on "simplicity" or "Higher Laws" and occasionally threatens to dominate an entire work, "Life Without Principle," but only rarely. More often the wit, the humor, the irony render Romantic idealism accessible as a guide to life at its best rather than a monstrous abstraction existentially, perhaps, worthless.

The companions of Henry Thoreau's literary walks achieve a concrete experience of Romantic idealism, perhaps ultimately inaccessible in any other way. The dynamism of Thoreau's best

writing takes us momentarily out of ourselves to that heaven-
approaching plane from which the world of normality is seen
and judged. We are reluctant to depart and, once there, perhaps
more reluctant to return. The movement of Thoreau's probe enables us to do both and thus extract the maximum benefit from
both the going and the coming back.

STANLEY EDGAR HYMAN (1919-   ) has written studies of Nathaniel West
and Flannery O'Connor, and has been a staff writer for *The New Yorker*.
He is best known for *The Armed Vision* (1948), a study of the methods
of modern literary criticism. "The first thing that we should insist on is
that Thoreau was a writer," Hyman asserts, "and not only a writer, but
a writer in the great stream of the American tradition, the mythic and
non-realist writers."

Henry Thoreau
In Our Time

STANLEY EDGAR HYMAN

The Promised End (Cleveland, Ohio: World Publishing Company, 1963), pp.
23-39.

In July, 1945, we celebrated the centennial of Henry David
Thoreau's retirement to Walden Pond. Almost twice as many
old ladies as usual made the pilgrimage to Concord, to see the
shrine containing his furniture, and to Walden, where they had
the privilege of adding a rock to the cairn where his hut once
stood and of opening a box lunch in the picnic ground that
stands as his monument. The American Museum of Natural
History staged a Walden Pond exhibit. The *Saturday Evening
Post* ran an illustrated article. And to add the final mortuary
touch, a professor of English published a slim volume called
Walden Revisited. All in all, it was a typical American literary
centennial. Henry Thoreau would probably not have enjoyed
it.

A more significant Thoreau centenary would have been
July, 1946, the hundredth anniversary of his going to jail. Every
reader of *Walden* knows the story. Thoreau had not paid a poll
tax for several years, as a sign that he had renounced his allegiance to a government that protected slavery and made war

on Mexico, and one day when he walked into Concord to get a mended shoe from the cobbler he was seized and put into jail. That night the tax was paid for him, and the next morning he was freed, obtained his mended shoe, and went back to the woods to pick some berries for dinner. While he was in jail, placidly meditating on the nature of state coercion, Emerson is supposed to have come by and asked: "Henry, what are you doing in *there*?" to which Thoreau is supposed to have replied: "Waldo, what are *you* doing *out there*?"

It takes not much investigation into the story to discover that the actual details of Thoreau's first great political gesture were largely ridiculous. For one thing the act itself was both safe and imitative, Bronson Alcott having given Thoreau the idea three years before by refusing to pay his taxes and going to jail, where he was treated quite well. For another, Thoreau in jail seems to have been not at all the philosophic muser he makes himself out to be, but, as the jailer later reported, "mad as the devil." For a third, Emerson certainly engaged in no such pat dialogue with him, for the jailer allowed no visitors, and Emerson's actual reaction to the event was to tell Alcott he thought it was "mean and skulking, and in bad taste." Finally, the person who "interfered" and paid his tax was Thoreau's old Aunt Maria, disguised with a shawl over her head so that Henry would not be angry with her for spoiling his gesture.

Why, then, celebrate the centenary of this absurd event? For only one reason. As a political warrior, Thoreau was a comic little figure with a receding chin, and not enough high style to carry off a gesture. As a political writer, he was the most ringing and magnificent polemicist America has ever produced. Three years later he made an essay called "Civil Disobedience" out of his prison experience, fusing the soft coal of his night in jail into solid diamond. "Civil Disobedience" has all the power and dignity that Thoreau's political act so signally lacked. "Under a government which imprisons any unjustly, the true place for a just man is also a prison," he writes in a line Debs later echoed, ". . . the only home in a slave state in which a free man can abide with honor." "I saw that the State was half-witted, that it was timid as a lone woman with her silver spoons, and that it did not know its friends from its foes, and I lost all my remaining respect for it, and pitied it." He summarizes his position, coolly, reasonably, even humorously, but with utter finality:

> I have never declined paying the highway tax, because I am as desirous of being a good neighbor as I am of being a bad subject; and as for supporting schools, I am doing my part to educate my fellow-countrymen now. It is for no particular item in the tax-bill that I refuse to pay it. I simply wish to refuse allegiance to the State, to withdraw and stand aloof from it effectually. I do not care to trace the course of my dollar, if I could, till it buys a man or a musket to shoot with,—the dollar is innocent,—but I am concerned to trace the effects of my allegiance. In fact, I quietly declare war with the State, after my fashion, though I will still make what use and get what advantage of her I can, as is usual in such cases.

"Civil Disobedience" has been tremendously influential. It powerfully marked the mind of Tolstoy, and changed the direction of his movement. It was the solitary source book on which Gandhi based his campaign of Civil Resistance in India, and Thoreau's ideas multiplied by millions of Indians came fairly close to shattering the power of the British Empire. It has been the bible of countless thousands in totalitarian concentration camps and democratic jails, of partisans and fighters in resistance movements, of men wherever they have found no weapon but principle with which to oppose tyranny. In the relative futility of Thoreau's political act and the real importance of his political essay based on it, we have an allegory for our time on the artist as politician: the artist as strong and serviceable in the earnest practice of his art as he is weak and faintly comic in direct political action. In a day when the pressure on the artist to forsake his art for his duties as a citizen is almost irresistible, when every painter is making posters on nutrition, when every composer is founding a society devoted to doing something about the atom bomb, when every writer is spending more time on committees than on the typewriter, we can use Henry Thoreau's example.

Our first task in creating a Thoreau we can use is distinguishing the real man, or the part of him we want, from the various cardboard Thoreaus commentators have created to fit their wishes or fears. To Emerson, who should have known him better than anyone and certainly didn't, he was a bloodless character distinguished for his ascetic renunciations, a cross between Zeno the Stoic and a cigar-store Indian. Emerson wrote:

> He was bred to no profession; he never married; he lived alone; he never went to church; he never voted; he refused to pay a tax to the State; he ate no flesh; he drank no wine; he never knew the use of tobacco; and, though a naturalist, he used neither trap nor gun.

To his poet-friend and biographer Ellery Channing, Thoreau was the Poet-Naturalist, a sweet singer of woodland beauty, and to his young Abolitionist friend and biographer Frank Sanborn, he was a Concord warrior, a later embattled farmer. To Lowell, an embattled Cambridge gentleman, he was a Transcendentalist crackpot and phony who insisted on going back to flint and steel when he had a matchbox in his pocket, a fellow to the loonies who thought bran or swearing or the substitution of hooks and eyes for buttons would save the world. To Stevenson, full of Victorian vigor and beans, Thoreau was a simple skulker.

In our century Thoreau has fared little better. To Paul Elmer More he was one of Rousseau's wild men, but moving toward the higher self-restraint of neo-Humanism's "inner check." John Macy, one of our early Socialist critics, found him a powerful literary radical, but a little too selfish and aloof to be a good Socialist. To Lewis Mumford he was the Father of our National and State Parks, and to Leon Bazalgette, a French biographer, he was a savage, one of Chateaubriand's noble redmen in the virgin forest. Parrington makes him a researcher in economics, and *Walden* a handbook of economy to refute Adam Smith. To Constance Rourke he is the slick Yankee peddler out of vaudeville, who turns the tables on smart alecks, and to Gilbert Seldes he is an Antinomian.

Ludwig Lewisohn, an amateur sexologist and the Peeping Tom of our criticism, assures us that Thoreau was a clammy prig, the result of being hopelessly inhibited to the point of psychical impotence, or else hopelessly undersexed. The mechanical Marxists of the thirties are about as useful. V. F. Calverton conceded that he was "the best individual product of the petty bourgeois ideology" of his period, but hopelessly distorted by "Anarcho-individualism" and a probable sexual abnormality. Granville Hicks dismisses him with an epigram: "Nothing in American literature is more admirable than Henry Thoreau's devotion to his principles, but the principles are, unfortunately, less significant than the devotion." Van Wyck Brooks gives us Thoreau as a quirky, rather charming New England eccentric, his only vigorous feature an entirely fictitous hostility to the Irish, projected from Brook's own discreet xenophobia. To Edward Dahlberg, a philosophic anarchist and disciple of D. H. Lawrence, Thoreau is a philosophic anarchist and earlier Lawrence. And Henry Seidel Canby, who manages to be one of the best biographers in America and almost the worst critic, sums up his excellent, definitive biography with the revelation that Thoreau was a neurotic, sublimating his passions in a loving study of nature.

From these cockeyed and contradictory extractions of Thoreau's "essence" we can reach two conclusions. One is that he is probably a subtler and more ambiguous character than anyone seems to have noticed. The other is that he must somehow still retain a powerful magic, or there would not be such a need to capture or destroy him, to canonize the shade or weight it down in the earth under a cairn of rocks. It seems obvious that we shall have to create a Thoreau for ourselves.

The first thing we should insist on is that Thoreau was a writer, not a man who lived in the woods or didn't pay taxes or went to jail. Other men did all these before him with more distinction. At his best Thoreau wrote the only really first-rate prose ever written by an American, with the possible exception of Abraham Lincoln. The "Plea for Captain John Brown," his most sustained lyric work, rings like *Areopagitica*, and like

Areopagitica is the product of passion combined with complete technical mastery. Here are two sentences:

> The momentary charge at Balaklava, in obedience to a blundering command, proving what a perfect machine the soldier is, has, properly enough, been celebrated by a poet laureate; but the steady, and for the most part successful, charge of this man, for some years, against the legions of Slavery, in obedience to an infinitely higher command, is as much more memorable than that as an intelligent and conscientious man is superior to a machine. Do you think that that will go unsung?

Thoreau was not only a writer, but a writer in the great stream of the American tradition, the mythic and nonrealist writers, Hawthorne and Melville, Twain and James, and, in our own day, as Malcolm Cowley has been most insistent in pointing out, Hemingway and Faulkner. In pointing out Hemingway's kinship, not to our relatively barren realists and naturalists, but to our "haunted and nocturnal writers, the men who dealt in images that were symbols of an inner world," Cowley demonstrates that the idyllic fishing landscape of such a story as "Big Two-Hearted River" is not a real landscape setting for a real fishing trip, but an enchanted landscape full of rituals and taboos, a metaphor or projection of an inner state. It would not be hard to demonstrate the same thing for the landscape in *Walden*. One defender of such a view would be Henry Thoreau, who writes in his *Journals*, along with innumerable tributes to the power of mythology, that the richest function of nature is to symbolize human life, to become fable and myth for man's inward experience. F. O. Matthiessen, probably the best critic we have devoting himself to American literature, has claimed that Thoreau's power lies precisely in his re-creation of basic myth, in his role as the protagonist in a great cyclic ritual drama.

Central to any interpretation of Thoreau is Walden, both the experience of living by the pond and the book that reported it. As he explains it in the book, it was an experiment in human ecology (and if Thoreau was a scientist in any field, it was ecology, though he preceded the term), an attempt to work out a satisfactory relationship between man and his environment. He writes:

> I went to the woods because I wished to live deliberately, to front only the essential facts of life, and see if I could not learn what it had to teach, and not, when I came to die, discover that I had not lived. I did not wish to live what was not life, living is so dear; nor did I wish to practice resignation, unless it was quite necessary. I wanted to live deep and suck out all the marrow of life, to live so sturdily and Spartan-like as to put to rout all that was not life, to cut a broad swath and shave close, to drive life into a corner, and reduce it to its lowest terms, and, if it proved to be mean, why then to get the whole and genuine meanness of it, and publish its meanness to the world; or if it were sublime, to know it by experience, and be able to give a true account of it in my next excursion.

And of his leaving:

> I left the woods for as good a reason as I went there. Perhaps it seemed to me that I had several more lives to live, and could not spare any more time for that one.

At Walden, Thoreau reports the experience of awakening one morning with the sense that some question had been put to him, which he had been endeavoring in vain to answer in his sleep. In his terms, that question would be the problem with which he begins "Life Without Principle": "Let us consider the way in which we spend our lives." His obsessive image, running through everything he ever wrote, is the myth of Apollo, glorious god of the sun, forced to labor on earth tending the flocks of King Admetus. In one sense, of course, the picture of Henry Thoreau forced to tend anyone's flocks is ironic, and Stevenson is right when he notes sarcastically: "Admetus never got less work out of any servant since the world began." In another sense the myth has a basic rightness, and is, like the Pied Piper of Hamelin, an archetypal allegory of the artist in a society that gives him no worthy function and no commensurate reward.

The sun is Thoreau's key symbol, and all of *Walden* is a development in the ambiguities of sun imagery. The book begins with the theme: "But alert and healthy natures remember that the sun rose clear," and ends: "There is more day to dawn. The sun is but a morning star." Thoreau's movement from an egocentric to a sociocentric view is the movement from "I have, as it were, my own sun, and moon, and stars, and a little world all to myself" to "The same sun which ripens my beans illumines at once a system of earths like ours." The sun is an old Platonist like Emerson that must set before Thoreau's true sun can rise, it is menaced by every variety of mist, haze, smoke, and darkness, it is Thoreau's brother, it is both his own cold affection and the threat of sensuality that would corrupt goodness as it taints meat, it is himself in a pun on s-o-n, s-u-n. When Abolitionism becomes a nagging demand Thoreau can no longer resist, a Negro woman is a dusky orb rising on Concord, and, when John Brown finally strikes his blow, for Thoreau the sun shines on him, and he works "in the clearest light that shines on the land." The final announcement of Thoreau's triumphant rebirth at Walden is the sun breaking through mists. It is not to our purpose here to explore the deep and complex ambiguities of Thoreau's sun symbol, or in fact to do more than note a few of many contexts, but no one can study the sun references in *Walden* without realizing that Thoreau is a deeper and more complicated writer than we have been told, and that the book is essentially dynamic rather than static, a movement *from* something *to* something, rather than the simple reporting of an experience.

Walden is, in fact, a vast rebirth ritual, the purest and most complete in our literature. We know rebirth rituals to operate characteristically by means of fire, ice, or decay, mountains and pits, but we are staggered by the amount and variety of these in the book. We see Thoreau build his shanty of boards he has first purified in the sun, record approvingly an Indian purification ritual of burning all the tribe's old belongings and provisions, and later go off into a description of the way he is cleansed and renewed by his own fireplace. We see him note the magic purity of the ice on Walden Pond, the fact that frozen water never turns stale, and the rebirth involved when the ice breaks up, all sins are forgiven, and "Walden was dead and is alive again." We see him exploring every phase and type of decay: rotting ice, decaying trees, moldy pitch pine and rotten wood, excrement, maggots, a vulture feeding on a dead horse, carrion, tainted meat, and putrid water. The whole of Walden runs to symbols of graves and coffins, with consequent rising from them, to wombs and emergence from them, and ends on the fable of a live insect resurrected from an egg long buried in wood. Each day at Walden Thoreau was reborn by his bath in the pond, a religious exercise he says he took for purification and renewal, and the whole two years and two months he compresses into the cycle of a year, to frame the book on the archetypal rebirth pattern of the death and renewal of vegetation, ending it with the magical emergence of spring.

On the thread of decay and rebirth Thoreau strings all his preoccupations. Meat is a symbol of evil, sensuality; its tainting symbolized goodness and affection corrupted: the shameful defilement of chastity smells like carrion (in which he agreed with Shakespeare); the eating of meat causes slavery and unjust war. (Thoreau, who was a vegetarian, sometimes felt so wild he was tempted to seize and devour a woodchuck raw, or yearned like a savage for the raw marrow of kudus— those were the periods when he wanted to seize the world by the neck and hold it under water like a dog until it drowned.) But even slavery and injustice are a decaying and death, and Thoreau concludes *Slavery in Massachusetts* with: "We do not complain that they *live*, but that they do not *get buried*. Let the living bury them; even they are good for manure." Always, in Thoreau's imagery, what this rotting meat will fertilize is fruit, ripe fruit. It is his chief good. He wanted "the flower and fruit of man," the "ripeness." The perfect and glorious state he forsees will bear men as fruit, suffering them to drop off as they ripen; John Brown's heroism is a good seed that will bear good fruit, a future crop of heroes. Ultimately Brown, in one of the most terrifying puns ever written, was "ripe" for the gallows. On the metaphor of the organic process of birth, growth, decay, and rebirth out of decay, Thoreau organizes his whole life and experience.

I have maintained that Walden is a dynamic process, a job of symbolic action, a moving *from* something *to* something. From what to what? On an abstract level, from individual isolation to collective identification, from, in Macaulay's terms, a Platonic philosophy of pure truth to a Baconian philosophy of use. It is interesting to note that the term Bacon used for the utilitarian ends of knowledge, for the relief of man's estate, is "fruit." The Thoreau who went to Walden was a pure Platonist, a man who could review a Utopian book and announce that it was too practical, that its chief fault was aiming "to secure the greatest degree of gross comfort and pleasure merely." The man who left Walden was the man who thought it was less important for John Brown to right a Greek accent slanting the wrong way than to right a falling slave. Early in the book Thoreau gives us his famous Platonic myth of having long ago lost a hound, a bay horse, and a turtle dove. Before he is through his symbolic quest is for a human being, and near the end of the book he reports of a hunter: "He had lost a dog but found a man." All through *Walden* Thoreau weighs Platonic and Baconian values: men keep chickens for the glorious sound of a crowing cock "to say nothing of the eggs and drumsticks"; a well reminds a man of the insignificance of his dry pursuits on a surface largely water, and also keeps the butter cool. By the end of the book he has brought Transcendentalism down to earth, has taken Emerson's castles in the air, to use his own figure, and built foundations under them.

Thoreau's political value, for us, is largely in terms of this transition from philosophic aloofness. We see in him the honest artist struggling for terms on which he can adjust to society *in his capacity as artist.* As might be expected from such a process, Thoreau's social statements are full of contradictions, and quotations can be amputated from the context of his work to bolster any position from absolute anarchism to ultimate Toryism, if indeed they are very far apart. At his worst, he is simply a nut reformer, one of the horde in his period, attempting to "improve" an Irish neighbor by lecturing him on abstinence from tea, coffee, and meat as the solution to all his problems, and the passage in *Walden* describing the experience is the most condescending and offensive in a sometimes infuriating book. At his best, Thoreau is the clearest voice for social ethics that ever spoke out in America.

One of the inevitable consequences of Emersonian idealism was the ease with which it could be used to sugar-coat social injustice, as a later generation was to discover when it saw robber barons piling up fortunes while intoning Emersonian slogans of Self-Reliance and Compensation. If the Lowell factory owner was more enslaved than one of his child laborers, there was little point in seeking to improve the lot of the child laborer, and frequently Emerson seemed to be preaching a principle that would forbid both the rich and the poor to sleep under bridges. Thoreau begins *Walden* in these terms, remarking that it is frivolous to attend "to the gross but somewhat foreign form of servitude called Negro Slavery when there are so many keen and subtle masters that enslave"; that the rich are a "seemingly wealthy, but most terribly impoverished class of all" since they are fettered by their gold and silver; that the day laborer is more independent than his employer, since his day ends with sundown, while his employer has no respite from one year to another; even that if you give a ragged man money he will perhaps buy more rags with it, since he is frequently gross, with a taste for rags.

Against this ingenious and certainly unintentional social palliation, *Walden* works through to sharp social criticism: of the New England textile factory system, whose object is "not that mankind may be well and honestly clad, but, unquestionably, that the corporations may be enriched"; of the degradation of the laboring class of his time, "living in sties," shrunken in mind and body; of the worse condition of the Southern slaves; of the lack of dignity and privacy in the lives of factory girls, "never alone, hardly in their dreams"; of the human consequences of commerce and technology; of the greed and corruption of the money-mad New England of his day, seeing the whole world in the bright reflecting surface of a dollar.

As his bitterness and awareness increased, Thoreau's direct action became transmuted. He had always, like his friends and

family, helped the Underground Railway run escaped slaves
to Canada. He devotes a sentence to one such experience in
Walden, and amplifies it in his *Journal*, turning a quiet and terrible irony on the man's attempt to buy his freedom from his
master, who was his father, and exercised paternal love by
holding out for more than the slave could pay. These actions,
however, in a man who disliked Abolitionism, seem to have
been simple reflexes of common decency, against his principles,
which would free the slave first by striking off his spiritual
chains. From this view, Thoreau works tortuously through to
his final identification of John Brown, the quintessence of direct
social action, with all beauty, music, poetry, philosophy, and
Christianity. Finally Brown becomes Christ, an indignant
militant who cleansed the temple, preached radical doctrines,
and was crucified by the slave owners. In what amounts almost to worship of Brown, Thoreau both deifies the action he
had tried to avoid and transcends it in passion. Brown died for
him, thus he need free no more slaves.

At the same time, Thoreau fought his way through the
Emersonian doctrine that a man might wash his hands of wrong,
providing he did not himself commit it. He writes in "Civil
Disobedience":

> It is not a man's duty, as a matter of course, to devote
> himself to the eradication of any, even the most enormous
> wrong; he may still properly have other concerns to en-
> gage him; but it is his duty, at least, to wash his hands
> of it, and, if he gives it no thought longer, not to give it
> practically his support. If I devote myself to other pur-
> suits and contemplations, I must first see, at least, that I
> do not pursue them sitting upon another man's shoulders.
> I must get off him first, that he may pursue his contempla-
> tions too.

Here he has recognized the fallacy of the Greek philosopher,
free because he is supported by the labor of slaves, and the
logic of this realization was to drive him, through the superiority and smugness of "God does not sympathize with the
popular movements," and "I came into this world, not chiefly

to make this a good place to live in, but to live in it, be it good or bad," to the militant fury of "My thoughts are murder to the State, and involuntarily go plotting against her."

Thoreau's progress also involved transcending his economics. The first chapter of *Walden*, entitled "Economy," is an elaborate attempt to justify his life and views in the money terms of New England commerce. He speaks of going to the woods as "going into business" on "slender capital," of his "enterprise"; gives the reader his "accounts," even to the half-penny, of what he spends and what he takes in; talks of "buying dear," of "paying compound interest," etc. Thoreau accepts the ledger principle, though he sneaks into the Credit category such unusual profits on his investment as "leisure and independence and health." His money metaphor begins to break down when he writes of the Massachusetts citizens who read of the unjust war against Mexico as sleepily as they read the prices current, and he cries out: "What is the price current of an honest man and patriot today?" By the time of the John Brown affair he has evolved two absolutely independent economies, a money economy and a moral economy. He writes:

> "But he won't gain anything by it." Well, no, I don't suppose he could get four-and-sixpence a day for being hung, take the year round; but then he stands a chance to save a considerable part of his soul,—and *such* a soul!—when *you* do not. No doubt you can get more in your market for a quart of milk than for a quart of blood, but that is not the market that heroes carry their blood to.

What, then, can we make of this complicated social pattern of our purposes? Following Emerson's doctrine and example, Thoreau was frequently freely inconsistent. (He was able to write in *Walden*, "I would rather sit on a pumpkin and have it all to myself, than to be crowded on a velvet cushion," and a few pages later, "None is so poor that he need sit on a pumpkin.") One of his chief contradictions was on the matter of reforming the world through his example. He could disclaim hoping to influence anyone with "I do not mean to prescribe rules to strong and valiant natures" and then take it back immediately with "I foresee that all men will at length establish their lives on that basis." Certainly to us his hatred of technological progress, of the division of labor, even of farming with draft animals and fertilizer, is backward-looking and reactionary. Certainly he distrusted co-operative action and all organization. But the example of Jefferson reminds us that a man may be economically backward-looking and still be our noblest spokesman just as Hamilton reminds us that a man may bring us reaction and injustice tied up in the bright issue of economic progress.

To the doctrine of naked expediency so tempting to our time, the worship of power and success for which the James Burnhams among us speak so plausibly, Thoreau opposes only one weapon—*principle*. Not policy or expediency must be the test, but justice and principle. "Read not the Times, read the Eternities." *Walden* has been a bible for the British labor movement since the days of William Morris. We might wonder what the British Labour Party, now that it is in power, or the rest of us, in and out of power, who claim to speak for principle, would make of Thoreau's doctrine: "If I have unjustly wrested a plank from a drowning man, I must restore it to him though I drown myself."

All of this takes us far afield from what must be Thoreau's chief importance to us, his writing. The resources of his craft warrant our study. One of his most eloquent devices, typified by the crack about the Times and Eternities, is a root use of words —resulting from his lifelong interest in language and etymology —fresh, shocking, and very close to the pun. We can see the etymological passion developing in the *Journal* notes that a "wild" man is actually a "willed" man, that our "fields" are "felled" woods. His early writings keep reminding us that a "saunterer" is going to a "Sainte Terre," a Holy Land; that three roads can make a village "trivial"; that when our center is outside us we are "eccentric"; that a "landlord" is literally a "lord of the land"; that he has been "breaking" silence for years and has hardly made a "rent" in it. By the time he wrote *Walden* this habit had developed into one of his most characteristic ironic devices: the insistence that telling his townsmen

about his life is not "impertinent" but "pertinent," that professors of philosophy are not philosophers, but people who "profess" it, that the "bent" of his genius is a very "crooked" one.
In the "Plea for Captain John Brown" the device achieves a
whiplash power. He says that Brown's "humanities" were the
freeing of slaves, not the study of grammar; that a Board of
Commissions is lumber of which he had only lately heard; of
the Governor of Massachusetts: "He was no Governor of mine.
He did not govern me." Sometimes these puns double and triple
to permit him to pack a number of complex meanings into a
single word, like the "dear" in "Living is so dear." The discord
of goose-honk and owl-cry he hears by the pond becomes a
"concord" that is at once musical harmony, his native town,
and concord as "peace."

Closely related to these serious puns in Thoreau is a serious
epigrammatic humor, wry quotable lines which pack a good
deal of meaning and tend to make their point by shifting
linguistic levels. "Some circumstantial evidence is very strong,
as when you find a trout in the milk." To a man who threatened
to plumb his depths: "I trust you will not strike your head
against the bottom." "The partridge loves peas, but not those
that go with her into the pot." On his habit of exaggeration:
"You must speak loud to those who are hard of hearing." He
reported that the question he feared was not "How much wood
did you burn?" but "What did you do while you were warm?"
Dying, he said to someone who wanted to talk about the next
world: "One world at a time"; and to another, who asked
whether he had made his peace with God: "We have never
quarrelled." When Emerson remarked that they taught all
branches of learning at Harvard: "All of the branches and none
of the roots." Refusing to pay a dollar for his Harvard diploma:
"Let every sheep keep but his own skin." Asked to write for
The Ladies' Companion: "I could not write anything compan-
ionable." Many of these are variants of the same joke, and in
a few cases, the humor is sour and forced, like the definition
of a pearl as "the hardened tear of a diseased clam, murdered
in its old age," or a soldier as "a fool made conspicuous by a
painted coat." But these are penalties any man who works for
humor must occasionally pay, and Thoreau believed this "in-

dispensable pledge of sanity" to be so important that without some leaven of it "the abstruse thinker may justly be suspected of mysticism, fanaticism or insanity." "Especially the transcendental philosophy needs the leaven of humor," he wrote, in what must go down as an understatement.

Thoreau was perhaps more precise about his own style and more preoccupied generally with literary craft than any American writer except Henry James. He rewrote endlessly, not only, like James, for greater precision, but unlike James, for greater simplicity. "Simplify, Simplify, Simplify," he gave as the three cardinal principles of both life and art. Emerson had said of Montaigne: "Cut these words and they would bleed" and Thoreau's is perhaps the only American style in his century of which this is true. Criticizing De Quincey, he stated his own prose aesthetic, "the *art* of writing," demanding sentences that are concentrated and nutty, that suggest far more than they say, that are kinked and knotted into something hard and significant, to be swallowed like a diamond without digesting. "Sentences which are expensive, towards which so many volumes, so much life, went; which lie like boulders on the page, up and down or across; which contain the seed of other sentences, not mere repetition, but creation; which a man might sell his grounds and castles to build." In another place he notes that writing must be done with gusto, must be vascular. A sense of Thoreau's preoccupation with craft comes with noting that when he lists "My faults" in the *Journal*, all seven of them turn out to be of his prose style. Writing for Thoreau was so obsessive, so vital a physical process, that at various times he describes it in the imagery of eating, procreation, excretion, mystic trance, and even his old favorite, the tree bearing ripe fruit. An anthology of Thoreau's passages on the art of writing would be as worth compiling as Henry James's *Prefaces*, and certainly as useful to both the writer and the reader.

Thoreau's somewhat granite pride and aloofness are at their most appealing, and very like James Joyce's, when he is defending his manuscripts against editorial bowdlerizing, when he stands as the embattled writer against the phalanx of cowardice and stupidity. He fought Emerson and Margaret Fuller on a line in one of his poems they printed in *The Dial,* and won. When the editor of *Putnam's Monthly* cut passages from an article, Thoreau wrote to a friend: "The editor requires the liberty to omit the heresies without consulting me, a privilege California is not rich enough to bid for" and he withdrew the series. His letter to Lowell, the editor of *The Atlantic,* when Lowell cut a "pantheistic" sentence out of cowardice, is a masterpiece of bitter fury, withering Lowell like a premature bud in a blast.

Henry Thoreau's and John Brown's personalities were as different as any two personalities can be; one the gentle, rather shy scholar who took children huckleberrying; the other the harsh military Puritan who could murder the children of slavers in cold blood on the Pottawatomie, making the fearful statement, "Nits grow to be lice." Almost the only things they had in common—that made Thoreau perceive that Brown was his man, his ideas in action, almost his Redeemer—were principle and literary style. Just as writers in our own day were drawn to Sacco and Vanzetti perhaps as much for the majesty of Vanzetti's untutored prose as for the obvious justice of their case, Thoreau somehow found the most convincing thing about Brown to be his speech to the court. At the end of his "Plea" he quotes Brown's "sweet and noble strain":

> I pity the poor in bondage that have none to help them; that is why I am here; not to gratify any personal animosity, revenge, or vindictive spirit. It is my sympathy with the oppressed and the wronged, that are as good as you, and as precious as the sight of God.

adding only: "You don't know your testament when you see it."

"This unlettered man's speaking and writing are standard English" he writes in another paper on Brown. "It suggests that the one great rule of composition—and if I were a professor of rhetoric I should insist on this—is, to *speak the truth.*" It was certainly Thoreau's great rule of composition. "He was a speaker and actor of the truth," Emerson said in his obituary of Thoreau. We have never had too many of those. He was also, perhaps as a consequence, a very great writer. We have never had too many of those, either.

JOSEPH MOLDENHAUER (1934-   ) is associate professor of English at the University of Texas. He has published articles on Faulkner, Poe, Marvell, and Emily Dickinson, as well as on Thoreau, in such journals as *Texas Studies in Literature and Language, The Graduate Journal, The Emerson Society Quarterly,* and *The Journal of American Folklore,* many of which have been reprinted. He is one of the editors of the forthcoming edition of Thoreau's works, to be published by the Princeton University Press.

Paradox in Walden

JOSEPH MOLDENHAUER

The Graduate Journal, Vol. 6 (Winter, 1964), 132-46. Reprinted with the author's revisions from *Twentieth Century Interpretations of Walden,* ed. Richard Ruland (Englewood Cliffs, N.J.: Prentice-Hall, Inc., 1968), pp. 73-84.

I fear chiefly lest my expression may not be extra-vagant *enough, may not wander far enough beyond the narrow limits of my daily experience, so as to be adequate to the truth of which I have been convinced.* Extra-vagance! *it depends on how you are yarded. . . . I desire to speak somewhere with-out bounds; like a man in a waking moment, to men in their waking moments; for I am convinced that I cannot exaggerate enough even to lay the foundation of a true expression.*[1]

I

The idiosyncrasies of Thoreau's personality and opinions are so absorbing that "paradox" has always been a key term in Thoreau scholarship. Critic of government and relentless re-porter of tortoises, Platonic dreamer and statistician of tree rings, Transcendental friend who calls for "pure hate" to un-derprop his love,[2] Thoreau invites description as paradoxical, enigmatic, or even perverse. But as Joseph Wood Krutch main-tains, "to unite without incongruity things ordinarily thought

[1] *The Writings of Henry David Thoreau,* Walden Edition, 20 vols. (Boston, 1906), II (*Walden*), 357.

[2] *Ibid.,* I, 305. See Perry Miller, *Consciousness in Concord* (Boston, 1958), pp. 80-103, for a full examination of the paradoxes in Transcendental friend-ship.

of as incongruous *is* the phenomenon called Thoreau."[3] In *Walden* this propensity toward the resolved contradiction may be observed in full flower. Here Thoreau talks only of himself, yet "brag[s] for humanity." Self-isolated in a spot as remote, he says, as Cassiopeia's Chair, he strolls to the village "every day or two." Renouncing materialism for a poetic and mystic life, he proudly reports his own prudential efficiency, and documents his "economic" success with balance sheets. Bewailing the limitations of science, he painstakingly measures the depth of the pond and counts the bubbles in its ice.

The dominant stylistic feature of *Walden* is paradox—paradox in such quantity and of such significance that we are reminded of the works of Donne, Sir Thomas Browne, and other English metaphysical writers. Thoreau's paradoxical assertion—for instance, "Much is published, but little printed"—seems self-contradictory and opposed to reason. As a poetic device it has intimate connections with metaphor, because it remains an absurdity only so long as we take the terms exclusively in their conventional discursive senses. The stumbling block disappears when we realize that Thoreau has shifted a meaning, has constructed a trope or a play on words. The pun, that highly compressed form of comparison in which two or more logically disparate meanings are forced to share the same phonemic unit, lends itself admirably to Thoreau's purpose and underlies many of his paradoxes, including the example cited above. The peculiar impact of the paradox lies in our recognition that an expected meaning has been dislocated by another, remaining within our field of vision but somewhat out of focus. We are given, in Kenneth Burke's splendid phrase, a "perspective by incongruity."

The user of paradox thus defines or declares by indirection, frustrating "rational" expectations about language. Shortly before the publication of *Walden*, another New England Transcendentalist, the theologian Horace Bushnell, affirmed the usefulness of the device, declaring that "we never come so near to a truly well rounded view of any truth, as when it is offered paradoxically; that is, under contradictions; that is, when under two or more dictions, which, when taken as dictions,

---

[3] Joseph Wood Krutch, *Henry David Thoreau* (New York, 1948), p. 286.

are contrary to one another."[4] In *Walden*, Thoreau wants to convey truths of the most unconventional sort—to bring other minds into proximity and agreement with his own attitudes and beliefs. He employs paradox not only for its galvanic effect in persuasion (i.e., as a verbal shock-treatment which reorients the audience), but for the special precision of statement it affords.

At the outset of Thoreau's literary career, his friend Emerson criticized the *"mannerism"* of "A Winter Walk," objecting most strenuously to the oxymorons: "for example, to call a cold place sultry, a solitude public, a wilderness *domestic.* . . ."[5] And we are not astonished to find that Thoreau himself deprecated the very instrument he used so skillfully. When he set down in the *Journal* a list of his "faults," the first item was "Paradoxes,—saying just the opposite,—a style which may be imitated."[6] On another occasion he complained that a companion, probably Ellery Channing, "tempts me to certain licenses of speech. . . . He asks for a paradox, an eccentric statement, and too often I give it to him."[7] But in spite of these warnings and hesitations (which, incidentally, are echoed in the reservations of some of his most sympathetic later critics), Thoreau did not abandon the paradoxical style. Richard Whately, the author of his college rhetoric text, had acknowledged, though rather reluctantly, the value of the device in argumentation. Thoreau's seventeenth-century reading illustrated its rich literary possibilities. Most important, his ironic sensibility embraced paradox. Thoreau wisely followed what he called the crooked bent of his genius and practiced a rhetoric appropriate to his aims.

These aims were in part determined by the character of Transcendental thinking, with its emphasis upon the perception of a spiritual reality behind the surfaces of things. Nature for the Transcendentalist was an expression of the divine mind; its phenomena, when rightly seen, revealed moral truths. By

---

[4] Horace Bushnell, *God in Christ: Three Discourses . . . with a Preliminary Dissertation on Language* (Hartford, 1849), p. 55; cited in Charles Feidelson, Jr., *Symbolism and American Literature* (Chicago, 1953), p. 156.

[5] Walter Harding and Carl Bode, eds., *The Correspondence of Henry David Thoreau* (New York, 1958), p. 137: RWE to HDT, Sept. 18, 1843.

[6] Thoreau, XIII, 7, n.

[7] *Ibid.*, XII, 165.

means of proper perception, said Emerson, "man has access to the entire mind of the Creator," and "is himself the creator" of his own world.[8] The pure, healthy, and self-reliant man, whose mind is in harmony with the Over-Soul, continually discerns the miraculous in the common. But for the timid or degraded man, whose eyes are clouded by convention, nature will appear a "ruin or . . . blank." Idealism is the Transcendentalist's necessary premise: it assures him that things conform to thoughts. By way of demonstration, Emerson tells his uninitiated reader to look through his legs at an inverted landscape. Thoreau was sufficiently tough-minded, and sufficiently interested in the details of natural phenomena, to resist the systematic translation of nature into ideas and moral precepts which Emersonian theory implied. He placed as much emphasis upon the "shams and delusions" which hinder men from "seeing" nature as upon the spiritual meanings of individual natural objects. But he always believed that to recognize one's relations with nature is the basis of moral insight; and he was convinced that the obstacles to this wisdom were removed by the simplification of life. Strip away the artificial, Thoreau tells the "desperate" man, and you will be able to read nature's language. Reality, the "secret of things," lurks under appearances, waiting to be seen. Describing his conversations with the French-Canadian woodchopper, Thoreau says he tried to "maneuver" him "to take the spiritual view of things."[9]

The language of *Walden* is, in a very immediate sense, strategic. The problem Thoreau faced there—and to some extent in all his writings—was to create in his audience the "waking moments" in which they could appreciate "the truth of which [he had] been convinced." In other words, he tries to wrench into line with his own the reader's attitudes toward the self, toward society, toward nature, and toward God. He "translates" the reader, raising him out of his conventional frame of reference into a higher one, in which extreme truths become intelligible. To these ends Thoreau employs a rhetoric of powerful exaggeration, antithesis, and incongruity. Habitu-

---

[8] *The Complete Works of Ralph Waldo Emerson*, Centenary Edition, 12 vols. (Boston, 1903), I, 64.

[9] Thoreau, II, 166.

ally aware of the "common sense," the dulled perception that desperate life produces, he could turn the world of his audience upside-down by rhetorical means. He explores new resources of meaning in their "rotten diction" and challenges ingrained habits of thought and action with ennobling alternatives: "Read not the Times," he exhorts in "Life Without Principle." "Read the Eternities."[10] With all the features of his characteristic extravagance—hyperbole, wordplay, paradox, mock-heroics, loaded questions, and the ironic manipulation of cliché, proverb, and allusion—Thoreau urges new perspectives upon his reader. These rhetorical distortions or dislocations, rather than Transcendental doctrines *per se*, are Thoreau's means of waking his neighbors up. They exasperate, provoke, tease, and cajole; they are the chanticleer's call to intellectual morning; they make *Walden*, in the words of John Burroughs, "the most delicious piece of brag in literature."[11]

II

Walden is not, of course, merely a sophisticated sermon. It is the story of an experiment; a narrative; a fable. In 1851, with his "life in the woods" four years behind him and the book which would celebrate that experience, which would give it a permanent artistic and moral focus, still far from finished, Thoreau wrote, "My facts shall be falsehoods to the common sense. I would so state facts that they shall be significant, shall be myths or mythologic."[12] Even the most hortatory sections of the book are grounded in this "mythology" or significant fiction. I hope to demonstrate that paradox is apposite to the literary design of *Walden:* its themes, symbols, characters, and plot.

As a number of literary theorists have maintained, we can to some extent isolate "a fictional hero with a fictional audience" in any literary work.[13] The "I" of *Walden*, Thoreau as its nar-

10 *Ibid.*, IV, 475.

11 Burroughs, "Henry D. Thoreau," *Indoor Studies* (Boston, 1895), p. 29.

12 Thoreau, IX, 99.

13 Northrop Frye, *Anatomy of Criticism* (Princeton, 1957), p. 53. See also W. K. Wimsatt, Jr., *The Verbal Icon* (Lexington, Ky., 1954), p. xv; John Crowe Ransom, *The World's Body* (New York, 1938), p. 247ff; René Wellek, "Closing Statement," *Style in Language*, ed. Thomas A. Sebeok (New York, 1960), p. 414.

rator and hero, is a deliberately created verbal personality. This dramatized Thoreau should not be confused in critical analysis with the surveyor and pencil-maker of Concord: the *persona* stands in the same relation to the man as *Walden*—the symbolic gesture, the imaginative re-creation—stands to the literal fact of the Walden adventure. The narrator is a man of various moods and rhetorical stances, among them the severe moralist, the genial companion, the bemused "hermit," and the whimsical trickster who regards his experiment as a sly joke on solid citizens. The mellowest of all his moods is the one we find, for instance, in "Baker Farm," "Brute Neighbors," and "House Warming," where he pokes fun at his own zeal as an idealist and reformer. In all his roles he conveys a sense of his uniqueness, the separateness of his vision from that of his townsmen.

The "fictional audience" of *Walden* likewise requires our attention. In defining it I take a hint from Burke, who in "Antony in Behalf of the Play" distinguishes between the play-mob and the spectator-mob as audiences for the oration in *Julius Caesar*. The reader of *Walden*, like Shakespeare's spectator, adopts a double perspective, weighing the speaker's statements both in terms of the fictional circumstance and in terms of their relevance to his own experience. I would distinguish a range of response *within* the dramatic context of *Walden* from an external or critical response. The reader in part projects himself into the role of a hypothetical "listener," whom the narrator addresses directly; and in part he stands at a remove, overhearing this address. Psychologically, we are "beside ourselves in a sane sense,"[14] both spectators who respond to *Walden* as an aesthetic entity and vicarious participants in the verbal action. As spectators, or what I will call "readers," we are sympathetic toward the witty and engaging narrator. As projected participants, or what I will term "audience," we must imagine ourselves committed to the prejudices and shortsightedness which the narrator reproves, and subject to the full tone of the address.

The rhetoric of *Walden*, reflecting in some measure the lecture origins of the early drafts, assumes an initially hostile audience. Thoreau sets up this role for us by characterizing, in

[14] Thoreau, II, 149.

the first third of "Economy," a mixed group of silent listeners who are suspicious of the speaking voice. He would address "poor students," "the mass of men who are discontented," and "that seemingly wealthy, but most terribly impoverished class of all, who have accumulated dross." In addition Thoreau creates individual characters who express attitudes to be refuted by the narrator, and who serve as foils for his wit. These are stylized figures, briefly but deftly sketched, who heckle or complain or interrogate. Their function is overtly to articulate the implicit doubts of the audience. "A certain class of unbelievers," "some inveterate cavillers," "housewives . . . and elderly people," "my tailoress," "the hard-featured farmer," "a factory-owner"—such lightly delineated types register their protests against Thoreau's farming techniques, his lack of charity, his conclusions about the pond's depth, his manner of making bread, and even the cleanliness of his bed linen. Their objections tend to be "impertinent," despite Thoreau's disclaimer early in "Economy," to the lower as well as the higher aspects of the experiment. He answers these animadversions with every form of wit: puns, irony, redefinition, paradoxes, twisted proverbs, over-statements, Biblical allusions (cited by a "heathen" to shame the Christian audience), and gymnastic leaps between the figurative and the literal. It is in this context of debate, of challenge and rejoinder, of provocation and rebuttal and exhortation, that the language of *Walden* must be understood. Thoreau's rhetoric is a direct consequence of the way he locates himself as narrator with respect to a hostile fictional audience. The dramatic status of the speaker and his hearers accounts for the extraordinary "audibility" of *Walden* as well as for the aesthetic distance between the author and reader.

Our bifurcation into spectator and participant is most intense in the hortatory and satirical passages. In the latter role, we are incredulous, shocked, and subject to the direct persuasive techniques of the argument. As spectator, on the other hand, we applaud Thoreau's rhetorical devastation of the premises of his fictional audience, and, if we find the instructive and polemical statements in *Walden* meaningful, as we most certainly can, we recognize that they are contained by the literary

structure and that they must, as statements about life, be understood first within that context. Even the reader who conforms
to the type of the fictional audience, and who brings to *Walden*
a full-blown set of prejudices against Thoreauvian "economy,"
does not stay long to quarrel with the narrator. The force of
Thoreau's ridicule encourages him to quit the stage. For the
participant, *Walden* is "an invitation to life's dance";[15] the
sympathetic reader dances with Thoreau from the start.

Thoreau's paradoxes are also congenial to the "comic"
themes and narrative movement of *Walden*. Using the distinctions of Northrop Frye, we can consider comedy one of the
four "mythoi" or recurrent patterns of plot development which
may appear in any genre. The "mythos of spring" or comic plot
is typified by a rising movement, "from a society controlled by
habit, ritual bondage, arbitrary law and the older characters to
a society controlled by youths and pragmatic freedom . . . a
movement from illusion to reality."[16] Frye's generalization may
call to mind a passage in "Conclusion" where Thoreau pro-
claims the joys of the "awakened" man: "new, universal, and
more liberal laws will begin to establish themselves around
and within him; or the old laws be expanded, and interpreted in
his favor in a more liberal sense, and he will live with the li-
cense of a higher order of beings." On the human level, *Walden's* narrator performs this ascent. On the level of nature, the
green life of spring and summer must rise from old winter's
bondage, repeating the hero's own movement and prefiguring
the spiritual transformation of his audience, "man in the larva
state."

Following a traditional comic pattern, Thoreau represents
in *Walden* two worlds: the narrator's private paradise and the
social wasteland he has abandoned. Each of these polar worlds
has its basic character type and body of symbols. The narrator
is the *Eiron*, the virtuous or witty character whose actions are
directed toward the establishment of an ideal order. The audience and hecklers, who take for granted "what are deemed

[15] E. B. White, "Walden—1954," *Yale Review*, XLIV (1954), 13. White does
not distinguish between reader and fictional audience.

[16] Frye, p. 169.

'the most sacred laws of society,' "[17] serve as the *Alazon* or impostor. This comic type is a braggart, misanthrope, or other mean-spirited figure, usually an older man, who resists the hero's efforts to establish harmony but who is often welcomed into the ideal order when the hero succeeds. The narrator of *Walden*, both clever and good, withdraws from a society of "skin-flint[s]" to a greenwood world at the pond. His pastoral sanctuary is represented in images of moisture, freedom, health, the waking state, fertility, and birth. The society he leaves behind is described in images of dust, imprisonment, disease, blindness, lethargy, and death. Upon these symbolic materials Thoreau builds many of his paradoxes. In his verbal attacks upon the old society, whose "idle and musty virtues" he finds as ridiculous as its vices, the narrator assumes a satirical or denunciatory pose. When he records his simple *vita nuova*, that is, in the idyllic passages, his tone becomes meditative or ecstatic.

III

But it is, after all, to the dusty world or wasteland that *Walden's* fictional audience belongs. Despite their dissatisfactions, they are committed to this life and its values, and blind to the practical as well as the spiritual advantages of the experiment. The narrator, far from being a misanthropic skulker, wishes to communicate his experience of a more harmonious and noble life. His language serves this end: the first rhetorical function of paradox is to make the audience entertain a crucial doubt. Do they value houses? Thoreau calls them prisons, almshouses, coffins, and family tombs. Farming? It is digging one's own grave. Equipment and livestock? Herds are the keepers of men, not men of herds; and men are "the tools of their tools." Traditional knowledge and a Harvard education? Thoreau describes them as impediments to wisdom. Financial security, or "something [laid up] against a sick day," is the cause of sickness in the man who works for it. Fine and fashionable clothing is a form of decoration more barbaric than tatooing, which is only "skin-deep." The landlord's sumptuous furnishings are really "traps" (an elaborate pun) which hold the

---

[17] Thoreau, II, 355.

holder captive. The railroad, marvel of the industrial age, is a means of transportation ultimately slower than going afoot. Religion, Thoreau tells his pious audience, is a "cursing of God" and distrust of themselves. "Good business," the bulwark of their culture, is the quickest way to the devil. In short, says Thoreau, "the greater part of what my neighbors call good I believe in my soul to be bad, and if I repent of anything, it is very likely to be my good behavior. What demon possessed me that I behaved so well?" These paradoxes, often executed with brilliant humor, jostle and tumble the listener's perspective. To be sure, the narrator is a self-acknowledged eccentric— but he is not a lunatic. Thoreau makes sense in his own terms, and the fictional audience no longer can in theirs.

At the same time as he makes nonsense of the audience's vocabulary with satirical paradoxes, Thoreau appropriates some of its key terms to describe the special values of his life in the woods. For example, though he despises commerce he would conduct a profitable "trade" with the "Celestial Empire." In this second body of rhetorical devices Thoreau again exploits polarities of symbol and idea, and not without irony. But these paradoxes differ sharply in their function from the satirical ones. They attach to the hero's world, to nature and simplified action, the deep connotations of worth which social involvements and material comforts evoke for the desperate man. Thoreau astounds and disarms the audience when he calls his experiment a "business" and renders his accounts to the half- and quarter-penny. By means of this appropriately inappropriate language he announces the incompatibility of his livelihood and his neighbor's and simultaneously suggests interesting resemblances. Thoreau's enterprise, like the businessman's, requires risks, demands perseverance, and holds out the lure of rewards. The statistical passages of "Economy" and "The Bean-Field" are equivocal. On the one hand, they prove the narrator's ability to beat the thrifty Yankee at his own game; on the other, they parody the Yankee's obsession with finance. Thoreau's argument that a man achieves success in proportion as he reduces his worldly needs is likewise paradoxical, a queer analogue to the commercial theory of increasing profits by lowering costs. He reinforces this unconventional economic princi-

ple by declaring that the simple life is to be carefully cultivated and jealously preserved: "Give me the poverty that enjoys true wealth." Similarly he contrasts the rich harvest which
a poet reaps from a farm with the *relatively* worthless cash
crop, and is eager to acquire the Hollowell place before its
owner destroys it with "improvements." I would also include in this category of paradoxes Thoreau's constant reference to fish, berries, and other common natural objects in the
language of coins, precious gems, and rare metals; his praise
of the humble simpleton as an exalted sage; his assertion that
the woods and ponds are religious sanctuaries; and his des-
scription of his labors as pastimes and his solitude as compan-
ionable. Some related statements carry the mystical overtones
of the New Testament: "Not till we are lost, in other words,
not till we have lost the world, do we begin to find ourselves."
"Walden was dead and is alive again." All these apparent contradictions support Thoreau's triumphant subjectivism in *Walden*, his running proclamation that "The universe constantly
and obediently answers to our conceptions."[18] The highest and
most sincere conception yields the noblest life.

By nature a dialectical instrument, the paradox is thus
stylistically integral to this severely dialectical work. Viewed
generally, the two large groups of paradoxes reflect the comic
structure of *Walden* and its two major themes: the futility of
the desperate life and the rewards of enlightened simplicity.
With the paradoxes of the first or satirical group, Thoreau declares that his listener's goods are evils, his freedom slavery, and
his life a death. Those of the second group, corresponding
rhetorically to the recurrent symbolism of metamorphosis, affirm that the values of the natural and Transcendental life
arise from what the audience would deprecate as valueless. In
these paradoxes, the beautiful is contained in the ugly, the
truly precious in the seemingly trivial, and the springs of life in
the apparently dead.

As *Walden* progresses the proportion of the first to the
second kind gradually changes. The rhetoric of the early chapters is very largely one of trenchant denunciation, directed
against the desperate life. That of the later chapters is predomi-

18 *Ibid.*, II, 108.

nantly serene, playful, and rapturous. Thoreau creates the impression of a growing concord between himself and his audience by allowing the caustic ironies and repudiations of "Economy" to shift by degrees to the affirmations of "Spring" and "Conclusion." Thoreau the outsider becomes Thoreau the magnanimous insider, around whom reasonable men and those who love life may gather. Rhetorically and thematically, as the book proceeds, the attack becomes the dance.

IV

One of the numerous extended passages in *Walden* which is dominated by oxymoron and which lends itself to close rhetorical analysis is the following, from "Where I Lived, and What I Lived For":

> We do not ride on the railroad; it rides upon us. Did you ever think what those sleepers are that underlie the railroad? Each one is a man, an Irishman, or a Yankee man. The rails are laid on them, and they are covered with sand, and the cars run smoothly over them. They are sound sleepers, I assure you. And every few years a new lot is laid down and run over; so that, if some have the pleasure of riding on a rail, others have the misfortune to be ridden upon. And when they run over a man that is walking in his sleep, a supernumerary sleeper in the wrong position, and wake him up, they suddenly stop the cars, and make a hue and cry about it, as if this were an exception. I am glad to know that it takes a gang of men for every five miles to keep the sleepers down and level in their beds . . . for this is a sign that they may sometime get up again.

In developing his initial paradox and the thesis of the passage, "We do not ride on the railroad; it rides upon us," Thoreau relies heavily upon a pun, for "sleepers" refers simultaneously to the railroad ties and to the benighted laborers who lay them. The repetitions in the short third sentence—"man . . . Irishman . . . Yankee man"—vigorously connect the miserable workers with the more fortunate riders of the cars; they are all in the human family. The train rides on mankind in the sense that a *man* would degrade his life in the railroad enterprise, working on the tracks all day for a pittance. His life is a form of death; symbolically he has been buried, like the wooden sleepers which he himself has covered with sand. He may stay "buried" or "asleep" for many years, perhaps as long as the wooden ties, the "sound sleepers," remain solid and unrotted. When Thoreau remarks, "if some have the pleasure of riding on a rail, others have the misfortune to be ridden upon," he ironically suggests a brutal insouciance on the part of those wealthy enough to travel over an extension of the track, laid by new workers. But in terms of the opening statement, the travelers share the misfortune of being ridden upon; they are to an extent themselves "sleepers" or unenlightened men. The occasional sleepwalker struck by the train is very likely an exhausted laborer, walking on the track in the mental and moral stupor typical of his way of life. Thoreau calls him a "supernumerary sleeper," equating once more the literal block of wood with the wooden man who places it. But "in the wrong position" involves a new paradox: instead of walking stupidly and sleepily on the track—preserving a merely physical uprightness—he should perhaps have wholly abandoned himself to his futile labor and lain down with the ties. Nevertheless, his calamity excites a "hue and cry." In terms of the railroad's "economy" he should have been at the same time a sleeper and not a sleeper. To be struck and run over by the train, or literally to assume the position of the wooden sleepers in man's last and permanent sleep, is to be withdrawn from the fruitless life of track-laying, or to be "awakened." For if the laborer's life is *figuratively* a death and a sleep, his *actual* death, the end of that existence, would be a birth or a waking. Finally, Thoreau sees in the restlessness of the ties, their tendency to shift in the roadbed, an intimation that the very workmen who keep the sleepers down and level may awaken to the dawn of their own moral day, and rise.

v

The principle of paradox likewise controls individual chapters, such as "Higher Laws," and fully developed arguments such as the discussion of philanthropy in the first chapter. It can also be discovered in the juxtaposed rhythms of rise and fall, ascent and descent, primitivism and transcendence which pervade the imagery and action of the book. In this last connection we might briefly note that the Transcendental distinction between what "*is*" and what "*appears to be*" is reflected in the recurrent contrasting of surface and subsurface phenomena. When the narrator chases the diving loon, or fishes for pouts at night, he acts out his pursuit of higher truth. Common sense will provide only superficial catches; the earnest truth-seeker, the "hunter and fisher of men," must search beneath appearances and within himself. The pond in its most consistent symbolic role is the self, the beholder's own profound nature. Here, as elsewhere, Thoreau ascends by descending: on dark nights his fishing line is lost in the black water below, and his line of thought wanders to "vast and cosmogonal themes in other spheres." The bite of the pout links him to nature again, and as the fish comes wriggling upward, the mind pins down an intuition to a perceived fact. "Thus I caught two fishes as it were with one hook." Legislators prescríbe the number of fishhooks to be permitted at Walden, "but they know nothing about the hook of hooks with which to angle for the pond itself, impaling the legislature for a bait." Thoreau, however, has mastered this fishing lore; he sacrifices social institutions in the quest for himself, for reality. In a similar paradox, Thoreau admits that "Snipes and woodcocks . . . may afford rare sport; but I trust it would be nobler game to shoot one's self."

"Conclusion," which is richer in paradoxes than any other chapter, announces the grand prospects of the awakened life: "In proportion as [a man] simplifies his life, the laws of the universe will appear less complex, and solitude will not be solitude, nor poverty poverty, nor weakness weakness." The chapter reaches its climax in two dramatized paradoxes, fables of metamorphosis. In the first, the timeless artist of Kouroo, like the liberated human spirit Thoreau is celebrating, creates a new and glorious world around himself. The second fable, more humble in its materials but not less marvelous in its import, is the anecdote of a bug which gnaws its way out of an old table, emerging from "society's most trivial and handselled furniture" to enjoy a beautiful and winged life after a long death. "Morning," Thoreau had declared earlier, "is when I am awake and there is a dawn in me." To an audience now capable of sharing his ecstatic vision, his wonder at the infinite possibilities open to the self, he makes his final appeal in the heightened language of paradox: "Only that day dawns to which we are awake. There is more day to dawn. The sun is but a morning star."

RICHARD DRINNON (1925-   ) is a member of the faculty of the University of California at Berkeley, and author of *Rebel in Paradise: A Biography of Emma Goldman* (1961). Professor Drinnon asserts that "The vision of individuals with spiritual development and the simple animal strength to affirm their bodies was one of the important contributions of this paradoxical celibate."

Thoreau's Politics
of The Upright Man

RICHARD DRINNON

Thoreau in Our Season, ed. John H. Hicks (Amherst, Mass: University of Massachusetts Press, 1966), pp. 154-68. Reprinted from the *Massachusetts Review*, Vol. 4 (Autumn, 1962).

"In imagination I hie me to Greece as to an enchanted ground," Thoreau declared in his *Journal* and then proved himself as good as his word in his lecture on "The Rights & Duties of the Individual in relation to Government." There was not a major figure in the classical background of anarchism whom Thoreau did not draw upon in some way. Though he may have been unaware of Zeno's strictures against Plato's omnicompetent state, he assuredly honored the Stoic for his individualism, his use of paradox, perhaps his belief in transcendent universal laws, certainly his serenity—"play high, play low," Thoreau observed with delight, "rain, sleet, or snow—it's all the same with the Stoic." He read Ovid with pleasure, used a quotation from the *Metamorphoses* an as epigraph for his *Week on the Concord and Merrimack Rivers*, and must have been well aware of Ovid's nostalgia for a time when there was no state and "everyone of his own will kept faith and did the right." But he found the most dramatic presentation of libertarian views in the

Antigone of Sophocles. In this great drama of rebellion the central conflict was between the spirited Antigone and her uncle Creon, a not unkind man who had just ascended the throne of Thebes. Corrupted a little already by his power, blinded more than a little by bureaucratic definitions of right and wrong, and advancing specious reasons of state as justification for his actions, Creon forbade the burial of the dead traitor Polynices. Driven by love for her slain brother and more by her awareness of the unambiguous commands of the gods to bury the dead, Antigone defied Creon's order. When she was brought before the king, she proudly avowed her defiance:

> For it was not Zeus who proclaimed these to me, nor Justice who dwells with the gods below; it was not they who established these laws among men. Nor did I think that your proclamations were so strong, as, being a mortal, to be able to transcend the unwritten and immovable laws of the gods. For not something now and yesterday, but forever these live, and no one knows from what time they appeared. I was not about to pay the penalty of violating these to the gods, fearing the presumption of any man.[1]

In his lecture on the individual and the state, which became the essay printed first as "Resistance to Civil Government" and later under the famous title "Civil Disobedience," Thoreau echoed Antigone's magnificent lines in his admission that "it costs me less in every sense to incur the penalty of disobedience to the State than it would to obey" and in his declaration that "they only can force me who obey a higher law than I." Like

---

[1] Thoreau's sturdy prose translations in the _Week, Writings_ (1906), I, 139-40, may be compared with Gilbert Murray's rhyming verse translation of _Antigone_ (London: Allen & Unwin, 1941), 37-38. As Murray remarked in the introduction, Sophocles seemed to have created the ideal virgin martyr of Greek tragedy almost in spite of his intention; it is highly improbable that he set out to create an anarchist heroine. Yet she demonstrated unforgettably a specific instance of the possible gap between justice and state law and the final responsibility the individual owes to those laws which are above and beyond the Creons of this world. In this ultimate sense Antigone was an anarchist heroine—with reason Henry Nevinson pointed this out years ago in an essay on "An Anarchist Play," _Essays in Freedom_ (London: Duckworth, 1911), 209-14.

Sophocles' heroine, Thoreau made quite clear his rejection of the Periclean argument of Creon that the highest responsibility of the individual must be to the state and his rejection of the later Platonic assumption of a pleasing harmony between the laws of man and the laws of the gods. The kernel of Thoreau's politics was his belief in a natural or higher law; for the formulation of his essay on this subject, his indebtedness to the Greek tragedian was considerable.

Yet no single work provided Thoreau with his key concept.[2] In his day the doctrine of a fundamental law still covered Massachusetts like a ground fog. It had survived the classical period, had become the eternal law of Aquinas, the anti-papal fundamental law of Wycliffe, and, through Calvin, Milton, and Locke, had flowed across the Atlantic to furnish the colonists with their indispensable "Word of God." The more secular emphasis of the eighteenth century on the "unalienable Rights" possessed by every individual in a state of nature made little difference in end result—little difference at least in doctrine, for all along men had thought it natural for a higher law to be the basis for legislation. In nineteenth-century Massachusetts the existence of a fundamental, higher law was accepted by radicals such as Alcott and Garrison, by liberals such as William Ellery Channing, and by conservatives such as Justice Joseph Story. These older countrymen of Thoreau were joined by Emerson, whose essay on "Politics," published five years be-

---

[2] Thanks to the careful researches of Ethel Seybold, *Thoreau: The Quest and the Classics* (New Haven: Yale University Press, 1951), 16, 17, 24, 66, 75, we know that Thoreau read the *Antigone* at Harvard and probably twice thereafter, once at the time he was working up his lecture on the dangers of civil disobedience and once in the 1850's. Unfortunately Miss Seybold overstates her case by making the *Antigone* "probably responsible for one whole section of Thoreau's thought and public expression. From it must have come his concept of the divine law as superior to the civil law, of human right as greater than legal right." I say "unfortunately," because her overstatement has allowed some students to dismiss her valid points with rather fatuous pronouncements that Thoreau was merely an "involuntary classicist," that he was a "romanticist" by nature—whatever all this means. That Thoreau could find plenty of "romance" in the revels of the great god Pan, the mysticism of Orpheus, and the naturalness of Homer seems clear to me. In any event, one major inspiration for "Civil Disobedience" was Sophocles' work, first presented about 441 B.C., well in advance of Étienne de Boétie's *Discourse sur la Servitude Voluntaire*, published in 1577 and suggested as the earliest important source by Edward L. Tinker, *New York Times Book Review*, 29 March 1942.

fore "Civil Disobedience," had a more direct influence on the young rebel. To be sure, Emerson approached the crass Toryism of Chancellor Kent in discussing "higher law" by attaching it to the power of property. But Emerson was usually much better—at his worst he could sound like an early incarnation of Bruce Barton—than his lines on wealth and property would suggest; most of "Politics" was on the higher ground of a radical Jeffersonianism:

> Hence the less government we have the better—the fewer laws and the less confided power. The antidote to this abuse of formal government is the influence of private character, the growth of the Individual . . . the appearance of the wise man; of whom the existing government is, it must be owned, but a shabby imitation. . . . To educate the wise man the State exists, and with the appearance of the wise man the State expires. The appearance of character makes the State unnecessary. The wise man is the State.[3]

Emerson even averred that "good men must not obey the laws too well."

The similarity of Emerson's point of view and even his language to Thoreau's must be clear to anyone who has carefully read "Civil Disobedience." Living where he did when he did, Thoreau could hardly have escaped the doctrine of a higher law. It was hardly fortuitous that *all* the most notable American individualist anarchists—Josiah Warren, Ezra Heywood, William B. Greene, Joshua K. Ingalls, Stephen Pearl Andrews, Lysander Spooner, and Benjamin Tucker—came from Thoreau's home state of Massachusetts and were his contemporaries. Tying the development of American anarchism to native traditions and conditions, Tucker uttered only a little white exaggeration when he claimed that he and his fellow anarchists were "simply unterrified Jeffersonian democrats."[4]

Thus the doctrine of higher law, as Benjamin Wright once

---

[3] *The Complete Essays* (New York: Modern Library, 1940), 431.

[4] Quoted in Rudolf Rocker, *Pioneers of American Freedom* (Los Angeles: Rocker Publications Committee, 1949), 150. A more recent and helpful study of early American anarchism is James J. Martin, *Men against the State* (DeKalb, Illinois: Adrian Allen Associates, 1953). The native American anar-

remarked, logically leads to philosophical anarchism. True, but this truth can be misleading without the warning note that the logic has to be followed out to the end. Half-way covenants can lead to something very different. John Cotton, for instance, believed in a higher law, yet came down on the side of authority and the Massachusetts establishment; Roger Williams believed no less in a higher law, yet came down on the side of freedom and the individual. Like all ideas, that of a higher law could become a weapon in the hands of groups and institutions. For Thomas Aquinas *lex aeterna* meant the supremacy of the church, for Thomas Hobbes the "Law of Nature" meant the supremacy of the state. For Jefferson and Paine, natural law meant revolution and the establishment of a counter state. But for Thoreau it meant no supremacy of church over state or vice versa, or of one state over another, or of one group over another. It meant rather the logical last step of *individual action*. Belief in higher law *plus* practice of individual direct action *equal* anarchism. "I must conclude that Conscience, if that be the name of it," wrote Thoreau in the *Week*, "was not given us for no purpose, or for a hindrance." From Antigone to Bronson Alcott, Thoreau, and Benjamin Tucker, the individuals who acted on the imperatives of their consciences, "cost what it may," were anarchists.[5]

---

chists shared with Thoreau yet another Yankee characteristic: they were all members of an entrepreneurial professional middle-class which was integral to a relatively simple economy based on farming and trade. Not unnaturally they tended to assume that the interests of all would be best promoted if the individual were left absolutely free to pursue his self-interest. That is to say, just as they developed higher law doctrine to its logical conclusion, so did they take laissez faire theory beyond the liberals to advocate a marketplace literally without political controls. Fortunately Thoreau did not join these anarchists in their preoccupation with currency manipulation, free banking, economic competition. Aside from being more interesting, the trail Thoreau cut for himself promised to lead somewhere.

[5] In 1875 Tucker followed Thoreau's example and refused to pay the poll tax of the town of Princeton, Massachusetts; he was imprisoned in Worcester a short while for his refusal—see Martin, *Men against the State*, pp. 203-04. It had almost become a habit in the area. Three years before Thoreau spent his night in jail, Alcott was arrested for not paying his poll tax. Thoreau was probably influenced by his example and by the civil disobedience agitation of William Lloyd Garrison and his followers—see Wendell Glick, " 'Civil Disobedience': Thoreau's Attack upon Relativism," *Western Humanities Review*, VII (Winter 1952-53), 35-42.

II

So much for the main sources and the master pillars of Thoreau's political position. I have argued that in those crucial matters in which expediency was not applicable, it added up to anarchism. But the question of whether this made him a workaday anarchist lands us in the middle of a tangle. Was Thoreau really an individualist, an anarchist, or both, or neither? Emma Goldman defined anarchism as "the philosophy of a new social order based on liberty unrestricted by man-made law" and once spent an evening in Concord vainly trying to persuade Franklin Sanborn that under this definition Thoreau was an anarchist. Joseph Wood Krutch doubts that Thoreau felt a direct responsibility for any social order, old or new, and stresses his "defiant individualism."[6] Sherman Paul, on the other hand laments that "one of the most persistent errors concerning Thoreau that has never been sufficiently dispelled is that Thoreau was an anarchical individualist."[7] Still, "Thoreau was not an anarchist but an individualist," argues John Haynes Holmes.[8] The tangle becomes impassable with Paul's additional observation that Thoreau "was not objecting to government but to what we now call the State."

There are two main reasons for this muddle. Thoreau was himself partially responsible. His sly satire, his liking for wide margins for his writing, and his fondness for paradox provided ammunition for widely divergent interpretations of "Civil Disobedience." Thus, governments being but expedients, he looks forward to a day when men will be prepared for the motto: "That government is best which governs not at all." The reader proceeds through some lines highly critical of the American government, only to be brought up sharp, in the third paragraph, by the sweet reasonableness of the author: "But to speak practically and as a citizen, unlike those who call themselves no-government men, I ask for, not at once no government, but

6 Krutch, *Henry David Thoreau* (New York: William Sloane, 1948), 133-35.

7 Paul, *The Shores of America: Thoreau's Inward Exploration* (Urbana: University of Illinois Press, 1958), 75-80, 377. Paul emphasizes Thoreau's willingness to have "governmental interference for the general welfare."

8 Holmes, "Thoreau's 'Civil Disobedience,'" *Christian Century*, LXVI (January-June 1949), 787-89.

at once a better government." Those who discount Thoreau's radicalism snap up this sentence which seems clear on the face of it: Do not think me an extremist like the Garrisonians and anarchists, he seems to be saying, but think of me as one who moderately desires a better government now. But is this all he wants? Might he not favor, *a little later,* no government? Shattered by this doubt, the reader is thrown forward into another bitter attack on the American government and on the generic state. It becomes increasingly clear that critics who have tried to put together a governmentalist from Thoreau's writings on politics have humorlessly missed the point. He does indeed say that he will take what he can get from the state, but he also twits himself a little for inconsistency: "In fact, I quietly declare war with the State, after my fashion, though I will still make what use and get what advantage of her I can, as is usual in such cases." Compare Thoreau's wry position here with that of Alex Comfort, the English anarchist, written a hundred years later: "We do not refuse to drive on the left hand side of the road or to subscribe to national health insurance. The sphere of our disobedience is limited to the sphere in which society exceeds its powers and its usefulness. . . ."[9] But let us back up a bit. What was the nature of the "better government" he wanted at once? Obviously it was one that would stay strictly in is place and ungrow—progressively cease to exist. What was the "best government" he could imagine? He has already told us and the essay as a whole supports his declaration: a government "which governs not at all."

But the main obstacle to any clear cut identification of Thoreau's politics has been the uncertain shifting borders of anarchism, liberalism, and socialism in the nineteenth century and after. No series of definitions has succeeded in decisively marking out their frontiers. Stephen Pearl Andrews, for instance, the erudite contemporary of Thoreau, conceived of himself as at one and the same time a believer in the socialism of

[9] Quoted by Nicolas Walter, "Disobedience and the New Pacifism," *Anarchy,* No. 14 (April 1962), 113. It is worth noting that Walter thinks "Thoreau wasn't an anarchist," though he believes that "the implications of his action and his essay are purely anarchist. . . ." I am sure that Thoreau would have chuckled or perhaps laughed in his full free way had he known this question would still be debated a hundred years after his death.

Charles Fourier and the anarchism of Josiah Warren. The intermingling of socialism and anarchism is further illustrated by Mikhail Bakunin, the founder of communist anarchism, who thought of himself as a socialist and fought Marx for the control of the First International. Even Marx has been called an ultimate anarchist, in the sense that he presumably favored anarchism after the state withered away. But perhaps the closest analogue to Thoreau was William Morris. Working closely with Peter Kropotkin for a number of years, Morris rejected the parliamentarians and joined forces with the libertarians in the Socialist League of the 1880's—the League was eventually taken over completely by anarchists!—and wrote *News from Nowhere* which was anarchist in tone and sentiment. Yet his explanation of why he refused to call himself an anarchist was obviously confused and showed that he was rejecting individualist anarchism and not Kropotkin's communist anarchism.[10]

A somewhat comparable confusion mars a recent attempt to analyze Thoreau's position. He was not "an anarchical individualist," argues Paul, because he went to Walden not "for himself alone but to serve mankind." It would be easy to quote passages from *Walden* which seem to call this contention into question. One example: "What *good* I do, in the common sense of that word, must be aside from my main path, and for the most part wholly unintended." Another: "While my townsmen and women are devoted in so many ways to the good of their fellows, I trust that one at least may be spared to other and less humane pursuits."[11] Yet this would be to read Thoreau literally. Unquestionably, as he informed us in "Civil Disobedience," he was "as desirous of being a good neighbor as I am of being a bad subject." The distinction was crucial. Though he served the state by declaring war on it, in his own way, he

10 George Woodcock and Ivan Avakumovic, *The Anarchist Prince* (London: T. V. Boardman, 1950), 216-19. Thoreau's great influence on the English left dates back to this period when many were filled with idealism and with admiration for the "sublime doctrine" of anarchism.

11 Since I have marked up my copy of *Walden* (New York: Modern Library, 1937), all my citations will be to this edition rather than to the appropriate Walden volume (II) of his *Works*. Here the quotations are from pp. 65, 66.

served society for a lifetime by trying to understand and explain Concord to itself. The manageable unit of society—unlike the vast abstraction in Washington or even Boston—was drawn to the human scale of Concord and other villages. If men lived simply and as neighbors, informal patterns of voluntary agreement would be established, there would be no need for police and military protection, since "thieving and robbery would be unknown,"[12] and there would be freedom and leisure to turn to the things that matter. Thoreau's community consciousness was the essential, dialectical *other* of his individuality. Consider the following from *Walden:*

> It is time that villages were universities, and their elder inhabitants the fellows of universities, with leisure . . . to pursue liberal studies the rest of their lives. Shall the world be confined to one Paris or one Oxford forever? Cannot students be boarded here and get a liberal education under the skies of Concord? . . . Why should our life be in any respect provincial? If we will read newspapers, why not skip the gossip of Boston and take the best newspaper in the world at once. . . . As the nobleman of cultivated taste surrounds himself with whatever conduces to his culture — genius—learning—wit—books—paintings—statuary—music —philosophical instruments and the like; so let the village do. . . . To act collectively is according to the spirit of our institutions. . . . Instead of noblemen, let us have noble villages of men.[13]

One nobleman who also agitated for noble villages was the anarchist Kropotkin. He could have agreed completely with

---

[12] *Walden*, 156.

[13] *Walden*, 98-100. By all means see Lewis Mumford's fine discussion of Thoreau in his chapter on "Renewal of the Landscape," in *The Brown Decades* (New York: Dover Publications, 1955), 64-72. Mumford credits Thoreau with the achievement of helping "to acclimate the mind of highly sensitive and civilized men to the natural possibilities of the environment" and gives him a major place in the history of regional planning in America. The influence of Thoreau on Paul Goodman, who describes himself as a "community anarchist," is apparent to anyone who has read his and his brother Percival's *Communitas* (Chicago: University of Chicago Press, 1947).

Thoreau's preoccupation with his locality and his readiness to act collectively "in the spirit of our institutions." In *Mutual Aid* (1902), Kropotkin celebrated the vital growth of society in the ancient Greek and medieval cities; he sadly outlined the consequences of the rise of centralization when the state "took possession, in the interest of minorities, of all the judicial, economical, and administrative functions which the village community already had exercised in the interest of all." Like Thoreau, Kropotkin advocated that the community's power be restored and that local individuality and creativity be left free to develop. The closeness of their views—though Kropotkin must have thought Thoreau too much an individualist like Ibsen!—points up the mistake of Sherman Paul and others in equating the "anti-social" with the "anarchical." Society and the state, as Thoreau and Kropotkin were very much aware, should not be confused or identified.

The definition of Emma Goldman quoted above will have to do for our purposes, then, though we must keep in mind its approximate nature and the greased-pole slipperiness of the political theory from which Thoreau's views are so often confidently said to have differed. Under this definition Thoreau was always an anarchist in matters of conscience, an ultimate anarchist for a time "when men are prepared for it," and in the meanwhile an anarchical decentralist. But enough of this attempt to stuff the poet and mystic in one political slot. Actually Thoreau's writings may yet help to explode all our conventional political categories.

III

"We scarcely know whether to call him the last of an older race of men, or the first of one that is to come," admitted an English critic in *The Times Literary Supplement* for 12 July, 1917. "He had the toughness, the stoicism, the unspoilt senses of an Indian, combined with the self-consciousness, the exacting discontent, the susceptibility of the most modern. At times he seems to reach beyond our human powers in what he perceives upon the horizon of humanity." With remarkable insight, the writer had perceived Thoreau's perplexing doubleness and had even touched the edge of his higher, profoundly exciting unity.

Of Thoreau's "unspoilt senses of an Indian" and his passion for the primitive there can be no question. "There is in my nature, methinks," he declared in the *Week*, "a singular yearning toward all wildness." To the end he was convinced that "life consists with wildness." But this conviction did not rest on a sentimental-romantic view of our "rude forefathers." The crude relics of the North American tribes, their improvident carelessness even in the woods, and their "coarse and imperfect use" of nature repelled him. His unpleasant experience of a moose-hunt in Maine led to the reflection: "No wonder that their race is so soon exterminated. I already, and for weeks afterwards, felt my nature the coarser for this part of my woodland experience, and was reminded that our life should be lived as tenderly and daintily as one would pluck a flower."[14] Yet Thoreau never gave up his conviction that, standing so close, Indians had a particularly intimate and vital relationship with nature. "We talk of civilizing the Indian," he wrote in the *Week*, "but that is not the name for his improvement. By the wary independence and aloofness of his dim forest life he preserves his intercourse with his native gods, and is admitted from time to time to a rare and peculiar society with nature. He has glances of starry recognition to which our saloons are strangers."

By way of contrast, "the white man comes, pale as the dawn, with a load of thought, with a slumbering intelligence as a fire raked up, knowing well what he knows, not guessing but calculating; strong in community, yielding obedience to authority; of experienced race; of wonderful, wonderful common sense; dull but capable, slow but persevering, severe but just, of little humor but genuine; a laboring man, despising game and sport; building a house that endures, a framed house. He buys the Indian's moccasins and baskets, then buys his hunting-grounds, and at length forgets where he is buried and plows up his bones."[15] In this list of the bourgeois virtues, the

[14] Quoted in Albert Keiser, *The Indian in American Literature* (New York: Oxford University Press, 1933), 227.

[15] *Works*, I, 52-53; see also 55.

keen, far-reaching social criticism of "Life Without Principle"
—first entitled "Higher Law"—and indeed of *Walden* itself is
anticipated. Calculating for the main chance, this obedient
white man had cut his way through thousands of Indians in
order to rush to the gold diggings in California, "reflect the
greatest disgrace on mankind," and "live by luck, and so get
the means of commanding the labor of others less lucky, without contributing any value to society! And that is called enterprise! I know of no more startling development of the immortality of trade. . . . The hog that gets his living by rooting,
stirring up the soil so, would be ashamed of such company."[16]
In this powerful essay on "Life Without Principle," he concluded that "there is nothing, not even crime, more opposed
to poetry, to philosophy, ay to life itself, than this incessant
business." An economist of importance, as the first chapter of
Walden may yet prove to a skeptical world, Thoreau saw
clearly that the accumulation of wealth really leads to the
cheapening of life, to the substitution for man of the less-than-
hog-like creature who calculates and lays up money and even
fails to root up the soil in the process. "What is called politics,"
he wrote in "Life Without Principle," "is comparatively something so superficial and unhuman, that practically I have never
fairly recognized that it concerns me at all." The war against
Mexico, the scramble for territory and power, and other de-
bauches in nationalism were, he trusted, a different manifest
destiny from his own. In his letter to Parker Pillsbury on the
eve of the fighting at Fort Sumter, he reported that he did "not
so much regret the present condition of things in this country
(provided I regret it at all) as I do that I ever heard of it. I
know one or 2 who have this year, for the first time, read a
president's message; but they do not see that this implies a fall
in themselves, rather than a rise in the president. Blessed were
the days before you read a president's message. Blessed are
the young for they do not read the president's message."[17] Yet,

---

[16] "Life without Principle," in *Walden*, 717.

[17] His reference to "manifest destiny" appeared in his letter to H. G. O. Blake,
27 February, 1853; his letter to Pillsbury was dated 10 April, 1861—*The
Correspondence of Henry David Thoreau*, eds. Walter Harding and Carl Bode
(New York: New York University Press, 1958), 296, 611.

despite all these devastating shafts aimed at the institutions reared up by the "pale as dawn" white man, Thoreau honored learning as much or more than any man in America. Far from advocating a return to some preliterate bliss, he advocated, in his chapter on "Reading" in *Walden*, a study of "the oldest and the best" books, whose "authors are a natural and irresistible aristocracy in every society, and, more than kings or emperors, exert an influence on mankind."

Thus Thoreau's doubleness, of which he was well aware: "I find an instinct in me conducting to a mystic spiritual life, and also another to a primitive savage life." It was one of his great achievements to go beyond the polarities of "Civilization and Barbarism"—alternatively attractive poles which drew most of Thoreau's contemporaries helplessly back and forth like metal particles—to come close to a creative fusion: "We go eastward to realize history and study the works of art and literature, retracing the steps of the race," he wrote in the serene summary of his walks. "We go westward as into the future, with a spirit of enterprise and adventure." Thoreau wanted the best for his countrymen from both nature and civilization, past and present. He perceived clearly the meaning of America. It was an opportunity for new beginnings: "The Atlantic is a Lethean stream, in our passage over which we have had an opportunity to forget the Old World and its institutions. If we do not succeed this time, there is perhaps one more chance for the race left before it arrives on the banks of the Styx; and that is in the Lethe of the Pacific, which is three times as wide." Had he lived with unflagging powers for another decade or so, he might have used his laboriously accumulated notebooks of "Extracts relating to the Indians" to show why the aborigines enjoyed "a rare and peculiar society with nature."[18] It is indisputable that his interest in classical mythology, ancient societies, and con-

---

[18] Keiser, *The Indian in American Literature*, 217-18, "cannot but believe that cruel fate robbed the world of a great work dealing in a sanely realistic yet sympathetic . . . manner with the child of nature on the American continent. . . ." Perhaps, though it is possible that the Civil War might have undone Thoreau along with so many others. It should be noted that Thoreau shows, in many passages, an intuitive sense of the distinction, made by such modern students as Mircea Eliade, between cyclical archaic time and progressive, cumulative modern time. His works were organized around the former. Indeed

temporary tribes was an anthropological concern for the enduring features of life in groups. His interest in savages was
much like that of Claude Lévi-Strauss and might have been
expressed in the latter's words: "The study of these savages does
not reveal a Utopian state in Nature; nor does it make us aware
of a perfect society hidden deep in the forests. It helps us to
construct a theoretical model of society which corresponds to
none that can be observed in reality, but will help us to disen-
tangle 'what in the present nature of Man is original, and what
is artificial.' "[19] Thoreau's theoretical model, which came from
all his efforts to drive life into a corner and get its measurements, made it clear that the efforts of his neighbors to live
for the superfluous made their lives superfluous. Through careful inspection of his model, he was able to see, years before
Lenin, that at bottom the state is a club. To cooperate with it,
especially in matters of importance, is to deny life, for the
state, like a standing army, is organized power and at the disposal of hate. "You must get your living by loving," confidently
declared this supposedly narrow village eccentric. Clearly, he
aspired to create for his countrymen a "new heaven and a new
earth," just as each of Greece's sons had done for her. The look
of this new heaven is suggested by a passage in the *Week*. On
Saturday, after he and John had made the long pull from
Ball's Hill to Carlisle Bridge, they saw "men haying far off in
the meadow, their heads waving like the grass which they cut.
In the distance the wind seemed to bend all alike. As the night
stole over, such a freshness was wafted across the meadow that
every blade of cut grass seemed to teem with life."

To this feeling of the correspondence of man to nature, "so
that he is at home in her," Thoreau added poetic intuitions of
an individualism to come. With his common sense, he realized
that the notorious common sense of his countrymen was in-
sane. The important questions were buried under daily rounds

---

the *Week* might be interpreted as an extended defense of Parmenides's thesis
of the permanence of the universe against the Heraclitean progressivism of a
nation of boosters (see esp. 54-56, 60, 128, 239, 347, 416). His constant
return to the problem of time and its obvious importance for his understanding
of man in nature invite a careful, systematic inquiry.

[19] Lévi-Strauss, "Tristes Tropiques," *Encounter*, XC (April 1961), 40.

of trivia. Living was constantly deferred. No joyful exuberance was allowed to slip by prudence. Thoreau could have joined William Blake in his belief that "Prudence is a rich, ugly old maid, courted by Incapacity." The incapacity was partly the result of a split between the head and the heart, thought and feeling, and the absurd belief that the intellect alone enables man to meet life. In his final summing up, in the essay "Walking," he warned that the most we can hope to achieve is "Sympathy with Intelligence . . . a discovery that there are more things in heaven and earth than are dreamed of in our philosophy." But his neighbors not only had an overfaith in abstract reasoning and in the general efficacy of the intellect; they also distrusted the body. William Blake could thrust through the prudishness of his time to rediscover the body; hemmed in by the moral sentimentalism of his family, by Emersonian etherealness, and his own confirmed virginity, Thoreau had more difficulty. His embarrassing admission—"what the essential difference between man and woman is, that they should be thus attracted to one another, no one has satisfactorily answered" —is indeed, as Krutch points out, "a real howler."[20] Nevertheless, he took a sensuous delight in his body, claiming in the *Week* that "we need pray for no higher heaven than the pure senses can furnish, a purely sensuous life. Our present senses are but rudiments of what they are destined to become." Here is a body mysticism which placed Thoreau in the tradition of Jacob Boehme and William Blake. It presupposed, Norman Brown observes, that "the consciousness strong enough to endure full life would be no longer Apollonian but Dionysian— consciousness which does not observe the limit, but overflows; consciousness which *does not negate any more*."[21] Shocked by phallic forms in nature, the stiff-backed Thoreau yet remarked that he worshipped most constantly at the shrine of Pan—Pan, the upright man of the Arcadian fertility cult, famous for his Dionysiac revels with the mountain nymphs![22] The vision of

[20] Krutch, *Thoreau*, 207.

[21] Brown, *Life against Death* (Middletown, Conn.: Wesleyan University Press, 1959), 308-11.

[22] *Works*, I, 65. I should not place any great reliance on this passage, which apparently was valued in part for its shock value, if it stood alone. It does not.

individuals with spiritual development and the simple animal strength to affirm their bodies was one of the important contributions of this paradoxical celibate. It was a vision sensed and acted upon, in their own ways, by Isadora Duncan and Emma Goldman and Randolph Bourne and Frank Lloyd Wright. It exerts its appeal to the poetic libertarian strain in radicalism, to men as diverse as e. e. cummings, Karl Shapiro, Henry Miller, Paul Goodman, Kenneth Patchen, Herbert Read, the late Albert Camus and Nicolas Berdyaev. A recent, rather extravagant form is perhaps Allen Ginsberg's notion of "Socialist-Co-op Anarchism." In any form it is revolutionary.

"One thing about Thoreau keeps him very near to me," Walt Whitman remarked. "I refer to his lawlessness—his dissent —his going his absolute own road let hell blaze all it chooses."[23] Thousands of young people know exactly what Whitman meant. A few perhaps can see that Thoreau's death was his greatest achievement, for it showed that his philosophy had taught him how to die—and therefore how to live. Some can appreciate and understand his two years at Walden Pond. But many are ready, like the young Indian lawyer in South Africa in 1907, to be impressed that Thoreau "taught nothing he was not prepared to practice in himself."[24] Like Gandhi, they are ready to draw on Thoreau's "Civil Disobedience" for "a new way" of handling political conflict. Thoreau thereby made another major contribution to radical politics, for anarchism and socialism have traditionally been strong on ends and weak or worse on means. It is true that Thoreau was himself unclear about violence, as his splendid tribute to John Brown and his occasional callow observations on war show—"it is a pity, he wrote a correspondent in 1855, "that we seem to require a war from time to time to assure us that there is any manhood still left in man."[25] Yet he went farther than most in thinking his way through this problem. More importantly, like Antigone

[23] Quoted by Walter Harding, *A Thoreau Handbook* (New York: New York University Press, 1959), 201.

[24] Quoted by George Hendrick, "The Influence of Thoreau's 'Civil Disobedience' on Gandhi's *Satyagraha*," *New England Quarterly*, XXIX (1956), 464.

[25] Letter to Thomas Cholmondeley, 7 February 1855—see *Correspondence of Thoreau*, 371.

he left us the powerful, burning, irresistible appeal of his example. It is as timely as the banner "Unjust Law Exists" which marched beside Camus' "Neither Victims Nor Executioners" in the recent Washington youth demonstrations. It is as timely as Bertrand Russell's sit-down in Trafalgar Square. It may even help us survive the disease called modern history.